Reading, thinking, and communicating.
(*Photograph by Harold M. Lambert*)

Teaching Children To Read

LILLIAN GRAY
SAN JOSE STATE COLLEGE

THIRD EDITION

THE RONALD PRESS COMPANY · NEW YORK

Library of Congress Catalog Card Number: 63–11837

PRINTED IN THE UNITED STATES OF AMERICA

This book is dedicated to my sister, Marguerite Pearson, in token of her unfailing patience and encouragement.

PREFACE

With all the attending benefits, the interesting work with children and the feeling of being needed, what does it take to be a good reading teacher? What special skills are required? What types of training? What factual background? *Teaching Children To Read,* Third Edition, is designed to answer these questions.

This book is intended as a text for courses in the teaching of elementary-school reading for education majors and liberal arts majors expecting to teach and will serve as a practical guide for the in-service and classroom teacher and for the reading specialist. For those confronted with guiding a child's reading growth through the school years, this text offers sound help based on both a careful study of scientific investigations in the field of reading and the long experience of the author. The chief goal of reading instruction is to promote personal development. This book directs itself to that goal, the integrating theme throughout being concern for the individual.

The Third Edition gives attention to such recent emphases as team teaching, instructional television, teaching machines, and speed reading. Separate chapters are devoted to phonics and to reading in relation to other language arts. Self-selective reading is evaluated in the light of recent research. The Third Edition also presents a variety of new-type lesson plans for reading instruction at all levels which are of particular value in work with student teachers.

For the photographs of children engaged in various reading activities, the author is indebted to the following officials: Curt Davis, Assistant Superintendent, Mrs. Ruth Palmer, General Supervisor, Mrs. Lucille Travis, Principal of Bascom Avenue School, Albert Schneider, Principal of Benjamin Cory School, Mrs. Marjorie Kurle, first-grade teacher, and Jerry Thornton, sixth-grade teacher, all of the San Jose (California) Unified School District; Mrs. Christina McDonald, Curriculum Assistant, El Rancho Unified School District, Pico Rivera, California; and Thomas Calabrese, Principal of Memorial Junior High School, Huntington Station, New York.

The author wishes to express gratitude for the aid in collecting and preparing other photographs to these faculty members at San Jose State College, San Jose, California: Dr. Richard Lewis, Head of the Audio-Visual Department; Mrs. Gaither Lee Martin, Coordinator of Television Services; and Marian Moreland, Associate Professor of the Commercial Art Department. The frontispiece was provided by the Harold Lambert Studios, the McGuffey facsimile by the Bettman Archive, and the photograph of Horace Mann by the Horace Mann Life Insurance Company, which owns the rights to it.

Special thanks for valuable reference material are due to Edith Smith, Alice Fales, Helene Wacek, William R. Rogers, Norma Baker, Paul Betten, Clay Andrews, and Gertrude Corcoran. Mrs. Dora Reese, with whom the author collaborated on the first two editions, had other commitments and felt it wise to withdraw from the work of the third revision. During the preparation of this edition, however, she has offered helpful counsel, and for this the author expresses warm appreciation.

The stimulation for writing this book has come from the many teachers and students with whom the author has been privileged to work.

LILLIAN GRAY

January, 1963

CONTENTS

Part IV. ADDITIONAL ASPECTS OF THE READING PROGRAM

PART I

BACKGROUND FACTORS
IN READING INSTRUCTION

1

READING AND AMERICAN LIFE

The ultimate aim of good teachers is to give America's children a sound education. Almost inevitably, this includes helping pupils to feel secure in the basic skill of reading. The child who does not learn to read well in the elementary school runs the risk of becoming an adult handicapped in many phases of living.

Once reminded of the importance of reading in school and in life, most prospective teachers display eagerness to learn how to give effective instruction in this strategic skill. On their part, those who have experience in education stand ready to share what they have learned about the best known ways to teach reading, as well as to point out experiments which may lead in the future to improved methods. Having an important stake in education, the majority of teachers in the field accept their dual role and maintain stability in the school offering, but respond to new demands. The population explosion, for example, which continues to create a problem of teacher shortages and overcrowded classrooms in many communities, has dictated various innovations such as team teaching and instructional television. The point particularly to be noted here, by reason of its implications for reading, is that whatever goes on within a given culture pattern sooner or later affects the school program.

THE USES OF READING IN LIFE

Quite fittingly, teachers in the United States take their cues for organizing a valid reading program from the kinds of reading essential to the welfare of our society. Only thus can the teacher provide classroom experiences which will develop desirable reading habits, attitudes, and skills. What, then, are the uses of reading in American life? An acceptable list includes reading as (1) an aid in meeting everyday needs, (2) a tool of citizenship, (3) a pursuit for leisure time, (4) a tool of vocation, (5) a source of spiritual refreshment, (6) an aid to enrichment of experience—including personal development and vicarious experiencing.

The Child's Introduction to the Usefulness of Reading. Today teachers find little difficulty in interesting the small child in learning to read. Printed matter is as much a part of the modern scene the child comes to know as automobiles, telephones, jet planes, deep freezers, and television sets. Many a child enters the first grade, and even the kindergarten, with the ability to react to certain printed stimuli. Usually, with a familiarity bred by repetition, he can recognize the name of his favorite candy bar on the wrapper. From tagging along after his mother as she pushes a shopping cart up and down the aisles of the supermarket, the child becomes acquainted with various printed labels on her choice of packaged or canned goods. Rides in the family car demonstrate for the small child how his father responds to printed highway and service-station signs. During the evening televiewing session, a youngster soon learns to connect certain oral announcements contained in television commercials with the brand names displayed on pictured packages. (A four-year-old of the author's acquaintance has such terms as *detergent* and *stannous fluoride toothpaste* in his repertoire of speaking and reading recognition.) It is not long before life experiences teach the child to read such vital printed information as: "Wet Paint," "Poison," "Fire Escape," etc.

Of course, the more subtle forms of reading used to cope with practical problems of everyday living may be beyond the young child's understanding. Thus, he may observe his father reading a bill or an income-tax blank, and watch his mother perusing a new recipe for meat loaf, with only the vaguest notion as to the purposes served by the black squiggles on white paper. But, through repeated exposure, Junior eventually winds up with built-in readiness for using reading to solve problems connected with daily living.

Similarly, through a series of related experiences, the child grows into an appreciation of the other uses of reading. When he observes his parents reading newspapers and sample ballots, though not aware of its real significance, he is being introduced to reading for civic enlightenment. As his parents read storybooks to him, or sit for several hours reading books and magazines for their own enjoyment, he is becoming acquainted with reading as a good pursuit to follow in leisure time. Looking at pictures in the Sunday-school leaflet and trying to guess what it says under each, asking an adult for help, and subsequently recalling part of what was read aloud, may be the child's first contact with reading as a source of spiritual growth. No matter to which earning group his father belongs—be it business, labor, or professional—the chances are that at one time or another the child will see him reading a vocational journal. The range is great, including journals for dentists, long-haul truck drivers, plumbers, farmers, and stockbrokers. The teaching profession, for example, has national, state, and subject-matter journals, useful in aiding members to keep up with the latest professional developments. When the child's mother or older sister reads aloud to the other from the woman's page of the daily newspaper hints on etiquette, clothes, beauty, entertaining, or traveling, Junior may not recognize that the category represented is personal enrichment, but here, again, he is learning that people use reading for many purposes.

By the time he enters school Junior has been exposed to a wide variety of reading uses. Aware of the importance of reading in school and in life, the teacher knows that she must teach Junior a great many reading skills, and tap for the purpose a wealth of books, new and old, informational and recreational. If reading goals are correlated with life uses, the teacher avoids the pitfall of teaching reading as an end in itself and does not get so bogged down in drills as to forget that they must be functional and related to the larger service of guiding the child to enjoy all the fun and ideas in print.

There is a bookshop called "The Treasures of Time" in one of our American towns. It seems well named. In a very real sense, books are treasures. When a teacher helps a child to learn to read them, she is insuring his inheritance of a rich fortune. Albert Schweitzer the great philanthropist once said, "Only those will be happy who have sought and found how to serve." It is true that the teacher of reading has found a worthy cause to serve, considering the wide usefulness of the skill to each individual in our culture.

THE READING HABITS OF AMERICANS

Evidence of Satisfactory Status. A heartening picture of the reading habits of Americans is presented by means of some available statistics. According to the United States Statistical Abstract for 1958, only 2.5 per cent of the population fourteen years of age or over were found to be illiterate. The total circulation for magazines reached 175,000,000 in 1956,[1] while 11,200 weekly and daily newspapers were supported, indicating that the record for magazine and newspaper reading is highly satisfactory. One investigation at the University of Minnesota showed, for example, that 95 per cent of the people in both rural and metropolitan areas read local newspapers.[2] Lyness' study of the newspaper reading habits of children from grades three through eleven in Des Moines, Iowa, revealed that 85 per cent of the youngest read some part of the newspaper and that the attention given to this form of reading increases with age.[3] More recent evidence from public-opinion polls, according to Lester Asheim, indicates that Americans "are still almost 100 per cent newspaper readers." [4] Though the year 1962 witnessed the demise of some evening newspapers in large cities, the morning papers in metropolitan areas and both evening and morning papers in smaller cities and towns easily held their own in advertising and circulation.

As for magazine reading, the Gilbert Youth Research Company made an investigation into the reading habits and tastes of teen-

[1] Peter S. Jennison, "Today's Challenge to the Book World," *Library Journal*, LXXXII, No. 17 (October 1, 1957), (New York: American Book Publishers Council) 2319.

[2] Malcolm S. MacLean, "Mass Media Audiences: City, Small City, Village and Farm," *Journalism Quarterly*, XXIX (Winter 1954), 271–82.

[3] Paul I. Lyness, "The Place of Mass Media in the Lives of Boys and Girls," *Journalism Quarterly*, XXIX (Summer 1952) 43.

[4] Lester Asheim, "What Do Adults Read–" *Adult Reading*, Fifty-fifth Yearbook, Part II. National Society for the Study of Education. Chicago: University of Chicago Press, 1956.

agers and in 1959 widely syndicated its findings. The fact was that 72 per cent of teen-agers read magazines each week. Though the "pulp" magazines led the field for many years for both adults and adolescents, a 1962 report by Martin Mayer shows that there has been considerable upgrading of taste recently. Numerous "pulp" magazines have suspended publication, whereas every "slick paper" magazine published today sells two to five times as many copies as it did twenty years ago, and most of the companies that advertised in magazines a decade ago still advertise in magazines today but are apt to buy less space.[5] Wolesley presents the encouraging news that popular women's magazines tend to offer more serious ideas than formerly.[6]

Showing laudable concern for children's growth in reading habits and attitudes, book clubs for adults have been augmented within the past decade by similar organizations for young Americans. For many years now, an annual Children's Book Week has been sponsored each November by the Children's Book Council, which distributes posters and otherwise publicizes and dramatizes the value of books. Each spring, the Children's Division of the American Library Association presents the Newberry and Caldecott medals for the most distinguished children's books of the year. Such organizations as the Boy Scouts of America and the Camp Fire Girls are headed by responsible people who wish to ensure the development of reading ability in the growing generation. They remind boys and girls of what they are missing if they do not use their library cards regularly. As motivation to increased book reading, these organizations offer merit badges and distribute reading lists. All these activities promise much good for the future.

Evidence of Less Satisfactory Status. There is another side to the portrait delineated above of the more hopeful aspects of the interest displayed by Americans in good reading. While the figures for magazine and newspaper reading are satisfactory, there is no

---

[5] Martin Mayer, "Television '62: Exploring Television's Impact on Life in the United States," *TV Guide*, X, No. 29 (July 21, 1962), 2–6.

[6] Roland E. Wolesley, "Women's Magazines—Dope or Dynamite," *Niemann Reports*, II (April 1957), 31–34.

immediate prospect—to judge by recent polls and surveys—that the United States will develop into a nation of bookworms.

Public librarians, at a recent convention, recognized a major anomaly in the reading pattern of Americans when they pointed out: (1) Literacy is a prerequisite of reading but does not necessarily guarantee it. (2) The majority of Americans accept the well-read person (i.e., the prolific book reader), but they do not admire him. And so it is not much that Johnny cannot read as that our culture pattern often fails to encourage book reading.

In 1950, American newspapers and news magazines gave wide publicity to the results of an international poll on reading habits. The poll revealed that the French were the most prolific readers, with 70 per cent of the French population questioned reading a book at the time of the poll. Other findings were less reassuring: Only 55 per cent of the English, 48 per cent of the Norwegians, 43 per cent of the Swedes, 40 per cent of the Canadians, and 20 per cent of the Americans were engaged in such reading. According to a Gallup poll in April, 1959, only 21 per cent of American adults questioned had read a book within the month,[7] not a very impressive gain for the nine-year period represented.

Book reading is emphasized in polls and surveys because more rewarding ideas are usually to be found between the covers of a book—provided it is a good book—than in even the finest articles and stories, crowded within the smothering mass of advertisements in a magazine. Thanks to greater length and richer use of detail, books usually present more substantial fare than that found in the fugitive reading matter represented by magazines and newspapers. The impact upon the reader, as a general rule, is correspondingly more vivid and memorable.

Records show that there is only one good bookstore for every 175,000 people in the United States. In spite of the increase of bookmobiles, there are 27,000,000 Americans without any form of public library service. The book industry is worth less in dollars, according to the *Library Journal*,[8] than the profit of a single major industrial enterprise.

It is, of course, impossible to learn to do anything well, whether it be cooking, typing, or ballet dancing, without adequate practice.

[7] Figures from the American Institute of Public Opinion.
[8] *Ibid.*, p. 2319.

Those who read little tend to read ineffectively. Deriving small pleasure from the activity, they spend less time and money on reading and more time and money on other forms of recreation. Though statistics reveal a rise from the 1/5 cent of the consumer dollar spent on books in 1957[9] to 1/2 cent of the consumer dollar in 1960,[10] book buying still represents a very small portion of the expenditures for individual recreation. In a listing of nine items, expenditures for television, radio, and phonographs rank highest; spectator amusements (movies, sports events), second; magazines and newspapers, third; non-durable toys, fourth; gardening, fifth; sporting goods, sixth; books and maps, seventh; bowling, cards, eighth; art hobbies, ninth.[11]

When the thoughtful teacher considers the great value of book reading and the lack of appreciation of it by the buying public, she is apt to redouble her efforts to stimulate increased use of this form of reading among her pupils. Speaking in favor of a home library containing the child's personal favorites, Phyllis Fenner the well-known public librarian said, "We want books that children will enjoy reading and rereading, and keep for their own children."[12]

Whether one is encouraged or depressed by the increase in sales of one form of book—the paperback—depends upon the interpretation made. Almost non-existent thirty years ago, paperbacks are sold today from the familiar revolving racks in drugstores and supermarkets in every neighborhood. However, the sale of millions of paperbacks weekly does not represent a clear gain for the cause of book buying and book reading. A Gallup poll estimated that 9 per cent of buyers of paperbacks account for 78 per cent of copies sold.

FORCES AFFECTING AMERICAN READING HABITS

Are there any special circumstances to explain the present relatively unsatisfactory status of book-reading habits in our country?

---

[9] "Books Continue To Take 1/5 Cent of U.S. Consumer Dollar," *Publishers Weekly*, LXXII (September 9, 1957), 46.

[10] *Editorial Research Reports* (December 20, 1961), 918.

[11] Staff article, "The Leisured Masses," *Business Week*, No. 1254 (September 12, 1953).

[12] Phyllis Fenner, *The Proof of the Pudding: What Children Read* (New York: John Day Co., Inc., 1957), p. 212.

Historically, a great many factors have contributed to the lack of appreciation of serious reading. Men of action established the American colonies and expanded the nation westward. There was not much time left over to indulge in the meditative and reflective arts. In the prevailing social climate a pattern was set which has continued as part of our culture. To the colonists and pioneers who had little time for book learning were added millions upon millions of immigrants. Seeking to earn a livelihood in a strange country, they, too, were forced to action rather than to studious pursuits. Problems for the teachers of America were in the making.

Lack of Reverence for the Mother Tongue. A persistent force affecting reading is connected with the fact that the United States is a "melting pot" nation populated by people from every land; many languages are spoken here. Children do not always hear English spoken correctly at home, because their parents may not have learned it properly from *their* parents who came to this country as immigrants. Since, for millions of people living here, English is not really the mother tongue, teachers have had to face the continuing problem of trying to educate, in English, children born to parents who lack experience with the subtleties of English syntax and vocabulary. Having no speech counterparts for a large number of words met in challenging books, many Americans become discouraged and avoid all but easy reading material.

Dearth of Reading in the Home. If people speak and read a language other than English in the home, they will not be inclined to buy books written in the adopted tongue. If the parents do not read, or read only in limited amount, the growing generation of potential readers is considerably handicapped in the development of its own lifetime reading habits. It makes a great deal of difference to the individual and, through him, to the nation if American children have incentives to read in the home. This kind of reading gives needed additional practice and helps to extend the school program.

Competition for Leisure Time. Another factor related to the present unsatisfactory level of reading habits is the unending competition for leisure time. In a country as rich as the United States, book reading as a recreational activity must compete with attending motion pictures, listening to radio and phonographs, watching television, and driving cars.

Most parents and teachers realize the extent to which popular communication media have subtracted from the study and reading time of teen-agers, but the retarding influence of cars upon scholarship ratings is not widely comprehended. The National Association of Secondary School Principals, in its publication *Spotlight*, revealed that, according to a survey carried on from 1955 to 1959 at Madison High School in Rexburg, Idaho, "No straight A student had the use of a car. Of the B students, 15 per cent owned or had the use of a car. But 41 per cent of the C students, 71 per cent of the D's and 13 per cent of the F, or failing, students owned automobiles."

When reminded of the values of book reading, young and old alike explain that there just is not time for it. Even this rationalization loses force in view of the following computation: A booklet entitled *Your Library Card—A Passport to World Knowledge* claims that, if the individual will read only fifteen minutes a day, he can read half a book a week, or two books a month, twenty books a year, a thousand books in a lifetime.[13] Skeptical of the claim, thirty members of a college class taught by the author embarked on personal investigations to check the validity of the first two items. Using some of the books found in the list in the Appendix, a third of the students in the class discovered that they could read more than the modest amount in the claim, chiefly because of a strong tendency to become so absorbed in the content during the first fifteen minutes that reading time was unconsciously extended. Instead of reading half a book a week, they found it comparatively easy to read a book a week.

National Tendency to Nervous Tension. A further obstacle to the growth of desirable reading tastes and appreciations is the rapid pace of American living. Everyone seems to be high keyed and in a great hurry. It naturally takes more time to read a good book of characterization, such as Clancy Sigal's prize-winning novel,

13 Prepared by the Channing-Bete Co., Greenfield, Mass.

Going Away,[14] than to read a brief paperback mystery or to glance through picture magazines, where reading assumes a secondary role. American culture is predicated on the ambition motif, a race to get ahead, to succeed, to amass material proof of prowess. Americans in the twentieth century have a deeply ingrained habit of nervous haste. Consequently, they want everything to be lively and to move in quick tempo. In their reading, the majority demand material that requires a minimum of mental effort. Difficult reading is thus not only often rejected but frequently resented.

Holding Standards Too Low. More often than not, the elementary reading program is geared to the child incapable of reading beyond the sixth-grade level. Yet an interesting study of a significantly large group of schoolchildren (2,000), whose reading achievement was measured in terms of mental ability, revealed that, shortly after their entrance into junior high school, only one out of four cannot go beyond the sixth grade in reading.[15] Perhaps in their concern for the fourth child, elementary teachers have been failing to challenge the other three pupils sufficiently. Some of the recognition and encouragement accorded to teachers of retarded pupils should be shared with teachers who motivate accelerated pupils to read more stimulating books.

Lack of Emphasis in the School Program. Still another factor contributing to the present status of reading interests is the lack of special attention to recreational reading. In many school systems, basic reading instruction is carefully planned but recreational reading is given only incidental emphasis. In the attempt to stimulate the growth of the book-reading habit, reliance upon casual recommendation is a mistake. All along the line, from primary grades through high school, planned guidance in raising the standards of appreciation and taste should be an accepted part of the total reading program.

A related factor inhibiting growth in recreational reading is the overemphasis in some school systems on social-studies reading, in the fields of geography, history, and civics. While of great impor-

[14] Published by Houghton Mifflin Co., Boston, 1962 (513 pages).
[15] George I. Thomas, "A Study of Reading in Terms of Mental Ability," *Elementary School Journal*, XLVII (September 1945), 28–33.

tance, this type of reading, dealing as it does with facts, should not be considered a substitute for the "literature of power," that is, the creative power inherent in imaginative literature. Thus, Friday book-club meetings in the intermediate and upper grades should not be used for social-studies reports. In helping the children to program these book-club meetings in the classroom, the effort should be made to direct their attention toward imaginative fiction such as *The Wind in the Willows* or *Charlotte's Web*.

AMERICAN TRIBUTES TO BOOKS AND READING

The present discussion of book-reading habits in the United States would be incomplete without the citation of a few of the countless tributes paid by Americans to books and reading over the years.

Benjamin Franklin was once asked, "What kind of man deserves the most pity?" Franklin replied, "A lonesome man on a rainy day who does not know how to read."

Ernest Hemingway the novelist is quoted as saying, "After you are finished reading [a good book,] you will feel that all *that* happened to you and afterwards it all belongs to you. The good and the bad, the ecstasy, the remorse and sorrow, the people and the places and how the weather was."

President Griswold of Yale University phrases his regard for reading this way: "Since reading maketh full men, when we stop reading we shall be empty men."

Along this same line, the Chinese-American philosopher Lin Yutang hints that people who have the habit of daily reading are prevented from being bores. In his book *The Importance of Living* he says, "A scholar who hasn't read anything for three days feels that his talk has no flavor." People who never nourish their minds by substantial reading tend to limit themselves to "maintenance talk" entailing a tiresome play-by-play account of their day's activities. Someone has aptly referred to this talk as a "grabbag of personal and domestic trivia," and it does not provide stimulating companionship.

Each human being can make his own discoveries in the world of books. Interesting surprises await the browser or seeker who chances upon a book, for example, by Franz Kafka, George Gissing, or Katherine Mansfield.

THE ROLE OF READING IN SCHOOL

If people use reading as an aid in solving problems connected with daily living, the schools must teach children how to read directions, how to find a wide variety of practical information, and so on. If·adult voters examine both sides of an issue, verify the accuracy of information, discount biases, and evaluate propaganda, children should be taught habits of critical appraisal in school. If people in daily life seek guidance in inspirational books, children should be helped to look for examples of decency and fair play in the stories they read. If adults read for diversion, children also should be guided to read for enjoyment. The teacher does well to keep in mind the broad social aims of reading and to relate them to stages of child development.

Reading and Child Development. People in the field of reading instruction continually urge teachers to respect each child's individual "timetable" of growth—to accept the child at his personal level of development and to begin instruction at that point. The whole reading-readiness program shows the keen concern educators have for the importance of the child's capacity; they do not require him to perform a reading task until he is sufficiently mature for it. The emphasis on reading in this text should therefore not be interpreted to preclude attention to stages of child development. In a later chapter it will be shown how child needs have dictated the very steps used in teaching a basic reading lesson.

Reading and Pupil Progress. When the importance of reading, in relation to life, was stressed, the point was made that our cultural pattern is predicated on literacy. For this reason American schools are, in the last analysis, reading schools, with the textbook an essential part of education. As John Gardner, of the Commission on National Goals in Education, asserted in 1960: "Some subjects are more important than others. Reading is the most important of all." Indeed, reading is intimately linked with every content area of the modern school curriculum. It is impossible to think of a child as good in geography and poor in reading. Most of what the child is supposed to learn, in social studies, science, art, music, and literature, depends on reading. This basic skill is a tool as well in solving arithmetic problems and in spelling and writing. So completely dependent is the child's success in school upon reading that many behavior problems stem from inability to read. When steps are taken to increase achievement in reading, an improvement in personal behavior usually follows. It stands to reason that, if a child's inability to read is exposed to the view of his more skilled classmates day after day, and year after year, something will happen to his attitude. Failure in reading is difficult to gloss over, and it must not be underestimated. Truly, reading is the first R.

QUESTIONS AND ACTIVITIES

1. What is the difference in emphasis between the section on "The Usefulness of Reading in Life" and the section entitled "The Reading Habits of Americans"?
2. Of the six uses of reading listed which have you employed this week?
3. What is the basic difference between teaching the mother tongue in France and in the United States?
4. Which of the facts included under the sidehead "Evidence of Satisfactory Status" did you find the most gratifying? Why?
5. Of the statistics listed under the sidehead "Evidence of Less Satisfactory Status" which one surprised you the most? Discuss.
6. A number of tributes to books and reading which the author has used in her college classes are listed in this chapter. Most of her students seem to prefer Benjamin Franklin's tribute. What would be your guess as to the second most popular tribute? Why not survey your class and discover the favorite? Try to analyze why it was chosen.
7. In the final section of the chapter, the claim is advanced that American schools are reading schools. Complete this statement: The child cannot be poor in _____ and good in _____.
8. One of the most effective ways to *study* is to make use of the SQ3R technique (Survey, Question, Read, Recite, Reread). To *review* a chapter after having studied it according to the five activities enu-

merated, making an outline is helpful. This way relationships between ideas are highlighted for improved retention. A partial outline
of the first chapter appears below, showing centerheads and sideheads used in the textbook. To make mental associations helpful in
remembering content, finish the partial outline below.

Chapter 1—Reading and American Life

Introduction
  I. The Uses of Reading in Life
        A. The Child's Introduction to the Usefulness of Reading
  II. The Reading Habits of Americans
        A. Evidence of Satisfactory Status
        B. Evidence of Less Satisfactory Status
  III. Forces Affecting American Reading Habits
        A. Lack of Reverence for the Mother Tongue
        B. Dearth of Reading in the Home
        C. Competition for Leisure Time
        D.
        E.
        F.
  IV.
  V.
        A.
        B.

Note that Roman numerals are used for centerheads and capital letters for first-level sideheads. This chapter did not contain material
for second-level sideheads, but these are usually introduced with
Arabic numerals 1, 2, etc. Since outlining is effective in both study
and review, the student is urged to utilize this technique in covering
the material in this text.

SELECTED REFERENCES

BURNETT, LEO. "The Mission of Magazines," *The Saturday Review,*
    XLII (December 1959), 22.
COMMISSION ON THE ENGLISH CURRICULUM, NATIONAL COUNCIL OF
    TEACHERS OF ENGLISH. *Language Arts for Today's Children.* New
    York: Appleton-Century-Crofts, Inc., 1954.
CONANT, JAMES B. *Learning To Read: A Report of a Conference of
    Reading Experts.* Princeton, N.J.: Educational Testing Service, July,
    1962.

DAWSON, MILDRED A., and HENRY A. BAMMAN. *Fundamentals of Basic Reading Instruction*. New York: Longmans, Green & Co., Inc., 1959.

DEBOER, JOHN J., and MARTHA DALLMANN. *The Teaching of Reading*. New York: Holt, Rinehart & Winston, Inc., 1960.

HEILMAN, ARTHUR W. *Principles and Practices of Teaching Reading*. Columbus, Ohio: Charles E. Merrill Books, Inc., 1961.

HOVLAND, CARL I. "Effects of the Mass Media of Communication," Chap. 28 in GARDNER LINDZEY (ed.) *Handbook of Social Psychology*. Vol. II. Cambridge, Mass.: Addison Wesley Publishing Co., Inc., 1954.

INTERNATIONAL READING CONFERENCE PROCEEDINGS. *Challenge and Experiment in Reading*. Vol. VII. New York: Scholastic Magazines, 1962.

NATIONAL SOCIETY FOR THE STUDY OF EDUCATION. *Sixtieth Yearbook: Development in and Through Reading*. Chicago: University of Chicago Press, 1961.

SCHLICK, FRANK I. *The Paperbound Book in America*. New York: R. R. Bowker Co., 1958.

SCHRAMM, WILBUR, JACK LYLE, and EDWIN B. PARKER. *Television in the Lives of Our Children*. Stanford, Calif.: Stanford University Press, 1961.

SELDES, GILBERT. *The Public Arts*. New York: Simon & Schuster, Inc., 1956.

SHAFFER, HELEN B. "Reading Boom: Books and Magazines," *Editorial Research Reports*, Vol. XI, No. 23 (December 20, 1961).

SQUIRE, JAMES R. "Literacy and Literature," *English Journal*. Vol. XLIX (March 1960), 154–60.

STRANG, RUTH, CONSTANCE M. McCULLOUGH, and ARTHUR E. TRAXLER. *The Improvement of Reading* (3d ed.). New York: McGraw-Hill Book Co., Inc., 1961.

WAPLES, DOUGLAS, BERNARD SERELSON, and FRANKLYN R. BRADSHAW. *What Reading Does to People*. Chicago: University of Chicago Press, 1950.

2

THINKING, READING,
AND OTHER LANGUAGE ARTS

Language has been termed man's greatest invention. It is not an inborn human skill but a form of behavior which has to be acquired by each individual through experience and imitation. Case studies of rare "wolf" children who have been lost to human contact since infancy reveal that they tend to grunt like animals when found, and show no signs of having developed any form of communication resembling language.[1]

LANGUAGE DEVELOPMENT

Language as a Code. One authority refers to "man's unique capacity for receiving abstract messages in a complex code through such perceptual channels as seeing and hearing."[2] Whether telegraphic, diplomatic, or what not, a code is a system of signals. To understand the "message" requires the ability to recognize the signals. The most prominent signal in the complicated code known as language is the *word*. Whether spoken or written, the word is what a given group (English, Spanish, French, and so on) "assign to stand for an object, action, feeling

[1] Arnold L. Gesell, *Wolf Child and Human Child* (New York: Harper & Row, 1941).
[2] Helen M. Robinson, "Word Perception," *Special Bulletin* (Chicago: Scott, Foresman & Co., 1962), p. 226.

relationship or combination thereof." According to linguistic theory,[3] when we see the printed word "dog," it "acts as a trigger that releases its oral counterpart, which, in turn, releases a meaning we already possess." The word assigned to represent *dog* in another system of signals (a foreign language) would be a mystery to us; we could not "decode" it. Thus, if we see the word "perro" in print, it triggers neither an oral counterpart nor a subsequent release of meaning, unless we know the Spanish language.

Language Growth in the Child's First Five Years. As child psychologists have pointed out, it is impossible to reassure a crying infant with words. He cannot reason. He just feels. The mental process of reasoning depends upon words. Since no one can think beyond the scope of his vocabulary, and since the infant has none, he stops crying not by reason of his mother's words, promising comfort and relief, but because of her accompanying actions. She picks him up, holds him, feeds him, or otherwise makes it possible for him to enjoy sensations of security. At first, all the infant hears are sounds. Eventually, the repetition of certain sound patterns, uttered by his mother in association with her soothing actions, will take on meaning. When the infant stops crying in response to certain words *un*accompanied by actions, the rudiments of thinking have begun for him, for now he is dealing with abstract symbols.

According to Smith's study,[4] the six-year-old has developed, through listening and speaking, meaning vocabularies ranging from 6,000 to 48,800 words, with 23,700 as the average. Today, authorities in the field of child growth and development believe that the magnitude of these figures could well be altered upward as the result of wide use of television and other mass media.

Applying the Linguistic Approach. The size of the listening and speaking vocabularies developed in the early part of the child's life forms an essential part of his linguistic maturity (readiness) for learning to read. The fact that the child hears and speaks many

[3] James P. Soffietti, "Why Children Fail To Read: A Linguistic Analysis," *Harvard Educational Review,* XXV (Spring 1955), 63–94.

[4] Mary Katherine Smith, "Measurement of the Size of General English Vocabulary Through the Elementary Grades and High School," Genetic Psychology Monographs XXIV, No. 344 (November 1941), p. 311.

words before he comes to school has been shown by linguistic research to have important implications for reading instruction. By capitalizing upon the child's knowledge of spoken words, the teaching of beginning reading is made easier. Certainly, it is useful to introduce words in print already intimately known to the child through listening and speaking.

In addition to helping the child to recognize words and concepts—to give a simple example: the difference between jelly and jam—speech insights, gained from listening and speaking before the child enters school, give him other important background for acquiring reading and writing skills. The ability to "relate *speech intonation* to the printed page," according to one authority,[5] "may be used to clarify, interpret and explain a written text." Before school entrance, the child has been speaking and hearing sentences expressed with meaningful intonation. This experience will help him in reading better because he already has the "key to our sentence system," i.e., the fact that "words do not assign meaning to the sentence, but rather, the sentence assigns meaning to words." Dr. Lloyd expresses the relationship of intonation to meanings graphically when he says, "Intonation is the glue that sticks words together." What we are thinking underlies our remarks as we make them and gives stress to certain words. In American English, usage has evolved a certain convention of stress. We say, "Birds FLY." "Cows give MILK." Mother called Tom "a GOOD boy." If a child reads these phrases aloud with the stress here indicated, he is relating reading to meanings familiar in speech. Smith and Dechant[6] point out that, since the "printed word itself possesses no meaning, the perceiver's reaction to the word depends on the quality and number of his prior experiences, his ability to reconstruct and combine experiences, and the general nature of the culture in which he has lived."

According to Helen M. Robinson, William S. Gray Research Professor of Reading, University of Chicago, "The good reader

[5] Donald J. Lloyd, "Reading American English Speech Patterns," paper read at the spring meeting, May 13, 1961, of the Chicago Area Reading Association (CARA), a regional council of the International Reading Association, published in Monograph No. 104. New York: Harper & Row, 1962.

[6] Henry P. Smith and Emerald V. Dechant, *Psychology in Teaching Reading* (Englewood Cliffs, N.J.: Prentice-Hall, Inc., 1961), 44.

learns to *see* word groups as he hears them spoken and his eyes achieve relationships of meaning that a word-by-word reader fails to recognize."[7] Children can more readily anticipate and identify words as they read if they have some knowledge of *word order*, and *idiomatic use of English*. If a child is beginning to understand how English sentences are "put together," he will know that, when he comes to the phrase "I like ——," a noun meaning will follow. If the phrase begins: "I like to ——," he naturally expects some action to follow. Dr. Robinson continues, "Similarly, a child who is accustomed to saying *has gone* instead of *has went* will read the words *has gone* more readily because the language pattern is familiar to him."

THE VALUE OF INTEGRATING THE LANGUAGE ARTS

Specifically, there are five language arts: listening, reading, speaking, writing, and thinking. Through listening and reading, experiences are gained; through speaking and writing, experiences are shared. Thinking is at the master switch, serving as a silent partner, in control of receiving and sending abstract messages in the complex code of language. All language arts make use of the same signals—words. The receptive arts, listening and reading, require similar patterns of thinking such as interpreting the main idea and noticing supporting details, grasping relationships, summarizing and organizing ideas, sensing emotions, etc. As the child learns to listen, speak, and write, he develops a vocabulary for thinking about people, places, things, and feelings. These language experiences, in turn, help the child to respond to signals in print and to form appropriate sensory images as he reads silently.

Oral reading, also, presents fewer problems if linguistic insights gained in speaking and listening are related. Wepman's studies[8] show that "those children who are unable to discriminate discrete units of speech sounds are frequently found to have articulatory defects and to experience difficulty in associating sounds with let-

[7] Helen M. Robinson, "Coordinating the Language Arts Saves Time in Teaching Reading," *Learn to Listen, Speak and Write* (teacher's ed.), Book 2/1 (Chicago: Scott, Foresman & Co., 1962).

[8] Joseph M. Wepman, "Auditory Discrimination, Speech and Reading," *Elementary School Journal*, LX (March 1960), 325–333.

ters"—another instance of the close relationship existing between hearing, speaking, reading, and thinking.

As regards a further problem connected with reading aloud, particularly at the primary level, W. Cabell Greet, Professor of English, Columbia University, and speech consultant, Columbia Broadcasting System, has this to say: "When the final *d* in *did* or *and* is exploded with extra emphasis, these words become did/a and an/da, incorrectly containing two syllables instead of one." Here, again, if the child is encouraged to remember how he says these words in everyday talking, he will tend to use natural pronunciation when he reads them aloud. Aside from the other advantages which have been enumerated, coordinating reading with speech helps to prevent word-by-word oral reading.

Though each of the language arts has its own particular skills, requiring appropriate teaching methods, four of them—speaking, writing, listening, and reading—overlap at several points. As was indicated in the introductory discussion above, pupils benefit if the teacher coordinates language-arts instruction whenever possible. All language arts have one relationship in common. Each is intimately involved with thinking and the tools of thought—words. To teach with full awareness of this basic relationship, as well as of the various interrelationships among the other four language arts, is to provide a more complete program. The remainder of the chapter will deal firstly with teaching the language arts in their relation to thinking and secondly with teaching the receptive and expressive language arts in an integrated program.

TEACHING THE LANGUAGE ARTS WITH EMPHASIS ON THEIR RELATION TO THINKING

Procedures To Improve Speaking Habits and Skills. The need for taking thought while speaking is highlighted by one of those amusing dialogues which take place in Lewis Carroll's classic *Alice's Adventures in Wonderland:*

"Really, now you ask me," said Alice, very much confused, "I don't think—"

"Then you shouldn't talk," said the Hatter.

In early childhood, Junior may not know what it means to "weigh one's words" or to "count ten before swearing," but he will learn to babble less thoughtlessly if the teacher helps him to be more selective in what he says. This desirable skill may be initiated by such questions as "What was the funniest thing you saw at the circus? What was your favorite part of this story?"

In a democracy, deciding about solutions to problems in group discussion is everybody's concern. All through the grades, teachers exert their best efforts to guide children to quote facts accurately, to stick to the point, to give evidence for sweeping claims, to allow others a turn to talk, to add to the last speaker's thought, and to disagree without being disagreeable.

Children should also be taught to keep their wits about them in situations less formal than group discussions, held to solve problems. It is important to think about what one is saying when making social introductions, handling guest-host relationships, receiving and returning compliments, giving directions, explaining mishaps, etc. (Lists of habits and skills in this chapter have been culled from various city, county, and state language-arts courses of study.)

To avoid embarrassment (poor grammar, like poor spelling is readily apparent), children should be given direct help in correcting specific grammatical slips. If a child says, "My mother gave popcorn to she and I," the teacher should encourage him to try each person separately: "My mother gave popcorn to her" and "My mother gave popcorn to me." Then the child is ready to combine for two what he would say for each separately: "My mother gave popcorn to her and (to) me."

Junior will gain in social acceptability if he is encouraged to express himself in an interesting way. Definite guidance in improving oral expression should be given to arouse children's pride in going beyond clichés. If a child ignores his stock of words and contents himself with trite choices, the teacher should occasionally guide him to replace tired, all-purpose terms with more apt ones. For example, suppose Junior remarks, "Last night on TV I saw a man pick up a big old sack of gold in a mine and try to get away with it." The teacher asks questions to elicit synonyms: "How did he get the sack up? Was it a light load? What was the man trying to do? Was it his gold?" Soon Junior is ready to give a revised version: "Last night on TV I saw a man lift a heavy sack of gold in a mine and try to escape with it." He will realize that the second version provides a clearer picture for the listener, and will feel a little glow of triumph since he was not told the words. As his teacher drew him out with pertinent questions, he supplied the more accurate and interesting terms himself. The process of eliciting revision should not be carried to the point of nagging, needless to say.

Procedures To Improve Written Expression. Another language art concerned with sharing experience is writing, which, according to Francis Bacon the seventeenth-century philosopher, "maketh an exact man." In speaking, gestures and facial expressions help to carry the burden of communication, but in written discourse exactly the right words must be chosen if meaning is to be clearly conveyed. The written message is down in black and white for all to judge—for contemporaries and perhaps even for generations to follow.

When a comparison is drawn between the greater exactitude demanded by writing and the less strict demands of speaking, the author is reminded of a little boy she taught some years ago in the third grade. An art exhibit had been planned by the eight-year-olds. Some of the children painted pictures; others modeled pet animals in clay; four, including Terry, elected to prepare plate gardens. On the day of the art exhibit, as Terry approached the school, by some mischance, he dropped his plate garden on the cement sidewalk. Everything was broken—the planter dish, the miniature Japanese bridge, the delicate figurines of cranes and people. Even the sprouting green carrot tops, to simulate shrubbery, were crushed. That afternoon, when the third-grade exhibit was over, the children decided to write news accounts about their show. Terry's is reproduced below.

Today we had an art show. Betty brought a Japanese garden. Tom brought a Japanese garden. Linda brought a Japanese garden. But nobody else brought any more Japanese gardens.

The author of this textbook has always treasured the little composition. Could anything more exactly describe the situation than that dignified last sentence? Terry had found in writing an outlet for his feeling of loss, as well as a chance to organize a personal experience.

Benjamin Franklin wrote in his *Autobiography* that "The next thing most like living one's life over again seems to be a recollection of that life made as durable as possible by putting it down in writing." More children should be encouraged to keep diaries. There is no telling how many lives of obscure people would form fascinating documents if they would only put down sincerely what they feel about work, love, religion, windfalls, disappointment, etc. Furthermore, such diaries might become instruments of self-discovery when reread years later.

Many opportunities should be provided for children to write brief accounts of their experiences as individuals and as members of a group. (The first-grade experience charts fall into the second type, though their chief purpose is to furnish experience in "reading them back.") Monday morning is a suitable choice of time, since the weekends often feature trips and special treats. In individual compositions, children should be encouraged to express themselves freely, creatively. Thus Jo-Ann, a seven-year-old, writes, in all the pride of discovery,

> I playd with my puppy Sunday.
> He hase teeth like litle pinns.

It is a good policy to correct only one mistake in each of the first few written efforts. Should all four of Jo-Ann's errors be red-penciled, it might inhibit her the next time from writing what she really would like to say. Some children become so wary of climbing out on a spelling limb, as it were, that they compromise and use inept words that they *are* sure about. It is a good idea to invite the children to ask for the spelling of words they want to use, as they are composing their written work. The teacher then steps quickly to the board and writes them.

As soon as children are ready to produce written social-studies reports, the teacher can expect to give many hours of patient guidance to helping the children to learn such basic skills as taking notes, making outlines with centerheads and first- and second-level sideheads, and composing a well-organized whole from the notes and the outline.

In addition to original compositions, diaries, and reports, children are helped to grow in writing skill through the motivation which springs from personal and social needs. A letter to a schoolmate absent because of illness, a thank-you note to grandmother for a present—these and other activities offer a functional setting for practice in written expression." Supervised experience with proofreading their own writing" helps to "internalize standards of usage," according to Marcus.[9] Her study was conducted with a control group who were taught usage by means of systematic instruction in grammar and syntax. The experimental group, exposed to supervised experience in proofreading their written work, made greater improvement.

Thinking and Listening. To pay attention, while directions are being given or announcements or introductions are being made, demands a different type of listening from that needed for conversations and stories. Reaction on the part of the hearer is more closely involved. Analyzing as one listens is required for lectures, political speeches, and sales pitches, in order to be alert to propaganda devices. Definite training can put listeners on guard against such verbal traps as emotional appeals, faulty reasoning, and dubious factual evidence. To obtain functional application, the teacher can guide the children to analyze different types of propaganda on tape recordings. Wachner[10] points out that it is just as important to provide "experience-listening" if we want learning to take place as it is to provide "experience-reading."

Listening attentively is also essential in more or less informal social relationships. Guidance in this form of listening has important implications for personal development. Unfortunately less thinking accompanies listening during the average conversation between friends, job associates, and acquaintances than in any other use of this particular language art. The trouble is that one party to a conversation often fails to pay attention to the other party's talk, because he is busily preparing what he will say next. To listen to another as though memorizing every precious word is

[9] Marie Marcus, "A Functional Language Program in Sixth Grade," *Elementary English* (October 1960), 273.

[10] Clarence Wachner, "Listening in an Integrated Language Arts Program," *Elementary English*, XXXIII (1956), 491–96.

to accord him a rare experience. Even at the primary level, children can be guided to look at the speaker, to keep attention on what is being said, and try not to interrupt.

Listening is, of course, rightly classed with reading as a receptive art. However, these companion arts differ in several respects. As someone has aptly said, "Reading is more private and personal." Attention is not divided by the need to adjust to another personality, as in the case of listening. Carried on alone, reading stimulates no feeling of social pressure. Rereading can conveniently take place; not so with relistening. It is often awkward and embarrassing to ask for repetition.

Thinking and Reading. It can safely be asserted that thinking must accompany reading or no actual reading is going on. With these two language arts an unusually strong two-way relationship is involved. Thinking makes reading for meaning possible, and reading, in turn, makes more thinking possible. Indeed, probably nothing is more helpful to thinking than reading, because thereby the thoughts of other people—in many cases geniuses—are received. In considering their thoughts in terms of personal experience, the reader's own thinking is greatly stimulated. Let the reader notice what happens to his own imagination as he reads Mark Twain's flight of fancy quoted below.

When I'm playful I use the meridians of longitude and parallels of latitude for a seine, and drag the Atlantic ocean for whales. I scratch my head with lightning and purr myself to sleep with thunder.[11]

Long before the age of astronauts Mark Twain's mind went into orbit.

In his studies in thinking and reading, Dr. Donald Durrell sets up three major types of thinking: (1) organizational thinking such as listing, classifying, outlining, etc.; (2) elaborational thinking such as seeing further possibilities, new ideas, and suggestions; (3) critical thinking such as evaluating, comparing, judging relevance of facts, etc.[12] The first two types of thinking in relation

[11] Life on the Mississippi (New York: Harper & Row), Chapter 3 in any of their editions from 1917 on.
[12] Defined for My Weekly Reader (teacher's ed.), XXXII, No. 17 (January 22, 1951), 1. (New York: American Education Publications).

to reading are self-explanatory and easy to see, but the third, critical thinking in relation to reading, requires some discussion.

CRITICAL THINKING IN RELATION TO READING. Since the teacher's grasp of any phase of reading influences the quality of instruction, it is reassuring to note the responses of a group of elementary-school teachers to this pair of survey questions:

1. How do you define critical thinking in relation to reading?
2. How would you *apply* critical thinking to the reading of these forms of content: restaurant menus, cookbook recipes, love letters, newspapers, textbooks, fiction?

Representative responses from a summer-session class, composed of both men and women teachers, appear in two sections below. To conserve space, individual contributions are merely separated by dots.

Selected Definitions of Critical Thinking in Relation to Reading.

To me, critical thinking while reading means the opposite of being gullible and believing everything in print. . . . It means reading on both sides of an issue. . . . Critical reading means seeking objective evidence for a statement in print. If an advertiser claims that his product is the longest, widest, I say: "Prove it." . . . Critical thinking while reading means estimating the suitability of material for a particular purpose. For instance, will this joke that I am reading be suitable to tell at the PTA meeting? . . . To me, critical reading means running down statements to the original source. "What *four* out of five doctors?" . . . Critical thinking means challenging the authority, talking back to the author. But that does not necessarily mean that the reader's word is law! The reader may be no more right than the author. It is essential to consult many sources for the truth. That is my criterion; I keep asking of what I read: "Is this true?"

Applications of Critical Reading to Different Types of Content.

1. Reading menus: The "yardstick" that I use in making a choice of a meal is the price. I read a menu from right to left, in other words. . . . I select a menu item in keeping with my purpose—to reduce. If a meal adds up to too many calories, I don't choose it. . . . I decide what will agree with my digestion and then I order. . . . I remember what I have had at the restaurant before and my standard of choice is what they prepare reasonably well. . . . My standard in choosing is my

appetite. If I am very hungry I read through the menu with that in mind and try to find something filling.

2. Reading cookbook recipes: As I read a cookbook recipe, I think how to enlarge or reduce it, depending upon the number of people I have to cook dinner for. . . . I use my own preferences and if the recipe calls for rosemary, I won't even try it because I don't like rosemary flavor. . . . If I am preparing a meal for guests I read recipes with the idea of impressing guests favorably with something unusual. . . . The yardstick I hold up to evaluate a recipe is: "Will it work?" . . . I judge a recipe by the ingredients it calls for. If there are too many and too fancy, I know it just isn't my dish. . . . My standard of selection when I read a recipe critically is: "Do I have the ingredients in the house?" Sometimes, though, if the recipe calls for bay leaves and I'm out of bay leaves, I'll make it without bay leaves.

3. Reading love letters: In my opinion it is almost impossible to be coolly objective in reading love letters because of the fact that a love letter is not usually written in a rational mood, and it isn't read in a rational mood. . . . The value of a love letter is nil unless it measures up to my criterion: sincerity. . . . There is no more critical reading than this. Anything with such personal involvement is bound to be read with close attention. . . . The reader of a love letter does not read critically. He believes what he wants to believe and is not limited to what is down in black and white. . . . The question I constantly hold up as a yardstick when I read a love letter is: Does this sound as though he loves me?

4. Reading newspapers: To know what to think about any issue in the newspaper, a reader needs to be well-informed on both sides of the question. . . . To me critical reading of the news means willingness to look up further information if puzzled by something in the paper that seems contradictory. . . . When I read claims I check with my own observations. . . . To read newspapers critically I consider the party preference of the owner. As I read I am on guard against slanted reporting. Then I try to balance what appears there by reading another paper or magazine owned by someone of an opposing political belief. . . . I am on guard against name-calling. . . . I try to see how actual facts square with the opinions stated. . . . If a politician who has lost an election criticizes the way problems are being handled by the candidate who won, I demand that the losing politician suggest feasible solutions instead of just criticizing.

5. Reading textbooks: This type of reading is complicated by the need to read not only from the student's viewpoint as to what he thinks worth remembering but also from the instructor's viewpoint, in order to pass the examination. . . . The set of criteria I use and by which I judge a textbook consists of the following: "Is it interesting? Is it written by someone with both theoretical and practical background?" . . .

One form of critical evaluation I use is to try to identify the school of educational thought to which the author belongs. Does he believe that the school program should suit the child, or does he believe that the child should suit the school program? Or does he avoid either extreme position and take a moderate view, choosing the best ideas from both schools of thought?

6. Reading fiction: As I read a novel I keep asking: "Is this plot plausible or is the long arm of coincidence stretched out of shape? Are the characters believable or overdrawn?" . . . I try to find hints in the dialogue, characters and setting to discover whether or not the author is drawing upon his own life experience. . . . If I am reading historical novels I always make comparison with actual historical facts. . . . I compare the way the characters act under stress with the way I have acted in somewhat similar situations. . . . I read to find personally helpful bits of philosophy, and so on, to change my moods. . . . I talk back to the book. For example, yesterday I read something a character in a novel said to the effect: "All sadness is wasted energy." I didn't agree, recalling that sometimes in a sad moment I have recognized some past unkindness, and repenting, resolved not to err again. I don't call such sadness wasted energy. . . . I tend to hold up literary yardsticks and measure the originality, felicitous choice of words and so on.

In one form or another, the teachers who participated in the above informal survey showed an understanding of the mental processes involved in critical thinking. Implicit in their responses are (1) the search for suitable data, (2) comparison of sources to determine which offers the most reliable authority, (3) estimation of worth according to some standard, after (4) obtaining sufficient background to quality for passing judgment.

It is in the last connection that children suffer a disadvantage. They have not lived long enough to build up a rich supply of standards to put to service in measuring values. However, even in the first grade, the teacher should help children to make a modest start at thinking critically. By successive steps other teachers in other grades should lead pupils to more complex levels. In reading a primer story the children may be challenged to decide, "Could this really happen? Is a puppy able to swim?" Each pupil then summons from the storehouse of his "little past" all that he knows about puppies, and uses that knowledge as a yardstick in deciding his answer. At the third-grade level children are capable of searching for relevant materials. Suppose they are asked to find out about the kinds of work done by Hopi Indians. The social-studies text may contain several pages about the food, shelter, clothing, and work of Hopi Indians. But the children are instructed to ignore passages that do not deal with the *work* of the Hopis, and focus attention upon those that feature it. Still later, in the intermediate and upper grades, children may be led to evaluate the accuracy of an item about astronauts or antimissile missiles in a science comic book by comparing it with a more reliable source such as a modern encyclopedia. There is no question but that from first grade onward it is essential for prospective citizens of our democracy to be able to pass competent judgment concerning matter in print. (See Index for page references to other aspects of critical thinking and reading.)

TEACHING THE LANGUAGE ARTS IN AN INTEGRATED PROGRAM

The language-arts program in American schools would be immeasurably strengthened if all teachers consciously planned instruction in one language art to reinforce the others. In order to read well, one must be able to think and to understand. Words and meanings already on hand are put to the service of interpreting ideas met in print. The reverse process is also to be encouraged in the classroom, i.e., transferring into the children's speaking and writing vocabularies the new words gained from reading. Most people tend to have a larger "recognition vocabulary" in reading than they have a "production vocabulary" in speaking and writing. It is, of course, easier to recognize words appearing before one in print than to call them up from memory. Indeed, authorities feel that the central problem for those aiming to speak or write well is the *transfer* of vocabulary from reading to one's permanent stock, where it may be tapped for purposes of expression. Reading, then, affects, and is affected by, the other arts of language.[13] Since one skill fortifies the others, teachers must integrate the language arts more consciously than in the past. However, this is not to say that reading instruction will lose its special

[13] Agatha Townsend, "Interrelationships Between Reading and Other Language Arts Areas," *Elementary English*, XXXI (February 1954), 99–109.

identity. Because the elementary school is dedicated to the promotion of literacy and because reading is literacy's chief tool, carefully planned instruction in reading skills must be not neglected but included daily.

In addition to recognizing the close family ties which exist among the various language arts, it is important to realize as well that growth in language power is related to the mental, physical, emotional, and social growth patterns of each individual child. As in any learning endeavor, for progress in the language arts, children must be given selective guidance. Not all advance at the same rate, and much patience is required to help children develop facility in the receptive and expressive language arts.

An Example of Integrated Instruction. An excellent example of a method of instruction which provides for the interplay of the language skills is the one the French use. According to report, the French sum up the relation between thinking, reading, speaking, listening, and writing by the declaration "Phraseology and thinking go together." This is but another way of stating that no one can think beyond the span of his vocabulary. To foster growth in vocabulary with the goal of sharpening the quality of thinking, French educators plan reading lessons to provide for the integration of the language skills. While American educators could not completely adopt French techniques for teaching reading in conjunction with the other language arts, nevertheless, a study of French methods may shed light on teaching English and permit teachers a clear view of wider services in the field of reading.

THE FRENCH READING LESSON. For many years, according to French state courses of study, the typical reading lesson in their schools has taken essentially the following form. (To make the description clear, some American educational terms have been substituted for the French.)

1. The teacher lists on the board some of the new words from the passage to be read and makes certain that the pupils are able to pronounce them and know their meanings. (We, also, follow this procedure in introducing a reading lesson.)

2. The teacher asks a guiding question to help the pupils find an important idea in a given part of the selection. The children read silently to find the answer to the teacher's question. One child is called upon to read his choice of answer orally. (This sequence of guiding all the pupils to read silently to find the right part, followed by having one read it aloud, is accepted technique in a great many American schools.)

3. The French teacher leads the children to explain what the passage means and to relate it to their own experience, or compare it with other selections they have read. (We follow this procedure also.)

4. The French teacher leads the children to appreciate the apt choice of a few of the key words in the passage. Shades of meaning are explored by comparing the words used in the selection with synonyms which the author might have used. (We could do a great deal more of this type of study to sharpen our children's feelings for words.) If the French selection contains a description of a "serene twilight," for example, the teacher helps the children to form a chain of mental associations with the adjective *serene*. Exact shades of meaning expressed in the passage are discovered as the children "tune in" different synonyms and note the effect. Will any of the synonyms "calm," "tranquil," "placid," "quiet," or "peaceful" be as effective as the word "serene" in describing the twilight? It will be noted that, as the children compare each of the five synonyms with the word "serene," they receive so much exposure to it and to the synonyms that they are not likely to forget them. In short, the emphasis is sufficient to transfer the new words to each pupil's permanent stock, available for use in thinking, speaking, and writing.

5. Having now read the passage silently and orally, discussed the meaning, and admired the style through attention to the choice of words, French pupils are next asked to make an oral reproduction of the gist of the passage. They are not told to tell in their own words what they have just read—a process that tends to maintain the status quo in vocabulary. They are asked to reproduce the heart of the passage, not by rote but in a *combination of*

their own phrasing *plus* some transferred key words and phrases from the original selection. (Opportunity for creative expression is given at another time.)

6. The French teacher makes it a point to mention specifically which new words were noted in the child's oral reproduction and to commend him for transferring them.

7. The children next make a *written* reproduction of the passage (with the book closed), resembling the oral one. Each child has a *cahier*, or notebook, for the purpose. Once again the teacher urges the pupils to transfer terms learned during the other steps, and reminds them to display pride in their mother tongue by using good grammar and syntax.

8. The teacher corrects the notebooks each day. (Time for making corrections is considered part of the teaching load because the French feel that a mistake uncorrected is a learning opportunity lost.) When the child receives his notebook, he must observe all corrections and write a fair copy ("without blemish" as the French say). This second version is, in turn, carefully checked by the teacher.

The French maintain that, through this multiple-exposure process, the pupil's vocabulary is "enlarged, sharpened and quickened." By the method of focusing on synonyms, concentrating on meaning and on oral and written reproduction, new words are retained and become so much a part of the pupil's life that they come instantly to mind when he needs them. At suitable difficulty levels, this type of instruction is carried on daily, from the primer classes through the upper levels. Lucidity and precision, coupled with grace, are emphasized in the writing. These standards carry over into speaking. Precise meanings are continually stressed in reading and listening. Correctly enough, French teachers never use oral reading as a test to discover whether or not the pupils know pronunciation. Rather, the French use oral reading as a means of guiding children to find ideas in print in order to communicate these through skillful oral reading.

EVALUATION OF THE METHOD. Regardless what one may think of French educational theory, this highly systematic method seems to have borne fruit rather than to have crushed out creativity. French masters of expression—La Fontaine, Lamartine, Daudet, Voltaire, Balzac, Gautier, Stendhal, Flaubert, Anatole France, De Maupassant, Gide, and Camus—were tireless in their efforts to express their thoughts with meticulous clarity. It is inspiring to read that Anatole France rewrote some paragraphs fifty times before he satisfied himself that his thinking and writing formed a lucid whole. His manuscripts showed that he changed words, transposed their order, then scratched them out. He covered pages with corrections, additions, and interlineations, his biographers tell us. He believed that only through a rich store of words could thought be brought sharply into focus. This wealth of working tools gave charm and grace to his writings. Clear thinking and writing make for "clear" reading, i.e., promote readability.

The French beliefs that words and ideas usually go together and that a word will often guide a child to a valuable idea have not only borne fruit in great French authors. The type of training which the children receive in reading, thinking, writing, listening, and speaking enables French people in every walk of life—barbers, messenger boys, janitors, cobblers, students, waitresses, and grocers—to express themselves with exceptional accuracy, and to take pride in the accomplishment.

ADAPTATION OF THE METHOD. American educators would not consider it feasible or desirable to adopt the French method of instruction in totality. Too many differences exist between the two countries. In France, with very little competition from other language groups, French reigns supreme as the mother tongue. Most children in France enjoy the initial advantage of hearing the French language spoken well from their earliest years, by parents and grandparents. As was pointed out in the first chapter, because of the "melting pot" nature of the population in the United States, many hear spoken as the mother tongue in their childhood homes not English but German, Italian, Norwegian, Swedish, Spanish, Portuguese, or some other language. If their parents and grandparents speak English at all, they speak it imperfectly, having learned it in adulthood. The handicap is passed along to the children. Hence the language-arts problem is complicated and, in a sense, self-perpetuating, in spite of the valiant efforts of teachers. The strongly centralized type of educational control which prevails in France, plus the fact that the country is not large, ensures uniformity of instruction in the mother tongue. With each local American school district chiefly responsible for what is taught, any one method would be difficult to introduce in the United States and considered by many to be contrary to American principles.

Since writing makes a person more exact in his thinking and expression, increased opportunities for written work should be given to American children. Using a modification of the French plan in order to coordinate language teaching in the schools of the United States would help correct much that is ambiguous and careless in current communication. Children must be convinced, of course, that they can utilize a good vocabulary to their advantage, and that reading is an important means of helping people to speak better, to think better, to know more, and, therefore, to stand a better chance of success in life.

Interest in Integration. In the United States the spread of the practice of linking basic reading to written expression, at least one period a week (an adaptation of the French method of language-arts instruction), promises to add many of the tools of thought to the children's permanent stock. The reciprocal relationship is not limited to basic reading. Recreational reading also can be most useful in stimulating worthwhile experiences in writing and speaking.

Reading and Written Expression. One teacher of an intermediate grade had the members of the class write a summary of the story they had read during the basic reading period. She had used guidance techniques and through adroit questioning had called attention to the apt choice of words in the basic-reader story. The paragraphs were written *after* the basic readers had been collected. In the resulting paragraphs composed by the children (three are reproduced below), a varying degree of transfer of vocabulary from reading to written language is apparent. The top reader in the class wrote the best paragraph, and the poorest reader produced the poorest written effort. The paragraphs reveal that there were three distinct levels of ability in this class, even though an uninformed school board insists on having every child in a given grade use the same reader. (Apt terms that were transferred by the children from the story in the basic reader to the written summary appear in italics.)

BETSY GOES TRAVELING

In *autumn* a letter came from Betsy's Aunt *who* lived forty miles away. The letter *invited* Betsy to come to the wedding of Betsy's *favorite cousin, whose* name was Sarah Dickens. Betsy was to bring her mother's wedding dress for Sarah to get married in. *While* Betsy was on the statecoach an *accident* happened. One of the wheels got stuck in the mud. While the *passengers* were waiting to have it *repaired,* a man asked them to his house *nearby. When* the wheel was fixed, they *carried* Betsy back to the coach, still sleeping. She forgot the bag with the wedding dress. But the man came with the bag later.

BETSY GOES TRAVELING

Betsy was the only one that got to go to the wedding. But Betsy *lost* the wedding dress and the *coachman* did not want to go back and she began to cride but the man came to give it to her and then got to the city.

BETSY GOSE TRAVELING

Betsy wanted to go to her *cousin.* Betsy was goning to the city.

To judge from this sampling, two-thirds of the class could profit greatly from more directed practice in written English. The use of a common experience such as the reading of a story in the basic reader offers a springboard for one form of written expression. It has the advantage that the teacher is able to trace the transfer of vocabulary from the reading to the written summary of the story. The children's recognized purpose was to gain practice in reviewing the story in order to tell it to someone at home later—a process not unrelated to writing out a speech as a preparation for delivering it at some future time.

In addition to giving the children practice at least once a week in the writing of summaries of stories in the basic reader, many teachers combine such reading with imaginative writing. Even in the second and third grades children enjoy writing new endings for stories they read, or turning out an entirely new version. Thus, when a third-grade group read in their basic reader a story about a train which kept stopping mysteriously because a baby elephant in the baggage car was raising its trunk and pulling the signal cord, several wrote other mysteries in a somewhat similar vein. One involved a farm family frightened by the appearance of a light in their barn one night. The guilt party turned out to be the family's pet goat, chewing on a string which was tied to a pull-chain light fixture.

Since vocabularly is important to all language arts, various exercises are designed for effecting the transfer of new words from the basic reader to the child's permanent stock. The columns below, copied by the author from the blackboard of a fourth-grade classroom, show one very popular exercise in the *transfer of vocabularly*.

Everday Way	*Book Way*
1. The *old lady* was *mad*.	1. The *elderly passenger* was *angry*.
2. Tom was *glad*.	2. Tom was *delighted*.
3. The conductor *said*—	3. The conductor *exclaimed*—

The teacher listed in a column at the left the all too common way of expressing the idea. Then she helped the children to find the same idea expressed more aptly in the story in the reader. The child who found the "book way" for improving upon the choice of words in the "everyday way" read it aloud, and the teacher wrote the apt expression opposite the trite one.

Further integration of reading—this time library reading—with written expression is often made possible when children are encouraged to keep individual "pay dirt" notebooks. They "mine" library books for "gold," i.e., for parts that prove to be especially enjoyable and worth remembering. These quotations are copied into the notebook, along with the book title and the name of the author. Some teachers lead the children to devote several pages at the back of the notebook to lists of new words and phrases encountered during silent reading. Recently the author glimpsed one such list maintained by a sixth-grade girl. Among others, it included these phrases: "ostentatious as a band majorette" and "the expectant crowd."

In their written work children at all levels beyond the primary should be taught to use other "go-ahead signals" than the overworked "and" or "so." According to English teachers, "go-ahead signals" advise that the writer is continuing a thought rather than introducing any new ideas. "Go-ahead signals" include words such as "also," "moreover," "furthermore," "likewise," "consequently," "therefore," "whereupon," etc. "Turn-about signals" warn that the writer is getting ready to introduce a change of thought, and include "on the other hand," "otherwise," "although," "though," "yet," etc. The word "but" is the overworked member of this classification.

ORAL READING AND SPEECH IMPROVEMENT. Linguistic authorities point out that since the teacher knows how to speak English, and most children know how to speak English, the problem of learning to read aloud well consists of reading English as it is spoken. However, for those children who do not know how to speak English well but who mumble and swallow syllables, careful guidance in oral reading may be needed. Several specialists have expressed concern to the author over the changing pattern of speech in the growing generation. Some authorities in the field characterize the speech of many teen-agers as nervous, jerky, overrapid, and marred by undersyllabication. Far from attaching any blame to the youths themselves, a combination of factors over which they have no control it held responsible, including (1) the "cold war" atmosphere, causing generalized anxiety; (2) both parents working, thus denying children sufficient contact with adults to imitate better language patterns; (3) lack of oral reading past the second grade.

While teachers have little control over the first two possible causes, they can easily provide more oral reading. Since there is a definite carry-over from distinct oral reading to distinct speech, children probably suffer from the absence of this form of training. In protest against mechanical oral reading around the class, taking turns, many school programs have altogether abandoned oral reading practice beyond the second grade, instead of improving the instruction itself. In the first place, the oral reading should be *motivated*. The teachers should ask thought-provoking questions to guide the reading. Oral reading should always be rereading. The pupils must read silently before reading aloud. Finally, the passage which each pupil reads aloud in answer to a guiding question must be kept brief. Never should the teacher direct the pupils to read the next line or page or paragraph. Instead, she should pose a challenging question which causes the child to read purposefully to *find* the answering part. By the form of her guiding questions or directions, the teacher provides the children with opportunities for reading orally to share, to prove a point, or to interpret; she might ask, for example, "Who was the most excited person in the wagon train on that morning in April, 1843?" After the children have read silently to find the answer and a child has been called upon, the teacher cautions; "Show with your voice how thrilled the boy felt to be starting west." Attention should be drawn to the thought in all oral-reading sessions, to the way people talk, i.e., with natural intonation, not merely to "smoothness" and "expression."

The custom of holding book-club meetings every Friday afternoon in grades past the first offers a fine opportunity for audience reading, i.e., one person reading material familiar to him but new to the other members of the group. Sharing enthusiasm for a given book provides a functional setting for the development of good oral-reading habits. In reading aloud enjoyable passages from favorite books, children learn to put the audience at ease by "speaking up" clearly in a voice that will carry, enunciating distinctly, though without distortion, pronouncing words correctly, and interpreting the passage with vitality.

Other rewards of oral reading, beyond improvement in speech habits and interpretation of meanings, include increased control of vocabulary, sentence structure, and grammar—not to mention growth in poise developed through facing a group. Adequate practice in oral reading, aided by dictionary work, promotes a high degree of security in speaking. Unless words are pronounced aloud at least once, children tend to avoid their use in speaking. Not unmindful of the prominent way in which a mispronounced word stands out, children exercise due caution and thus fail to transfer words from silent reading to their speaking vocabularly. In oral reading the new words get pronounced.

The End Product: Clear Communication. In a democracy the people are the government. If the people cannot read and listen with understanding, if they cannot express themselves lucidly in communications to representatives, the government will not be truly representative. Though each American, no matter what his walk in life, helps to shape and influence the destiny of the nation by the quality of individual thinking, the responsibility for establishing operations to improve the language arts has been accepted by the schools. Over the years teachers have fought to preserve our embattled mother tongue. It is to their everlasting credit that, in spite of the mixed nationalities composing our population, and the strong competition coming from the slang and colloquialism prevalent in mass media, good English is still spoken, written, listened to, and read in the United States.

QUESTIONS AND ACTIVITIES

1. Why is the ability to use the language arts well an important duty of citizenship?
2. Name and discuss factors in the United States which create problems in teaching the language arts.
3. Observe a child for a sufficient time to diagnose his speech behavior. Outline a program of activities to aid him.
4. What are some of the characteristics of interesting conversation? What steps can be taken in the elementary school to help improve speaking and listening abilities?
5. Look up the index of *The Reading Teacher* magazine in your school library. Select for study a recent article on linguistic theory as applied to reading instruction. Survey the article. Outline it. Summarize it. Share it in class.
6. What are some of the characteristics of critical thinking?
7. In class discuss how the French method of coordinating instruction in language arts can be adapted in the United States.
8. What is your reaction to the French assertion that "phraseology and thinking go together"?

SELECTED REFERENCES

ARTLEY, A. STERL. "Critical Reading in the Content Areas," *Elementary English*, XXXXI (February 1959), 122–130.

COMMISSION ON THE ENGLISH CURRICULUM, NATIONAL COUNCIL OF TEACHERS OF ENGLISH. *Language Arts for Today's Children*. New York: Appleton-Century-Crofts, Inc., 1954.

DURRELL, DONALD. "An Appraisal of the Teaching of Reading in Our Schools and Suggested Improvement," in *Vital Issues in Education*, ARTHUR TRAXLER (ed.). Twenty-first Educational Conference, Educational Record Bureau and American Council on Education, Washington, D.C., 1956, pp. 152–58.

ELLER, WILLIAM. "Fundamentals of Critical Reading," in *The Reading Teacher's Reader*, OSCAR S. CAUSEY (ed.). New York: The Ronald Press Co., 1958.

GLEASON, HENRY, *An Introduction to Descriptive Linguistics*. New York: Holt, Rinehart & Winston, Inc., 1955.

HENLE, PAUL (ed.). *Language, Thought and Culture*. Ann Arbor, Mich.: University of Michigan Press, 1958.

HUSBANDS, KENNETH (ed.). *Teaching Elementary School Subjects*. New York: The Ronald Press Co., 1961.

LeFEVRE, CARL. "Reading Instruction Related to Primary Language Learnings: A Linguistic View." Paper read at the Golden Anniversary Convention of the National Council of Teachers of English, Chicago, November 25, 1960. Published in *The Journal of Developmental Reading* (Spring 1961).

LLOYD, DONALD J., and HARRY R. WARFEL. *American English in Its Cultural Setting*. New York: Alfred A. Knopf (a division of Random House, Inc.), 1956.

McKEE, PAUL G. *Teaching of Reading in the Elementary School*. Boston: Houghton Mifflin Co., 1948.

SMITH, NILA BANTON. "New Vistas in Reading," in *Frontiers of Elementary Education V*. Syracuse, N.Y.: Syracuse University Press, 1958.

3

READING THEN AND NOW

The reading of history is somewhat like entering a theater when the curtain has been up on a play for quite a while. Too late to see the first act, the tardy arrival is inclined to turn to a person in the next seat and ask, "What has happened up to now? What did I miss?" Such demands show a need to know what has gone before in order to understand what is going on now. This chapter is written for the purpose of "filling in" the student concerning the history of American reading instruction. It is hoped that a brief glimpse of the past will enable him to gain a somewhat clearer picture of today's aims, methods, and materials.

METHODS, REFORMS, AND INFLUENCES IN TEACHING READING

Aims, Methods, and Materials. When the first permanent English settlement in America was founded in Jamestown, Virginia, in 1607, the purpose of teaching children to read was to further religious growth, the method was the "alphabet-oral," and the materials were adapted from the Bible. Thus, when little colonials attended "dame schools," conducted in their kitchens by women who could read and write, the *New England Primer* was used. That small volume contained rhymed quotations of Biblical content, considered suitable for five- and six-year-old children. Below are two examples:

> In Adam's fall
> We sinned all.

Thy life to mend
This Book attend.

As soon as the colonies declared their independence in 1776, a new motive for learning to read was added to the religious and moral goals, the pupose now being to unify the former colonies by developing a national consciousness and a national language. Since the first colonists were English, all those who followed—the Dutch in New York and Pennsylvania, the Swedes in New Jersey, the French in Maryland—had to relinquish their mother tongues and learn English, the official language because it had been the first to arrive.

With the hindsight permitted by the passage of time, we can look back upon assorted instructional techniques and realize that some of them represented extremes. Unfortunately, educational excesses seldom result in educational successes. Methods of teaching reading have veered from too much emphasis on oral reading in Horace Mann's day to so little at the present time that the speech patterns of some of the members of the oncoming generation may be seriously affected, from an overdependence on phonics to a neglect of word analysis, from too little humane concern with readiness for reading to overzealous application of a principle which is of priceless value when used with discrimination.

A brief glance at some of the ill-advised reading practices of the past may serve to warn against further excesses. Equally, such a backward glance may develop respect for the value of some of the reforms which have proved of lasting benefit. Thus, the informed student of educational history may well view with a cautious eye any attempt to foster reliance on a single method. In addition to warning against going to extremes in teaching and "throwing away the baby with the bath water," a knowledge of the history of reading can also serve to prevent a revival of methods which in the past have proved fallacious. For example, a student of educational history, acquainted with the pitfalls inherent in the old "rugged phonics," is not so apt to make the blunder of trying to teach beginning reading solely by such means.

Historical examples have a fascinating way of showing the relations between aims, methods, and materials of reading and the social order in which they are used. From the study of history evidence can be found confirming the wisdom of adopting a many-sided program of reading instruction for our rich, many-sided civilization. By inference, reliance on any one extreme is condemned.

Alphabet-Spelling System. During the colonial period (1607–1776), the most famous reading book, as was indicated earlier in this chapter, was the *New England Primer*. It's small pages opened with the alphabet. To remove any doubt concerning the importance of mastering it, the children were confronted with this consoling stanza:

> He who will ne'er learn his ABC
> Forever will a blockhead be.

John and Priscilla started reading by learning that *a* is *a*, and that *b* is *b*. What thoughts the letters of the alphabet aroused is not a matter of record. But, after the children had mastered their ABC's, they were allowed the inestimable boon of fitting them together to form such fragments as *ab, eb, ib, ob, ub,* and, in reverse, *ba, be, bi, bo,* and *bu.* The children would chant these in unison, "droning at their lessons like the hum of a beehive," according to Washington Irving's report in his amusing story about Ichabod Crane. After some months of tedious drilling, the children progressed to reading verses of the religious type quoted at the start of this chapter. The last thing colonial pupils got in the whole process was the thought. The thought is, of course, the logical starting point, but it is doubtful if the thoughts that were expressed in the *New England Primer* carried much real meaning to the children, even though the sound was ominous enough to chill them to the marrow. "Rachel doth mourn for her first born," ran one verse, which scarcely seems suitable content for a six-year-old.

Overdramatic Oral Reading. The alphabet-spelling method was retained after 1776, but reading aloud, with all the fire of a famous patriot orator like Patrick Henry, was added to the system of instruction. Although the religious materials of the colonial period were still used, with a slightly watered-down moralism, the reading content of the period tended to favor a somewhat self-conscious patriotism—not unnatural in a country so recently released from being an English colony. Instruction was focused on eloquent oral reading, often accompanied by what today might be termed "sound effects." If a poem about a Roman chariot race was read at the time, it received a full treatment of "significant gestures" as they were called, even to the stamping of the reader's feet to simulate the pounding of the horses' hoofs. This was "reading with expression" with a vengeance, and it suggests that modern teachers who insist upon having the children engage in elocutionary oral reading instead of using the natural intonations of daily speech are harking back to a procedure which belongs historically to the period of 1776–1840. If attention is called to the meaning of a passage instead of to the reader thereof, oral interpretation usually takes care of itself.

The Speller-Readers. The most popular of the speller-readers from 1782 to about 1845 was Webster's *American Spelling Book*, a little volume which "taught millions to read and not one to sin." It opened with the alphabet and went on to the "sounds" *ab, ba, eb, be,* etc., combining vowels and consonants. Then came pages devoted to column after column of spelling words, increasing in difficulty until by page 131 (1842 edition) the word "antiscorbutic" appears. Sometimes during the long period of its popularity Webster's speller-reader was the only book used in country schools. Children had it from the first grade through the eighth, spelling most of the time unrelated lists of words, with only occasional opportunities to read sentences—also unrelated in content: "Some fishes are very bony," "Do not sit on the damp ground," etc. As a reward for their stamina in remaining with the book throughout their elementary-school career, the graduates were favored with four fables at the end of the book. Each had a moral attached. The most famous fable had to do with a vain and frivolous girl who tossed her head proudly, thus causing the eggs she was carrying there to be addled.

No recognition was given to the fact that reading and spelling are different processes. George Hilliard's speller-reader, *The Franklin Primer,* contained a verse which demonstrates how strongly held was faith in the efficacy of spelling:

And if you can't read
Pray endeavour to spell,

For by frequently spelling
You'll learn to read well.

With such materials as the speller-readers, discipline was a major problem. The schoolmasters (more men than women taught elementary schools in those days) were often forced to engage in fights with the older boys. The story is told of a rural schoolmaster who came to his new job in 1830 as thin as a beanstalk and left it a stout man only a year or so later. He had gained weight by the simple expedient of eating the lunch of any scholar who misbehaved during the reading class.

A Needed Reform: The Word Method. The analytical alphabet-spelling method was superseded by the introduction of the word method in 1838. Horace Mann, an educator of vision and foresight, was chiefly responsible for introducing the change. He criticized the alphabet method and advised the adoption of the word method in his famous report to the Board of Education in Massachusetts in 1838:

Presenting the children with the alphabet is giving them what they never saw, heard, or thought before. . . . But the printed names of known things (dog, cat, doll) are the signs of sounds which their ears have been accustomed to hear, and their organs of speech to utter. Therefore a child can learn to name 26 familiar *words* sooner than the unknown, unheard of and unthought of *letters* of the alphabet.

Under Horace Mann's vigorous leadership, interest in adopting the word method gradually increased. Words are certainly more concrete than "a" or "b." The word "candy," for example, ties to a pleasant substance that a child knows, while "a" can be associated with nothing but the letter.

Though the word method represented a great improvement over the alphabet method as an approach to reading, it had several faults. First, children had to drill on isolated words before being allowed to recognize sentences. The emphasis upon words encouraged children to form the habit of reading word by word, just the opposite of what is desirable in reading. The efficient reader takes in several words at a glance, enough to form a thought unit. Comprehension and speed are improved when children form the habit of reading in meaningful phrases. Furthermore, the word method lacked economy. When children have to learn all words by sight, they lack an independent means of word recognition.

THE INFLUENCE OF HORACE MANN. Despite the drawbacks of the word method, Horace Mann's feat in introducing this reform of the alphabet-spelling method should be fully appreciated. It might be said that Horace Mann helped to break a spell. He saw the wisdom of accustoming children when reading to look upon words as units, instead of staring at each letter in a word separately, as in spelling.

In spite of the objections to the alphabet method as a means of *introducing* children to beginning reading, not the least of which is its tendency to slow up the reading rate, some parents today— more than a hundred years after Horace Mann's reform—ask why reading is not started with the ABC's. Faith in the efficacy of beginning with letter-name knowledge dies a slow death. The wise teacher will help parents of beginning first-grade children to understand that the word method, or, as it is called today, the look-and-say method, used as an approach to reading, is not exactly a new fad but dates back to a reform instituted by Horace Mann over 125 years ago.

Horace Mann also made an important contribution to improved instruction in reading throughout the elementary school when he condemned meaningless oral reading as "a barren action of the organs of speech upon the atmosphere." The goal in his time seemed to be to give each child a turn to stand and read a paragraph or a page orally each day. Horace Mann condemned the emphasis upon pronouncing with a neglect of comprehension. He urged the teacher to "put questions to the children, directing them to read silently until they locate the answer." Then and only then was any pupil to stand and read the pertinent part aloud. Questions directed toward content, he averred, caused children to think as they read. Without using the terminology to which we are accustomed today, he was in favor of *motivated oral reading,* preceded by silent reading.

McGuffey and His Readers: A Reform. Another man who influenced reading instruction, though for some reason he has not had as

many schools named after him as Horace Mann, was William H.
McGuffey, the author of the first truly successful graded series of
readers. *The McGuffey Eclectic Readers* were written for children at all grade levels from first through eighth and were a great
improvement on the Webster speller-reader. However, McGuffey
showed no awareness of Horace Mann's plea for using the word
method in beginning reading. McGuffey started off with the alphabet and syllables. But his stories departed somewhat from the
adult type of content characteristic of the time. He is purported to
have approached the scientific method of selecting materials by
trying out his stories on a group of neighborhood children. If a
child of six expressed a preference for a story, McGuffey included
the story in his primer; if a child of ten showed a strong liking for
a story, he earmarked it for book five. Though he introduced materials more interesting to children, he did not break entirely from
the prevailing concept of a child as a miniature adult. An examination of a woodcut illustration (shown in this chapter) from *Mc-
Guffey's First Reader* (1840 edition) will reveal that twenty-four
new words were introduced in one story—quite a heavy load of vocabulary for a child of six or seven. The last three lines emphasize
the moralistic point of view which dominated his readers, sharing
space with selections containing other types of content, namely,
economic, nationalistic, militaristic, international, and religious.

The "Culture" Extreme. According to a number of historians, the
United States from 1870 to 1917 (American entry into World War
I) displayed a certain meretricious snobbishness. Possibly this
element gradually crept into the culture pattern because of a self-
conscious attitude, caused in part by the scathing criticisms by
European writers such as Charles Dickens and Mrs. Trollope, who
proclaimed that the big growing country across the Atlantic was as
crude and uncouth as some of the frontiersmen along its expanding borders. However stimulated, the desire for culture was present to motivate interest in reading as a cultural asset.

Reflecting the prevailing social climate, the chief aim of reading
at this time, among an influential group of educators in the United
States was to emphasize literature appreciation, especially of the
classics, at all levels. Certainly not without its good points, the

program of instruction was carried to extremes, and literature appreciation deteriorated into a tedious form of literature analysis. Reading periods were spent in cross-examining pupils concerning the fine points of *Horatius at the Bridge, The Lady of the Lake,* etc. Weeks were spent in overanalysis of archaic terms, customs of other days, and so on. Only the most talented pupils could cope with some of the difficult materials and adult-level methods. Series of readers published during this period displayed titles which reflected the nation's interest in "culture" through the use of "literature." The words "pathway," "road" and "literature" figured prominently in them. No one denies the value of acquaintance with literary masterpieces, but to spend a school term reading and discussing *Hiawatha,* for example, seems extreme and calculated to kill interest in "culture" rather than to promote it.

The "Rugged Phonics" Excess. At approximately the same period (1870–1917) another type of "analysis" appeared. Elaborate schemes of phonics flourished: the Ward System, the Pollard System, the Beacon System, the Gordon System, and others. These systems were formal and mechanical. Indeed, this approach to reading was more difficult and uninteresting, if possible, than the old alphabet-spelling methods. The use of phonics systems developed slow laborious readers who were so busy attending to the mechanics and identifying the *up* family (*up, slup, dup, cup, nup*), or honking out in staccato fashion the *acs, ics, ocs,* that meaning was completely lost sight of. These phonics systems were irrelevant, superimposed, and practiced in isolation from interesting, meaningful content. Those who advocate a return to rugged phonics today would profit by a study of history, which records them as tried but scarcely true. In fact, these methods were discovered to be so unsound that they were abandoned.

The Look-and-Say Excess. In the United States, teachers are nothing if not thorough. Rugged phonics yielded such poor results that the pendulum swung to the opposite extreme, and for a time teachers eliminated any form of word analysis. From the excessively artificial emphasis on sounds or fragments of words in the era of rugged phonics, they turned to the equally illogical avoidance of vowel rules, syllabication principles, and so on. The child had to learn every word as a sight word from looking at the whole word and saying it a great many times—the look-and-say method. If by some happy accident the child incidentally noticed similarities and differences helpful in recognizing new words, well and good but direct instruction in promoting the skill of word analysis was forbidden. Since experiment usually shows that direct instruction gives surer results than incidental opportunism, this excess of the use of look-and-say bred some unsatisfactory situations. One mother remarked during this era, "I'm sending my child to a progressive school where they don't teach phonics at all. Of course, she won't be able to read, but she'll be happy about it."

Word analysis in the modern reading program will be considered at length later. The present position[1] is to use the sight-word or look-and-say method only as an approach to beginning reading in the first grade. As soon as the child has a stock of sight words, he is ready to make comparisons, to carry on consonant substitution, and to generalize enough to understand vowel and syllabication principles. For the child to learn *all* words as sight words is uneconomical and unnecessary. Some words in English are phonetic and others, at least partially phonetic; the rest have to be learned by attention to word form and other clues including structural analysis.

The Silent-Reading Excess. The Army Alpha tests, administered to servicemen in World War I to test their silent-reading ability, produced standardized measurements of silent-reading skills. These tests revealed that overwhelming numbers of young Americans had inferior silent-reading habits. Oral word-calling methods, unsuitably difficult literary materials, mechanical drills, and other factors were blamed for the poor showing on the tests.

With their conscientious tendency to go to the opposite extreme, educators began to emphasize silent reading. Oral reading was swept out of some school systems, and, since tests were more easily devised to measure retention of facts than to evaluate literary appreciation, school readers were now designed to feature silent-

[1] James B. Conant *et al.*, *Learning To Read: A Report of a Conference of Reading Experts.* Princeton, N.J.: Educational Testing Service, July, 1962.

St. Francis College

Fort Wayne, Indiana

reading materials of an informational nature. The use of literary materials for reading instruction became unpopular. Many teachers felt guilty if they used either oral reading or literary content. As an offshoot of the emphasis on silent reading, non-oral methods were advocated even for beginning reading. Teachers held up signs which displayed printed directions, and the children read them silently and carried out the directions by running, jumping, skipping, hopping, walking, and so on. Visitors to non-oral classes reported that not a word was uttered during the reading period. In fact, it was like walking in on a class in which both the teacher and pupils were deaf-mutes. Educators hoped that this method of using no voice at the start would eliminate inner speech, which slows down silent reading. Since the children had been talking outside of school from the age of two, the objective was not gained, and tension of the vocal cords, or incipient inner speech, was still present during silent reading.

The Influence of Tests. The Army Alpha was but the first of many tests. Some startling evidence was uncovered concerning the great range of differences between individuals. The wide achievements in reading of children in the same grade spurred the profession to make worthwhile changes in classroom organization and instruction. A whole new program recommending ability grouping (top, average, low), flexible promotions, and differentiated assignments was developed. This type of "individualized instruction" (1919–1930) was quite different from the plan for "individualized guidance or self-selective reading" recommended by innovators in the late fifties. The earlier version of the Dalton plan was copied widely. The traditional curriculum was subdivided into "contract units" for individual pupils to do alone. The children worked through individual assignments, reporting to the teacher from time to time. Necessarily there was a great deal of paper and pencil work, with the children filling out blanks in notebooks. There was little or no group work in reading under the Dalton plan, the Winnetka plan, and others.

Attention to individual differences also brought to light the need for remedial reading. During that era Dr. Grace Fernald worked out her kinesthetic method of learning to read words by tracing and saying them. To visual and auditory reception she added "muscle memory." Much research was carried on at this period to discover causes of reading difficulties, explore diagnostic measures, and experiment with corrective procedures.

Finally, as a result of the testing movement, in 1926 the International Kindergarten Union, working with the United States Bureau of Education, conducted an investigation concerning "pupils' readiness for reading instruction upon entrance to first grade." Only a year later, the periodical *Childhood Education* picked up this term readiness and in a number of articles added the word "reading" to form the now famous phrase "reading readiness."[2] To demand that a child of six begin the difficult task of reading just because he is six chronologically and, therefore, legally of an age to enrol in first grade is now considered unsound by the majority of teachers. There is wide acceptance of the need for determining not only mental but physical, emotional, social, and language readiness before plunging the child into the world of abstract symbols.

A BALANCED READING PROGRAM TYPICAL TODAY

No One Aspect Emphasized. Having learned from the past, the majority of educators today neither spend all the time and energy available on teaching oral reading nor restrict instruction to silent reading. The school reading program does not eschew either factual or imaginative content; it makes use of both study-type and recreational reading. Educators try to give America's children rich experiences in dealing with specific types of reading activities.

From historical examples, teachers have learned that the emphasis should be placed on meaning. Instead of starting a child off with twenty-six strange letters, words familiar to the child from his spoken vocabulary are used in his first contacts with reading. Though phonics is not used in the very first stages of reading, teachers today introduce a modern type of analysis at the application level as early as the children are *ready* for it. After

[2] Nila Banton Smith, "What Have We Accomplished in Reading?" reprinted from *Elementary English*, March, 1961, by the National Council of Teachers of English, Champaign, Ill., p. 145.

children have acquired a stock of sight words, they are shown how to use these sight words to "unlock" new words. A familiar beginning sound in a known word is compared to the same element in a new word to enable the child to develop independence in word attack, etc.

Improvement in Primary-Grade Methods. The first five years of the child's life are marked by a wealth of new experiences of all kinds. Modern teachers believe that these experiences should be used in starting the child off in reading. Well-planned activities are provided in school for those who have a meager background of concepts. Enriched oral vocabulary, not drill on isolated letters, is stressed. The ability of the child to express himself in sentences is considered an important forerunner of reading. The reading-readiness activities the school provides can help the child develop understandings and appreciations that he can use in interpreting what he reads, especially if the teacher follows through with an experience record.

Suppose a teacher plans a tour of the school building and grounds for her first graders. (A trip of this sort is far from prosaic to an eager six-year-old.) On the tour the children meet the principal, peek into the sacred realm of the sixth grade, visit the custodian in the furnace room. They discover that many people help to make their school home a comfortable place. When the children return from the excursion, they are, like all travelers, full of the subject. They chatter about what they have seen and heard and the teacher helps them make up a story about their experience. She writes on the blackboard some of their remarks about the trip, revising them if necessary so that they carry the same meaning. She uses only one line of writing because run-over lines confuse beginners. The children see that the marks made with white chalk on the board mean what they have just said.

With the teacher's help the children read back the written record of their experience. Of course, this first reading does not constitute actual reading, since the children are only remembering what happened, what they said about what happened, what the teacher wrote down, and where she wrote it. Later the teacher reproduces the children's story on a big chart of tagboard or news-

print, and the children draw a picture for it. A collection of these experience stories becomes a book—their book—and the children can reread and enjoy these stories they have composed and share them with others.

This process is just the reverse of the way the child of colonial times or of the era of rugged phonics learned to read. Children today begin with the thought and are concerned with the alphabet only when they begin to write, to spell, and to use the dictionary, encyclopedia, and other reference materials. Primary reading methods can be considered to have taken a decided turn for the better.

Improvement in Upper-Grade Methods. Reading instruction and materials at levels beyond the primary have also improved. In 1835 many children in the upper grades were exposed to Lindley Murray's *Pronouncing English Reader,* which was stiffly organized into "didactick, pathetick, publick, argumentative" pieces. The method of teaching was oral, and it is difficult to imagine a more mechanical procedure. Sentences were marked off to show when the voice was to rise and when to drop. Today the emphasis is on content in line with the child's interest, and reading for meaning is the goal.

Old-fashioned educators did not understand that, for retention to take place, silent reading of the study type must be purposeful. Great faith was once shown in the procedure of repeatedly rereading a selection. This was followed not by an evaluation of the main ideas but by an attempt to memorize it and regurgitate it in recitation. Old manuals illustrate the teaching directions typically given: "Read your lesson until you know it. Read it six times." Today teachers ask children stimulating questions about content chosen to meet their interests. They are given the opportunity to express opinions about the ideas found in their books, and encouraged to apply what they read to their own thinking and action.

When it came to oral reading in other times, the teacher called up the various classes in order to hear them read, as the process was fittingly termed. The teacher instructed the children to toe the mark, thus ensuring a straight line and placing further empha-

sis on formality rather than on thought. Then the children took turns reading orally. When the need arose, the teacher issued admonitions such as "Mind the stops!" (observe the punctuation) or "Mind your p's and q's!" (be careful to read correctly letters that are hard to tell apart).

In many schools in the United States, oral reading around the class, using the start-stop method, amply satisfied instructional demands. After one child had rattled off a few lines the teacher stopped him, roused the next child, and started him off on his turn. A steady diet of this, and the emphasis for the teacher and pupils alike fell on determining whether or not the child knew all the words. Often, each child knew that the teacher would call for paragraph reading in order, and he would count ahead to his paragraph and lapse into a coma until it was his turn. Meaning did not matter, and discussion of the ideas was beyond the realm of reading. Now the emphasis is on understanding, enjoyment, and appreciation. The goal is to make reading a stimulating social activity. In addition to promoting growth in reading ability, the reading lesson contributes to the child's personal development, helping him to enjoy vicarious experiences and to gain new interests, attitudes, and understandings.

THE NEED FOR A VARIETY OF READING SKILLS

Under the teacher's guidance, children learn to read critically, linking what they read with actual experience. Reading is not just a single activity. It is a complex procedure, involving many skills and specific abilities, which range from the rapid reading characteristic of skimming to the careful reading required in studying. Vocabulary study, phonetic and structural analysis, and syllabication are taught as a means to an end—greater power in carrying on independent reading and in utilizing knowledge.

Many different types of reading are required in modern life, and different skills are needed for each. To meet everyday needs, the individual must be able to change his rate and vary his attention to suit his purpose and the types of content serving it.

For convenience, even though there is some inevitable overlapping, reading is usually categorized as *recreational*, done for

pleasure or appreciation, and *informational,* carried on in a different frame of mind from that prevailing in recreational reading. With recreational reading, the reader makes his own interpretation, and what he retains is his own concern. With informational reading, the reader is expected to retain ideas in their original form. Reading an income-tax blank would scarcely be classed as pleasure reading. Nor would the government appreciate a free interpretation of the directions for reporting taxes. Informational reading has been variously classified as *work-type, study-type,* and *assimilative.* The terms *informational, study-type,* and *work-type* will be used interchangeably here. The chief purpose of this form of reading is to gain some type of information, and the mood of reading is better described as studious and attentive rather than relaxed. Usually, the reading is for profit.

Informational Skills. Informational reading subdivides into many activities, among them reading to find the central thought, to note supporting details, to locate specific pieces of information, to se lect and to organize materials, to draw inferences, and to predict outcomes. Many modes of attack are required for informational reading. Some require a fast rate; others, a slow rate. Some demand a careful perusal of each step; others are characterized by the need to skip around. Informational materials are usually more factual in nature than recreational materials, although facts can be found in both. With informational content, the reader's attack tends to be more aggressive, active, studious, non-emotional, and analytical.

READING TO FOLLOW DIRECTIONS. This kind of reading is not inspiring or amusing; often it is tedious. People will do almost anything to avoid pinning themselves down to the study of a set of directions. Reading to follow directions demands attention to detail, comprehension of facts in order, and the habit of reading back for verification. In short, this reading requires getting the literal-sense meaning. Examples: reading directions for installing a gas-heater vent to prevent suffocation from carbon monoxide, for cutting out a dress pattern, for taking medicines, for using insect sprays, for the care of an automobile.

READING FOR THE CENTRAL IDEA AND SUPPORTING DETAILS. In this type of reading it is necessary to be able to locate the main emphasis—the big idea. After that, details or smaller ideas supporting the main one are recognized. If a paragraph in a natural-science book is read that describes in detail the various shapes of needles found on pine, spruce, hemlock, and cedar, even fifth-grade children should be able to locate the main idea (the type of needles helps to identify many evergreens) instead of being sidetracked by a detail (the foliage of the pine tree is long, slender, and hard).

READING TO REMEMBER. The individual may find an anecdote so well worded, or an article so full of verbal ammunition in support of his point of view, that he may wish to read to retain much of it to use later. For this type of reading it is necessary to maintain a high degree of interest throughout, notice topic headings, reject the non-essentials, set a time limit, rule out distractions, notice key words and phrases, engage in self-recitations, and reread to improve retention.

SKIMMING. Reading to find a specific piece of information is highly purposive; although such reading is more rapid than reading to remember, retention must be exact. Examples include indexes, tables of contents, *Readers' Guide,* telephone directory, dictionary, encyclopedia, railroad timetables, radio and television program schedules, course-of-study catalogs, and restaurant menus.

This type of reading requires knowledge of the alphabet, ability to follow cross-references, capacity for rejecting the irrelevant and concentrating on the relevant, background for judging the reliability of a reference. In locational skimming, the eye moves rapidly over the page in search of pertinent data. The reader must sternly resist any tendency to lose valuable time dawdling over side issues, in favor of pushing ahead to find the specific piece of desired information.

Recreational Skills. Recreational reading is generally faster, more fluent, and more emotional than informational reading. Instead of striving for accurate or detailed retention, a general impression of content and ideas is usually sufficient. Enjoyment and appreciation are characteristic, although, of course, factual material too is sometimes read in a relaxed recreational mood.

To clarify further the concept that different types of reading are demanded of the modern reader, some uses of recreatory reading are described here.

READING FOR PLEASURE AND RELAXATION. Fiction, autobiography, current periodicals, and belles-lettres are perused at a fairly rapid rate without any of the twinges of conscience that occur when study-type materials are passed over quickly. Occasionally, the reader may go back and reread a particularly enjoyable bit, or he may read it aloud to a companion. (Involved in this is the need for reading with clarity and good oral interpretation.

RECREATIONAL SKIMMING. Recreational skimming occurs daily. A reader often glances through a magazine or book to gain a general impression of the contents or to pick out a story or chapter to read, or perhaps to hunt a passage to re-enjoy.

READING IN SEARCH OF ARTISTIC EFFECTS. The reader may slow his rate in order to savor a felicitously worded phrase or well-expressed thought. He may wish to collate two translations or to otherwise compare artistic effects.

READING TO JUDGE LITERARY VALUES. This reading is akin to the type just described. Questions arise in the mind of the reader: Is this interesting? Is the plot clear? Has this universality of appeal? Can I identify myself with the characters? Is the suspense element well handled? Is this honest? Does it ring true, or is it fatuous?

READING TO SUPPLEMENT THOUGHT AND FOLLOW INTERESTS. For personal guidance and to promote interests in art, music, fashions, health, sports, travel, this reading might be considered as classifying itself in the informational-reading category. But, even though the reader is dealing with factual material, he is approaching it in the recreational mood of anticipating enjoyment.

The Characteristics of a Good Reader. To some, reading is a perpetual delight; to others, even the simplest type of reading is a painful ordeal to be sidestepped whenever possible. Reading is as essential to members of the first group as eating. Just as they need three square meals a day for physical nourishment, they require "three square books" a week for mental nutrition. Members of the second group, on the other hand, are prone to regard reading uneasily as something printed on paper. It cornered, they read in gloomy fits and starts of abstraction. They have acquired the tool but not the ability to use it effectively.

There appear to be two activities in which humans will persist without a particle of success to crown their efforts—golf and bridge. When it comes to reading, there is a marked tendency to avoid it if it is difficult. Thus the poor reader perpetuates his lack of proficiency. Herein lies the challenge to the teacher to give instruction in all types of reading with so much skill that the child will want to use the implement he is acquiring. These are some of the characteristics of the good reader. He

1. Reads by himself without asking help in recognizing new words; uses context clues, word analysis, the dictionary for new words
2. Groups words into thought units
3. Reads rapidly but without sacrificing comprehension
4. Reads with a definite purpose in mind
5. Uses reading to solve daily problems
6. Develops a wide variety of background understandings to make his reading more meaningful
7. Applies what he reads to motivate ambitions, control moods, change attitudes

8. Demands sense, not nonsense, from what he reads; uses semantics and critical appraisal in testing validity
9. Reads a great variety of material
10. Makes time for reading, even though it means turning off the television an hour earlier in the evening or getting up an hour earlier in the morning

Mortimer J. Alder offers a diverting but no less instructive example of what he considers to be the most effective reading to be found in daily life:

If we consider men and women generally, and apart from their professions or occupations, there is only one situation I can think of in which they almost pull themselves up by their bootstraps, making an effort to read better than they usually do. When they are in love and are reading a love letter, they read for all they are worth. They read every word three ways; they read between the lines and in the margins: they read the whole in terms of the parts, and each part in terms of the whole; they grow sensitive to context and ambiguity; to insinuation and implication; they perceive the color of words, the odor of phrases, and the weight of sentences. They may even take the punctuation into account. Then, if never before or after, they read.[3]

Of course, it would be difficult to find in all types of reading the motivation for close attention and study that exists in love letters. The individual who can carry on this type of reading with skill, however, may hope to engage in others with acceptable success if he is sufficiently motivated and trained.

A fifth-grade teacher indicated that the good reader

1. Does not pause often on a line
2. Does not go back and reread often
3. Does not carry on a great deal of inner speech
4. Can make out words on his own
5. Reads smothly and rhythmically, not in uneven jerks
6. Knows how to adjust reading rate to suit the material and purpose
7. Remembers what is important from what he reads

The poor reader reads painful contradictions without challenge, showing that his critical faculties are dormant. He is notorious for

[3] *How To Read a Book* (New York: Simon & Schuster, Inc., 1955), p. 63. Used by permission obtained in 1962.

making a single-track response. Recognizing only one word at a time is about all the retarded reader can do without special training, and so he tends to mangle meaning in his strenuous battle of word attack. The good reader, on the other hand, is anything but a word caller. He is able to carry on a complicated series of activities simultaneously. As he comprehends the meaning of what he reads, he is able to engage in critical, expressional, and appreciational activities. That is, he can comprehend the author's meaning and can react emotionally at the same time to the ideas presented. Some of his appreciation is of literary form, some of thought, some of self-criticism, as he compares himself with the characters in a piece of fiction, or his ideas with an author's in a didactic piece. The skilled reader processes each selection he reads by putting on, as it were, the spectacles of his background of experiences and reading through them. It is precisely because good comprehension in reading involves countless associations of the higher mental processes that great skill is demanded for doing it well, and, by the same token, great skill is needed for teaching it effectively.

THE NEED FOR GUIDANCE IN DEVELOPING SKILLS

In classwork, children engage in the types of reading which adults use for carrying on life activities. Training in these must be comprehensive and systematic. Competent instruction is valuable in learning any skill. Compare, for example, the technique of a self-taught typist with the smooth performance of one who has received instruction in the touch system from a capable teacher. In reading, more than in learning less complicated skills, direct guidance is important; a whole constellation of mental processes is involved. Because a person possesses skill in one type of reading, there is no guaranty that he will have skill in others. To promote development in any specific reading skill, specific instruction must be given.

Children do not automatically learn how to organize what they read. Such skills as recognizing the relation of ideas, anticipating content, arranging ideas in order, outlining, and summarizing are not learned spontaneously, although these skills can be acquired with direct instruction on an elementary level by the elementary-school child. The advantages of direct, planned guidance over incidental teaching cannot be emphasized too strongly. If children are to learn to locate what is essential, to appraise and to organize ideas, to retain what is useful in serving their personal needs, the teacher must provide specific guidance.

Experienced teachers know that some children can comprehend as they go along but cannot remember what they read after they are through. Others are able to reproduce ideas on the printed page but cannot use them in any original way. Because so little uniformity in reading development exists, the teacher obviously needs to provide special training to meet individual needs.

Some children are able to retain material read for immediate recall but cannot recall even the gist of a given passage after time has elapsed. There is also the contrast between verbal and ideational memory. Some readers seem to have the special power to remember the exact words in which ideas were expressed (what actors call a quick study); others can remember the ideas but practically none of the exact words.

Often the teacher is so fully occupied in teaching the mechanics of reading that she fails to teach its uses and skills. Satisfied with the children's achievement on a standardized reading test, she may not realize that success in aided recall, with several choices written out plainly to jog the memory, is not the same thing as having to call up out of a welter of memories the specific answer needed for a question. Impressed by a high score in reading of the type which asks the student to find a specific answer to a question, the teacher may not realize that the same student may need help in carrying on self-criticism while reading fiction. To be able to compare one's self with the characters about whom one is reading is a highly edifying use of critical thinking. The average child does not understand, without being shown, that reading literature is one thing and reading factual material is another. The teacher must provide activities to give the children practice in all types of reading.

Guidance in Informational Reading. Retention is a prime factor in informational reading. It can be aided by interest, a vivid first impression, frequent reviews with good attention, distributed practice, and the attitude of intending to remember. Superior results are obtained when the teacher motivates interest, provides for clear original registration by using visual aids and discussion, guides the children to make self-recitation, and schedules practice sessions, short but regularly spaced over a fairly long period of time. If the children are helped to recognize the importance of intending to learn, as well, retention will be better than if none of these instructional activities are carried on. It is important to give exercises in outlining, organizing, and summarizing. Children are materially aided in retaining factual material when they are given guidance in using a key topic as a rallying point for a cluster of details and ideas. As the publication of books, magazines, and newspapers is constantly increasing, it becomes more and more important to help children to retain an adequate amount of content after a single reading.

Guidance in Recreational Reading. Children cannot be taught to read effectively for appreciation purposes in a work-type atmosphere. Reading for enjoyment and appreciation is a subjective process and therefore difficult to measure. Because this type of reading deals with intangible associations, the art of developing it is often neglected by teachers. However, the fact that instruction in this type of reading is not widely understood does not mean that it is not given at all.

Guidance in Reading Appreciation. For an eighth-grade reading lesson of the appreciation type, a teacher asked the children to collate two translations of a story by Alphonse Daudet. She told them to place the versions side by side and to compare them for the purpose of deciding which translation they enjoyed more. The first translation said,

Ah, Monsieur Seguin's little goat, how pretty she was! How pretty she was, with her soft eyes, her beard like a corporal's, her shiny black hoofs, her horns striped like a zebra, and her long white hair which formed a kind of great coat.

The second:

Ah, how pretty Monsieur Seguin's little goat was! How pretty she was, with her soft eyes, her beard like a noncommissioned officer's, her

Horace Mann (1796–1859). (*Courtesy of Horace Mann Life Insurance Co.*)

McGUFFEY'S FIRST READER.

LESSON I.

can	has	the	read	John	name
her	two	that	keep	book	there
see	you	with	Jane	hand	clean
boy	how	girls	they	must	learn

Do you see that boy?
There are two girls with him.
The name of the boy is John.
Jane has a book in her hand.
They can all read from the book.
They must keep the book clean.
They must see how fast they can learn.

Woodcut—1840 edition of *McGuffey's First Reader.* (*The Bettman Archive*)

Developing readiness for discriminating similarities and differences in abstract forms and letters. (*Cory School, San Jose, Calif.*)

A reading circle early in the first grade, when readiness for reading is still being developed by means of picture reading. (*Cory School, San Jose, Calif.*)

black and shining hoofs, her striped horns like a zebra's and her long white hair which covered her like a great coat.

The teacher first asked the children to read each translation through silently. Then she asked for an oral reading of each. Following this she guided the children to consider parallel phrases. The children read the phrase "her beard like a corporal's" and compared it with the phrase "her beard like a noncommissioned officer's" and decided that the first had a better sound because the adjective describing the soldier in the second version sounded too long-winded and awkward. The children then considered the phrases "her shiny black hoofs" and "her black and shining hoofs," "her long white hair which formed a kind of great coat" and "her long white hair which covered her like a great coat."

After discussing the sound and sense of each translation, the children expressed a preference for the first one, defending their choice by pointing out that the second version contained longer, "bumpier" phrases. Thus, without confusing the eighth-grade children by the use of such abstract terms as *diction, syntax,* or *cadence,* the teacher led them to pass a sound literary judgment and projected them a step further along the road of good taste in literary matters.

Guidance in Critical Thinking and Comprehension. Critical appraisal is continuously present in the capable handling of either informational or recreational reading. In informational reading, the critical faculty is exercised when the reader decides whether or not the information is reliable and relevant to his needs. In recreational reading, critical thinking is employed in interpreting passages in terms of one's own experience, including enjoyment, and in making literary judgments or otherwise applying intellectual and esthetic yardsticks. The capable reader constantly "talks back to the book."

Comprehension, if its multiple and complex role is thoughtfully considered, is little short of a miracle. The eye passes sensations along to the mind; the mind interprets them, interpolating additions and inventions from the reader's experiences and interests to supplement the written material.

As with other skills, the development of comprehension is aided by exercises in comprehension. Modern manuals which accompany basic readers recommend that teachers guide the child to read for definite purposes. Guiding questions are listed in the lesson plans to encourage the child to read, to supplement the author's thought, to supply examples, to look up difficult words, to take notes, to summarize, to review, to get the main thought, to find new ideas, and to evaluate them. The use of direct guidance in specific reading abalities will improve the ability to comprehend.

Children read with better comprehension when teachers not only help them approach different types of reading appropriately but also see to it that reading is associated with concrete experience. The use of activities and visual aids in the classroom, supplemented by a variety of excursions about the neighborhood and community, helps the children to develop understandings which enable them to interpret what they read in terms of their own experience. Personal identification with content is a potent means of ensuring comprehension and thus promoting better retention. Since what is retained usually becomes a part of the reader's subsequent thinking and acting, the importance of teaching the interwoven skills under discussion can scarcely be overemphasized.

Guiding principles and techniques for the teaching of reading which have stood the practical test of modern usage are described in subsequent chapters. A knowledge of these principles and techniques will enable the teacher to go forward confidently with instruction. If, having attained a grasp of these fundamentals, the teacher is also a craftsman in love with her work, she can proceed toward the desirable goal of making each reading lesson a work of art to be thoroughly enjoyed, rather than stoically endured, by her pupils.

RECENT TRENDS IN THE TEACHING OF READING

The first main section of this chapter was devoted to the past history of reading instruction. The second and third main sections dealt with acceptable teaching practices of the present. These discussions would seem to cover the topics of *then* and *now*. But this chapter would be incomplete without mention of still another aspect of the topic—that of emerging trends.

However, instead of attempting to discuss recent, or fairly recent, developments all in one chapter, it seems advisable to divert treatment to appropriate chapters in which can be shown the functional relationships to various phases of reading instruction at the grade levels affected.

In keeping with this plan of organization, all that will be offered here is an alphabetical listing of newer emphases in the field of reading, with an indication of the chapter or chapters in which each is discussed: instructional television (Chapter 10), individualized guidance (Chapter 8), language-experience approach (Chapter 8), linguistic emphasis (Chapter 2), phonics—the perennial controversy (Chapters 3, 8, 11), reading readiness—a re-estimate (Chapters 5, 6), speed reading (Chapters 7, 10), teaching machines (Chapter 10), team teaching (Chapter 10).

What the future holds for these developments, no one can safely predict. Research in some has been contradictory or inconclusive. Only time will tell whether interest in all, or none, will continue or abate. This series of developments must still be classified at this moment as history in the making.

QUESTIONS AND ACTIVITIES

1. This chapter discusses excesses and reforms in teaching reading. Below is a jumbled list. In the left margin, label the extremes with a capital E and the reforms with a capital R. If any seem to classify under both headings, mark ER.

> Alphabet-spelling method
> The speller-readers
> Horace Mann's word method
> McGuffey's graded readers
> Rugged phonics
> Elocutionary oral reading
> Look-and-say method
> Emphasis on analysis of classics
> Silent-reading emphasis
> Remedial reading
> Reading readiness
> Balanced reading—no one method

2. The second main section of the chapter discusses two large classifications of reading. See labeled columns below, and list skills appropriate to each:

Informational-reading skills   *Recreational-reading Skills*
1.   1.
2. etc.   2. etc.

3. Of the characteristics of a good reader listed in this chapter, which do you consider to go "deeper" than mere mastery of skills? Explain.
4. Contrast the activities of the skilled reader with those of the poor reader.
5. This chapter describes four kinds of guidance in building skills in informational and recreational reading. Characterize each of the four types with explanatory statements.
6. Give examples of informational reading which you have carried on this week. Of recreational reading. As you read books, news items, or magazine articles, what specific skills can you now identify?

SELECTED REFERENCES

ALTICK, RICHARD D. *The English Common Reader: A Social History of the Mass Reading Public, 1800–19——*. Chicago: University of Chicago Press, 1957.

ANDERSON, PAUL S. "McGuffey vs. The Moderns in Character Training," *Phi Delta Kappan*, XXXVIII (November 1956), 53–58.

BOYD, WILLIAM. *From Locke to Montessori*. London: George H. Harrap & Co., Ltd., 1914.

CAUSEY, OSCAR S. *The Reading Teacher's Reader*. New York: The Ronald Press Co., 1958.

CONANT, JAMES B., *et al. Learning To Read: A Report of a Conference of Reading Experts*. Princeton, N.J.: Educational Testing Service, July, 1962.

FORD, PAUL. *The New England Primer*. New York: Dodd Mead & Co., Inc., 1897.

MILLER, GEORGE A. *Language and Communication*. New York: McGraw-Hill Book Co., Inc., 1951.

MINNICH, HARVEY C. *William Holmes McGuffey and His Readers*. New York: American Book Co., 1936.

RUSSELL, DAVID. *Children Learn To Read* (2d ed.). Boston: Ginn & Co., 1961.

SHAFFER, HELEN B. *Three Centuries of Reading in America*. Editorial Research Reports, Vol. XI, No. 23 (December 20, 1961), Washington, D.C.

SMITH, NILA BANTON. *American Reading Instruction.* Morristown, N.J.:
Silver Burdett Co., 1934.

SMITH, NILA BANTON. "What Have We Accomplished in Reading?"
Reprinted from *Elementary English* (March 1961), National Council of Teachers of English, Champaign, Ill., 145.

THORNDIKE, EDWARD LEE. *Man and His Works.* Cambridge, Mass.:
Harvard University Press, 1943.

4

THE INFLUENCE OF READING ON
ADJUSTMENT AND PERSONALITY

A disk jockey with a reputation for dry humour who conducts an early-morning radio program announced, "It is 6:21 A.M. and I'm still adjusted! But just give me a little more time, listeners. By 9 A.M. I'm sure to antagonize somebody and be my old maladjusted self." No matter what interpretation is placed upon his facetious statements, the conclusion is inescapable that he regards adjustment as something temporary and subject to fluctuation.

A more positive approach to understanding the term *adjustment* as it is used in the title of this chapter can be found in the definition of the verb form *to adjust*. According to *Webster's New Collegiate Dictionary*, it means to bring into harmony or agreement, to accommodate, to reconcile, to suit, to fit, to adapt. The last synonym, however, suggests pliability, whereas to *adjust* suggests less of pliability and tact and more of internal harmony. The person who simply *adapts* may be full of conflict, feeling one way and, for the sake of social expediency, acting quite another. A well-adjusted individual, on the other hand, has come to terms with life, and there is consistency between his inner drives and the outward expression of them. In other words, with adjustment there is unity of response. According to educational psychology, the individual is "internally well balanced if he has learned to live harmoniously with others and yet retain his personal identity, secure in the knowledge that he, like each of them, has something individual, unique, distinctive to contribute to the group in which he lives."

Since maladjusted individuals, full of inner conflicts and strate-
gies—whether they be sixteen-year-old delinquents or sixtyish dic-
tators—are responsible for a great variety of the social ills afflicting
our world today, it is important for teachers to learn how to help
pupils adjust effectively to life. Is reading an aid in bringing about
desirable adjustment? This chapter attempts to answer the question, dealing as well with the influence of reading on personality.

THE RELATION BETWEEN READING AND ADJUSTMENT

This is an age of tension and turmoil. As inventions have increased, human problems seem to have multiplied. Scientific war-
fare introduced an era of terrifying insecurity. In a brief span of
time, the people of the United States have had to face problems
brought on by World War II, the Korean War, the cold war, the
threat of megaton bombs, competition for the conquest of outer
space, large population shifts, displacement by automation, the
population explosion, overcrowded schools, and teacher shortages.
It would be naïve to expect children not to sense anxiety and un-
easiness in the adults they know. If, in addition to background
tensions, the child has to face failure in school because of poor
ability in reading, he may become emotionally disturbed to the
point of serious maladjustment. Arthur I. Gates, Professor of Education at Columbia, has said that failure in reading is as serious
in its consequences to the child as financial or marital failure to
the adult.

The Effect of Incompetence in Reading. The child growing up in
the American culture pattern is made to feel that his chief task
in school is to learn to read. If he fails, he inevitably suffers loss
of prestige and of self-respect. In his effort to compensate the child
may, and often does, become rude, discourteous, and a bully, thus
trying to win attention by the "back door." Another mode of escape is to react with apathy and indifference. Whether belligerent
or passive the child is a behavior problem, using a temperamental
reaction as a "buffer" between a hurt ego and failure in reading.
Teachers complain that retarded readers are "more impulsive,
easily distracted, self-centered, inclined to daydream; less inclined

to adapt to other personalities, and display any interest in hobbies." They frequently lack even an approach to a sense of humor. Dull and lifeless or boisterous and aggressive (or gradations in between), few retarded readers like their teachers or are liked by them. In addition to displaying difficulty with vocabulary, comprehension, and speed in reading, these poor children seldom use reading as an outlet. In fact, they will do anything rather than read and are among our most indiscriminate viewers of television.

Since reading is one facet of language, it is reasonable to assume that failure in reading will reduce the child's possibilities for full personal development. He will not be able to read to supplement or interpret his own experience. As a consequence of being cut off in this way, he will be poorly informed and lack the saving perspective which comes from reading. He will, in turn, have little to offer others. In a very real sense, he will suffer poverty of mind and spirit.

There is no department of living—whether it is learning, earning, worshiping, marrying, raising children, or retiring—in which reading does not perform a useful service by furnishing information, guidance, and inspiration. Obviously, a retarded reader could perform some of the activities listed in this paragraph without reading a thing, but, in order to enjoy these human activities fully and richly, he must be able to read well. Anyone who grows up unacquainted with good books suffers real loss of enjoyment, as well as missing the instrumental benefits of reading. Uninformed, narrow, lacking in depth, such a person robs himself and, in his ignorance, may even harm others.

The difference in maturity between those who read and those who do not is well-nigh incredible. As an appreciative reader once phrased it: "Books let you in on the details of living." Those who worry over feeling different are enabled to see that they are not alone. Through books, it is possible to gain insight into personal problems, to evaluate them, and perhaps to set up new and more realistic goals. By means of books, a person can travel to many lands, meet people in all walks of life, enjoy with the heroes and heroines vicarious adventures that add color, variety, and zest to the imagination. Through the activity of reading, as in no other experience, it is possible for the individual to savor moments of profound insight which, in turn, often touch off an exquisite sense of well-being. The background stored up by reading constitutes a never ending source, ready at hand for dipping into when the need arises "to judge, sympathize, analyze or criticize." Teachers should realize that the child will need competence in reading if he is to understand himself and others in this world.

The Value of Personality and Mental-Health Tests. In view of the relationship between reading and mental health, the teacher should supplement her subjective judgment of a pupil's adjustment or lack of it by the use of standardized forms which yield objective data of great value in a guidance program. Most of these tests are based on a psychology which holds that personality can be modified and that adjustment can be improved. Instead of accepting the belief that personality is completely determined by natural inheritance, those responsible for making these tests maintain that personality also depends upon the development of understandings, attitudes, and skills acquired in coping with oneself and other people.

THE MENTAL HEALTH ANALYSIS. This is a group test for grades four to eight, designed by Professors, Thorpe, Clark, and Tiegs for the California Test Bureau, in Los Angeles. The test requires forty-five minutes to administer and gives an analysis of the child's mental-health liabilities and assets. The mental-health liabilities include (1) immature behavior, (2) emotional instability, (3) feelings of inadequacy, (4) physical defects, and (5) nervous manifestations. The mental-health assets include (1) close personal relationships, (2) interpersonal skills, (3) social participation, (4) satisfying work and recreation, and (5) adequate outlook and goals.

A helpful series of definitions for each of the above ten categories is given in the *Manual of Directions* which accompanies the Mental Health Analysis. A sample profile is also offered, which gives the teacher a gauge of the child's adjustment or lack of it.

THE CALIFORNIA TEST OF PERSONALITY. This test, designed by the same authors who devised the Mental Health Analysis, appraises such components of personality as the following:

Components of Self-adjustment	*Components of Social Adjustment*
1. Self-reliance	1. Social standards and skills
2. Sense of personal worth	2. Freedom from antisocial tend-
3. Sense of personal freedom	encies
4. Feeling of belonging	3. Family relations
5. Freedom from withdrawing	4. School relations
tendencies	5. Community relations

Because few people give truthful answers when directly questioned about their feelings, the California Test of Personality disguises many of the items on this form. The following questions, for example, uncover an attitude by approaching it from different directions: "Are the boys and girls mean to you?" "Are most of the boys and girls mean to you?" "Are the people near your home often mean?" "Are there people near your home who are not nice?" Individuals who feel that they are surrounded by hostility cannot be said to be well adjusted. Some of the meanness they report in their response of "yes" may pertain to "mean" people actually known, but if suspicion of people prevails almost to the point of a persecution complex, the child is definitely maladjusted in at least this area. Personnel giving this test and interpreting results must have certain qualifications.

OTHER MEASURES OF ADJUSTMENT. Other measures available for assessing the individual's psychological makeup have been selected for listing below. Since educational authorities question their validity in some cases, it is absolutely necessary that only experienced persons administer these measures and evaluate the results. An example of an "adjustment inventory" is the Heston Personal Adjustment Inventory. The Haggerty-Olson-Wickman Behavior Rating Scale and the Allport-Vernon Study of Values are examples of behavior, interest, and opinion inventories. "Situation tests" call for judgment by one or more qualified observers of the individual's behavior in simulated lifelike situations.

Still another method of personality study is one in which the subject "responds as he chooses" to pictures, unfinished sentences, and ink blots. By means of this "projective technique" the individual throws out responses supposed to be so revealing of his personality that they can be interpreted by an expert and yield a basic adjustment picture. Thus, if the subject is faced with an incomplete sentence such as "The big boy was the first to _____," his personal outlook will be at least partially revealed in the way he finishes it. One child may complete the sentence by saying "throw a rock," whereas another, with a different personality organization, may furnish "make a home run." As the subject gives spontaneous answers, values are unconsciously revealed. The Rorschach Ink Blot Test is the most widely known instrument making use of the projective technique. It consists of ten separate ink blots on pieces of paper. The subject is shown the blots and is graded by a professional on what he sees or fails to see in the blot shapes. The purpose of this test is to provide a situation which cannot be solved in the conventional manner, because the subject has no previous experience in describing what he sees or does not see. Although the subject does not know what he is supposed to describe, Rorschach has provided a guidepost of normal and abnormal reactions through preliminary work in testing thousands of subjects with ink blots. A clear view of the personality of anyone is usually clouded by habits, mannerisms, and customs that people build up to mask their true feelings. This defensive surface barrier is extremely difficult to penetrate. But when subjected to the ink-blot series in which he is supposed to "see" something, the individual cannot rely on his protective "front" and must tell the truth as to what they mean to him.

Needless to say, complete reliance upon inventories, scales, situation tests, and projective techniques in judging an individual's psychological makeup would be a highly questionable procedure. One must always come back to the fact that human beings are extremely complicated and unpredictable. However, analyses, personality tests, and some of the other measures described, at least help to throw some light upon the problem of the individual's adjustment.

THE NECESSITY OF GUIDANCE FOR THE MALADJUSTED READER

The Relationship Between Emotions and Reading. If a child is so tense and anxious that he looks at every word half a dozen times before reading it aloud, for fear of making a mistake, his reading difficulty may be rooted in a neurosis of which inability to read at normal speed is merely a surface symptom. When remedial work is given to this child, more is needed than drill. He may have nagging parents who demand nothing short of perfection from him, thus causing him to be fearfully cautious in pronouncing each word. In this case a home-school conference is in order. Parents are apt to make comparisons between their children. If a younger child is reproached for not doing as well in school as an older brother or sister, he will tend to conform more and more to this unflattering image. The child develops a fear of failure in such a situation and his grades suffer. Frustration mounts and he refuses to exert himself. Since he cannot read, he is hindered from developing fresh concepts which might lead to personal growth. Indeed, his whole personality may be blunted. As Ruth Strang[1] and her coauthors state: "Without adequate reading proficiency the individual lacks access to one of the most important avenues of learning. Thus, poor reading indirectly affects an individual's personal development by blocking paths he might otherwise have taken and decreasing self-esteem and self-confidence."

Since likes and dislikes can be cultivated, the teacher should pay special attention to motivation in dealing with emotionally disturbed children. It is well to arouse interests and develop hobbies. The teacher should make it a point to talk to the retarded reader, tell him part of a story, read part of it to him, and then suggest that he finish it to find out what happened. Successful guidance for emotionally disturbed children includes what Hirschberg[2] terms "planned ego development." The child should be accepted as a person regardless of his poor achievement in reading. Recognition can be provided for other possible achievements besides reading. It is often necessary to establish more sympathetic rapport between him and his classmates. Above all, "planned ego development should aim toward the development of skills and mastery." Therefore, the teacher should choose material of high

[1] Ruth Strang, Constance M. McCullough, and Arthur E. Traxler, *The Improvement of Reading* (3d ed.) (New York: McGraw-Hill Book Co., Inc., 1961), p. 340.
[2] J. Cotter Hirschberg, "The Role of Education in the Treatment of Emotionally Disturbed Children Through Planned Ego Development," *American Journal of Orthopsychiatry*, XXIII (1953) 684–90.

interest value and easy vocabulary in order to make it possible for the child to experience some success in reading.

Attention to mental hygiene should be continuous in child development. At the first-grade level the teacher must avoid rushing the child into reading *before he is ready,* or the converse, *holding him back* from reading *when he is ready.* In the intermediate grades the teacher should also give much individual attention to the child, both as a person and as a reader. Since success in the upper grades in other subject-matter areas is dependent upon reading, failure to learn to read adequately produces deep frustrations. Unless the teacher can recognize the signs of maladjustment and is acquainted with tests to assist in the diagnosis of a child's particular needs, she cannot provide the proper guidance.

The Relationship Between Drives and Reading. It is of prime importance for the teacher to understand as much as possible about the factors which promote good mental hygiene. The dynamic basis of human conduct, psychologists tell us, is represented by two large classes of fundamental drives:

Physiological Drives	*Social Drives*
1. Hunger	1. Recognition
2. Thirst	2. Security
3. Elimination	3. Mastery (achievement)
4. Temperature maintenance	4. Change and novelty
5. Sex	5. Conformity and consistency.
6. Rest	
7. Movement	
8. Sleep	

It is comparatively simple to understand that failure to satisfy the needs for food, water, rest, and so on can cause disintegration of the personality. It is not so often recognized that the absence of success in meeting social needs also exercises a detrimental effect. Interference with the satisfaction of the *social drives* may lead to maladjustment. Psychologists point out that an individual normally behaves in such a manner as to win attention, recognition, and approval. If the individual cannot attract attention legitimately, he may compensate by becoming noisy and showing off or by resorting to a worrisome apathy. By some means or other the need for *recognition* is satisfied.

Each normal individual desires *security*—one of the instincts upon which psychologists usually agree is the early appearance of the infant's fear of falling, of losing the support and security of his mother's arms. As the individual grows older, security in the economic sense is demanded, but far more important is the need to feel secure in the love or approval of others. It is scarcely necessary to remind a teacher that failure in reading is almost certain to affect the individual's sense of security.

The desire for *mastery* and *achievement* is surely violated when the child fails at an activity as important to school success as reading. Here, again, if the desire for notice cannot be satisfied by fair means, the child may seek it by playing truant, annoying his classmates, or resorting to other antisocial conduct.

After sitting in one position for a while, change through movement becomes a *physical* necessity. Our culture pattern seems to breed a strong *mental* drive for *novelty* and *change* as well. Indeed, this acquired need seems to be almost as strong as the opposite drive for security. Since reading furnishes limitless possibilities for enjoying vicarious experiences, it offers an avenue of refreshing change from the tedium of everyday activities. Denied this readily available outlet, the individual is apt to become restless to the point of maladjustment.

The normal individual wants to be *consistent* in thinking and conduct, finding conflicts difficult to bear. He usually wants to do the expected thing, and, if thwarted in a realization of this particular drive, he may take recourse to rationalization and an "I don't care" attitude. The normal individual seeks companions to share interests and experiences. If the child cannot read, his failure is shown up several times each day. He cannot read about boys, what they do, and what they do not do, and thus receive guidance in developing his own role as a boy. His is a triple loss: He cannot *conform* to school demands academically and fit into the reading group. Therefore, he is likely to lose the esteem of his peer group. Finally, his own personal image suffers.

In addition to the social drives mentioned above, it might be wise to add an occasional impulse toward non-conformity. Not to be overlooked are the many non-conformists—religious leaders, scientists, educators, artists, statesmen—who have contributed enormously to human progress. Many of them were frowned upon by those intent upon maintaining the status quo. There is a growing tendency in the American social order to overemphasize the importance of doing things with a group. So pronounced is this emphasis, in spite of the continual stipulation in the schools to honor individual differences, that the wish to be alone is regarded by many today as a sign of maladjustment. With hermits it is, of course, but, when people, upon occasion, draw apart to meditate and concentrate in solitude, they should not be suspect. Beethoven did not compose his musical masterpieces in a committee! In viewing the contributions of many of those who have worked alone, one surely cannot condemn them as antisocial. Obviously, the distinction must be made between withdrawal to escape from life's responsibilities and withdrawal for productive purposes.

In view of the close relation between reading and success in school, it is not difficult to realize why the teacher of reading must do everything possible to further such adjustment, and thus help to decrease frustration, withdrawal, and antagonism.

THE INFLUENCE OF BOOKS AND READING ON PERSONALITY

Psychologists sometimes define personality as the "individual's social stimulus value." As a wit once said, "You can't be alone and say, 'My goodness, how much personality I have!' Someone else has to be present to admit it." More and more psychologists support the school of thought which advocates the cultivation of a breadth of interests, on the theory that the more interests the individual has, the more interesting he will be to others.

Aldous Huxley the brilliant modern novelist suggests in *Eyeless in Gaza* that personality is feeling and thought, that sometimes the individual himself selects what to think and feel from all that happens to him, and that sometimes the collective wisdom or unwisdom of a class or a whole society dictates what the individual shall feel and think and become. "To a certain extent," Huxley concludes, " 'personality' is not even personal property."

Probably the safest definition is that "personality includes and combines inherited traits, and is subsequently influenced by the type of body with which a person is born, the environment of his growth and development, and all of his thoughts and emotions, felt secretly or openly expressed."

Evidence of Research Concerning the Effects of Reading. Together with the home, school, and church, books have been called by some the architects of human personality. In what way can this assertion be proved? Evidence of changes in personality traits caused by reading is difficult to find and when found is often considered too subtle and introspective to be valid. However, by means of questionnaires, free-written reports, "open-end" questions and "reading autobiographies," a small body of research has accrued which is encouraging. For example, in a study by Weingarten[3] of the responses of 1,256 college students to a questionnaire, it was demonstrated that, in reading, these young people could attain understanding of themselves, a worthy concept of self, recognition of an ideal person to emulate, understanding of other persons' motives, and awareness of others' solutions to their problems. A study of the impact of reading on a group of elementary-school teachers is reported by Russell.[4] In writing about the effects of reading on their lives, they indicated that, in their childhood reading, the most frequent effects were identification with character(s), enjoyment of humor and adventure, enrichment of everyday experiences, enjoyment of fantasy, and added knowledge. Smith[5] stated that, as a result of reading, 60 per cent of the elementary-school pupils she studied reported changes in attitude, 30 per cent, changes in their ideas, but that only 9 per cent of the group reported changes in their behavior.

The Instrumental Value of Reading Doubted. In the last research finding above lies an explanation why many people express doubt concerning the power of books to influence personal development. The trouble is that readers do not *apply* what they read. In the absence of observable changes in *behavior,* onlookers become

[3] Samuel Weingarten, "Developmental Values in Voluntary Reading," *School Review,* LXII (April 1954), 222–30.

[4] David H. Russell, "Contributions of Reading to Personal Development," *Teachers' College Record,* LXI (May 1960), 435–42.

[5] Nila Banton Smith, "Some Effects of Reading on Children," *Elementary English,* XXV (May 1948), 271–78.

skeptical of the instrumental values of reading. The easiest books to evaluate in terms of their effects are the "how to" books, offering printed advice regarding ways to improve posture, weight control, manners, etc. Yet the majority of those who read them constitute very poor advertisements for the counsel presented. As a college girl complained: "My room-mate has been reading a book on charm for a week and she isn't charming yet." It is, of course, apparent that no one can reduce weight, for example, simply by reading a book about controlling appetite. Application is a necessary concomitant.

However, it is not with these "prescription-type" books that teachers are chiefly concerned in dealing with children. Such books, written, as it were, "to order," handle problems "head on" with a lamentable lack of art and subtlety. As a consequence, they are probably a good deal less effective in influencing personal development than those that deal with a problem from the "inside out rather than from the outside in." For example, a book that makes a frontal attack on courage cannot possibly have the impact of a novel like Hugh Walpole's *Fortitude*. In the latter, the reader finds subtlety and depth; there is no awkward surface belaboring of the easy slogan type. Consequently, it makes an impression.

The Functional Value Supported. The skeptics notwithstanding, many persons attribute to books and reading great power in influencing and modifying human behavior.

THE EVIDENCE OF TESTS, COURSES, AND WRITERS. An interesting study[6] was made of the effect of immediate experience on the responses of second-grade children to the California Test of Personality. After the children were given the test, a story pertaining to two children with excellent personalities was read twice to the class. The class was then given the test again to see whether their answers would reflect the attitudes and personalities of the model children. The many differences between the answers on the first and second test seemed to indicate that responses on a personality test are affected by recent reading material.

[6] Grace Therese Curran, "The Effect of Immediate Experiences upon Responses on the California Personality Test," *Journal of Educational Research*, XLVIII (December 1954), 289.

Courses offered in the "great books" support the theory that books are powerful agents in molding the thought and actions of the reader. Reduced to simplest terms, the philosophy of the Great Books Foundation seems to be that if students will study the great minds of all ages as they are preserved in the classics, at least some of this thought will be assimilated to influence contemporary conduct, with resulting benefit to society.

Josette Frank, who works directly with books and children, reminds teachers that books can perform wonderful services for young people. In her *Your Child's Reading Today* she shows how a child's shyness can be minimized by reading such a book as Cathleen Schurr's *The Shy Little Kitten,* how the story *Adopted Jane* can soften the discovery that one is not a real son or daughter. At a different age level, a girl who has just failed to receive a bid to join a sorority can be helped to face her disappointment by reading a factual article which explains that admission to sororities does not depend solely on the girl's own qualifications. Such factors as being a daughter or a sister of a member, having strong alumnae support, or having as friends active members of the chapter are extremely important qualifications. The disappointed girl will also learn that only a handful of "pledges" can be taken in each year.

Modern writers, concerned with how people react to poverty, sickness, windfall, pathos, romance, success, failure, are quick to credit books with powers of personal development. For example, in *The Disenchanted,*[7] Budd Schulberg writes of a man, also an author, who is thoroughly disgusted with himself for being "a dabbler, a trifler." In his thirties, this man turns to reading, hoping, one infers, to find something to help him to improve his work habits.

Other people use stories and jokes to indicate their belief in the power of reading to affect human conduct. There is the anecdote about the meeting between two men: "How is your mother?" asked the first. "Feeling very poorly," replied the second. "What's the matter?" inquired the first. "She has acute frontal sinusitis," replied the second. "Where did she get that?" asked the first. "From *The Reader's Digest,*" said the second. "She read a very convincing article about it last month."

[7] New York: Random House, Inc., 1953, p. 214.

THE EFFECT OF EXHORTATION. No matter how enthusiastic book-lovers are concerning the power of the printed word to bring about changes in personality, it is doubtful if many of them would place much faith in mere exhortation,[8] which serves only to create "a temporary emotional upsurge" at which it is "futile to try to 'peg' the individual." Improvement in personality must be "internalized" and not laid on like an embrocation. One of the main faults of "success literature" lies in its tendency to exhort the reader to triumph over odds, to laugh at setbacks, and to believe that failure is impossible, and then to assume that all will be well. Thinking divorced from action is not likely to bring about any tangible change for the better in the behavior of even the most earnest reader. Generalizations that encourage the use of the "will power," and exhortations to be serene and not worry are useless unless individuals are placed in dynamic situations that stimulate the remaking of habits. The effective method is to combine the verbal approach with action. For example, after reading an article on wastefulness, one might mentally lecture oneself to be less wasteful, and then follow this good advice by conserving what one has and resisting the impulse to buy new gadgets. Those who follow this middle course of linking good reading with doing are closer to the solution of the delicate problem of changing habits than are those who pin their faith on exhortation, or those who deny the power of print to influence human behavior.

THE EFFECT OF DRIP-BLOOP TECHNIQUES. The advertising world has long recognized the fact that varied repetition wins customers. Novelty of appeal and reiteration are basic to most advertising campaigns. In television, for example, millions of dollars worth of network revenue a month may be dedicated to the repetition of food commercials at fifteen-minute and half-hour intervals in a great variety of ways—the object being to influence the buying behavior of the American public. It might be helpful to think of this powerful form of repetition as the "drip-bloop" technique. Anyone who has heard a dripping water faucet knows that it has a steady, implacable force that cannot be ignored by even the most philosophical. If a faucet leaks persistently enough and if

---

[8] Carl R. Rogers, *Counseling and Psychotherapy* (Boston: Houghton Mifflin Co., 1942), p. 20.

it alternates a nerve-wracking *drip* with a tension-building *bloop,* it will make its influence felt, and the auditor will be spurred to some form of activity. He may close a door to deaden the recurring sounds or he may telephone a plumber, but he will do something.

For inspirational or how-to reading materials to take effect, the drip-bloop method must be utilized, with repetition turning up in a number of challenging and attention-fixing guises. The drip-bloop technique instigates action in a sequence similar to that contained in this anecdote: A friend recommends a certain book, and you say, "Really?" Another friends recommends the same book, and you say, "Goodness, I must read it!" Then a third friend recommends the book, and you *do* read it. Variety and repetition are components of successful persuasion anywhere.

Another illustration of the importance of receiving motivation from a number of sources is the story of the woman who read an article extolling the virtues of oil painting as a means of relaxation. Unconvinced, though slightly interested, she made no move toward adopting oil painting as a hobby. In the first place, she did not know how to start, and, in the second, she had a vivid recollection of the C-minus grades she had consistently received in art courses at school. But the drip-bloop technique came into play when she ran across another article, quoting Winston Churchill's many reasons for liking to paint. This second exposure made a deeper impression. She began to toy with the idea of trying oil painting herself. A week later, while browsing in the library, she found a book entitled *Grandma Moses, American Primitive.* It was about the wonderful old lady who took up amateur painting at the age of seventy-six and who at the age of ninety-four had painted 1,600 oils, most of them purchased by museums and collectors, thus placing her in the ranks of America's leading artists. After reading the biography of Grandma Moses, the borderline hobbyist found a library book entitled *Get in There and Paint.* She did! This final drip-bloop was thus decisive. Reading had definitely influenced a course of action. Painting is now an active hobby and has modified the woman's outlook and influenced her personality to some extent.

Here is a final example of the influence of repetition when coupled with variety. A young man learned he had failed to pass the state bar examination. He felt aimless and unimportant; indeed, he was so overwhelmed with self-pity that he contemplated suicide. Fortunately, he had often found that reading helped banish his despondent moods. So he sought distraction in the university library. After browsing for something to help him face his disappointment philosophically, he chanced upon a book on existentialism. After scanning it pessimistically, his attention was attracted to the description of a symbol used to illustrate the advisability of living each day fully and gratefully. The selection read as follows:

After an accidental fall a man found himself trapped on a high ledge just wide enough for standing. The ocean tide was rising swiftly. Above, and on each side, sheer, steep cliffs rose, utterly impossible to scale. Below were jagged rocks and storm-tossed waves. No human being was within shouting distance.

The young man then read a number of challenging questions following the selection: At that moment was the man on the ledge worrying about success, money, prestige? Or was it life—very life itself—that he was busy valuing as he had never valued it before? Had not life become infinitely precious to him? As he stood on that narrow ledge, waiting for the tide to engulf him, did anything else matter to him but the great gift of life? The article ended with a recommendation that the reader try imagining personal disaster such as the loss of an arm, a leg, or an eye and then be glad and grateful that the loss was only imagined.

The depressed student read the passage twice and was aware of a slight abeyance of self-pity. But more drip-bloop repetition was necessary to help him formulate an emotionally healthy attitude. He told his best friend that reading about the existentialist symbol and the suggestion to imagine disaster had helped, but only temporarily. At this his friend recalled a parable he had read that seemed to come back to him when he needed solace. It ran

One day Adam had been weeding industriously in the Garden of Eden when the serpent came along and asked Adam why he was working so hard.

"What's the use?" said the serpent. "You are not going to live forever."

"I'm not?" said Adam in amazement. "I thought I was. That's why it has been worthwhile doing all this hard work."

Said the serpent, "Your time on earth is limited. Why fix up the Garden so nicely? You are going to die some day and leave it all."

At this Adam stopped weeding, and when Eve came along the garden path a little later, she found him fast asleep. She woke him and said, "Adam, why aren't you weeding?"

"What's the use?" said Adam. "I just learned today that I'm not going to live forever."

"Adam,'" said Eve sternly, "even if you have only one more day left to live, keep weeding!"

"Not a bad philosophy," agreed the young ex-law student. Several times during the following week he deliberately recalled Eve's wholesome advice whenever he caught himself sinking into the cynicism that prompted him to demand, "What's the use of living if I can't be what I want to be—a lawyer?" He was discovering that career frustration is one of the scourges created by the modern culture pattern. But luckily he found another drip-bloop reinforcement in an article quoting Justice Holmes's fundamental attitude toward life at the age of ninety:

Life is an end in itself, and the only question as to whether it is worth living is whether you have enough of it.

Finally the young man understood at last that he must not think that his life was over because of one failure. He realized that he must begin to work. For the first time since failing the bar examination, he began to consider a career in public accounting—his second job choice after legal work. "Keep weeding, old boy," he told himself ruefully.

It would be gratifying to report that these few exposures to wholesome viewpoints were all the young man needed to effect a change in him. However, a few days later, the bitter mood of futility and self-pity returned. He had been exposed to several helpful passages, but he had not really accepted their fundamental thesis; he was not practicing new mental habits yet. He only knew about them; he had not made them a part of himself.

After a bleak day devoted almost entirely to pampering his self-pity, he picked up his roommate's copy of the current *The Saturday Review* and skimmed through it in desultory fashion. There he noted an article about an eighty-four-year-old French writer. The student had never heard the man's name and he could not even pronounce it. What did interest him was one passage the old man had written in his diary:

Ecstasy is my normal state. I have made the great decision. I have given up my reluctance to abandon self-pity for self-respect. Knowing that one crowds out the other, I have made the choice. Now, there is no room for self-pity. I will be strong. Never again will I pity myself. Ah, now at last, I can respect myself.

The student's reaction to this passage was immediate. "Well!" he exclaimed aloud, "if a man of eighty could say that, what of a man of twenty-four, with his whole life ahead of him?" And he felt a deep shame for having adopted despair as *his* normal state.

Thus, by degrees—by drip-bloop, if you please—this young man's reading had an impact upon him, leading him to a more wholesome attitude toward life. Reading had thus provided insight and information, had led him to compare himself with others, and had helped him to organize concepts in a new way, focusing his attention on the need for change and inducing him to set up new goals. In short, reading had made it easier for him to live with himself and had made him a better person, easier for others to live with.

The Method Applied in the Classroom. Suppose that the teacher of the sixth-grade class wishes to teach better posture. How can she use reading to serve this purpose? Needless to say, she will try a variety of procedures. She may first elicit from the children their ideas concerning good posture. "What is good posture?" she may ask. "What is the value to health of good posture?" After communicating what they already know, the children can be encouraged to supplement their knowledge by reading works on posture and health placed on the reading table. Undoubtedly, the teacher will make use of visual aids and show the children how to keep a record of their progress in achieving good standing, sitting, and walking posture. The teacher may use "before and after" snapshots or cutouts of the children's life-sized silhouettes (obtained by casting shadows with the help of a flashlight and a hanging sheet) for added motivation. She may also emphasize how much better clothes fit when the back is erect and the stomach held in. A program of dancing and rhythm to encourage balance and poise can be used effectively. Thus the teacher can emphasize posture in a variety of interesting ways, including reading. At the same time many of the children in the classroom may display a greatly improved attitude of self-respect, better health, and increased personal effectiveness, as well as improved posture.

This kind of lesson would seem to meet the criteria for effective learning experience set up by Professor Stephen Corey, of Teachers College, Columbia University, that the "learning of children, if it is to be functional" involves doing something in a very literal sense, i.e., use of "bodily activity . . . fruitful use of ears and the eyes and the muscles." He warns that "talk and reading are educative only if the words that are spoken and read are rooted in a substantial amount of direct, first-hand, perceptual experience."[9]

Taking a slightly different point of view, but not necessarily contradicting the desirability of learning by doing whenever feasible, Clifton Fadiman[10] writes, "An early familiarity with books unconsciously introduces the child to a fundamental, liberating truth: that the largest part of the entire universe of space and time can never be apprehended by direct, first-hand experience."

The Selection of Books for Personal Enrichment. Since lifelong opinions are often formed during early reading, it becomes a task of primary importance to study the child's personality, both by objective tests and by subjective means, in order to discover his strengths and weaknesses and furnish him the right kinds of guidance.

THE CRITERIA FOR CHOICES. If the teacher knows how far the child's reading has advanced, she will be in a better position to recommend books to serve his needs. She must not do this obtrusively, of course, but in the spirit of sharing something enjoyable. To influence the child's personal growth, the teacher should provide a well-balanced supply of books which offer guidance along a wide variety of lines. Suppose the teacher has a child who

[9] "Some Criteria for a Maximally Effective Learning Experience," Supplementary Educational Monographs, *Reading in Relation to Experience and Language*, edited by W. S. Gray, Vol. 6, No. 58 (Chicago: University of Chicago Press), p. 9.

[10] *Holiday Magazine*, XXX, No. 5 (November 1961), 147.

is too factually minded. Probably he should be encouraged to read imaginative selections now and then to develop a more balanced personality. The humorless might well profit from some of Lewis Carroll's whimsey in *Alice in Wonderland.*

One teacher tells of a literal-minded boy who menaced the peace and quiet of the sixth-grade classroom with a volume called *27000 Little-Known Facts.* In her attempt to guide the boy, she stressed the importance of a balance between his fact-finding tendencies and the exercise of his imagination. Through *The Peterkin Papers* she showed him how humorless literal-minded people can be to themselves, how disconcerting to others. Through the books *Tom Sawyer* and *Huckleberry Finn* she introduced the child to two boys who never hesitated to use their imagination. Next she let him wander in the exciting world of hiding and pursuit represented by James Fenimore Cooper's *The Spy.* Imperceptibly, book by book and story by story, she guided the boy to react favorably to imaginative sequences in print, until she had helped him to form new reading tastes. This teacher believed that if a child reads better books he will inevitably become a better person. This approach is in keeping with writer Josette Frank's comment at an educational meeting: "If the idea is accepted that reading about gangsters in comic books will breed young gangsters, the converse must be accepted that reading books about wholesome personalities will inspire children to imitate them." It is true, of course, that "the idea of utilizing books to promote certain personality traits is not new—only the tendency to doubt it."

No one can guarantee that a given book will accomplish a definite end. There is no certainty that any one book will be the key to a child's personality problems. Desirable changes in personality involve thinking, feeling, and acting. Yet, even though the teacher cannot measure the exact amount of change which a wholesome program of reading may make in the personality of a child, it is reassuring to reflect that some change probably occurs and that the child may remember all his life the flavor and form, the emotional impact, of some of the reading he has done. Naturally, the teacher should be alert for books that appear especially helpful to personal development. Adopting a particular hobby as the result of reading a persuasive book may promote a sense of achievement. Learning a great deal about etiquette, for example, through reading books about good manners may help to develop poise—an important source of security—if the counsel read is practiced. Truly, reading coupled with doing can work wonders.

Books for Personal Enrichment. Presented below are suggested readings which have been found valuable in promoting a well-rounded development of interests and hobbies for children at the middle and upper grade levels. When displaying these books in the library corner, the teacher will find it helpful to print separate placards to label the books according to the various personal-enrichment classifications.

Humor

ATWATER, RICHARD, and ATWATER, FLORENCE. *Mr. Popper's Penguins.* Boston: Little Brown & Co.

CARROLL, LEWIS. *Alice's Adventures in Wonderland.* New York: The Macmillan Co., Publishers (a division of the Crowell-Collier Publishing Co.).

HALE, LUCRETIA. *The Peterkin Papers.* Boston: Houghton Mifflin Co.

McCLOSKY, ROBERT. *Homer Price.* New York: The Viking Press, Inc.

TRAVIS, P. L. *Mary Poppins.* New York: Harcourt, Brace & World, Inc.

SHEPHERD, ESTHER. *Paul Bunyan* (tall tales). New York: Harcourt, Brace & World, Inc.

WHITE, E. B. *Charlotte's Web.* New York: Harper & Row.

Hobbies

BATES, ALFRED. *The Gardener's First Year.* New York: Longmans, Green & Co., Inc.

TEALE, EDWIN WAY. *The Boys' Book of Photography.* New York: E. P. Dutton & Co., Inc.

TURNER, JOHN S. *Let's Start a Stamp Collection.* Philadelphia: F. A. Stokes Co.

Etiquette

BETZ, BETTY. *Your Manners Are Showing.* New York: Grosset & Dunlap, Inc.

LEAF, MUNRO. *The Watchbirds: A Picture Book of Behavior.* Philadelphia: F. A. Stokes Co.

PIERCE, BEATRICE. *It's More Fun When You Know the Rules.* New York: Farrar & Rinehart, Inc.

Nature

GUBERLET, MURIEL L. *The Seashore Parade.* New York: The Ronald Press Co.

MORRIS, PERCY A. *Boy's Book of Snakes*. New York: The Ronald Press Co.

NEEDHAM, JAMES G. *Introducing Insects*. New York: The Ronald Press Co.

WOOD, L. N. *Raymond L. Ditmars: His Exciting Career with Reptiles, Animals, and Insects*. New York: Julian Messner, Inc.

Travel

SOMEREN, VAN. *Young Traveler in Holland*. New York: E. P. Dutton & Co., Inc.

HOGG, B., and HOGG, G. *Young Traveler in Norway*. New York: E. P. Dutton & Co., Inc.

NOTE: There is a series of these books taking the "Young Traveler" to many other countries.

Biography

FOSTER, GENEVIEVE. *George Washington's World*. New York: Charles Scribner's Sons.

FOSTER, GENEVIEVE. *Abraham Lincoln's World*. New York: Charles Scribner's Sons.

VAN LOON, HENDRIK WILLEM. *The Life and Times of Simon Bolivar*. New York: Dodd, Mead & Co.

Music

LACEY, N. *Picture Book of Musical Instruments*. New York: Lothrop, Lee & Shephard Co.

WHEELER, OPAL. *Musical Biographies*. New York: E. P. Dutton & Co., Inc.

Art

GIBSON, KATHARINE. *Pictures To Grow Up With*. London: Studio Publications (for the Junior Literary Guild).

HOLME, GEOFFREY. *The Children's Art Book*. London: Studio Publications.

PARKER, PETERSHAM KAY. *What and What-not: A Picture Story of Art*. Boston: Houghton Mifflin Co.

Sports

ARCHIBALD, W. F. *Fighting Quarterback*. New York: Steck Publishing Co.

BONNER, R. *Baseball Rookies Who Made Good*. New York: Alfred A. Knopf (a division of Random House, Inc.).

QUESTIONS AND ACTIVITIES

1. Several definitions of adjustment are given at the beginning of this chapter. Which do you find most acceptable? If none of them satisfy you, how would you define adjustment?
2. Trace some of the effects of incompetence in reading.

3. What factors promote mental health?
4. What is the relationship between emotions and progress in reading?
5. Which of the definitions of personality do you prefer? Why? How would you define personality?
6. Why are some critics reluctant to admit that reading can modify personality?
7. Give an example of the "drip-bloop" method from your own experience.
8. How might a teacher help children to improve posture, manners, speech, through use of repetition plus novelty? Give the titles of actual reading selections which might be profitably used.
9. Reread the specific "personal messages" which the would-be suicide received as the result of applying the "drip-bloop" method of reading to his problem. Why is the "technique of imagined disaster" probably capable of wider application than some of the others?

SELECTED REFERENCES

DeBoer, John, "Literature and Human Behavior," *The English Journal*, XXXIX (February 1959), 76–82.

Development in and Through Reading. The Sixteenth Yearbook of the National Society for the Study of Education, Part I. Chicago: University of Chicago Press, 1961.

Ellison, Jerome, and Franklin T. Gosser. "Non-fiction Magazine Articles: A Content Analysis Study in Personal Development," *Journalism Quarterly*, XXXVI (Winter 1959), 27–34.

Ephron, Beulah Kanter. *Emotional Difficulties in Reading.* New York: The Julian Press, Inc., 1953.

Fenner, Phyllis. *The Proof of the Pudding: What Children Read.* New York: John Day Co., Inc., 1957.

Frank, Josette. *Your Child's Reading Today.* New York: Doubleday & Co., Inc., 1954.

Glasser, William. *Mental Health or Mental Illness.* New York: Harper & Row, 1960.

Great Books Program—A National Survey, White Plains, N.Y.; 1959.

Kircher, Clara. *Character Formation Through Books: A Bibliography* (rev. ed.). Washington, D.C.: Catholic University of America Press, 1952.

Larrick, Nancy. *A Teacher's Guide in Children's Books.* Columbus, Ohio: Charles E. Merrill Books, Inc., 1960.

Lodge, Helen C. "The Influence of Biography on the Moral Ideology of the Adolescent at the Eighth Grade Level." Unpublished Ph.D. dissertation, University of California, 1953.

MEHLING, REUBEN. "Attitude-changing Effect of News," *Journalism Quarterly*, XXXVI (Spring 1959), 189–90.

NEISSER, EDITH G. *The Eldest Child*. New York: Harper & Row, 1957.

RUSSELL, DAVID H. "Personal Values in Reading," *The Reading Teacher*, XII (October 1958), 3–9.

RUSSELL, DAVID H. *Children Learn to Read*. Boston: Ginn & Co., 1961.

SHRODES, CAROLINE. "Bibliotherapy: A Theoretical and Clinical Experimental Study." Unpublished Ph.D. dissertation, University of California, 1949.

SMITH, NILA BANTON. "Personal and Social Values of Reading," *Elementary English*, XXV (December 1948), 490–500.

STRANG, RUTH, CONSTANCE M. McCULLOUGH, and ARTHUR B. TRAXLER. *The Improvement of Reading* (3d ed.). New York: McGraw-Hill Book Co., Inc., 1961.

THORPE, LOUIS P. *Child Psychology and Development* (3d ed.). New York: The Ronald Press Co., 1962.

ZOLKOS, HELENA A. "What Research Says About Emotional Factors in Retardation in Reading," *Elementary School Journal*, LI (1951), 512–18.

PART II

READING READINESS

5

RECOGNIZING READINESS
FOR READING

Today the majority of first-grade teachers indorse the reading-readiness program in one form or another. The main tenet of this humane program is that a little child shall not be asked to begin reading until he is equal to the difficult task—ready, that is, mentally, physically, emotionally, socially, and linguistically.

Before the reading-readiness concept evolved, children were expected to be ready to read when they started school at the age of six. Chronological age was the only measure of readiness used. As a consequence of this arbitrary policy many children who entered first grade with high hopes in September found themselves classed as reading failures by Thanksgiving Day. Beginning in 1925, however, a group interested in early childhood education suggested that children should not be asked to read until mature enough mentally to cope with abstract symbols. What makes reading so difficult for little children is that the word "dog," for example, does not remotely resemble the animal it stands for.

In 1931, two investigators[1] published data showing that, of approximately a hundred children who had attained an M.A. (mental age) of six years and six months, or higher, 78 per cent made satisfactory progress in reading. But children in part of the group studied, who were below this mental age, did poorly in first-grade reading. Largely on the basis of this one study, a mental age of six

[1] Mabel V. Morphett and Carleton Washburne, "When Should Children Begin To Read?" *Elementary School Journal*, XXXI (1931), 496–503.

years and six months came to be regarded as essential before children could learn to read.

However, a few years later, Gates[2] published a study of four first-grade classes which revealed considerable discrepancy in the correlations between mental age and reading achievement, a discrepancy that could be accounted for by differences in instructional procedures. In checking upon the validity of the earlier study, Gates was not attempting to deny the need for mental capacity in reading, but merely objecting to reliance upon a fixed point such as 6.6 on the mental-age continuum. The result of his study should have caused teachers to view mental age in its proper perspective as one of many factors affecting a child's reading success, but faith in the validity of the mental-age minimum, established by the comparatively meager research in the early investigation by Morphett and Washburne, still persists in many quarters.

To sum up the present position, while reading authorities are not inclined to state arbitrarily what *exact* mental age is necessary, two investigators (Irving H. Anderson and Walter F. Dearborn, *The Psychology of Teaching Reading.* New York: The Ronald Press Co., 1952. Pp. 79–80) remind us, on the basis of many studies, that a "distinct relationship does exist between reading achievement and mental status."

A fairly recent investigation by R. E. Edmiston and Bessie Peyton[3] showed that some children with a mental age of only five years who had an enriched twelve-week readiness program were able to achieve up to national norms in first-grade reading. Moreover, a number of children who made poor scores on readiness tests, and for whom poor achievement was predicted, achieved up to grade following specific reading-readiness instruction. Here the importance of a readiness program in giving children a foundation for success in reading is reiterated. However, to insist that *all* children be given a readiness program, for a set number of weeks, is almost as misguided as requiring *all* children to begin reading at the chronological age of six.

[2] Arthur I. Gates, "The Necessary Mental Age for Beginning Reading," *Elementary School Journal*, XXXVII (1937), 497–508.

[3] "Improving First Grade Achievement by Readiness Instruction," *School and Society*, LXXI (1950), 230–32.

There are other relevant factors to consider in identifying what is required for learning to read, factors for which current mental tests seem inadequate. As a case in point, Durkin[4] reports some of the data resulting from her longitudinal study of forty-nine California children. These children must have had exceptional readiness for reading, because they could already read at levels from first to fourth grade when they entered school. She states that "the majority of them had exceptionally good memories and ability to concentrate. They were curious, conscientious, serious-minded, persistent and self-reliant. Furthermore, all of the children in the study had been read to regularly at home, in some instances from age two."

In addition to listing the above characteristics, which are not measured by mental tests but which apparently served as important factors in promoting the unusual degree of readiness enjoyed by the young children in her investigation, Durkin suggests another vital factor that affects the child's chance of success in reading. The child's "own perception of what it means to 'read' influences his attitude toward learning to read, and, consequently affects his achievements." For example, "One child may view reading as a symbol of growing up, while another sees it as a kind of unwanted independence." Such attitudes toward learning have been noted by many primary-school teachers. It is not uncommon for a young child, motivated by the desire to compete with older brothers and sisters, to strive hard to excel in reading, the ultimate goal being to win parental approval.

In view of research, it seems wise to recognize as many aspects of the child's readiness for reading as possible. Involved are physical readiness (visual and auditory), experiential background, emotional control, and, of course, always remembering to regard it in its proper perspective in a constellation of factors, mental readiness. Though listed as a separate form of readiness, language proficiency is used as an index of mental growth—so closely are the two related.

The fact is generally recognized that children vary a great deal in each area of readiness. Today, when a teacher faces twenty-

[4] Dolores Durkin, "Children Who Read Before Grade One," *The Reading Teacher*, XIV, No. 3 (January 1961), 163–66.

five or thirty children entering first grade, she is well aware that perhaps only a third have achieved the maturity needed for beginning to unravel the mysteries of the printed pattern. Some first-grade children may enjoy good general health; others may be too frail to be burdened immediately with so complicated a skill as learning to read. Some may have the necessary auditory acuity and speech-production accuracy; others may still be using baby talk and lisping "toat" for the word "coat." In some, a prolongation of infantile farsightedness may prevent focus on near objects such as print in a book. Some children may be so shy that standing before the group plunges them into emotional turmoil; others may be so accustomed to being the center of attention at home that they stage tantrums when denied the same monopoly at school. Beginning first-grade children also display varying degrees of skill in social readiness. Some know how to say "please" and "thank you," while others lack these social graces. As far as language readiness is concerned, the son of a doctor may know the term *patella*, whereas his neighbor from a home where a foreign language is spoken may not know the term *knee* from *leg*.

Though very few teachers now expect children to begin the formal reading of printed matter upon entrance to first grade, many parents demand that reading be started without delay. They often interpret this to mean teaching their children the alphabet and proceeding quickly from there to words and sentences—the more the merrier. It becomes the duty of the first-grade teacher to explain why she wishes to discover readiness for reading, or the lack of it, before starting the teaching process. In addition, it is necessary for her to make clear that she intends to provide a wealth of experiences to compensate for a given child's lack of readiness. Parents must be helped to realize that a program of reading readiness in the primary grades based on a recognition of children's differences in maturity may well result in fewer remedial problems at levels beyond the primary. When a teacher explains to a parent, "Your child has to mature more before he can read," she is being a better friend to the child than the teacher who is disinclined to delay reading, preferring to launch instruction at the start. There is some evidence that early pressures for reading may have unfavorable effects upon the child's later success.[5]

The remainder of this chapter deals with the ways in which the teacher discovers and lists the strongest and weakest qualities of each of the children in order to determine the types of help which will be needed to develop readiness for reading—the subject of the chapter following this.

RECOGNIZING THE MENTAL AGE FOR READINESS

Because reading makes heavy demands upon the intelligence, it is obvious that intelligence tests are useful in appraising certain phases of reading readiness. The tests designed for use in early childhood do not involve reading ability. The teacher gives the directions orally, and the children respond by putting marks on pictures.

The Use of Group Intelligence Tests. Several such group tests are available for use in obtaining information concerning the mental ability of each child in the class. At least one of these standardized measures of intelligence should be made early in the first year.

THE PINTNER-CUNNINGHAM PRIMARY MENTAL TEST (Harcourt, Brace & World, Inc.). This non-language group test requires thirty minutes to administer. It may be given from the kindergarten through the second grade. It tests the child's skill in observing, in judging relative size, in recognizing picture parts, in carrying out picture completion, and in performing dot drawing. The results show his ability to grasp relationships, recognize simple concepts, and hold the eye steady on the written line—all necessary reading skills. The child's achievement is rated against a standard test score compiled from the achievement record of a great many children.

THE DETROIT BEGINNING, FIRST GRADE TEST (Harcourt, Brace & World, Inc.). This group intelligence test, designed for children of

[5] D. E. M. Gardner, *Testing Results in the Infant School* (2d ed.) London: Methuen & Co., Ltd., 1948.

five years nine months to seven years nine months, requires thirty minutes to administer. It is a non-verbal test and hence is extremely useful at the beginning first-grade level. The mental tasks required of children by this test include matching forms and following directions. The first checks ability to discriminate similarities and differences, and the other measures capacity to understand a set of directions and give appropriate responses—both skills basic to reading.

THE LORGE-THORNDIKE I.Q. TEST (Houghton Mifflin Co.). The non-verbal group test for kindergarten and grade one requires thirty-five minutes to administer in two or three sessions. Published in 1957, this test was standardized on 136,000 children in a great many different communities throughout the United States.

The Use of Individual Intelligence Tests. Although group tests are useful in determining the individual mental abilities of first-grade children, more accurate measures can be obtained in problem cases through the use of individual intelligence tests. Since these tests must be administered and interpreted by a trained examiner, such tests cannot be described in detail here. However, the teacher should be familiar with the names of the two most widely used at the primary level: the Terman-Merrill Revision of the Stanford-Binet Intelligence Test (Houghton Mifflin Co.), and the Wechsler-Bellevue Intelligence Scales (Psychological Corp.). Both measure the child's mental development and thus enable the teacher to gauge the child's reading readiness.

Another individual test is the Arthur Performance Scale (The Commonwealth Fund). In this test the child is asked to perform identifications such as pointing to his mouth which give a clue to his stock of concepts. The teacher then is enabled to compare his mental and language quotients with those standard for his age group. This test is also suitable for children with a foreign-language handicap.

The Use of Reading-Readiness Tests. Investigators have found that the results of standardized reading-readiness tests have a high correlation with those of intelligence tests and are quite as reliable in predicting the child's probable success in reading. Indeed, some schools depend solely on reading-readiness tests to determine mental readiness for reading. Three of the most widely used tests in this category are listed and described below.

GATES' READING READINESS TESTS (Teachers College, Bureau of Publications, Columbia University). This group test requiring forty minutes to give, consists of four major tests: picture directions, word matching, word-card matching, and rhyming. The scores are translated into percentile scores and prediction of success in learning to read.

LEE-CLARK READING READINESS TEST (California Test Bureau). This group test also requires thirty minutes to administer. The test consists of matching letter symbols, understanding concepts, vocabulary, and following directions, as well as identifying letters and words. The scores are translated into percentile ranking and grade placement equivalents and are a useful tool in determining the child's achievement.

MARION MONROE READING APTITUDE TEST, Primary Form (Houghton Mifflin Co.). The first six pages of this test may be administered in thirty minutes as a group test; the last two pages require individual testing and take twenty minutes more. There are eight separate tests in the Monroe booklet, each designed to predict and analyze both reading abilities and reading deficiencies. A virtue of the test is that it very quickly tests a good many readiness factors: Visual, motor, auditory, knowledge of concepts, articulation ability, sentence length, ability to classify and retain ideas (idea count).

The Use of Informal Tests of Mental Readiness. From time to time the author has been privileged to examine various informal mental tests, devised by experienced first-grade teachers. The following have been used to good effect in judging mental readiness for reading:

1. The teacher asks a child to draw a picture of daddy or grandfather or of a neighbor. She has found that those children who draw a man with five fingers on each hand, and with head, torso,

feet, and legs separated clearly—instead of having all extremities springing unnaturally from a round-moon head—are more alert, observant, and intelligent, and hence more ready for reading.

2. The teacher asks a child to tell a story from a picture, noting vocabulary and complexity of sentence structure.

3. The teacher listens for questions, since a questioning attitude usually denotes an active mind.

4. The teacher writes the word "happy" on the blackboard without saying it or trying to have it read and simply traces one continuous line around it, following its contour exactly. Then she writes the word "chair" and proceeds in the same way, making allowances, of course, for the difference in its contour. Then she erases the words within the outlines, leaving the profiles intact. Finally, she writes the words "happy" and "chair" on the other side of the board and asks a child to draw a line from the word to the shape it will fit. This offers a good test of mental ability, since the child who is mentally immature is often baffled by the whole procedure.

The Use of Non-I.Q., or "Creativity," Tests. For half a century, mental tests have measured intelligence quotients in terms of such mental abilities as choosing the right answer (true-false), filling in the correct term, memorizing certain data exactly, and other measures of non-creative, non-experimental thinking. Recently a number of psychologists, among them Paul E. Torrence, of the University of Minnesota, and Calvin W. Taylor, of the University of Utah, have been developing non-I.Q., or "creativity," tests to measure another type of mental capacity. These new tests have been used experimentally with children at all age levels, including entering first graders. To stimulate the imagination more than is required for recognition of the right answer on the conventional intelligence tests, the new creativity tests try in various ways to obtain flexible, non-convergent responses. For example, the child being tested is given an incomplete figure and asked to draw a finish for it. One boy completed a perfectly straight vertical line by drawing a spider at the lower end; he then added the oral explanation: "The spider is playing that he is a yo-yo." (This child, incidentally, had scored very low on a conventional intelligence test.) As another test of the ability to make a creative response, the child is shown a pile of bricks and asked, "What could you do with them?" One child may answer that he would use them to build a house; another may say that he would make a barbecue pit of the bricks; still another may reply that he would make a fence or a bookcase. Psychologists have discovered that it is not the child with the highest rating on a conventional I.Q. test who is able to make up the longest list of ways in which to use any of the materials suggested. Rather it is the youngster with imagination.

Since the intellect is complex, in order to obtain the fullest picture possible of the child's mentality, it is felt by many educators that these non-I.Q. tests should be used to supplement the more conventional measures of intelligence. At the very least the teacher should be aware that there are different types of mentality and that the creative mentally calls for a flexible, as opposed to a more predictable, mind. Certainly the mental power of imagination and the ability to make many rich new associations and elaborate upon ideas in print are useful in reading. In any assessment of mental readiness for reading, teachers cannot afford to neglect identification of those children who have this important capacity of creativeness.

RECOGNIZING PHYSICAL READINESS

Willard C. Olson[6] and others believe that a composite measure of physical growth is closely related to reading development. They therefore believe that instruction in reading must be geared to the child's *organismic,* or total, development. In other words, in determining readiness for reading, they take into account not only mental age but such measures of physical growth as height age, weight age, grip age, dental age, and metacarpal age (an X-ray of a six-year-old wrist may show cartilage where bone structure will later appear). However, the validity of the "organismic age" concept developed by Olson has been sharply challenged by Anderson,[7] who has questioned the "propriety of averaging together dis-

---

[6] *Child Development* (2d ed.), Boston: D. C. Heath & Co., 1959.

[7] John E. Anderson, "Methods of Child Psychology," in *Manual of Child Psychology* (2d ed.) (edited by Leonard Carmichael) (New York: John Wiley & Sons, Inc., 1954), p. 8.

similar measures with differing reliabilities into a single scale of equal weights." Blommers, Knief, and Stroud[8] also disagree with Olson's conclusion. They have brought together research studies showing that the only substantial correlation found in all the items listed by Olson was between *mental* age and reading. In the light of their studies, when it comes to a consideration of physical readiness, it seems more sensible to relate reading development to aspects of physical development directly involved in the skill of reading, such as eyes sufficiently developed to focus on near objects (print in a book), hearing acuity, and speech-production accuracy.

The teacher should be alert to the physical condition of all the children in her room. She can readily observe whether a child has a well-nourished appearance. If a child is literally too tired to keep his head off the desk, as the result of having stayed up too late the night before, watching television, his parents should be consulted about extending his sleeping time. However, the teacher needs the services of a school nurse or doctor to obtain an accurate diagnosis of the child's health. She should avail herself of all such special services in collecting accurate data concerning the physical well-being of her children. In addition, she must be constantly sensitive to each child's daily health needs. Does he suffer from chronic colds, throat or ear infections? If the child is not in good physical condition, the teacher should realize that, even though he may be able to force himself to learn to read, to do so would be to tax his already overburdened little body. A child's physical needs must be cared for if he is to sustain attention on abstract symbols —an imperative activity in reading.

Eye Maturation and Reading Readiness. A child's readiness for reading is often determined by the condition of his eyes. Are they developed sufficiently beyond the stage of infantile farsightedness to permit him to read at close range without strain? At birth the eye is only one-third of its adult size. Such underdevelopment prevents perfect focus on the retina. While infantile farsightedness decreases gradually with the growth and lengthening of the eye-

[8] Paul Blommers, Lotus M. Knief, and J. B. Stroud, "The Organismic Age Concept," *Journal of Educational Psychology*, XLVI (1955), 142–50.

ball, some children do not develop the ability to focus on objects at close range until they are seven or eight years old.

The small number of children who need to wear glasses in the first grade, as compared with the greatly increased number in junior high school, is a suspicious circumstance to be considered. Some eye specialists believe that requiring children to read at close range at too early an age may be responsible for this undesirable condition.

The teacher should take careful note of the visual behavior of her students in the schoolroom. If she detects in a child a strong tendency to squint, frown, or blink excessively, she should refer the case to an eye specialist. Children who exhibit such signs of eyestrain as encrusted, red lids, a sty, or watery eyes should likewise be referred to a specialist.

The teacher should know about the vision and hearing tests listed below but should not be asked to give them.

Vision Tests. It is customary to appraise sharpness of vision by standing the child twenty feet from a wall chart on which are displayed letters of various sizes and having him identify letters. But such an eye test has little significance for reading, which is done at a distance sixteen inches from the page to the eyes, for the demands upon the eyes are different at various distances. The muscle posture and control for near-point vision are not the same as those required for seeing at a distance. Reading requires the two eyes to focus clearly upon an image at near-point distance. Tests, therefore, should be given at reading distance with the eyes actively engaged in seeing selected symbols the size of primer type.

The Betts Ready-To-Read Tests (Keystone View Co.). These tests are used in identifying visual readiness for reading and in discovering causes contributing to reading difficulties. They require from twenty to thirty minutes to administer, depending upon how many of the tests are used. These tests require the use of an instrument similar to a stereoscope, called an ophthalmic telebinocular. Since this is a very accurate instrument, children who do not pass the telebinocular test should be referred to an eye specialist. Most school systems assign health-department representatives to administer the test.

The Eames Eye Test (Harcourt, Brace & World Inc.). This test is composed of four subtests and takes about fifteen minutes to administer, except in cases where rechecking is desirable. The test reveals farsightedness, nearsightedness, dimness of vision, degree of eye coordination, and fusion. Two supplementary tests check eye dominance and astigmatism. A complete manual of directions for giving and interpreting the test is included. This test helps screen out children badly in need of eye correction requiring glasses or eye exercises.

Hearing and Readiness. In determining reading readiness, a child's hearing is also of vital importance. When a child experiences partial deafness, he cannot detect sounds normally, and, as a consequence, he does much guessing in completing the visual-auditory associations needed for reading. An auditory loss from physical impairment calls for a special seat in the classroom and individual help for the child. The earlier a case of hearing loss is discovered and medical treatment started, the greater the hope of correcting a physical condition which may also create a problem of emotional insecurity. Durrell and Murphy[9] report that the problem of being a poor reader because of inability to notice separate sounds in spoken words is not due to a hearing loss but stems from an inability to discriminate between slight differences in speech sounds. Hester,[10] reporting data collected on 200 children, stresses the fact that blending of consonant sounds was difficult for some impaired readers. In such cases, remedial work aimed at sharpening discrimination for minute differences in sounds is indicated.

Hearing Tests. The most widely used instrument for discovering the pupils who have hearing impairments is the Western Electric 4C Audiometer (Graybar Electric Co.). It resembles a special phonograph with earphones. The time required for the test varies with the subject. In this test, children listen to numbers given in

[9] Donald D. Durrell and Helen Murphy, "The Auditory Discrimination Factor in Reading Readiness and Reading Disability," *Education,* LXXIII (1953), 556–60.

[10] Kathleen B. Hester, "A Study of Phonetic Difficulties in Reading," *Elementary School Journal,* XLIII (1942) 171–73.

varying degrees of loudness and write down what they hear, or have the tester record their answers. Through referring a child for a test by the audiometer, the teacher learns the degree of the child's hearing impairment and the areas—high-frequency or low-frequency—in which the deficiency occurs. Those children who fall below the standard should be referred to an ear specialist.

Speech and Readiness. Is the child's speech difficult to understand? Is he enunciating words correctly, or is he still using baby talk? The loss of the two front upper baby teeth produces some pronunciation problems, especially in words that begin with f. Quite a few children have difficulty in pronouncing r and l and say "wabbit" for "rabbit" and "witto" for "little." One little boy whose name was Robert continued to call himself "Wobert" even when he reached the high first grade. So flagrant was his mispronunciation that one of the girls in his class said with unconscious humor, "I wonder why his mother named him Robert, when he can't say it."

Correct articulation and pronunciation are only half the battle. Can the child express himself in complete thought units, that is, in sentences? To be able to read simple sentences, he must, of course, be able to speak them first; a child who speaks in an easy, fluent manner has already achieved one requisite for good reading. Does he say, "May I have the book, please?" rather than using a sentence fragment such as "Want book."? Has he enough self-confidence to speak up so that he can be heard and understood by others? The teacher should be able to answer these questions in the affirmative, or the child is not ready to read. If he is using one type of speech pattern and the printed pattern in the book presents an entirely different pattern, his problems in reading will approximate those met by someone attempting to read a foreign language.

Another speech problem the teacher may encounter is stammering. While the problem is primarily an emotional one (many research specialists believe that all "nonfluent speech" stems from deep-seated insecurity and nervous strain), this defect does have definite implications for reading progress. Since children who stammer tend to avoid certain words such as those beginning with a hard c, they will often lack experience and familiarity with the spoken counterparts for many of the words they encounter in print.

A very effective test for use with children from kindergarten through grade school is the Speech Survey, by Bryn Bryngelson and H. Glaspey (The Expression Co.). This individual test, which takes from two to ten minutes to administer, is composed of forty-eight pictures on sixteen cards. The child names the objects in the pictures; his replies are a test of all the consonant sounds. It is an effective screening test to reveal basic articulatory deficiencies. If the child can produce a satisfactory sound for all but three or four consonants, his difficulty is usually interpreted as a transient developmental condition. But if there is a complete failure to reproduce sounds satisfactorily, immediate remedial work should be given by a specialist in faulty noun articulation. A great many articulation problems have an emotional origin. If a mother squeezes a child affectionately because he sounds cute every time he says, "Div' me my toat," she is likely to retard his speech development. The child links the affectionate response with baby talk and will unconsciously seek repetition of the pleasurable situation by continuing the immature speech pattern.

In his book *Baby Talk* (Springfield, Ill.: Charles C Thomas, Publishers, 1960), Morris Val Jones, professor of speech and hearing therapy, writes, "Studies show that speech problems are closely related to reading problems. How can a child learn to read efficiently if he has failed to master the sounds of American English?" (page 12).

Physical Activity and Readiness. Often children are not ready to begin reading because they cannot sit still long enough to concentrate on printed symbols. The high rate of basal metabolism may be one reason for this, though the rate is high for all children. (Metabolism refers to physical and chemical changes in the body associated with the production and use of energy.) An awareness of individual differences in this physical trait is important to teachers, especially at the primary level, where they are faced with the important task of determining all aspects of physical readiness before introducing reading to children. Pupils will be happier and the teaching of beginning reading easier if teachers recognize that some children are driven more relentlessly than others to release their pent-up energy in the form of restlessness and inattention. Common sense dictates that the teacher know her pupils so well that she will alternate quiet work with periods of physical activity, particularly for children who require many opportunities for physical release.

The teacher should obtain all possible information about each child's health history and physical characteristics before starting him on reading. Some teachers visit the home of each child during the course of the first term. This usually helps them understand the various degrees of readiness their children have achieved. In some situations parents are invited to the school for a conference with the teacher. Such a conference may reveal many facts about the child's health history, as well as many other facts important in judging reading readiness.

Information concerning the child should be assembled so that it can be studied and analyzed. The following information blank, adapted from Fay Adams and Edith Noblitt's Manual for Teachers in Elementary Education, has proved helpful to many teachers:

Background Record

1. Name_____ Address_____ Telephone_____
2. I.Q._____ M.A._____
3. Date of birth_____ Nationality_____
4. With whom child lives_____ Languages spoken at home_____
_____

5. Father's name_____
6. Mother's name_____
7. Number of rooms in home _____ Radios _____ TV's_____
8. Number of brothers and sisters in school_____
9. Number of brothers and sisters out of school_____
10. Father's occupation, training, and special talents_____
_____

11. Mother's occupation, training, and special talents_____
_____

12. Height_____
13. Weight_____
14. Surgeries_____

15. Diseases of childhood_____

16. Things child likes to do outside of school_____
   _____

17. What would child like to be_____

18. Weekly allowance_____

19. Library card_____

20. Work after school_____

21. Duties around home_____

22. Travel_____

23. Outside opportunities_____
      a. Dancing lessons_____
      b. Music lessons_____
      c. Singing lessons_____
      d. Others_____

24. Special comments and observations_____
   _____

Physical Environment and Readiness. The teacher should be sensitive to the needs of her children in the lighting, seating, heating, and ventilating of her classroom. She should either check these herself or enlist the services of the maintenance director or custodian. The teacher should note the position of the chairs to determine whether or not the light will fall over the child's left shoulder —a seating arrangement which prevents him from working in his own shadow. Glare should be eliminated to ensure a favorable lighting condition for reading. Children should be placed as nearly as possible in front of reading charts, blackboards, and pictures, with the material displayed at eye level. Pupils should be assigned to tables and chairs of proper height. If a child's feet dangle, or if he tries to perform exercises in the reading-readiness picture book while seated in a chair either too high or too low for comfort, his attention wavers and his power of concentration suffers.

When children become restless and irritable, the first things to check are the room temperature and the ventilation. A teacher's sensitiveness to these factors can often forestall behavior problems that subtract from the time that might be spent in developing reading readiness. The room should be kept at a temperature between 68 and 72 degrees Fahrenheit. Windows should be opened from the top or so guarded that a direct draft does not reach the child.

RECOGNIZING EMOTIONAL READINESS

Children are human beings with basic psychological needs similar to those of adults. The important influence which emotions exert upon every phase of the child's activity is not fully appreciated by many classroom teachers. The child who is anxious and insecure when he enters the first grade is not ready to profit from instruction. If he is pushed into reading before he is ready for this complicated type of learning, his emotional tension will be increased. Authorities believe that emotional maladjustments should be studied closely by the teacher to locate their cause, for only then can she attempt successfully to help the maladjusted child fit into the group. If he remains anxious and fearful, his learning will inevitably suffer.

Factors that produce emotional instability include parental neglect, at one extreme, and parental overprotection (spoiling the child), at the other; jealousy of little brothers and sisters who (the child believes) have transplanted him in the affection of his parents; parental demands for perfection in the child's every performance and activity; fear of temperamental outbursts and even physical punishment at home; economic insecurity such as that caused by the father's being unemployed; and timidity and shyness or their opposites, hostility and aggression.

Children emotionally disturbed by any of these factors are usually not ready to adjust to the mental discipline which learning to read demands. One of the first tasks of the teacher is to study the child's home background and to hold conferences with the parents to identify the causes of the child's emotional disturbance and to try to work out a remedy. The emotionally disturbed child is obviously not as well prepared to read as the child who is happy and well adjusted emotionally. If the causes of emotional disturbances are revealed in such conferences, the next step may be to refer the child to a psychometrist.

Tests of Emotional Stability. There are a number of individual tests designed to probe important aspects of the child's emotional life and to furnish answers to these questions: How does he see himself in relation to others? How does he react to discipline?

How does he see the mother figure, the father figure, siblings in the family, teachers, and other children? From an analysis the examiner is able to construct the total picture of the child. Since the scoring of tests of emotional stability is very complicated, special training is needed in marking and interpreting such tests. They are not ordinarily given by the teacher.

CHILDREN'S APPERCEPTION TEST (Harvard University Press). This test is administered individually and has no time limit. It is designed for very young children through those in early adolescence. To prevent self-consciousness, pictures of animals are used, such as those of the papa bear, mama bear, and little bear doing various everyday activities about the house. The children are asked to explain what the animals in the family are doing. As the child describes each picture, his responses often reveal facts about the organization of his emotional life with reference to his position in his own family. There are no "correct" answers in the test, but, in analyzing his remarks about feeding, sibling jealousies, mother-father relations, aggression, and other childhood experiences, the special examiner is able to discover any marked personality disturbances to report to the teacher.

PICTURE FRUSTRATION STUDY, CHILDREN'S FORM (Journal Press). This test, formulated by Saul Rosenzweig, is an individual test which can be used for children from four to thirteen. A booklet of pictures of children faced with a common stress situation is displayed. As the child reacts to each, it is assumed that he will identify himself with the frustrated child in the picture. There is no time limit. The test presents twenty-four cartoon-like drawings depicting situations familiar to children. In each picture one person is shown saying something to a child; the words may be accusatory, depriving, disciplining, apologizing, and so on. The child is asked to tell what the other person replies. The test is scored according to a manual. From the total number of responses, the examiner is able to measure the child's reactions in terms of extrapunitiveness, intropunitiveness, dominance, ego defense, and need persistence. As interpreted by psychometrists, it provides clues to these questions: How much did the actual situation hinder the child's mastery of the problem? How much did the child feel personally responsible for the situation? How much does he depend on others for the solution to his problems?

Informal Appraisal. It is possible to tell a great deal about a child's emotional life by looking at his drawings and paintings. For example, a child who draws the father three or four times larger than the mother may be revealing his feeling of being dominated by the father. A child who uses only an inch or two of a large piece of paper may be restricted in his emotional life. The colors a child uses are also indicative of how he sees the world. Very often a child unconsciously uses symbols of his inner emotions in his drawings. Admittedly, this is a very abstract method to determine personality problems and should be used cautiously and weighed against other types of appraisal.

Children in their play often reveal a great deal about themselves. When a child is playing house, for instance, the examiner often is able to identify the child's interpretation of the roles played in his life by his father and mother. The interaction between the two parents often sheds a great deal of light on his personality organization. But again, there are limitations in such methods of studying the child's emotional life, and they should play only a small part in the complete analysis of the whole child.

Psychometrists warn that emotional and personality tests must be regarded as indications of problems rather than as concrete evidence of emotional disturbance. Subjective observation by the teacher over a long period, as well as conferences with the parents, must still be utilized. By displaying sympathy and understanding to the child, the teacher can do much to decrease the child's emotional tension.

RECOGNIZING SOCIAL READINESS

Social readiness is closely related to emotional readiness but is usually treated separately by reading authorities for clarity and emphasis. Here the child is not considered so much from the standpoint of his individual entity as in the light of his relations with others. Obviously, if he cannot adjust socially to the group, emotional conflicts will develop. The child must feel accepted by the teacher and the other pupils to enjoy a real sense of being a part of the group; otherwise his progress in school is adversely affected.

The Desire for Social Approval. The desire of a first-grade child for social approval is a strong motivation in the child's daily performance in the learning-to-read stage. Children need to feel that they have the respect and approval of their parents, their siblings, their teachers, and their classmates; they need to feel that they belong, that they are not different and isolated. An attitude of wholesome self-respect is essential to good mental health and reading readiness. When children perform the activities related to reading creditably, they also enjoy the approval of their associates. Social approval is a powerful force in determining personality and behavior.

The following incident, which happened to a child named Hilda on her first day at school, illustrates how a teacher may thoughtlessly use a reading-readiness technique with harmful results. After the children had played a game in which they used the words "run," "skip," and "jump," they drew pictures illustrating these activities. If they recognized each of these words when they were written on flash cards, they were allowed to take their pictures home at the end of the day. Several of the children, including Hilda, failed to recognize all the words. Hilda left school feeling extremely unhappy and crying; she felt disgraced in the eyes of her teacher and classmates. She tossed restlessly in bed that night and dreaded the return to school the next morning. Although she had an I.Q. of 130, she did only average work throughout her first year. It may not be a sound generalization to say that success during the entire year hinged on that one experience, but she did receive a very poor start, and her status in the group and her self-confidence were undermined. Being a sensitive and intelligent child, the damaging effect of the experience lasted longer than it might have with other children.

Sociometric studies indicate that the child's status in the group affects his attitude toward school and suggests that the more pleasurable social experiences the child has, the happier he is.

Since it has proved extremely difficult to correct the poor group relations of maladjusted children in the upper grades, an early attempt should be made to improve the child's adjustment. A sympathetic teacher can do much each day to draw the child into the group and lead him to participate in social activities.

Teachers should be sensitive to abnormal behavior within the growth pattern of the six-year-old. Social misfits in the first grade have been described as those who are:

1. Unable to make friends
2. Always quarreling
3. Immediately on the defensive
4. Excessively, self-righteously good
5. Overconcerned about the behavior of others
6. Apt to cry too easily
7. Too noisy
8. Shy and withdrawn
9. Nervous and fearful

Teachers must recognize their responsibility for identifying children hampered by such antisocial characteristics, if they are to guide them toward better adjustment. It is highly important that teachers of primary-grade children pause from time to time to consider carefully their own relation with each child. The pressure of the demands of the group sometimes obscures the important individual needs of a disturbed child. Such was the case with Hilda, who felt herself a failure at reading so early in her school career.

The Desire for Security. Although teachers have heard and read a great deal in recent years about the necessity for security, the very nature of modern life and the problems resulting from world events have inevitably brought insecurity to today's children. It is the joint responsibility of the home and the school to do everything possible to counteract the many influences that create situations with which children are unable to cope and which increase their anxiety and insecurity. The desires for affection from family and for wholesome personal relations originate in the physiological needs of the infant. These desires are closely related to, but not identical with, the derivation of the need for social approval. With divorce rates rising and increasing numbers of children coming from broken homes, the first-grade teacher has the responsibility of contributing a measure of stability to the child's unstable world through her understanding and careful planning. If, instead, she augments and aggravates the child's insecurity by demanding difficult tasks of him before he is ready, such as that of learning to read, a "delayed-action mine of childhood" may be laid to explode with disastrous repercussions later.

The Desire for Individuality. Some children are so overprotected at home that their individuality is stunted and they develop such retiring personalities that they cannot take their rightful place in the social group. These children assert their individuality and self-esteem in a contradictory variety of ways. Some may fly into tantrums to win the desired attention; others may cry if a challenging task is asked of them, thus expressing self-pity at the slightest provocation. Such children need guidance to become helpful, cooperative members of the group. Unless a child can participate in the reading circle, for example, without acting up in one way or another, he will disrupt the orderly atmosphere essential for learning.

The Desire for Success. The urges to excel, to succeed, to overcome obstacles, to achieve a goal, to solve a problem, to dominate a situation—all are manifestations of an over-all desire to succeed. In a far-reaching skill like reading, which penetrates into every area of schoolwork, it is essential that the work be so arranged and organized that children feel successful and equal to the reading task at each step. Success develops self-confidence and satisfies the desire for mastery in reading. A child with average ability and abundant self-confidence often progresses faster than a fearful child with more innate ability. There is no surer way of undermining a child's self-confidence than to force him into reading before he is ready to undertake the task, or to give him reading material which is too difficult for him.

The Desire for Change and Novelty. Exploratory patterns, curiosity, and concern with the new, the strange, and the unfamiliar seem basic to human beings. Novelty exerts a constant appeal: A fixed routine can be followed for only a relatively short time before boredom occurs and the urge toward change and novelty exerts itself. A reading-readiness program should not fail to capitalize on this strong factor in motivation. The rapt attention which children accord to something new and interesting is one of the things which makes teaching the young so delightful an experience. And it provides a clue to planning work in reading readiness to include a variety of interesting activities.

RECOGNIZING LANGUAGE READINESS

It will be recalled from Chapter 2 that Smith's study of the meaning vocabularies of six-year-olds showed a tremendous range from lowest to highest number of words known. In the preschool period approximately 70 per cent of a child's meaning vocabulary consists of names of things he sees, according to Judd,[11] showing that the experiences which attract the child's attention are the "concrete experiences gained from things and persons." By the time he enters kindergarten or first grade, the child gives attention not only to persons and things about him but to their appearance and behavior. A conspicuous deficiency in a child's early language is the absence of words expressing *relationships*. According to Judd, "The ability to group objects in thought and think of relations is acquired later than the ability to discriminate objects and persons and recall their names." When the author overheard a sample of a first-grade girl's conversation on the playground, she asked the teacher curiously about the child's intelligence rating and background. What the child had said to her playmate was: "This morning, when I came downstairs for breakfast, my usually selfish big brother offered me the largest sweet roll, whereupon I was so touched that I handed it back to him." This little girl's use of the introductory adverbial clause, coupled with the combination of adverb and adjective apparent in her description of her brother, were remarkable enough in a child so young, but when, in addition, she used the adverb *whereupon* in its correct relation-

[11] Charles H. Judd, *Educational Psychology* (Boston: Houghton Mifflin Co., 1939), p. 161.

ship and displayed the ability to choose precise verbs, the author suspected that one or both of the child's parents were teachers or writers. It turned out that her father was a teacher in the local college and that her language quotient on a test was very high. Here was an example of a case of the influence of home environment on language development.

A study of the background facts quoted so far in this section suggests that children who come from environments which provide them with rich and interesting experiences and offer numerous opportunities for increasing the store of meaningful concepts are more apt to be ready for reading than children from underprivileged homes, where such opportunities for learning are restricted or completely missing. There are no figures to justify this conclusion, but common sense leads one to suspect that those who, according to Smith's aforementioned study, knew the meanings of only 6,000 words, as compared with 48,800 for the highest and 23,700 for the average, probably came from poverty-stricken environments where certain kinds of experiences were denied them. Language is a form of behavior acquired by imitation. Children whose parents are college graduates are usually more fortunate; they are often surrounded by books, taken on trips, provided educational toys, and benefit from being read to and from listening to the example of standard English set by their parents. The children's stocks of concepts grow, and they have wider ranges of concepts to bring to beginning reading than do children from more meager backgrounds of experience. Therefore, it is essential that the teacher study the home backgrounds of her pupil before beginning to teach them reading. Only in this way can she plan to compensate for the more limited experiences—and, therefore, limited linguistic development—of the underpriviledged children in her group by providing a well-rounded program of activities.

SUMMARIZING TYPES OF READINESS

The teacher may find it helpful to use a check list similar to the one presented below to summarize her findings concerning each child's reading readiness.

Reading-Readiness Appraisal List

Name   Robert J.   Chronological Age   6.5
                                               Mental Age   6.7

Does the child score well on a mental test?	Yes	No
Does the child score well on a reading-readiness test?	Yes	No
Is the child emotionally adjusted? (Parent conference)	Yes	No
Is the child's health normal? (Doctor's evaluation)	Yes	No
Is eye maturation normal? (Eye test)	Yes	No
Is hearing normal? (Audiometer test)	Yes	No
Does the child have an adequate vocabulary? (Observation)	Yes	No
Does the child have an adequate background of experiences? (Parent conferences and tests)	Yes	No
Can the child see likenesses and differences? (Reading-readiness test)	Yes	No
Can the child see relationships? (Intelligence test)	Yes	No
Can the child comprehend a sequence of ideas? (Reactions to stories told)	Yes	No
Are the child's work habits good? (Does he begin promptly and stay with a task?)	Yes	No
Can the child sustain attention? (Is he restless or alert? Can he answer questions directed to him?)	Yes	No
Can the child solve simple, everyday problems?	Yes	No
Can the child follow directions? (Readiness test and observation)	Yes	No
Does the child want to read?	Yes	No

Summary. Robert is a child who has many of the qualities needed for beginning reading, but he lacks an adequate background of experiences and an adequate vocabulary. Because of this, he is limited in his ability to solve problems which call for information beyond his meager experience. He is full of vitality and is well adjusted emotionally. He comes from a sturdy second-generation-American background, where the family, basically industrious and honest, have had little time for what they call the "frills."

Recommendation. A period of readiness work in hearing and learning stories, poems, and songs, in seeing many pictures and discussing them, and in sharing problem solving with the other children of his class as they carry on a unit of work will help prepare him for reading. Test responses and other records indicate that he should eventually rate in the upper third of the first grade.

QUESTIONS AND ACTIVITIES

Imagine that you have been elected to a first-grade position. You are aware that your influence as a teacher is greater than that of any teacher with whom your children will ever have contact. As you plan your work, these questions are important guides:

1. Why is it undesirable to introduce a child to reading before he is ready?
2. What are some of the measures for determining mental readiness for reading?
3. How does physical health affect readiness for reading? What health factors must be considered?
4. How should the teacher check on such physical aspects of readiness as vision, hearing, and speech?
5. What basic psychological needs do all children have? How are these related to reading readiness?
6. Why is it important for the teacher to be familiar with the child's emotional status?
7. How can the teacher determine the child's degree of social adjustment?

SELECTED REFERENCES

Bond, Guy L., and Eva B. Wagner. *Teaching the Child to Read* (3d ed.). New York: The Macmillan Co., Publishers (a division of the Crowell-Collier Publishing Co.), 1960.

Broom, M. E., *et al. Effective Reading Instruction in Elementary Schools* (2d ed.). New York: McGraw-Hill Book Co., Inc., 1951.

Gans, Roma. "How Do We Know When Children Are Ready To Read?" *Childhood Education*, XXVI (December 1949), pp. 152–55.

Gates, Arthur I. *The Improvement of Reading* (3d ed.). New York: The Macmillan Co., 1947.

Harris, Albert J. *How To Increase Reading Ability* (4th ed.). New York: Longmans, Green & Co., Inc., 1961.

Heilman, Arthur W. *Principles and Practices of Teaching Reading.* Columbus, Ohio: Charles E. Merrill Books, Inc., 1961.

Hester, Kathleen B. *Teaching Every Child To Read.* New York: Harper & Row, 1955.

Hildreth, Gertrude. *Readiness for School.* Harcourt, Brace & World, Inc., 1957.

Karlin, Robert. "The Prediction of Reading Success and Reading Readiness Tests," *Elementary English*, XXX (May 1957), 320–22.

McCracken, Glenn. "Have We Over-emphasized the Readiness Factor?" *Elementary English,* XXXIV (May 1952), 271–76.

McKee, Paul. *The Teaching of Reading in the Elementary School.* Boston: Houghton Mifflin Co., 1948.

Ragan, William B. *Modern Elementary Curriculum.* New York: Holt, Rinehart & Winston, Inc., 1954.

Russell, David H. *Children Learn To Read* (2d ed.). Boston: Ginn & Co., 1961.

Stone, Clarence R. *Progress in Primary Reading.* St. Louis: Webster Publishing Co., 1950.

Wepman, Joseph M. "Auditory Discrimination, Speech and Reading," *Elementary School Journal,* LX (March 1961), 325–33.

Williams, Gertrude H. "What Does Research Tell Us About Readiness for Beginning Reading?" *The Reading Teacher,* VI (May 1953), 34–40.

Yoakam, Gerald. *Basal Reading Instruction.* New York: McGraw-Hill Book Co., Inc., 1955.

6

DEVELOPING READINESS TO READ

Once the underlying mental, physical, emotional, social, and language needs of a child have been recognized by the teacher, she can use the list of his "readinesses" and "unreadinesses" to make plans for developing those of the former that he lacks. Children need growth in many abilities before they can interpret meaning from the printed page. This chapter is designed to help teachers plan a typical program of activities that promote readiness to read. Before listing and describing them, however, it is only fair to explain opposing points of view and new trends in the area of reading readiness.

OPPOSING POINTS OF VIEW

Opposition to the Concept of "Building" Readiness. Among the members of the profession there is substantial agreement that readiness should be determined and appraised, but the idea that the teacher can help to develop or "build" readiness has been attacked by a group largely interested in nursery-school and kindergarten education. The members of this group emphasize that readiness is not subject to exterior pressure but must "initiate within the child." In other words, these educators believe that children respond to instruction only when *time* has wrought the necessary development for learning specific skills. Much is made of waiting for "life" to develop readiness naturally. The teacher must not try to hurry the process. Consistency would seem to suggest that the only alternative left open to the teacher is to sit back until "life" has shaped the language facilities which the child needs for reading, for example. Yet this very group of educators who object to the concept of *developing* readiness for reading seems to find it permissible (by drawing a fine distinction) to "capitalize" upon the readiness already there.

New Trends in the Field of Reading Readiness. Great interest has been shown recently in the early introduction of reading instruction. In an increasing number of communities this instruction is already under way in the kindergarten. Publishers maintain that the pressure placed upon them by kindergarten teachers to produce reading-readiness workbooks for that early level became so intense that they were forced to comply. Some in this group even scoff at the need for developing readiness in children before beginning the work in reading. They seem impatient at the least delay and justify early instruction in reading on the basis that it is given *in response to public demand*. There must be some truth in their claim. Witness Durkin's study[1] of forty-nine children who entered first grade already able to read at grade levels from first up through fourth. Some have questioned the need for developing readiness, maintaining that TV has helped to create so sophisticated a group of youngsters that they have on hand an almost embarrassing supply of concepts. The argument is set forth by some that in other English-speaking countries such as New Zealand, England and Scotland children are started in organized reading at the age of five, when they enter school. According to Dr. Bond's report, based on firsthand investigation, the program "resembles our kindergarten instruction but is more specifically directed toward developing the necessary prerequisites to systematic reading instruction. After three to six months of this pre-reading program at age five, which includes some experience with actual reading, the children are started in the organized, basic instructional reading program." In evaluation Dr. Bond offers a shrewd reminder: "We can modify our reading programs to fit the

[1] Dolores Durkin, "Children Who Read Before Grade One," *The Reading Teacher*, XIV, No. 3 (January 1961), pp. 163–66.

children we teach but the less mature the child, the more individual attention he will need."[2]

Quite recently newspapers and news magazines gave wide publicity to the experiment conducted by sociologist Omar K. Moore, of Yale University. According to one account,[3] Dr. Moore showed that "normal children of two, three, four and five years of age can learn to read . . . with ease." However the ratio was one teacher for each child, according to reports and to the film of the experiment which the author viewed. When the ratio is one teacher to every twenty-five or thirty pupils, the phrase "with ease" would have to be modified. It has not yet been proved that there are any lasting benefits resulting to the child from such an early start. As Russell writes: "It seems probable that three-year-olds can be doing more profitable things than learning to read."[4]

One wonders what social purpose a youngster of two or three has for reading? Vocational? To meet daily problems? Another challenge concerning the wisdom of introducing children at such an early age to abstract symbols comes from those who wonder about the effect of such a course upon their social and emotional adjustment. A further question which often arises is this: Will the child who starts to read ahead of the others stay ahead? Research may find the answer to these queries.

In Support of the Typical Program. A third and by far the largest group, composed of people working in the field of reading instruction, firmly believes that readiness can be developed through a program of carefully planned activities. These people exclude physical readiness, however, which of course depends upon the child's stage of growth and is not subject to instruction. Each child seems to achieve readiness in his own good time for sitting up, crawling, walking, and taking solid food.

By following a typical readiness program, it is possible to arrange a rich variety of experiences which will help to accelerate the child's control of language and build up a stock of words and

[2] Guy L. Bond, "Differences in Reading Instruction in English-Speaking Countries," *The Reading Teacher*, XIV, No. 3 (January 1961), p. 154.

[3] Council for Basic Education *Bulletin*, June 1961.

[4] David H. Russell, *Children Learn To Read* (2d ed.) (Boston: Ginn & Co.), p. 186.

concepts useful in reading. For example, *a unit of work* not only stimulates language growth as the children make up stories and poems and engage in imitative play but aids in the development of social and emotional readiness as well. When the children plan excursions and construct things to represent ideas gleaned during the course of a neighborhood trip, mental readiness is promoted. Reading-readiness books provide a beginning in critical thinking as the children spot absurdities, exaggerations, and missing elements in pictures. Of course, critical thinking is only one of the skills useful to reading which are given practice in readiness books without actually demanding the reading of print. With all the types of readinesses listed, a solemn caution should be observed by the teacher never to *schedule* a *fixed number of weeks* for developing each. How can one know in the face of the children's individual differences what amount of time will be needed?

TEACHING TECHNIQUES

Developing Language Skills. Since reading depends so heavily upon language skills, the teachers must provide a program calling for language expression. Children differ widely in the preparatory program they require. Some of the children may have enjoyed the boon of being read to by their parents. Listening to stories read aids the children in seeing what enjoyment comes from books, and their vocabulary expands while their concepts become clearer. Certainly such children will have greater readiness for reading than those from bookless homes with non-reading parents. Some children may have been taken on trips and encouraged to discuss them. As a result, they have a variety of experiences that provide a wide range of meanings. Other children may be limited by a more narrow range of experiences and possess a meager stock of words and concepts. These children are the ones who have a special need of a carefully planned program of activities designed to enrich their verbal resources and thus to ready them for the challenge of reading.

VOCABULARY AND CONCEPTS. In discussing words and meanings it is important to remember that new experiences usually add new words to the individual's stock. Provision of a program of varied experiences will generally contribute, therefore, to the development of language readiness for reading. It goes almost without saying that the child's vocabulary is one of the most potent factors in his reading success.

Some distinction must be drawn between *words* and *concepts* before a program for developing language readiness is outlined. A child may recognize a *word* but have only limited understanding of its meaning. *Concept* refers to the extensiveness of meanings. Many words have at least half a dozen meanings, and a whole span of life may be required before the individual explores a concept fully. The amount and kinds of meanings which a child attaches to a particular word depend upon the ideas which the child can associate with the word. The ideas, in turn, depend upon the child's experiences. At first a small child's concept of the word "run" is associated with the experience, perhaps, of having his mother say to him, "*Run* out in the yard and play. Mother is busy." Only gradually will he extend this concept by adding to his store of meanings connected with the word. He may learn about *runs* in stockings by hearing his Mother refer to them; he may hear about a *home run* from his older brother; on TV he is exposed to the term *running for president;* he may hear his teacher say that she is "*running* out of paste"; a movie may show him a *deer run* or a *run on the bank*. Thus grows his concept of the word "run."

One of the teacher's responsibilities is to develop concepts useful in interpreting the stories which will be met in the preprimer. Do the children sense classification, for example, such as the difference between a pet kitten and a toy kitten? Do they know the primary colors? Do they know the names of things about which they will be asked to read with understanding? Nor should the teacher assume that a child understands certain concepts, as is shown in these two cases which occurred in a primary class: In the first case, a teacher was discussing the preparation which animals make for winter. A boy in the group said, "They store nuts to eat in winter." "Oh, that's not so," objected another boy, "A store is where you buy groceries." In the second case a child was repeating an old nursery rhyme as he understood it, showing his pathetic attempts to make sense out of a number of unfamiliar concepts:

Little Boy Blue
Come blow your horn.
The sheep are in the middle,
The cows are in the corner.

There is, of course, a wide variation in the experience and meaning vocabulary. Compare this child, who did not have any concept of either *meadow* or *corn,* with the little girl in the same grade who was told by her mother that it was time to go to bed. "Oh, let's reminisce awhile before I go," she suggested. Though she could use a word of three syllables correctly, her brother who was a year older referred to a malady from which he was suffering as "chicken pops," and one day, when his father was reading a story to him about a "furtive fox," he volunteered that he knew what it meant: "An animal that has fur on it." Teachers know better than to take the child's grasp of concepts for granted.

Everyday Experiences. In the ordinary everyday life of the classroom, many means can be utilized to help develop language expression and background concepts. Through the use of explanations, discussions, dramatizations, models, games, construction materials, blocks, and science and art materials, the teacher makes it possible for the first-grade children to see, taste, touch, listen, and manipulate. Often the teacher can work out a program for developing language concepts around the simplest events of the day. One teacher planned a program around a windy day in this fashion: She first wrote on the board, "This is a windy day" and read the sentence for the children. Then she asked them what they noticed about the wind. The children recalled the difficulty they had in keeping their caps on as they got off the school bus. The teacher asked each child to tell something about the wind. One said, "It is a hard wind." The teacher led the children to discuss the difference between a hard wind, a hard stone, and hard work. Later they clarified other concepts related to wind, such as dusty, rushing, noisy, bitter, and cold.

Field Trips and Excursions. Another valuable way to build a background of meanings is through the use of planned trips about the school or neighborhood. Thus, the children may be taken to see the nurse's room, the principal's office, the school library, the cafeteria, a firebox on the corner, a firehouse a few blocks away, a pet shop, a flower shop, the post office, a railroad station or roundhouse, a caboose, a house being built, a dairy, a circus, or the city zoo. Planning for a trip requires several important class discussions. Since notes must be sent home to the mothers in order for the children to be allowed to visit any place beyond the school grounds, the children learn facts about safety, thoughtfulness, and compliance with a law requiring the parent's permission to go on excursions. All these experiences inevitably expand the child's range of concepts and meaning vocabulary.

Experience Stories. After any experience, the children like to talk it over. Then this talk may be recorded by the teacher at the children's dictation. Whether the experience be passing out straws for the morning milk, sharpening pencils, watering the plants, feeding the fish, attending a birthday party in the class, or seeing Mary's little cocker spaniel following her to school one day, the children derive much benefit from the process of dictating four- or five-line stories about the interesting happening. The children are led by the teacher to review their new vocabulary as they compose a few sentences orally about what they saw or did first, next, and so on. These sentences are printed on the blackboard by the teacher. (Print is used, since it is unwise to burden the inexperienced reader with script before he is familiar with print.) The children enjoy "seeing the chalk say what their lips have just said." In some cases when the children deliver long rambling sentences, the teacher "edits" by suggesting a shorter way to say the same thing. Once the sentence is in print, the teacher reads aloud what she has just written at the children's dictation. Then the children play at reading the line. After the first recording on the blackboard, experience stories are usually lettered by the teacher on oak tag, a durable grade of paper. Thus they are recorded in more permanent chart form. These stories are usually illustrated by the children, the favorite drawing being chosen by class vote for a place of honor on the chart. The collection of chart stories based on group experiences often bears the title *Our Big Book.* (Mimeographed copies of each experience story may be made and collected into individual booklets for each child. These may be illustrated by his own drawings.) The *Big Book* may be displayed for visitors to enjoy, keeping them abreast of the doings in the class.

Sometimes the children "reread" their *Big Book*, although the chart stories are not meant to provide valid practice in reading. No one should overestimate the speed with which a child can master recognition of a new word. "Once over lightly" is scarcely enough, especially with the vocabulary in these experience stories. Necessarily varied because of a wide diversity of experiences, the vocabulary piles up too fast to permit sufficient repetition in *looking* at the words and *saying* them for mastery to result. The children are merely "reading back," that is, remembering what happened, what they said about the events, and what the teacher wrote at their dictation. Thus experience stories on big charts are primarily *reading-readiness* exercises. As such they have genuine value: They stimulate interest in the choice of words to express ideas; they enable the children to gain familiarity with the process of recording fleeting experiences in the more lasting form of the printed word. Then, too, experiences preserved in print make for an easy transition from the process of speaking words to the process of reading them. Since the children have experienced the events on which the chart story is based, have talked about them, and have dictated the material for the teacher to write, they have none of the exaggerated fear often present when first meeting new material in print. (Past generations of beginning readers were often handicapped by such fears.)

The Unit Plan. One of the most prolific sources of vocabulary and concept development is the type of group experience known as a "unit of work." The unit has been defined as an organization of learning activities, experiences, and types of learning around a central theme, problem, or purpose, developed cooperatively by a group of pupils under the teacher's leadership. To launch a unit, the teacher usually arranges environmental factors to motivate the children's interest. For example, she may bring in pictures and objects or use an excursion to turn the children's attention in a certain direction. Then, after the children's interest has been aroused, the teacher generally helps to "spark" a decision to express it in some form of group project. Entering first-grade children have successfully carried on a great variety of activities or "units of work." Sometimes they are motivated to build a play-house and furnish it, or a fire truck or a bus and "play" that they are riding in them, or a doll booth containing stuffed paper dolls (also part of the first grade do-it-yourself program). The author has seen circuses, zoos, pet shops, grocery stores, flower shops represented. As the children talk and plan and work together on the various construction phases of any unit, the teacher observes language patterns, individual habits of attention and concentration, not to mention interchild relationships. She may unobtrusively bring out the shy child; "tone down" the show-off, bluffer, or boaster; or attempt to find the cause of lying, temper tantrums, or other indications of lack of social and emotional adjustment. During the unit there are various opportunities for the children to express ideas not only in language but in other communication forms—as in drawing pictures or engaging in dramatic play.

A unit of work integrates many important concept-building activities during its course. In order to make clear how a unit is conducted at the first-grade level, a step-by-step description is offered below:

1. *Launching the bakery unit:* A first-grade class was motivated to discuss the importance of bread in the daily diet. Led by the teacher the children began to plan a visit to a real bakery to learn how bread is baked.

2. *Preparing for the excursion:* The teacher visited the bakery herself several days before the class was to go, making plans with the proprietor for the visit. Proper safety measures were also decided upon during the conference. The teacher sent notes to all the mothers in which she explained the trip and the transportation arrangements. She asked each mother to sign a permission slip for her child to participate in the excursion.

3. *Working out details of the trip:* With encouragement from the teacher, each child decided what question he wanted to ask when he arrived at the bakery. Each also understood that he could ask as many more questions as he wished during the visit. Here are some of the questions the children got ready: "How many

kinds of food does the baker make?" "How much flour does the baker use in a day?" "How many loaves of bread are baked each day?" "How are the ovens heated?" "Does the baker bake all day long?" "What kinds of cookies are baked?" "How do they make frosting for cakes?" "How many people work in the bakery?" Each child agreed to be responsible for remembering the answer to his particular question and to be ready on his return to share it with his classmates. Before starting on the expedition, the children also talked about how they would conduct themselves. They selected one member of the group to thank the baker.

4. *Experiences at the bakery:* When the children made their first community visit as a group, the excursion went off profitably and without mishap—thanks to the teacher's careful planning. The children had a happy time amidst the enticing odors of baking bread, pies, cakes, and cookies. They peeked eagerly into huge barrels of flour and stood on tiptoe to examine great mixing vats of dough. They marveled at the enormous ovens and long rows of crisp brown loaves of bread inside. After the tour, they interviewed the baker and his helpers and learned many more interesting things about bakeries from them. Best of all, they received generous samples of oatmeal, chocolate-chip, and sugar cookies. When, at noon, the children climbed into the bus to return to school, they brought back from this firsthand experience a wealth of new concepts.

5. *Experience stories about the trip and related work:* In the days following the trip to the bakery, the children were led to review their new vocabulary as they composed little three- or four-line stories to describe the interesting things that had happened in the course of their excursion. With the children dictating what they wanted to say about their experiences, the teacher printed the stories on the blackboard to be later printed by her on a chart and illustrated by a drawing, done by one of the children, showing the children descending from the school bus in front of the bakery. Here is an example of such a story:

Our Trip to the Bakery

We went to a big bakery.
We went at ten o'clock.
Mr. Richter said, "Come in."

After several experience stories had covered various phases of the excursion to the bakery, the teacher asked the children to inspect the charts for pairs of words which began alike such as "big," "bakery"; "to," "ten"; "cookies," "come." Language and art expression were combined as the children planned and drew a big frieze of their trip to the bakery. Conceptual memory was involved, since the children had to show in the frieze that they remembered the order of places they visited at the bakery, that is, first the office, then the supply room, baking ovens, wrapping room, shipping department, and salesroom.

6. *Setting up a "play" bakery in the classroom:* After the children had enjoyed their excursion, chart stories, and art experiences, the teacher adroitly led them to make the decision to reproduce the real bakery with a "play" bakery in the classroom, showing the salesroom. The teacher saw in such a construction activity many opportunities for utilizing language skills and other types of experiences of value in promoting reading readiness. Once the decision to have a "play" bakery had been reached by the children, committees were formed, giving the members worthwhile practice in working together toward the realization of a common goal. One corner of the classroom was set aside to represent the bakery salesroom and was furnished with cardboard cartons and cellophane to represent display cases, counters, and shelves. The children fashioned very lifelike cookies, doughnuts, bread, and cakes of papier-mâché painted in appropriate colors. When the "bakery" was ready for playing in, the children had an excellent opportunity to learn to attack and solve simple problems through dramatic play. Questions such as the following arose and required solution: Who shall be the clerk, the customer? What price should be asked for each item? Should string or rubber bands go around the cake boxes? What size sack should be used for two doughnuts? For half a dozen? The natural leaders wanted to monopolize the important roles in the dramatic play, but they were taught to share and to be guided by group decision.

7. *Making real cookies and having a party:* With a little encouragement from the teacher, the children decided to bake some real cookies. To prepare for the event, they decided to make

baker's caps and aprons for themselves. After the teacher arranged for the use of the school kitchen, the children made some real cookies, which they served at a party for the mothers. Each mother also received as a party "favor" a mimeographed copy of various compositions prepared by the children with the help of their teacher:

To Our Mothers

We baked the cookies.
Some are rabbits.
Some are chickens.
We had fun baking them.
Did you have fun eating them?

Our Poems

Down to the bakery we go.
Where they bake pies out of dough.
Rolls and cakes they make too.
We like them, yes we do.
Gingerbread boys of brown,
You are the best in town.

Other Ideas. The following are some additional ways to help children increase their meaning vocabularies:

1. Play preposition games such as Put the ball *into* the bag, or Put the eraser *above* the books on the shelf. In the same way use the prepositions "under," "beside," "below," "between," "behind," and "after."

2. Play adverb games such as Walk to the door *slowly* (*quietly, noisily, quickly*).

3. Play verb games. Have the children fill in a good word. "A cow can ————" (*moo, walk, run, eat*—when a wrong word is used, the teacher should help the children understand why it is wrong.) Play the same game with "Baby can————" "Mother can————"

4. Play adjective games. Think of something in the room that is *big, little, pretty, round, soft, hard*. Show pictures of baby animals and identify the ones which can be described as *hungry, busy, furry, fluffy, sleepy*.

5. Play a noun game. Show a farm picture and have the children name the *silo, haymow, dairy barn, windmill*.

6. Have the children tell the stories of pictures they have drawn.

7. Have the children retell and dramatize stories which have been read or told to them, or retell long stories in a continued-story fashion, having one child continue where another leaves off.

8. Show motion pictures, film strips, or slides to teach new words and their meanings.

9. Have the children memorize songs, poems, and rhymes.

10. Allow the children to tell about their out-of-school life so that they may learn from an exchange of experiences.

11. Help the children to be word-conscious. When a child uses a good word which many other children may not use, say something like this: "Didn't you like the word Robert used when he said the ocean was *calm* when he was at the beach yesterday?"

SENTENCE SPEAKING. Just as a child must have a vocabulary in order to express his thoughts, so must he have the ability to speak sentences in simple English before he can hope to read them. To encourage such expression, the teacher should plan conversation time for sharing ideas. The free period at the beginning of the day is a good time for this pooling of experience. The teacher has the children talk briefly on any subject they wish, guiding them from time to time in sentence formation. From this conversation time the children learn to listen to each other attentively, acquire new concepts, and learn new words. For example, during conversation time Bill might tell about a lake-shore picnic trip he took with his parents. After his story a child might ask, "Where did you go then, Bill?" He is likely to reply, "Home." At this point, the teacher might suggest that he say, "We went home by the lake road," or "We went home after the picnic." If the children speak in well-formed sentences, the teacher should recognize this achievement and comment favorably on it to encourage further use of such speech. A child may consider it important news that he has lost a front tooth, and, for a few moments at least, he becomes a person of importance in the class. The teacher may thus encourage the children to describe some of the happenings in their lives in school and at home. Little stories like those below may appear in the "news corner" of the first-grade classroom and stimulate interest in reading.

Paul has a new baby sister.
Her name is Helen.

Marjorie's dog came to school.
He hid the ball.
We liked the joke.

Here, in reading the items in the news corner, as in reading the stories recorded on experience story charts, the children are seeing that those "squiggles" on the big sheets of paper are about themselves.

Another major value of the conversation time is that it helps the shy child to break through his shyness by sharing a toy or a book with the group. In their joy over a new possession, timid children may forget themselves and talk in complete sentences. During conversation time an able child may tell an imaginative story; another may recite a song or a poem he has learned; a third child may show and tell about a picture he has drawn. Children do not tire of this conversation time, for it affords them an opportunity to discuss what is dear to their hearts.

To stimulate language growth, the teacher should encourage the children to talk by her own talent for listening as though she were memorizing every word they utter, read many stories to the children, permit the children to act out the stories, allow the children to retell the stories, and commend them for using new words. She should encourage the children to draw their favorite scenes, take them on many interesting excursions, and set a good example by her own speech.

Developing Visual Skills. Reading is primarily a visual process. One essential visual skill is the ability to distinguish among forms. Hence it is essential to provide experiences to help a child recognize likenesses and differences, classify things together that look alike, observe internal details, see part-to-whole relationship, associate ideas in a sequence, and make associations to help create visual imagery.

An adult has only to attempt to read a newspaper or book written in an unfamiliar foreign language to approximate the bewilderment a child faces in a page of print. Both the adult and the child see a succession of unfamiliar forms. It is not easy for an adult unfamiliar with Spanish, for example, to distinguish between "haciendo" and "hacienda." Yet a distinction is very important in reading meanings, because the first word signifies doing and the second the name of a large ranch. Good habits of visual observation, as well as left-to-right directional progression, must be taught.

READING-READINESS BOOKS. Among their other purposes, pre-reading books are carefully designed to furnish an introduction to the visual skills needed in reading, without actually demanding that the children read printed words. In grandmother's day it was thought that a knowledge of the alphabet and phonograms was basic to all reading skills. Today the approach is very different, and reading-readiness books serve to make the modern method very effective. The titles of some of these reading-readiness books clearly explain their content: *We Read Pictures, Look and Learn, Getting Ready,* etc.

A major skill needed for beginning reading is the ability to see likenesses and differences. To the uninitiated child a printed page must look like a jumble of black dots and marks; yet every word is different in some respect from the others. To get the spaces between the lines and letters, and dots and other marks to convey meaning is a gradual process, and reading-readiness booklets are specifically designed to aid in these tasks of visual discrimination.

Some prereading books have exercises in which a row of four pictured objects display one different element, i.e., three objects may be the same size but one larger, or three may face the same way and one the reverse. The child is supposed to circle the one that is not like the rest. Other beginning books have similar exercises that involve only letters and words, the principle in operation being that children should learn the kind of discrimination that reading demands. Such a reading-readiness book is found in the Reading for Meaning Series.[5] It provides exercises for "early and frequent training in making visual discriminations among letter forms, the symbols in which reading matter is printed, and word forms." The first page on visual discrimination shows four

[5] Paul McKee and M. Lucile Harrison, *Getting Ready: A Reading Readiness Book* (rev. ed.) (Boston: Houghton Mifflin Co., 1957), Introduction and exercises indicated.

page-wide "boxes" framed in different colors. The children are asked to find the first pair of letters (A A) and, without naming them, are asked if they are "just alike." The children place a mark under them to show *likeness.* The next pair of letters (B R) lead the children to note *difference.* Another type of visual-discrimination exercise is the "letter game." In this, cards are matched to the ones exposed by the teacher (not in alphabetical order) and the children learn to name the letters.

Other series stick to pictures for promoting the ability to recognize similarities and differences in objects or geometrical forms (circles, squares, and variations). Usually exercises combining visual and auditory discrimination are offered. Pictures of objects the names of which rhyme are mixed with a "foil" for example. The child is asked to look at the pictures to find two that rhyme, for example, a picture of a *fish* and one of a *dish.* Beginning sounds are also identified as the children are asked to find a picture of something that begins the same way *b*all starts (*b*aby, *b*asket).

PICTURE STORYBOOKS. A well-planned program of visual discrimination should include a rich offering of picture books which the children may peruse for themselves, identifying and discussing what they see in the pictures. The children gain more value from the pictures if they are first introduced by the teacher when she reads the story part of the book. (See lesson plan, page 148, and, for a list of picture books suitable for use at the primary level, see page 152.) One of the specific activities which develops reading readiness is experience in gleaning ideas from pictures. The degree to which a child grasps essentials in a picture storybook will be governed by his ability to observe effectively. To see relationships within a given picture in a picture storybook, and then perceive relationships from picture sequence to picture sequence, requires a considerable degree of maturity in effective observation. Certainly the child who is able to tell the story as it is pictured and to draw inferences from observation of the significant elements is more ready to deal with ideas in print than the child who cannot make meaningful associations with pictures.

While the contribution picture storybooks make to the growth of the visual skill of effective observation is stressed here, it should be made clear that these books stimulate growth of a whole hierarchy of skills. In looking through the pictures and talking about them, the child also receives much practice in language skills. His stock of mental concepts and his vocabulary are both enriched in this process. If the teacher reads aloud the little printed story accompanying the pictures, the child's auditory ability is also developed. The teacher, for example, may pose a "listening question" to motivate closer listening for the details of the story. However, by their very nature and purpose, picture storybooks rely heavily on visual skills for their appeal. For this reason the discussion of their value in promoting reading readiness is included in this particular section.

OTHER IDEAS. The teacher can help children develop the visual skills needed in reading in many other ways:

1. Call attention to likenesses and differences in the appearance of children's names, as in the case of Roy and Ronald. Explain, "Both of these names look alike at the beginning, but Ronald is the longer name."

2. After several experience stories have been built up around activities connected with a given unit, have the children look for the pairs of words which end alike such as "toy," "boy"; "booth," "tooth"; "rag," "tag."

3. To establish the proper eye movements, sweep the hand rapidly from left to right when indicating a line of print in the experience story or under a picture in the picture storybook. Never point to one word at a time, for this will lead to word-by-word reading. Phrases can be framed to form suitable meaning groups by cupping the hands at the beginning and end.

4. Cut up a picture for a jigsaw puzzle from pieces of construction paper in different shapes and colors (for example, a dog, a house, or a clown) and paste it on a nine-by-twelve-inch oak tag. Give the child a complete outline model of the picture and an envelope containing the pieces of the puzzle. Then ask him to reconstruct the picture. Include several incorrect pieces in the envelope so that the child must note likenesses and differences,

and concentrate upon the problem. Vary these problems from simple puzzles containing only the primary colors to difficult ones containing many colors.

Developing Auditory Skills. Children are sensitive to likenesses and differences in sounds to some degree; otherwise they could not have learned to talk. When they approach word recognition in reading, they will need to develop discriminatory abilities of a higher order. A teacher can use many different techniques to help develop auditory skills.

One technique to follow is to ask children to listen for rhymes such as Jill and hill in the well-known nursery jingle, or to listen for words that begin with the same sound in a sequence of words such as "candy," "cookies," "cake," "apples." Ask the children to tell which word does not belong. Another way the teacher can develop auditory skills is to distribute pictures of, say, a horse and a house, or a window and a toy whistle. The teacher then calls out one of these words, and the children circle the proper picture. If the circlings are correct, the teacher can assume that the children are recognizing words through auditory skill. Several additional suggestions follow:

1. After establishing a listening mood, say, "I know a boy whose name is Marvin. Will all the children whose names start with the same sound as the name Marvin please stand?" Have the children prove the similarity by saying, "Marvin-Margo," for example. Then pair David and Marvin, and ask the children if these names start alike or have a different sound at the beginning.

2. Ask the children to listen carefully and mark with a crayon the sounds that they hear. Tell them to close their eyes and listen to a tapping. Tell them to make a dot on a paper every time they hear a tap. Then tap a pencil sharply twice, pause, and tap twice again. If the children have heard correctly their visual interpretation should show a pair of dots close together, perhaps a dash, then another pair of dots.

Allow the children to make pictures of a varying pattern of taps with colored crayons. In each case, have them close their eyes as they listen for the taps, then open their eyes and draw dots in the appropriate pattern. If a teacher starts with a simple combination of taps and progresses to harder ones, she soon discovers the children who need help in listening and hearing.

3. Use auditory exercises in the reading-readiness booklets to build skill in rhyming. Ask the children to find a picture on the page that rhymes with "Dick" (stick"), with "Jane" ("cane"), and so on.

Developing Mental Readiness. Achievement in reading is more closely related to intelligence than to any other factor. Reading is thinking, according to leading investigators in the field. If the mind is keen, skill in reading follows, except in special cases, for example, when children with high mathematical quotients may possess a specific disability in reading. Such mental activities as recognizing relationships, sensing sequence, solving problems, and following directions are present both in thinking and in reading. While not all mental skills can be taught directly, the ones which have been mentioned can be developed, as will be seen from the suggestions listed below for developing them in preparation for reading readiness.

RECOGNIZING RELATIONSHIPS. One of the signs of clear thinking is the ability to classify and put things together that belong together. Some techniques for developing the ability to classify follow:

1. Present a variety of pictures such as those of a car, a house, a barn, a lake, and a pillow. On a table place a second set of pictures related to the first, such as a tire, a bed, a horse, and a boat. The children are to select from the table the picture which is related to one of the pictures on the chart and to explain why the selection has been made. The child may properly answer, "Tire and car go together." The other children listen to decide if the pairing has been correctly done.

2. Prepare a set of pictures of clothing, including shoes and hats, clipped from magazine advertisements. Collect pictures of people of all ages. Then ask the children to match the clothing and the people who would probably wear them.

3. Cut pictures from an inexpensive storybook and mount them on oak tag. Place the pictures out of order on the chalk tray. Then tell the story, and as each part of the story is completed have the children select the picture related to it. When the story is finished, the pictures should be in order. As an added exercise in recognizing relationships, the children may retell the story, each matching the part of the story related to a picture. Through this exercise the teacher can soon discover those who cannot relate a picture to a story paragraph.

4. Select a suitable picture and have the children observe it carefully. Then ask, "If you were one of the children in this picture, what would you do next?" Help the children decide if their answers suggest logical outcomes.

SENSING THE SEQUENCE OF IDEAS. The ability to sense the sequence of ideas is promoted by telling stories, learning poems, relating experiences, and giving directions. Here is a list of activities calculated to develop the ability to sense story sequence:

1. After reading a story of the children, ask them how a series of events happened in the story. Use such queries as these: "In the story where did David go after he saw the school bus?" or "Where did David go when he missed the bus?"

2. Have the children repeat from memory a set of directions, in sequence, for carrying on some activity in the classroom.

3. Let the children draw a frieze showing the order of places they visited in school during the first week.

4. Show a series of pictures telling a story. Withhold the last picture and see if any child can predict what the last one in the sequence will show. Then show the last picture for verification.

5. Adopting the plan of an idea count, read a short paragraph or story to the children. Ask them to tell what happened. If only half the ideas are retained, help the children recall the rest. Tell the children how many ideas there were altogether. The next time the technique is used the children are likely to listen more closely and to carefully note the sequence.

SOLVING PROBLEMS. Much problem solving, whether applied to simple problems in reading readiness or the more complicated ones of adult life, follows this progression: recognizing the problem, gathering information related to the problem, analyzing and using this information, and arriving at a conclusion. Sometimes the mere recognition of a problem results in the use of a previously learned solution. However, imagine that the children in a reading-readiness group are looking at a picture and the teacher asks, "Can you tell what time of the day it is?" The pupils are more likely to reply correctly if the teacher has instilled these steps in problem solving.

The following example shows how one first-grade teacher conducts a lesson at this level to develop her children's ability in solving problems. This teacher was using a science picture book during the reading-readiness work period. The children opened their books to a page where there were several pictures of people working. In each picture two ways of doing the same work were illustrated. For example, in one picture one field was being plowed by a tractor, another by horses pulling a plow; in another picture soil was being removed by a steam shovel, in one instance, and by a man shoveling by hand, in another. The caption read "Find the Easy Way." The problem the teacher set for the group was: "After we study these pictures, let us see if we can find out what makes one way easier than the other way."

As each picture was analyzed there was plenty of opportunity to make comparisons, to add other examples of easy ways, to discuss if the easy way is always the most fun (cooking on a picnic outdoor fire or on an electric range). Vocabulary work and seeing of relationships were included in this exercise. The children and the teacher then arrived at the solution of the problem by listing on the board all the things that help to make the easy ways, such as electricity, engines, wheels. The teacher presented a collection of colored mounted pictures of ways of doing things. Different children looked at the pictures and decided if the pictures illustrated an easy or hard way; the others evaluated these conclusions. Just for fun, some pictures of humorous ways of doing things were included. The children especially enjoyed isolating these.

These are some other suggestions to develop the ability to attack and solve simple problems:

1. Have the children make picture charts classified according to subjects such as farm animals, pets, toys, furniture, fruits, and vegetables.

2. Play this game: "It is true because _____" Examples: "It is a nice day because it is sunshiny"; "it is warm"; "the children are happy"; "Johnny has a new tooth"; "Mary is back in school."

3. If a group of children decides to play house, questions arise that need to be answered: Who should play the mother? The father? The children? What work will the mother do in the play-house? The father? The children? The more aggressive children usually want to assume the important roles in imitative play, but all of the pupils should be given the chance to be leaders as well as followers.

The teacher will find countless opportunities each day to include the problems of group living as well as individual problems. It is very important that children be taught to think for themselves, since it is an excellent foundation for success in reading.

FOLLOWING DIRECTIONS. To be successful here a child must be able to control himself well enough to listen carefully to the directions. He must recognize clearly what he is to do; he must be attentive while the directions are read. A few ideas to promote self-direction follow:

1. Have the children take pencil and paper and draw a picture, following directions. The exercise at first may require only a simple direction like "Draw the picture of a house." After children have learned to follow one step easily, include two steps in the next exercise, for example, "Draw a picture of a house with two windows." Then progress to several directions: "Draw a square. Put a circle in each corner and an X in each circle."

2. Play games which are built on directions, for example, "Listen very carefully. See if you can do exactly what I say. I will tell you what to do only once. Ready? Go to the blackboard. Draw a large circle. Put a dot in the middle of the circle."

The school day is full of opportunities which can be used to teach children to follow directions. They can be shown how to get paste from the paste jar, how to feed the hamsters, how to get ready to paint, and many other activities.

PLANNING THE LESSON

The lesson plan presented here uses the accompanying reading readiness exercise and contains many of the elements of reading readiness discussed in this chapter. Remember that, when teaching from a reading-readiness book, it is also important to use the accompanying teacher's guidebook, where one is provided. Otherwise the teacher should study carefully the "Notes to the Teacher" included in the readiness booklet.

READING-READINESS LESSON PLAN

I. What (subject matter)

Reading-readiness exercise; teacher-prepared seatwork

II. Why (aims)

A. Reading-readiness skills

1. To teach auditory discrimination of beginning consonants *b, c, m,* without actually naming them—the similar beginning sound will simply be emphasized in saying "banana," "basket"; "candle," "cake"; "milk mug," "mat."
2. To help the child to remember nine different pictures by means of strengthening his *associations* and mentally joining together objects that belong together

B. Content aims

To teach new concepts like the names of things in the pictures, in case these are not known, such as "mug" and "mat"

C. Social aims

To guide the children to appreciate orderliness, i.e., placing the banana in the basket and protecting varnish of the table by placing the milk mug on the mat

III. How (method)

A. Preparation for picture reading
Invite all the children to have fun doing this page.

B. Guiding the picture reading

1. Ask the children to look at the first picture on the left; ask: "What do you see? What is in the second picture in the top line? Where could you put the banana? Tell me in a sentence. Where is the banana in the third picture?"

2. Continue similarly with the other pictures from left to right, realizing the aims listed above. Be sure the children pronounce "milk" correctly. A great many children say "melk." Compliment them if the endings in "mat," "milk," "basket" are enunciated clearly.

3. After all three lines have been covered, as in number 1 above, turn the page away and ask the children to try to remember what was in the first picture in the top line, what was in the second, what was in the third. Since all these main objects involve food or drink, the children have an organization point, or "peg," about which to cluster a sequence of memories. Were these pictures not

connected by doing things with the first object in each, it would be exceedingly difficult for little children to remember nine objects. With the powerful links of association formed, they can do so quite easily.

C. Drill (seatwork)

To check retention, distribute mimeographed forms to the children, showing pictures in two columns to be matched by drawing lines. The children may then color the pictures.

picture of banana	picture of cake
picture of candle	picture of mat
picture of milk mug	picture of basket

D. Follow-up

Distribute color crayons and blank sheets folded in thirds across and ask the children to draw from memory what they saw on the three rows of the reading-readiness seatwork above. (Nine pictures should thus be drawn in order.)

IV. Evaluation

The student teacher should look back at the three types of aims (skills, content, and social) and determine which were achieved and which remain to be achieved. What facts, habits, attitudes, and skills were taught in this lesson?

PICTURE-STORYBOOK LESSON PLAN

I. What (subject matter)

A. "Story time" during the reading-readiness period

B. *Finders Keepers* by William Lipkind. (New York: Harcourt, Brace & World, Inc.)

C. The fanciful story of two shaggy dogs who had many strange adventures trying to decide the ownership of a bone

II. Why (aims)

1. To teach visual observation
2. To develop good listening habits
3. To learn new terms such as *goat, bucking*
4. To appreciate humor
5. To discover that working together is better than quarreling

6. To improve vocabulary
7. To be able to tell the real from the fanciful

III. How (method)

A. Introducing the story

1. Show the picture of the two dogs busily digging in the ground. Then say, "What do you see in this picture?" (The children discuss the picture as it is held up by the teacher.) "Do you think these dogs are friends? Why? What are they doing? Do you have any idea what they may find?"

2. Show the next picture. Then say, "Let us look at this. What seems to be the matter here? Which dog do you think will get the bone?" (The children venture to surmise.)

B. Asking the listening question

"These two funny dogs are called Nap and Winkle. Listen to the story while I read it, and see who gets the bone and why."

C. Reading the story to the children

Show pictures of the farmer, the goat, the barber, and the big dog during the oral reading. Ask questions to elicit reactions from the children. If pupils are not sure what a goat is, for example, explain about its horns and bucking.

IV. Evaluation

List children's linguistic, mental, and social gains.

PLANNING THE SCHOOL DAY

It would be helpful, particularly to the beginning teacher, to see how such an activity as the bakery unit (see pages 131–135) can be fitted into the day's work. A suggested daily program for a first grade is given below:

9:00 to 9:20   Sharing time. Children talk about any subject they wish—personal happenings, their bits of news. Experience stories may be recorded. Plans for activity period are set up.

9:20 to 9:30   Health and attendance check. Collect lunch money.

9:30 to 10:00	Reading-readiness book. Immature and average groups.
10:00 to 10:20	Relaxation, bathroom, games, outdoor play.
10:20 to 10:35	Reading-readiness book. Mature group.
10:35 to 11:25	Activity period. The "play" bakery. The bakery unit includes art, poetry, making up experience stories, and constructing things for the bakery.
11:25 to 11:30	Preparation for noon dismissal.
11:30 to 1:00	Lunch and recreation.
1:00 to 1:15	Rest period.
1:15 to 1:35	Music and rhythms.
1:35 to 1:50	Miscellaneous activities. Might include reading experience stories, evaluating activities in progress, completing reading-readiness book.
1:50 to 2:00	Playtime—outdoors if possible.
2:00 to 2:30	Story time, dramatization, poetry, pictures, films, slides, record playing, and art.

Such a daily program should be used by the teacher only as a guide; the program may vary with the needs of the children. The amount of time indicated for each activity is flexible, for even the length of time first graders are in school varies in different sections of the country. This program merely serves as an example.

PLANNING WITH PARENTS

The teacher should recognize the necessity of informing the parents about the nature of reading readiness; otherwise many protests may be aimed at the program. Among the methods being used for parent education, the most successful is the conference. Two types of parent conferences are becoming established as methods of home-school cooperation: the group conference and the individual conference.

The Group Conference. This type of conference is usually held early in the year. The parents of the children in a particular room are invited to the school in a group. The teacher explains the needs of the children and describes how these needs are met. She interprets present-day readiness methods. The parents have an opportunity to ask questions and become acquainted with the child's school environment. During this conference the teacher also displays reading-readiness materials and shows how the unit plan is utilized to develop a whole hierarchy of readinesses through mental, social, and language experiences.

The Individual Conference. This second type of parent-teacher conference is usually held later. The parents of each child come at a prearranged time to meet with the teacher. As a result of the previous group conference, the parents should have a general idea of the objectives of their child's school experiences, but it is sometimes necessary to reiterate during the individual conference the reasons for delaying a child's reading. If a mother has learned that the son of a neighbor (in the same first grade) is now reading the preprimer, while her own boy is still limited to reading-readiness books, or if invidious comparisons are being made with the more skilled older brothers or sisters in the family, the teacher should explain the reasons. The following is a reproduction of a first-grade teacher's persuasive arguments during such a parent conference:

It is not enough to know that your Jimmy is six years old. You tell me that his two older brothers both began to read when they were six. Perhaps Jimmy did not walk or talk as soon as they did? He needed a little longer to *grow* in order to be ready to walk and talk. He now also needs a little longer time to grow in order to be ready for reading. You did not try to force him to walk or talk before he was mature enough to do so, because it would have been useless, or even harmful, since forcing goes against nature—the same holds true for reading.

Of course, it is not easy to convince these anxious parents, who often seem to be in a great hurry to plunge their child into reading the day school starts, that it is wiser to provide the child with a good, well-rounded development—mental, physical, emotional, social, and experiential—than it is to try to begin by teaching him the alphabet.

Parents are usually quick to understand that the child's health can affect his progress in reading, but they are not so apt to recognize the importance of social development to the child's success in learning this difficult skill. The teacher may have to interpret this new viewpoint to the parent by explaining that children have to read together in groups in school, taking turns, listening courteously, and so on. Tactfully, she must make it clear that sometimes the youngest child in the family is "babied" too much, thus hampering his emotional and social development. The teacher may then suggest that overprotection causes children to prolong infantile reactions and that therefore the child should be given responsibilities at home which will help him feel competent and capable, such as putting away his clothes and toys and helping with various small tasks about the house not beyond his ability.

If the child's store of concepts and vocabulary is inadequate, the teacher may show the parents how they can help by reading to the child each evening. During the conference, the teacher should make it clear that a good speaking vocabulary helps reading vocabulary later. She may suggest the value here of family trips to the zoo, to farms, to pet shops, to picnic grounds, and parks.

Teachers who believe in the readiness concept must convince the parent that to delay reading until the child is ready to cope with it not only pays immediate dividends in greater comfort for the child but brings long-term rewards as well. This was the attitude of the teacher whose conference arguments were mentioned previously. She told the parents:

> You are worried because your boy has been in school several months and is not reading yet. But what are a few months or even a year to a little child? You would not think of putting up a house without first laying a firm foundation. The readiness work is the firm foundation for reading. It would be an easy matter for me, as Jimmy's teacher, to put him in one of my three reading groups. But he would not really be reading. Do you want him to be one of those children who sit in every class all the way through school, unable to take part in the work because he did not get a good start in reading? If we do not help him now, someone will have to try later to help him make up what he is missing. It is easier to develop reading readiness now. If he tries to read he will fail, because he is not mature enough yet to deal with abstract symbols. Is it fair to him to be labeled a failure in his very first year in school? Please let me help him reach the point where he will really be ready to read!

SELECTED LIST OF PICTURE STORYBOOKS

The following list includes books which are generously illustrated. Though many others could be mentioned, the teacher will probably find some books here to supplement her room library.

BEMELMANS, LUDWIG. *Madeline.* New York: The Viking Press, Inc.

BROWN, MARGARET WISE. *The Duck.* New York: Harper & Row

BURTON, VIRGINIA LEE. *Calico, the Wonder Horse.* Boston: Houghton Mifflin Co.

CERF, BENNETT. *Book of Laughs.* New York: Random House, Inc.

CHANDLER, EDNA WALKER. *Cowboy Sam.* New York: Beckley-Cardy Co.

CONDEY, ALICE E. *Here Come the Raccoons!* New York: Charles Scribner's Sons

DR. SEUSS. *The Cat in the Hat.* New York: Random House, Inc.

DR. SEUSS. *If I Ran a Circus.* New York: Random House, Inc.

DUVOISIN, ROGER. *Petunia.* New York: Alfred A. Knopf (a division of Random House, Inc.)

FARJEON, ELEANOR. *The Little Bookroom.* New York: Henry Z. Walck, Inc.

FATIO, LOUISE. *The Happy Lion.* New York: McGraw-Hill Book Co., Inc.

GRAMATKY, HARDIE. *Hercules.* New York: G. P. Putnam's Sons, Inc.

GRAMATKY, HARDIE. *Little Toot.* New York: G. P. Putnam's Sons, Inc.

HAYWOOD, CAROLYN. *Little Eddie.* New York: William Morrow & Co., Inc.

LANGSTAFF, JOHN. *Frog Went A-courting.* New York: Harcourt, Brace & World, Inc.

LENSKI, LOIS. *Little Airplane.* New York: Henry Z. Walck, Inc.

McCLOSKEY, ROBERT. *Make Way for Ducklings.* New York: The Viking Press, Inc.

McGINLEY, PHYLLIS. *All Around the Town.* Philadelphia: J. B. Lippincott Co.

MILNE, A. A. *The House at Pooh Corner.* New York: E. P. Dutton & Co., Inc.

MILNE, A. A. *Winnie The Pooh.* New York: E. P. Dutton & Co., Inc.

REY, H. A. *Curious George.* Boston: Houghton Mifflin Co.

TYMAN, LORETTA MARIE. *Michael McGillicuddy.* New York: Abelard-Schuman, Ltd.

ZAFFO, GEORGE J. *The Big Book of Real Fire Engines.* New York: Grosset & Dunlap, Inc.

ZION, GENE. *Harry, the Dirty Dog.* New York: Harper & Row.

QUESTIONS AND ACTIVITIES

1. How can the teacher capitalize upon everyday experiences in the classroom to develop vocabulary and concepts?
2. How valuable are field trips and excursions in adding to the child's stock of meaning gained at first hand?

3. List three values of the experience-chart story in developing readiness for reading.

4. Obtain a copy of a reading-readiness book. (They are large in size and usually paperbound, containing a variety of pictured exercises, each designed to build some reading skill, without actually requiring the reading of print. Each usually has the lesson plans or notes to the teacher offered at the front of the book and the types of exercises, labeled by skill categories and indexed by pages, at the close.) Examine a reading-readiness book to note exercises designed to promote mental readiness, visual readiness, auditory readiness.

5. How will participation in a unit of work help the child to develop a rich store of vocabulary and concepts?

6. How is a concept developed? (Review the example for *run*, and try to recollect some particular concept in your own experience which had gradual development.)

7. Find the topic heading "Developing Mental Readiness" in this chapter. Note the subtopics: "Recognizing Relationships," "Sensing the Sequence of Ideas," "Solving Problems," and "Following Directions." Choose one suggested activity under each heading to use with a child six years of age in your neighborhood.

8. Two types of parent conferences are recommended to acquaint parents with the goals and methods of the reading-readiness program. Why are such conferences necessary?

9. Since parents identify so closely with their children, how is it possible to explain *tactfully* that a child is being overprotected or pressured too hard to excel in school? Which are better terms to use at conference time with parents?

a. You must . . .	a. You should . . .
b. Lazy child	b. Can do more if he tries
c. Stupid	c. Can do better with help
d. Mean	d. Can learn to get along better with others
e. Sloppy	e. Could be neater
f. Below average	f. Working at his own level
g. Selfish	g. Should learn to share with others

10. Look up other examples of tactless and tactful ways of talking to parents in the National Education Association bulletin: *Conference Time for Teachers and Parents.*

SELECTED REFERENCES

ARTLEY, A. STERL. *Your Child Learns To Read.* Chicago: Scott, Foresman & Co., 1953.

AUSUBEL, DAVID. *Theory and Problems of Child Development.* New York: Grune & Stratton, Inc., 1958.

DAWSON, MILDRED A., and HENRY BAMMAN. *Fundamentals of Basic Reading Instruction.* New York: Longmans, Green & Co., Inc., 1959.

DEBOER, JOHN J., and MARTHA DALLMAN. *The Teaching of Reading.* New York: Holt, Rinehart & Winston, Inc., 1960.

DURKIN, DOLORES. "Reading Instruction and the Five-year-old Child," *Challenge and Experiment in Reading. International Reading Association Conference Proceedings.* New York: The Scholastic Magazines, 1962, pp. 23–26.

HANNA, LAVONNE, GLADYS POTTER, and NEVA HAGAMAN. *Unit Teaching in the Elementary School.* New York: Holt, Rinehart & Winston, Inc., 1955.

HEILMAN, ARTHUR W. *Principles and Practices of Teaching Reading.* Columbus, Ohio: Charles E. Merrill Books, Inc., 1961.

HESTER, KATHLEEN B. *Teaching Every Child To Read.* New York: Harper & Row, 1955.

HYMES, JAMES L., JR. *Before the Child Reads.* New York: Harper & Row, 1958.

LEE, J. MURRAY, et al. "Measuring Reading Readiness," *Elementary School Journal,* XXXIV (May 1934), 656–66.

McKEE, PAUL. *The Teaching of Reading in the Elementary School.* Boston: Houghton Mifflin Co., 1948.

MEHL, MARIE A., HUBERT H. MILLS, and HARL R. DOUGLASS. *Teaching in Elementary School* (2d ed.). New York: The Ronald Press Co., 1958.

MULDER, ROBERT L., and JAMES CURTIN. "Vocal Phonic Ability and Silent Reading Achievement: A First Report," *Elementary School Journal,* LVI (November 1955), 121–23.

ROBINSON, HELEN M. "Factors Which Affect Success in Reading," *Elementary School Journal,* LV (January 1955), 263–69.

STONE, CLARENCE R. *Progress in Primary Reading.* St. Louis: Webster Publishing Co., 1950.

YOAKAM, GERALD. *Basal Reading Instruction.* New York: McGraw-Hill Book Co., Inc., 1955.

PART III

THE BASIC PROGRAM
OF READING INSTRUCTION

7

EXAMINING THE BASIC
READING PROGRAM

There are four fields of reading instruction: basic reading, reading in the subject-matter fields (geography, history, science, etc.), recreational reading, and remedial reading. This chapter deals with the first field—basic reading instruction—by far the most important because it is designed to teach the basic skills. Since teaching basic reading is quite intricate, a complete form for a Basic Lesson Plan for Student Teachers is presented at the end of this chapter.

According to the abstract, among other findings of an interesting study conducted by Gerold W. Brekke,[1] of the University of North Dakota, in 1961 it was shown that the basal reading approach to the teaching of reading was used to some extent by 99.5 per cent of the 8,000 separate grades in the 1,224 schools of his sample. An over-all increase of sixty-eight minutes weekly was found between the average weekly identified time allotment for basal reading in his sample and the average of eight earlier studies. This seems to indicate that, in spite of the wide publicity given to other methods since 1955, more time is now being allotted to basal reading than formerly.

[1] "A Comparison of Time Allotments for Basal and Other Reading with the Recommendations of Reading Authorities" (Doctoral dissertation, The University of North Dakota, 1962).

In support of the value of the basic reader approach, Heilman[2] lists ten advantages. Some of the ones he mentions are as follows: systematic instruction, excellent teacher guides for step-by-step teaching program, practice of new skills introduced at the proper time and in the proper sequence, prepared materials to save the teacher's time, etc.

In a recent article in *The Reading Teacher,* written after first-hand observation of reading practices in various English-speaking countries, Guy L. Bond[3] appears to favor the basic approach when he states: "The other countries have avoided falling into the error of thinking that reading is discovered . . . in an incidental way while doing independent reading." He goes on to say that the teachers in the countries he visited (England, Scotland, New Zealand, Australia, etc.) "use to a greater degree basic reading texts; they read the manuals that accompany them, and do what the manuals suggest."

If used correctly, the basal reader series deals with all phases of the reading program, thus avoiding neglect of some or overemphasis of others. There is no reason why the work in basic reading instruction should not provide a stimulating environment for learning, if the activities radiating from the reading of the basic selection are followed. A wealth of such enriching experiences are suggested in the correlated-activities (also called followup activities) step in the basic lesson plan (see page 194).

As was stated above, most modern basic readers, with their teacher's guidebooks and children's workbooks, are carefully arranged to introduce skills gradually, so that one develops out of another. A new skill is not introduced until the child has mastered a previous skill, which thus serves as a foundation. For example, the child is not asked to syllabicate words until he has developed an understanding of vowel principles. But it is important that the teacher give equal attention to the development of the child in teaching the sequential development of important reading skills.

[2] Arthur W. Heilman, *Principles and Practices of Teaching Reading* (Columbus, Ohio: Charles E. Merrill Books, Inc., 1961), p. 110.

[3] "Differences in Reading Instruction in English-speaking Countries," *The Reading Teacher,* XIV, No. 3 (January 1961), 154.

CHILD DEVELOPMENT AND BASIC READING

It was common practice, not many years ago, to list typical sequences in the child's growth and development. Descriptions of normality and lists of behavior expectations for certain age groups were earnestly consulted by parents and teachers. Statements often appeared in education literature to the effect that five-year-olds are full of energy or that nine-year-olds love stories about frontier heroes.

But such generalizations too often ignored the fact that children's behavior is unpredictable. For example, it was not the nine-year-old group that adopted the Davy Crockett headgear—in worshipful emulation of the hero of the Alamo—but much younger children of five, six, and seven.

Forces Influencing Child Development. Milton Senn, of Yale University, has found that many forces influence the child's development. Because of dietetic research, for instance, American children today confound Arnold Gesell's norms by being taller and heavier. As for typical interests at a given stage of development, motion pictures, television, picture magazines, comic books, and advertisements now bring children into constant contact with the adult world. The teacher cannot assume uniformity in sequence of development but must study each individual child and accept him as he is, with his particular inherited traits, his body type, and his stock of experiences and concepts. Psychologists point out that, to predict a child's behavior, one must understand his personal fears, prejudices, superstitions, reactions to authority, and ability to endure frustration. This is not an easy task. As an astronomer once confessed, "I can foretell with reasonable accuracy where a given star will be fifty years from now, but I cannot predict where my eighteen-year-old daughter will be tonight."

Because of individual differences, the teacher must fit the reading program to the child, rather than attempt to fit the child into a hard-and-fast program. Systematic instruction must assuredly be present, but the time and the pace must be geared to the child's ability to profit from each reading experience. If the child is asked to do more than he is able, it will retard, rather than promote, his development. The readiness of the teacher to give instruction in a given skill is important, but even more important is the readiness of the child—mentally, physically, emotionally, and socially—to deal with a new learning experience.

The teacher must also consider similarities in development, as well as differences, since children have many needs in common. Certainly the needs for security, affection, acceptance, and achievement are basic needs in the American culture pattern. Knowing about these basic hungers helps to give direction to the teacher's efforts.

Stages of Reading Development. Children's reading development follows certain recognizable stages. While not sharply set off, these stages indicate to the teacher general levels of achievement. Allowing for exceptions and differences in degree, teachers can outline, with reasonable certainty, what these stages of development will be in the reading of many children. There may be some deviations, of course—as in the case of child prodigies—but teachers are safe in assuming that six-year-olds are not apt to be capable of reading such things as Thackeray's *Vanity Fair*. To comprehend such a book, the child must first pass through four stages of reading development. And this development takes time.

The stages of reading development have been described in many publications by the late William S. Gray, the leading authority in the field. With a few additions to the descriptive passages, the following are his classifications:

1. The stage at which readiness for reading is acquired.

   This usually includes the preschool years, the nursery school, kindergarten, and, usually, the first part of the first grade. Some children need only a few weeks' work in school to develop readiness for reading; some require many months.

2. The initial stage of learning to read.

   This usually occurs in the first grade. However, some children cannot begin reading until the second grade, or even later. Children who have achieved the initial stage are able to read simple materials in which the vocabulary is controlled, that is, only a few new words are introduced, and each is used so many times that the children soon learn to recognize it. The work with phonics is introduced gradually.

3. The stage of rapid progress in fundamental reading skills, habits, attitudes, and tastes.

Depending upon the child, of course, this stage is usually reached at the second- or third-grade levels. A number of children may not achieve it until the fourth. This is a stage of rapid progress in the fundamental reading skills. Silent reading is more rapid than oral reading now, and the children are able to read with considerable ease, understanding, and pleasure the informational and recreational material found in carefully prepared basic readers for the third and fourth grades.

4. The stage of learning to use reading as a tool.

This stage occurs, as a rule, at the fifth- and sixth-grade levels. When this stage has been achieved, the child is more mature and can read reference materials. He has techniques for making out words on his own. His interests have broadened, and practice over a number of years has increased his proficiency and excellence in reading.

5. The stage of refinement and extension of reading interests, skills, habits, and tastes.

This stage is reached in various grades at the junior- and senior-high-school levels and ideally should end only with death. By now sufficient experience in reading and life has enabled the reader to appreciate the subtle delights of literature, which might earlier have escaped him.

Child Needs and Lesson Steps. Children have many mental, emotional, and social needs. Among these are the need for security, the desire for social approval, the desire for individuality, the need to display self-reliance, the desire to achieve, the need to be interested, the need to recognize a purpose for doing something, etc. Certain of these needs are met by the four main steps widely used in teaching a basic reading lesson. The steps are usually designated as in the list that follows.

1. Preparation or introduction
2. Guided reading
3. Drill
4. Follow-up

It is worth noting that these lesson steps have arisen in response to *child needs*. Not one of the steps conforms to any preconceived adult concept of what should be done in conducting a reading lesson. A brief description of the connections between certain child needs and the lesson steps specifically formulated to take care of them is given below.

The child needs to be *interested*. To meet this need, an introduction is carried on before the reading of a story in the basic book begins. The teacher tries in some way to link the story to be read with the child's past experience. She may show an appropriate picture or object that elicits discussion from the pupils, in terms of their own experiences. She may place the title on the board and focus attention on one word in it, asking the children what it makes them think of. She may describe a character to touch off curiosity. Or she may tell part of the story to build suspense. All these means and others are designed to arouse interest in reading the story in the basic reader.

The child feels the need of *recognizing a purpose*—of seeing a *reason* for doing something. To meet this need, the teacher guides the reading by a series of purposeful questions or directions, which stimulate the child to find the answers. Usually, after the teacher has guided the reading of two or three pages, the child is "involved" in the story and reads the remainder without guidance or direction. An example of guiding the reading would be for the teacher to say, "Read until you find how many things happened when the bus stopped." (All read silently to find the pertinent part. Then one child reads it aloud.)

The child needs to feel *secure*. Although children do not voluntarily seek drill as such, they do experience a need for *security*. Using this need as a point of departure, the skillful teacher will help her pupils to recognize the value of repetition. To avoid drill (even the word is not mentioned in some circles) because children are not interested in it is to place responsibility on the irresponsible. Too often children's needs are confused with children's likes and dislikes. In any case, children must become acquainted with drill before their reactions can be judged. John Dewey the great philosopher once said, in a lecture given years ago at Columbia Teacher's College, that his attitude toward interest and effort had been misconstrued by well-meaning professionals. He did not intend to advocate humoring children at all cost. There is always this to consider, too: After a child has gone a little way with a new drill, he no longer considers the drill leading toward mastery of a skill as drudgery but begins to take a lively personal interest in his security and feels a sense of triumph in overcoming difficulty. May Hill Arbuthnot, author of many books on children's literature, has said that "children know what things they like, but not all the things they are *capable* of liking," such as practical drills leading toward important skills.

The child feels the need for *self-expression*. The follow-up step has evolved to help him to realize this end. At the conclusion of the reading of the story, "leads" to further activity are given. The children are encouraged to pursue the idea or theme of the story and to discuss it in relation to their own experience, and to other stories they have read in the basic reader or elsewhere. They may draw their favorite scenes, prepare a dramatization or puppet show, write a new ending for the story, or in other ways follow up the reading by some form of individual use or self-expression.

To summarize this section, note the relation between the matching columns below:

Child Needs	*Lesson Steps*
Interest	Preparation
Purpose	Guided reading
Security	Drill
Self-expression	Follow-up

READING HABITS AND SKILLS IN THE BASIC PROGRAM

The basic program seeks to help the child to develop necessary reading habits and skills. Used for the purpose of systematic teaching are the *readers*, containing stories; the *teacher's guidebook* or *manual*, offering lesson plans; and the *children's workbook*, presenting exercises and drills. As is always the case with habits and skills, there is unavoidable overlapping between the two. Of course, fundamental reading habits have to be introduced in skill-building sessions. When each skill is firmly established, it becomes a habit.

Fundamental Reading Habits. One of the veritable classics in the field of reading instruction is *The Twenty-fourth Yearbook*,[4] published by the National Committee on Reading, in 1925. It identified the fundamental reading habits listed below. These mental and visual activities were so designated because they underlie all reading. Whether the individual is skimming a magazine, enjoying a mystery novel, scrutinizing a report, or studying an income-tax form, he makes use of the fundamental reading habits. (It should be noted that the visual activities are basic to reading in English. Some oriental books are read from bottom to top and from right to left.)

1. Eye movements from left to right, top to bottom, and an accurate return sweep from the end of one line on the right to the beginning of the next line below on the left
2. Correct and independent recognition of words
3. Correct recognition of phrases at one fixation
4. Adequate speed of recognition
5. Rhythmical (not jerky) progress along the line

A review of the fundamental reading habits listed above will show the relation between two processes—the visual and the mental. Research through eye-movement photography by Dr. Guy Buswell, of the University of Chicago, in the twenties and thirties has furnished us information about the way the eyes move and speed of reading.[5]

EYE MOVEMENTS AND RATE OF READING. Buswell found that the eyes do not sweep smoothly across a line of print but start and stop. It is during the fixations, or pauses, that the words are actually seen, not while the eyes are moving. During the stop, an

---

[4] William S. Gray (ed.), Part I: *Report of the National Committee on Reading* (Bloomington, Ill.: Public School Publishing Co.).

[5] Guy Thomas Buswell, *Fundamental Reading Habits: A Study of Their Development*, Supplementary Educational Monograph, No. 21 (Chicago: University of Chicago Press, 1922), p. 78.

image is transmitted to the brain and words are read. Buswell made it clear that "eye movements are mere symptoms. The eyes are servants of the brain. They are the receiving organs, not the interpreting centers. But they are so near the interpreting centers that they reflect very directly what is happening in the seat of neural processes, the brain." Slow readers stop often, taking in one word at a time, whereas fast readers stop less often and take in several words in a thought unit with each fixation. What is more, slow readers tend to verbalize, a process related to oral reading, when each word must be pronounced. Some poor readers mumble to themselves as they read. Though "inner speech" is supposed to be present in most silent reading, fast readers seem to have reduced its use almost to the vanishing point. Finally, eye-movement photography shows that poor readers "go back," i.e., regress, many times—eleven to sixteen times per line is not unusual. Naturally, going back compulsively in a sort of "word worship," as one phase has been called, slows the forward speed of reading.

A child who is beginning to learn to read sees a line in pieces, that is, his eyes move across the page in uncertain jumps. While the eye must be trained to move from left to right and to make an accurate return sweep from the end of one line to the beginning of the next, it is the *mind's* eye which dictates the width of the child's eye span. The untrained or anxious reader regresses to a previous point on the line, or perhaps he has not really looked at that part of the line, or perhaps his mind has not grasped the full meaning connections. Dr. Beulah Ephron,[6] psychologist, has said that a child with perfectionist parents may develop the "nagging feeling that his reading is not perfect and therefore he must regress to pick up every single word." Needless to say he is a slow reader.

THE IMPLICATIONS OF THE EMPHASIS ON SPEED READING. Speed in reading is, of course, a desirable goal. With the great wealth of material in print, the slow reader is penalized. Methods which increase the rate of recognition are useful, and the teacher's guidebooks in the basic series explain such techniques in detail. Build-

[6] *Emotional Difficulties in Reading* (New York: The Julian Press, Inc., 1953), p. 88.

ing a large vocabulary, for example, is an almost certain means of reading faster, not only in a foreign language but also in one's own. Helping the child cut down on the habit of inner speech (some even recommend biting on a pencil while reading), giving practice in phrase perception, and setting a time limit for reading a particular passage are other methods suggested in basic manuals to improve reading speed.

Though Maclatchy[7] reported for example, improvement in phrase reading through the use of a tachistoscope in the primary grades, one would expect to find such a speed-up device to be of greater value at the middle grade levels. From the fourth grade on, there is a vast increase in the amount of informational reading to be done. The need to cover a quantity of social-studies and natural-science materials heightens interest in improving rate.

At these levels some use has been made of rate-training aids such as the tachistoscope, or flasher, which flashes word groups and phrases on a screen at speeds of up to 1/100 of a second (the time required for an eye blink), to help in overcoming word-by-word reading. Another reading machine is the pacer, or accelerator, which sends a battery-operated moving ruler down the page at a speed slightly faster than the pupil's comfortable one. "A hand-operated shutter device opens and closes over printed cards at adjustable time intervals."

A study by Marvel[8] of reading rate in the sixth grade, using a Speed-i-o-Scope for the experimental group, and other reading materials for the control group, failed to show significant differences in rate and comprehension between the two groups. However, the experimenter felt that failure to control the materials used made it impossible to conclude that the experimental training with the tachistoscope produced no effect. A gain in *motivation* was reported.

Other studies have reiterated the finding that such machines stimulate interest and hold attention. But the machines are not books, and, having used the machines to motivate interest and

[7] Josephine H. Maclatchy, "Bexley Reading Study," *Educational Research Bulletin,* XXV (September 18, 1946), 141–68.

[8] John A. Marvel, "Acquisition and Retention of Reading Performance on Two Response Dimensions as Related to 'Set' and Tachistoscopic Training," *Journal of Educational Research,* LII (February 1959), 232–37.

demonstrate the possibility of reading faster, the teacher should plan to return the children to the normal reading situation.

Doubling one's reading rate is entirely possible for the average reader,[9] but not everyone should expect to attain the incredible speeds presently being reported. The claim that machines and other high-speed methods will increase the rate of reading to 6,000 or more words a minute seem freakish. What such a reader is doing—and this form of "occupational skimming" is certainly of value to a businessman or professional facing mounds of letters and other printed matter—is reading hundreds of words, not thousands. For, as he looks down the center of the page in the approved manner, he is spotting only "key" words and a few on each side of the imaginary vertical line, in order to get the general drift.

To quote the number of words read per minute does not have any more actual significance than to quote one driving speed for all types of traffic. To paraphrase an excellent summary by Heilman,[10] the factors on which *rate* of reading *depends* include the reader's background knowledge of the content; the reader's purpose; his physiological and psychological states (tired, nervous, relaxed, assured); the amount of time at the reader's disposal; the size of the print; the glare or lack of light; surrounding noises or other distracting stimuli; and the readability of the book, i.e., vocabulary, sentence structure, style, etc.

No matter what the level—elementary or adult—speed should never be considered apart from comprehension. The meanings must be taken in by the mind. To be a better reader in the fullest sense does not necessarily mean to be a faster reader. Good reading consists of developing a variety of reading skills and applying them according to the type of material and the purpose for which it is being read. For example, one should not expect to read Robert Frost's poems in the same way one skims the daily headlines. To appreciate beautiful passages in literature requires selecting an appropriate reading rate.

[9] John S. Tuckey, "Seven Years of Acceleration," *Journal of Developmental Reading*, III, No. 4 (Summer 1960), 221.

[10] Arthur Heilman, *Principles and Practices of Teaching Reading*, (Columbus, Ohio: Charles E. Merrill Books, Inc., 1961), p. 283.

Basic Reading Skills. The use of the *teacher's guidebook* and the *children's workbook,* along with the *basic reader,* insures continuity and avoids gaps in the mastery of reading skills. Children benefit from direct, planned instruction. Nothing should be left to chance or treated in a haphazard, casual, permissive way. "Once over lightly," as we have been frequently reminded by disappointing reading-achievement scores, is not enough. Definite lessons should be devoted to the development of strategic skills required for effective reading.

WORD ANALYSIS. If a child has to keep running up to the teacher to ask, "What's this word?" he can scarcely be said to be "on his own" in reading. Deficiency in word analysis prevents the use of any other reading skills. Most basic reading series today make use of a *combination* of methods in helping children to figure out new words, rather than depending, as in the past, upon a supply of sight words learned by the look-and-say method. In addition to being trained to use word form and context clues, children are gradually introduced to word analysis. The latter process is the more modern and comprehensive method which has replaced separate "systems" of phonics. Word analysis includes both phonetic and structural analysis. Phonetic analysis refers to the sounds of vowels (short, long, etc.) and consonants (hard, soft). The root "phone" gives the derivation of "phonetic." The student will recall the same root in other words dealing with sounds, such as "telephone," "dictaphone," and "phonograph." Phonetic analysis involves training in the use of rhyming clues, ending sounds, consonant substitution, the vowel rules, and so on (see Chapter 11). Structural analysis involves working with the parts of the total word structure, such as root words, prefixes, suffixes, inflected endings, and syllables. But the ability to recognize and pronounce words is only the first part of the skills story. Words are not of much use unless they communicate meaning. Concept recognition is the subject of the next section.

RECOGNITION OF WORD MEANINGS. Success in reading depends upon the accumulation of a large meaning vocabulary. It is not enough to have the skill of *identifying* words. To know what words *mean* is an essential skill, developed in the basic reading program.

Through rich and varied experiences including those gained vicariously through wide reading, the individual builds up his stock of concepts. The good reader has mastered so many words and concepts that he rarely meets an unfamiliar term that acts as a "roadblock" to comprehension. The words he meets convey thoughts to him rapidly. But the process is different for the poor reader with a limited vocabulary. As Norman Lewis points out in *How To Read Better and Faster,* "Many of the words he meets represent a mystery to be puzzled out before ideas can be grasped and appreciated." A passage from a contemporary English novel well illustrates the point: "There were no charabancs nor liloes on the beach. So we ate our lunch of bubble and squeak in a spinney." Even if the reader can pronounce every word in the sentence, can he be said to be "reading" when at least four, possibly five, words have no meaning for him? If he cannot visualize a *charabanc,* a *lilo,* or a *spinney,* and if he does not know whether to sympathize with the characters because they ate a lunch of *bubble* and *squeak,* the meaning of the passage is, at best, obscured to him.

Semantics, the science of word meanings, is a fascinating field to explore. The depth of meaning attached to a given concept varies with the individual's experiences, both direct and vicarious. How, for instance, is a concept of ice built up in the mind of a child who lives in the southern part of the United States? Probably his first contact with ice is the sight of ice cubes from the family refrigerator. He notices their transparency and colorlessness, though he may not use these terms to describe them. Probably he thinks "I can see through it." He may arrive at the concept of coldness by contrast, when he decides that ice is certainly not warm. He may note its tendency to melt or to frost over, depending on circumstances. Later, from books, pictures, and, perhaps, personal experiences, he will increase his store of meanings clustered about this verbal symbol by learning about icebergs or the Ice Age. No doubt, sooner or later, he will meet a figurative use of the term, as in the description of an icy stare. This is the way concepts are built. The teacher's job in the basic program is to clarify those concepts the children meet in the reader. To do so she may use photographs, films, excursions, actual objects, or discussion.

The fact that language deficiency retards reading success serves to emphasize the relation between language development and reading. To appreciate this, one has only to recall how slowly one reads a foreign language, or a selection with a new type of content, such as a book using many psychiatric terms. Unfamiliar material is read much more slowly than material written in a familiar vocabulary.

For the first few years, children are busy learning to walk and talk and find out the names of the things around them in a "big, booming, buzzing confusion," as psychologist William James termed it. If the child hears English spoken fluently in the home, he enjoys a tremendous advantage in reading English. The child's abilities to think, read, and listen intelligently are dependent upon his vocabulary. The close relationship between size of vocabulary and school achievement has been shown in many research studies.

COMPREHENSION. "Getting thought from the printed page" is a simple definition of the skill of comprehension in reading. Words, phrases, and sentences are symbols of thought. The teacher's job is to teach the child to respond with matching meanings when he sees symbols in written form. However, comprehension is not a single skill. It is made up of a complex blend of habits and skills, visual and mental processes, some overlapping into the skill of interpretation. In one of his summaries of investigations in the field of reading, the late William S. Gray listed as involved in comprehension during silent reading the abilities to (1) use background experience to connect the reader's stock of meanings with what the author is saying; (2) recognize common words automatically; (3) attack new words by context clues, roots, and phonetic analysis; (4) with proper eye movements, not pausing often but taking in several words in each fixation, and not reading back; (5) react to what the author is saying by drawing inferences, passing judgment, and drawing conclusions.

If oral reading follows silent reading, other thinking abilities are called into play, such as selecting the "sock" words to lend meaningful emphasis when reading aloud, pronouncing the words correctly, articulating clearly, and pitching the voice so as to be heard by the audience without strain.

CRITICAL THINKING. In a democracy, it is extremely important to teach the skills connected with critical thinking while reading, to prevent individuals from reacting with blind confidence to what is in print. Some of the skills involved in critical thinking and reading include the abilities to (1) pass judgment by holding up some "yardstick" to compare excellence or value, (2) determine usefulness of data, (3) exercise caution concerning validity, (4) demand objective evidence, (5) check authority, (6) recognize faulty generalizations from an insufficient sampling. In guiding the reading of a story in the basic reader, the teacher can word her questions so as to bring the critical faculty into play. The children may read to prove a point, to select the main happening, to see if there is a character they would like for a friend, to verify statements, etc. The teacher's guidebook is an invaluable aid when it comes to suggestions for such skill building. The children's workbook also gives practice exercises in critical thinking. For example, it often presents passages of a paragraph or so, followed by a statement. Below this appear three choices which promote thinking: (1) true according to the article, (2) false according to the article, (3) not stated in the article. The child has to decide if he is justified in checking true, false, or "does not say."

RETENTION. Since the child does not feel the need of practice for retention, it is necessary to keep the drill sessions short and full of variety as well as to acquaint the child with the purpose of each. For example, the purpose may be to retain the sequence of a story, anecdote, or joke for retelling. Faced with the purpose of reproducing what he has read, the reader decides on the parts to be remembered. In the case of a joke, he would notice certain pertinent words to be transferred, especially the wording of the point. Technique for securing retention includes rereading and marking the passage into segments for memorizing, outlining, listing, underlining, keeping in mind some memorable similarity, and making use of mnemonics, or a system for assisting the memory. For example, some people who are confused by daylight saving time changes, not knowing whether to move their clocks forward or back in the spring and fall, find it helpful to use the scheme of repeating two sentences: "Spring forward. Fall back." The double meaning of each serves as a "peg" upon which to hang memory. Similarly, many elementary-school pupils who find it difficult to know where to put the "e" in the words "receive" and "believe" can set up associations to help them to remember by finding the little word "lie" in "believe" and then saying, "Never *believe* a *lie*." Since "receive" is spelled in just the opposite way, the problem of remembering how to spell these two words, at least, is solved. Of course, comprehension is basic to remembrance. There is no point in memorizing what one does not understand.

THE TOOLS AND THEIR USE IN READING INSTRUCTION

The Graded Series of Basic Readers. The term *basic readers* signifies the set of readers, selected by the city, county, or state educational authorities, used in regular daily instruction periods to teach the fundamental reading skills from grades one through eight. The basic series is composed of one or more reading-readiness booklets, one or more preprimers, a primer, a book one, a book two, and so on, through a book eight.

Basic readers should be distributed to the children as each group meets with the teacher. The basic readers should not be carried home or left in the school desks. They are designed to be used under the teacher's guidance in a sharing situation. Children profit from a common experience of reading in a group, if the group is not too large. With the teacher as their guide, essential meanings are not likely to escape the children. These social reading sessions are sorely missed when the basic readers are taken home, or read at odd times during the school day. Moreover, if the children are allowed to keep the basic books in their possession and read ahead, the teacher's interesting motivations for the stories (triggered by lesson plan suggestions in the manual) may not be effective and the children's enthusiasm for reading to find answers to the teacher's questions may be missing. The children may be allowed to carry home supplementary and library books, but not the basic readers. (They may, however, be allowed to do so after all the stories in them have been read under the teacher's guidance during the regular basic reading periods.)

The Content Plan of the Basic Readers. No matter what the series, and there are a dozen or more companies publishing the best known, basic readers are planned sequentially, that is, graded to give systematic development in reading skills, habits, attitudes, and tastes. Thus, book five is designed to follow book four, maintaining skills introduced in the earlier readers and developing new skills on these foundations. Continuity of growth is the aim.

The child and his experience are fully taken into account in the preparation of a series of readers. As far as content is concerned, the typical reader may cover such subjects as the following.

FIRST-LEVEL READERS. Most of the picture stories in the reading-readiness booklets and the printed stories in the preprimers, the primer, and book one are at the children's experience level. Children at this age are not required to deal with concepts beyond their immediate experience in the home, school, and neighborhood environment. The stories reflect the child's everyday world and cover such subjects as father, mother, pets, and expeditions to the supermarket, zoo, farm, or gas station. These stories contain repetitions and refrains. Only one or two words are introduced in each story of four pages in the preprimers, and the child is not burdened with a heavy vocabulary influx in the other primary books.

SECOND- AND THIRD-GRADE READERS. Story content in these basic readers often goes beyond the child's immediate experience. Units of five or six stories employing city backgrounds may be offered to broaden the experience of children living in a rural community; or, on the other hand, rural units may be offered to enlighten city children about cows, pigs, and cornfields. Rather than featuring familiar pets, stories at these levels include unfamiliar animals such as deer, bears, and raccoons. Folk tales about princesses, trolls, and wizards are common because the child now has enough concepts based on actual experiences to interpret unfamiliar experiences imaginatively. The selections are longer, and a more difficult vocabulary invites the children to try to make out new words by applying phonetic and structural analysis.

FOURTH-, FIFTH-, AND SIXTH-GRADE READERS. For those who have achieved the stage of being able to use reading as a tool, the whole process is stepped up. Much geographical and historical material may appear in the stories. A glossary is usually found at the back of the reader for greater independence in word attack. Units in the basic readers at this level offer stories which open up a wide variety of interests. They offer various themes such as the westward movement, pioneer adventures, biographies of famous heroes, tales of wild animals, and stories of children of other lands. Sixth-grade readers often introduce stories featuring humor, invention, exploration, and the defense of freedom. Readers at this level usually include a few famous classics in greatly abridged form. Apt and appropriate choice of words is recognized by pupils at this level if carefully pointed out by the teacher. This practice advances the child beyond attention to mere word meanings.

SEVENTH- AND EIGHTH-GRADE READERS. For the young teen-age group, the content of the basic readers offers a rich variety. Included are stories about the lives of famous people, high adventure and mystery, science and discovery, sports, hobbies, and special interests. Excerpts from such famous classics as Sir Arthur Conan Doyle's *Adventures of Sherlock Holmes,* Mark Twain's *Roughing It,* or Washington Irving's *The Legend of Sleepy Hollow* may be found in readers at this level. While critical thinking should be indivisible from reading, since reading is thinking (according to the view of many authorities), it is at this stage that children gain increased skill in evaluating reading material, verifying facts in print, and applying what they read to the solution of personal problems. Some teen-agers display tastes usually associated with far greater maturity. Top readers in this age group may take an interest in the lives of authors—sometimes even probe the author's purpose, note the simpler elements of style—and make more or less conscious use of books to pursue interests and solve problems.

The Teacher's Guidebook or Manual. Each basic series provides a teacher's guidebook or manual to accompany each of the readers. The manual includes suggestions and aids in instruction, as well as lesson plans for each of the stories in the reader.

Consultation of the guidebook for help in planning reading lessons does not indicate insecurity or inexperience on the part of the teacher. The guidebook offers a wealth of suggestions for making the best possible use of each story in each reader of the basic series. These manuals are prepared by the authors of a series of readers, and the teacher can gain from them an idea of the underlying philosophy of the instructional program. If the teacher follows the suggestions outlined for teaching reading, there will be fewer gaps in the child's progress and his needs will be met more systematically.

The teacher's guidebook makes careful provision in the *drill* section of the lesson steps for growth in word analysis through an interesting variety of practice exercises to be used at the blackboard or in mimeographed seatwork. The drills designed to promote growth in word analysis should be selected from either the basic guidebook or the children's workbook. It would be a great mistake to combine the basic program with some outside phonics system from a different source book that recommends the use of one, and only one, method of attacking new words. If the many suggestions in the teacher's guidebook for drills (i.e., Step 3 in most basic plans) are followed faithfully each day, growth in word recognition will be systematically provided, and arbitrary systems of phonics, isolated from the basic readers, not only in vocabulary control but also in educational philosophy, will not be needed.

The Children's Workbooks. In addition to the readers and the teacher's guidebook, the basic reading series also furnishes a children's workbook for each level. These workbooks offer exercises designed to give the child extra practice in every reading skill, from word recognition to critical thinking. Words first introduced in one context in the reader appear in the workbook with expanded meanings. For example, in a story about a train, the word "cord'" refers to a signal cord. The workbook discusses cord as a pile of wood and describes the vocal cords.

The basic workbooks rest on a broader base than phonics systems recommended by various self-styled phonics experts. Experiments have indicated that, when children *begin* to read, words are best learned as wholes. The simplest unit in language is a meaningful word, not a single sound. It is far easier to deal with the familiar concept represented by the word "cat" than to begin with the abstract, sounded-out distortion "cuh-aaa-tt." Advocates of the "sound out" method tend to forget that in English one letter may have several sounds. For example, think of the differing roles played by the "o" in "bomb," "tomb," and "comb." The method presented in basic workbooks consists of beginning with the whole word and later introducing its parts. This plan is easier than beginning with the abstract parts—the letters and the sounds. It is much more logical for a child of six to learn "come" as a sight word; he has seen it in many little stories, with the meaning of "come" clearly indicated in the action shown in pictures that carry the plot. The sound-out method confronts the beginner with a honked "cuh-ome," which does not remind him of anything. Some of these phonics systems, isolated from the basic program with its varied approach to word recognition, require the child to memorize over 160 fragments of sound. This tedious and uninteresting return to a method Horace Mann condemned over 125 years ago should be soberly questioned.

Narrow stress on one method of word attack is avoided in basic workbooks. Exercises are not limited to skills in word analysis alone. Help is given in attention to word-form and contextual clues. Furthermore, a great many exercises are designed to promote improvement in skills other than word recognition, such as comprehension, retention, and critical thinking. For instance, one fourth-grade reader tells the story of a lazy boy in Argentina. The workbook comprehension exercise, through a series of multiple choices, stimulates the children to critical thinking. They are led to see that it is not fair to think, on the basis of this one story, that all boys in Argentina are lazy. Thus, they are made to understand that it is dangerous to generalize from one example.

Other Materials of the Basic Program. Most of the companies which publish basic reading series venture creatively beyond the three major tools: the reader, the teacher's manual, and the children's workbook. Accouterments to the basic program include the Big Book, supplementary readers, vocabulary tests, phonograph records, word cards (especially for use in the first grade), cutout figures of the child characters featured in the series, film strips to give additional practice in word analysis, a correlated speech program, and helpful bibliographies of related materials. All these materials help to expand and enrich the basic program.

ORGANIZATION FOR READING INSTRUCTION

The Three-Group Organization. By far the most common practice for carrying on basic instruction in reading is the use of the three-group organization. After a reading survey test has been given, the class is divided into three groups on the basis of test scores: the fast-moving, the average-moving, and the slow-moving. A few children in the class may score so low that they do not fit into any group; these must be helped individually.

The composition of these reading groups must not be rigidly fixed, however. If it is found that a member of the average-moving group has made sufficient progress, he is then moved to the fast-moving, or top, group. On the other hand, because abilities vary, some children in the sixth grade cannot read with facility in a sixth-grade reader; a few may even be reading in third or even second readers. This situation is far from ideal, of course, but no cause for despair. The important thing is that each child must be allowed to progress at his own rate. If he makes progress commensurate with his ability, an important educational goal is being achieved. As Josette Frank has ably stated, "In other areas than reading we have never assumed that every child can learn every skill equally well. . . . If our boy does not excel in carpentry, we accept the fact that this is not his dish. Yet when it comes to reading, we seem to expect that all children can learn to read with equal or nearly equal skill." [11] The teacher should remember that some children are not temperamentally geared to reading, as in

11 *Your Child's Reading Today* (New York: Doubleday & Co., Inc., 1954), p. 53.

the case of the active child, who may lack the patience to sit down and quietly read for any length of time.

There are many areas of learning inadequacy. Some people are poor in music; yet they face the fact realistically and usually accept their inadequacy. Some lack mathematical proficiency; still others are extremely inept at mechanical activities. Obviously, those who are poor in reading have to deal with a more pervasive problem, since reading enters into many areas of daily life; yet here, too, the sensible course is to avoid brooding over the weakness, to try to do as well as possible and to progress beyond the present level of achievement, whatever it is.

NAMING THE GROUPS. The problem of how to designate the three reading groups in a class often troubles new teachers. Formerly, teachers assigned names to each group to disguise the ability level represented; the result was such terms as the Elves, the Sprites, or the Gnomes. One somewhat misguided teacher, faced with two reading groups, disposed of the problem of nomenclature by calling them the Weeds and the Flowers. Occasionally teachers have used such sports terms as the Red Sox or the Rams, though this is not recommended. Some teachers have named an entire reading group after one child in it. The most serious objection to calling a group Billy's Group is that such a designation is inaccurate and gives one child unwarranted prestige. Nor does the rotation of different children's names for the honor solve the problem; it merely involves endless and pointless bookkeeping.

The best and simplest practice seems to be either to label the groups the first, second, and third, or 1a, 1b, 1c, or to use the name of the basic book they are reading to designate the group; for instance, the *Once upon a Storytime* Group. Some teachers try to protect the feelings of the third, or slow, group by calling it the first group. But the children in the third group almost inevitably are well aware of their poor achievement in reading and are not deluded by the euphemism. If these children are helped by the teacher to feel that there is hope that they may learn to read better, while at the same time they are given the opportunity to excel in other directions, they usually accept the situation quite realistically.

SCHEDULING THE GROUPS. Since the habit of watching television for an average of two or three hours each day has curtailed the amount of reading practice children receive in the home, the teacher must take special care to provide ample time in school for practicing this essential skill. Experience has shown that at least an hour should be devoted to reading in the morning, and half an hour in the afternoon. The teacher should try to divide her time equally among the three groups, spending twenty minutes of the morning hour and ten minutes of the afternoon half-hour with each. Of course, the children are supposed to be reading to themselves while the teacher is working directly with another group. This system provides ninety minutes of reading time daily for each child in each class. The stipulated times do not include instruction in social studies or other content-field reading; nor do they include recreational reading. Separate provision should be made for these. At the very minimum, an hour and a half should be allotted each day to basic reading. Children require at least these ninety minutes to gain practice in essential reading skills.

The best times to schedule reading sessions are in the morning between 9:00 and 11:30 and shortly after 2:00 in the afternoon; the worst times, at 11:30, when the pangs of hunger prevent necessary concentration, and at 1:00, when the post-luncheon torpor sets in.

INSTRUCTING THE GROUPS. Ideally, the teacher should give equal time to each reading group. Sometimes, however, the work has to be staggered, and the teacher may spend more time with one group on one day than with the other two. But in the end she tries to even up the time spent with each group. In the past there was too often a tendency to neglect the top group and to give the slow group twice as much time. For the teacher to get around to each group once, and sometimes twice, during an hour-long session requires skillful planning. "It is like a combination of table-hopping and a three-ring circus!" said one visiting parent who observed such a lesson in the sixth grade. (If teaching three reading groups seems complicated, imagine the task of teaching reading skills, habits, and attitudes to thirty-nine children individually.)

What is likely to happen in a morning reading session in a typical sixth-grade class composed of thirty-nine pupils? In this hypothetical class, ten of the children are in the first group (the fast-moving) and are able to read in the sixth basic reader; twelve are members of the second group (average-moving) and are reading at the fifth reader level; and fourteen children belong to the third group (slow-moving) and are reading in a fourth reader. The remaining three pupils tested so low that they must be given remedial help outside the basic periods.

In this particular morning session, the teacher goes to the first group (fast-moving) and tells the children to look up the new words for the story they are to read today. She has listed six new words on the blackboard. She tells the children to use the glossary at the back of the sixth reader and to note pronunciation and meanings of the new vocabulary.

The teacher then leaves this group and moves to the second group (average-moving) to present five new words by means of clarifying pictures. She then asks the major motivating question, and the children set to work immediately to read the entire story to find the answer.

The teacher now returns to the first group to see if they have looked up their six new words during the ten minutes she spent with the second group. Next, she asks the major motivating question and indicates four thought-provoking questions that she has written on the board to be answered in writing after the children have read the story in their reader.

The teacher then goes to the third group (slow-moving). Until now the members of this group have been reading easy library books. (To manage three groups at different ability levels, it is very helpful to provide library books for the children to keep in their desks to read until the teacher can work with them directly in basic reading instruction.) Now the teacher presents some of the new words for the story by writing them on the blackboard and shows a number of pictures she has collected and mounted to clarify word meaning and to develop background for the story. After this preparation, she asks the major motivating question and does the guided-reading step, asking *who, what, why, when, where,* and *how* questions to help the children comprehend story plot and characters. The children read silently. They may ask about the pronunciation of some of the difficult words. Then the teacher calls upon some child to read aloud the part he believes answers the teacher's question. Often the teacher gives help in oral reading. After the teacher has guided the reading of the story in the third-grade reader, she assigns the seatwork. Today she made the preparation step brief and spent the bulk of her twenty minutes guiding the reading of this group.

Now the teacher returns to the second group and has the children answer their major motivating question and find certain parts of the story to read aloud in answer to her *post check questions.* (These check comprehension and retention *after* the silent reading of a fairly long passage. *Guided-reading questions,* on the other hand, come *before* the silent reading of rather brief passages.) She now explains their seatwork to this group and they get to work on it.

The teacher returns for the third time to the first group and spends a few more minutes with them. (In all, she has worked with them for a total of twenty minutes, in split shifts.) She asks for the answer to the major motivating question. Since even the top group needs practice in oral reading to ensure exercise in accurate pronunciation, articulation, and enunciation, the teacher has the children read several of the conversations aloud, allowing different children to read the parts of the various characters, with another child handling the narrative, or the "in-between part," as children often term it. Following this valuable practice in meaningful oral reading, the teacher sets the group to work on an accompanying exercise in the basic workbook.

During the afternoon half-hour session of this hypothetical sixth grade, the teacher calls up the third group (slow-moving) for ten minutes and helps it check the seatwork assigned that morning. Noting that this group is still having difficulty with attacking new words independently through the use of phonetic analysis, the teacher drills quite thoroughly on the application of the short-vowel rule. She has planned to emphasize one vowel rule each day and to review its application in a great many examples. She then writes on the board five words containing short vowels and mixes them with words containing long vowels. The children are to write them in columns to demonstrate that they know the difference.

The teacher next calls up the second group (average-moving) and checks over the responses to the multiple-choice questions in its workbook assignment. After the exercise is correctly scored, this group is allowed to go to the library corner for free reading.

The teacher then calls up the first group (fast-moving) and checks its seatwork, which today involves diacritical marking at a much higher level than the other two groups are capable of attaining. The scoring requires but a few minutes. One of the girls suggests that sides be chosen, with a captain for each, to hold a brief competition in diacritical marking. The five girls in this first group wish to challenge the five boys. The children want the teacher to call out a word at a time, which the captain of each team is to write on the board and, after a huddle with teammates, mark correctly for pronunciation. The children want to score one point for each correct breve, macron, accent, syllabication vertical, or underlined root word they identify. The teacher agrees that it is a worthwhile game because reading is not lost sight of, and the children are allowed to play it for a few minutes. The girls are leading by one point until the teacher calls out the word "steeple." Instead of splitting it before the *ple,* the team of five girls tells their captain to underline *steep,* erroneously treating it as a root word. Meanwhile, the boys divide "steeple" correctly, and the teacher declares the contest a tie.

After this, the teacher returns to check the slow group and finds that they are having no difficulty with the task of listing the words containing long vowels in one column and those containing short vowels in another. So she now closes the reading drill period for the afternoon, secure in the knowledge that the children know a little more about reading than they did at the start of the period.

When giving instruction in phonetic and structural analysis or, as earlier, in sight word drills, it is best to avoid gadgetry games. The competition described above, the "huddle system," did not lose sight of reading—the words remained words. But too often children are asked to regard words as such things as stepping stones, which, if successfully pronounced, enable the pupil to "cross" the brook drawn on the blackboard. Or again, a ladder is drawn on the board and a word written on each rung. As the children call the words correctly they "climb" the ladder. These and other equally extrinsic devices subordinate reading skill to an artificial activity and hence are of doubtful value. They do not hold the interest of the children long enough to warrant being called motivation. Modern manuals do not recommend extrinsic devices, as a rule. But they present many feasible drills for fixing new words and skills.

TECHNIQUES AND THEIR USE IN DEVELOPING SKILLS

Many skills are utilized to understand material in print, and children need direct instruction in each. What steps can the teacher take to provide a rick background of experience to increase their stock of meaning vocabulary? How can she stimulate a thoughtful attitude in reading? How does she utilize the basic program to improve comprehension in silent reading and skillful interpretation in oral reading? What can she use to improve retention and encourage application?

Ideas from Guidebooks. Specific techniques for promoting essential reading skills, habits, and attitudes, as well as tastes in reading, are presented sequentially in the lesson plans in the teacher's guidebooks at each level of the basic series. Since most guidebooks recognize the need for developing comprehension skills systematically, the teacher should use this helpful source regularly in planning her reading lessons. In this way she will assure the children practice in skimming (partial reading), getting the main idea, noticing supporting details, following a sequence of events, following directions, generalizing, drawing conclusions, anticipating outcomes, and reading critically.

The preparation step of the basic reading lesson helps increase the child's vocabulary. The child also learns new words and concepts during the skills-and-drills step. The guided-reading step shows how many types of comprehension can be stimulated by the proper questioning. As the teacher leads the children through the stories, her questions help facilitate complete understanding of the ideas involved.

Types of Guiding Questions. The teacher should not guide the reading in a basic session with such unchallenging directions as "Read the next line." "Read what he said." "Read the next paragraph." "Read the next page." This type of dry-as-dust guidance is not very helpful, since it places the emphasis on the location of a passage rather than on its meaning. Such guidance does not contribute to the child's development. The child should be helped to decide himself which part of the passage answers the teacher's question. With the help of the teacher's guidebook, supplemented by her knowledge of the needs of her particular group, the successful teacher guides the reading by a rich variety of interesting questions. These questions should be phrased to promote total comprehension; they should be significant, not pointless. Guiding questions for promoting comprehension of the stories in the basic readers should be phrased to help the children

1. To visualize character:	"Read until you find who Jonathan was."
2. To visualize time:	"Read until you find in what year the wagon trains started west."
3. To visualize scene:	"Read to find three parts that describe how the pioneers camped."
4. To identify with the emotions of characters:	"Why was the guide worried about the orphan boy?"
5. To experience sensory images, taste, sound:	"Read to find out how the buffalo steak tasted." (succulent)
6. To notice apt words:	"Which word describes the buffalo's coat better than 'rough'?" (shaggy)
7. To infer, or read between the lines:	"Why did the guide not tell Jonathan that he was lost?"
8. To reason:	"What plans did Jonathan make that showed he was resourceful?"
9. To enjoy the humor:	"The song the pioneers sang around the campfire said that Clementine wore 'herring boxes without topses' for shoes. How do you picture her walking in them?"

Of course, this list does not begin to exhaust the possibilities for promoting good comprehension; but perhaps enough examples have been given to help the teacher form an idea of the scope of the questions. The lesson plans in the teacher's guidebook offer a rich treasury of guiding questions, loaded with skill-building possibilities in comprehension and other elements of reading.

Sequence for Guided Reading. After the teacher has asked a guiding question, the children read silently before they read orally. Children should not be called upon to read orally at sight except in a testing situation such as in the 100-Words Test (see page 393). Reading silently first is a necessary and important preparation for oral reading. (Both forms should be practiced at all grade levels. The tendency to neglect oral reading past the second grade means that children miss receiving such oral-reading advantages as improvement in enunciation, pronunciation, vocabulary, grammar, and sentence structure, as well as such social advantages as development of poise in standing and facing a group and sharing an interpretation.)

A typical session in basic guided reading might follow this sequence. The teacher asks a question to promote a certain type of understanding. The children read silently to find the part that answers the question. (They should not skim the passage but should read everything up to and including the pertinent part.) During the silent reading, they may ask for the pronunciation of some of the words. The teacher furnishes help quickly. She calls on someone to read aloud the part he thinks answers her question. The children momentarily close their books and listen to see if they agree. The teacher may aid in oral reading when the child stumbles or reads word by word in a monotonous voice. The teacher may demonstrate how to read the two- or three-line passage, or she may ask the child which are the most essential, or "sock," words. The teacher may lead a brief discussion to relate the story happenings to the children's personal experiences. She praises the children enthusiastically if they use some of the new words from the story in making comparisons with their own experiences.

Procedure for Corrections. When is it desirable to correct mispronunciations made by the child in his oral reading during a basic reading period? Though correcting the child immediately—

no matter how gently—may cause him momentary distraction from the sense of the passage, it seems better to do so to prevent the wrong pattern of pronunciation being learned by the rest of the class. If the teacher postpones correction until later, she may forget to do so or lack the proper opportunity. Children expect to receive help; they are not so sensitive that they will not accept correction. If children are allowed to go through life mispronouncing words, they will eventually be corrected, perhaps in a most humiliating manner. Extremists may maintain that it threatens a child's security to correct him at the point of error; but security and self-confidence stem from certainty of knowledge, not from ignorance. Teachers should give corrections with a kindly attitude. To kindliness and sympathy should be added a bright, energetic manner, a sense of humor, and loving patience. The teacher's speech, while audible and distinct, should have an encouraging quality. The timid, uncertain, and vacillating teacher will not inspire her pupils. Since children are sensitive to impressions, it behooves the teacher to cultivate vitality and an enthusiastic, purposeful air if she expects the children to show interest. If the teacher sighs wearily and says, "Will the second group come to the reading circle now? Let's try to *finish* the story today," the children are not likely to display much eagerness for participating in basic reading.

Outline of a Sample Lesson Plan Form. To assist the student in grasping relationships between the various parts of a typical basic reading lesson plan, the skeleton outline below has been prepared. It offers the advantage of showing aims, steps, etc., at a glance. Immediately after this short form appears the *detailed* basic reading lesson plan form for student teachers.

OUTLINE OF A BASIC READING LESSON PLAN

I. What (subject matter)

    A. Basic reader:

        For grade:

        Title of story:

        Page of story:

        Page of lesson plan in manual:

      B. Visual aids:

II. Why (aims)

      A. Story—content aims:

          1.

          2. etc.

      B. Reading—skill aims:

          1.

          2. etc.

      C. Social aims:

          1.

          2. etc.

      D. Workbook aims:

          1.

          2. etc.

III. How (method)

      A. Preparation step

          1.

          2.

          3. etc.

      B. Guided—reading step

          Page:

          Page: etc.

      C. Drills step

          1.

          2. etc.

      D. Follow-up step

          1.

          2. etc.

IV. Evaluation

      A. Children's gains:

      B. Teacher's gains:

Sample Basic Lesson Plan Form. This discussion of basic reading is concluded with a form for a basic reading lesson plan intended for student teachers. If it seems long, please remember that it is a *three*-day plan and should be divided, therefore, into three teaching sessions. The student teacher is well aware that the only way to learn effectively is by doing. Therefore, she would enjoy a valuable learning experience by looking up a story in a *basic reader*, finding the lesson plan provided for it in the *teacher's manual*, and then trying her luck at filling out the blanks in the student teacher's lesson plan form below.

FORM FOR A BASIC READING LESSON PLAN
FOR STUDENT TEACHERS

I. What (subject matter)

    A. Basic reader _____

        For grade_____

        Title of the story_____ . _____

        Page of the story_____ Page of lesson plan in manual_____

    B. Visual aids, such as_____

II. Why (aims)

    A. Content aims (story plot and characters)

        1. To visualize the character of_____ aged_____
           and of_____ who is_____

        2. To visualize the time of the story_____
           and the place_____

        3. To identify the emotions of the characters, such as_____
           _____ in order to read the way they
           feel.

        4. To visualize the action depicting_____
           _____

        5. To transfer the following new words from the story to the
           child's permanent stock:_____

    B. Skill aims (to enable the children to use reading skills to get at the content of the story. NOTE: Many other skill aims could be substituted.)

        1. To infer from_____ actions or speechs that
           _____will happen.

        2. To carry on critical thinking, bringing out that a given printed passage_____ does or does not accord with life, experience, or other reading because_____
        _____

3. To read orally the way people talk, expressing the emotions described in the story, such as_____
_____ and_____
_____

4. To apply serial substitution in recognizing new words such as_____

5. To apply vowel rules and syllabication rules in recognizing new words such as_____
_____

C. Social aims (affecting manners, morals, attitudes, interests; or teaching facts required by the social pattern)

1. To learn the fact that_____
2. To awaken interest in_____
3. To locate the "pay dirt," the "nuggets of wisdom," or point of the story to utilize for personal improvement, for example,_____

D. Workbook aims (see aims printed in the margin of the commercial workbook accompanying the basic reader being used)

1. _____
2. _____

III. How (method)

A. Preparation for reading a story in the basic reader

1. Interest will be motivated by means of a discussion of _____ or questions about _____

2. Concepts will be clarified by a display of pictures of_____
_____ or actual objects such as_____

3. Presenting vocabulary
a. Five or six new words from the story will be written on the board. The teacher may tell them outright or, by adroit questioning, she may draw them from the children. Pictures help to elicit new words sometimes. They should be used in the same sense as they are found in the story.

_____ _____ _____
_____ _____ _____

4. Checking retention of new words
   a. "I'm thinking of a word on the board that means the same as_____"
   b. "I'm thinking of a word on the board that means the opposite of_____"
   c. "I'm thinking of a word on the board that matches this picture of a_____"
   d. "I'm thinking of a word of two syllables that means _____" (Use variety in the vocabulary check to maintain interest.)

B. Guiding the reading of the story in the basic reader
   1. Ask the major motivating question as follows:_____
   _____
   2. Have the major motivating question repeated by one child in the reading group.
   3. Ask guiding questions as follows:
   Page_____ Ask a question (for example) to help the children visualize character_____
   _____

   Page_____ Ask questions to help the children visualize the scene_____
   _____
   _____

   Page_____ ⎤ Ask questions to help the children visualize
   Page_____ ⎬ the action and to identify themselves with the
   Page_____ ⎦ emotions of the characters.
   Page_____ Ask a question to help the children to "play detective," that is, to anticipate, or read between the lines. For example, "What is the first hint on this page that makes you think that Bob was a polite boy? Read to find the part that tells about the most thoughtful thing he did."

   1st note: When half or three-fourths of the group have found the answer, call for oral reading by one child.
   2nd note: If there is not time to guide all the reading with oral questions, write some on the board.
   3rd note: If a child reads haltingly, or monotonously, *do not* say, "Read with expression." Say, for example, "How does Bob feel? Well, show with your voice

that he is surprised." Remind the children that television and radio announcers try to convince their audiences by emphasizing certain words in a loud voice. (These are called "sock" words.)

C. Skills and drills (selected from the guidebook. Use those most needed by the group.)

  1. Rereading (a few examples)

    a. "Let us reread to find all the parts that show when the characters in the story were feeling anxious to get to the city." (list pages)

    b. "Let us read all the parts that show when they were surprised." (list pages)

    c. "Let us reread the story in parts to get ready a dramatization of the scene showing——————————————
————————————————————————————— "

  2. Drilling and practicing on consonant substitution for the first and second grades, using these words:———————
—————————————————————————————

  3. Drilling on vowel rules, using these words from the story:
—————————————————————————————

(See teacher's guidebook and feed in the word-analysis exercises as it suggests.)

  4. Improving vocabulary by having the children substitute some apt words from the story for weak all-purpose words (useful for blackboard exercises).

Everyday Way	*Book Way*
he said	he exclaimed
he felt scared	he suffered terror
to go and see	to visit
she was mad	she was indignant
to beg and beg	to beseech

    NOTE: The children will be asked to go to the board and draw connecting lines between ordinary, everyday phrases and more apt phrases quoted from the story. The list can be mimeographed for seatwork as well.

  5. Fixing a word by mixing it in with "foils" (words like it in shape), as in the following: ————————————————
(This particular drill is suitable for first grade only.)

6. Working to improve oral reading by using the "look away" technique. Have the child look away from the book and repeat this sentence from the story: _____ _____. This will help to banish word-by-word reading.
7. Demonstrating to the child how to phrase and how to emphasize "sock" words. Have him do it afterward, using these sentences from the story:

_____

_____

8. Workbook pages. Explain aims for doing the exercises in the workbook, and make directions perfectly clear.

D. Follow-up of the story in the basic reader
   1. Let the children discuss the point of the story, which is that

   _____

   _____

   and relate the point to their experience. Call on two or three to describe experiences similar to those in the story.
   2. Bring in stories or poems with a theme similar to the story, such as_____

   _____

   3. Have the children prepare a dramatization of the story in the reader if it lends itself to this type of follow-up. Use paper-bag masks or simple costumes and properties. Divide the story into scenes and choose the cast from those who remember best what characters said and did.
   4. Let the children draw their favorite scene such as_____

   _____

   _____

IV. Evaluation

   A. Children's gains
      1. Facts learned, such as_____
      2. Habits practiced, such as_____
      3. Skills introduced, such as_____
      4. Interests stimulated, such as_____
      5. Attitudes encouraged, such as_____
      6. Experiences enjoyed, such as_____

   B. The Teacher's gains (in professional skills)
      1. Evidence of growth in holding interest_____

2. Evidence of growth in making explanations clear and using examples understandable to the children————————

3. Evidence of improvement in timing————————————
4. Evidence of growth in the ability to elicit more participation from the children————————————————

QUESTIONS AND ACTIVITIES

1. What are the four fields of reading?
2. What is the relationship between reading and child development?
3. What child needs are met by the four main steps of a basic plan?
4. What comprehension skills should be taught through the basic reading work?
5. What are the implications, if any, of the new emphasis on speed reading for instruction in the intermediate grades?
6. Examine a basic manual and children's workbook to verify the claims made for their skill-building functions.
7. What is the most widely used plan for organizing reading groups?
8. Why is it not advisable to import isolated phonics systems? What advantages can you name for using the word-analysis program outlined in the teacher's guidebook lesson plans?
9. Nine types of guiding questions are listed. Why should there be such a variety?
10. In your opinion, what is the best time during the school day to teach reading?
11. What is more effective in oral-reading instruction than cautioning children to "read with expression"?
12. Secure a reader and the teacher's manual and children's workbook accompanying it, and fill out the blanks in the Form for a Basic Reading Lesson Plan for Student Teachers. (See page 190, and also refer to the short form immediately preceding it to see at a glance what is involved.)

SELECTED REFERENCES

DAWSON, MILDRED A., and HARRY A. BAMMAN. *Fundamentals of Basic Reading Instruction.* New York: Longmans, Green & Co., Inc., 1959.

DURRELL, DONALD D. *Improving Reading Instruction.* New York: Harcourt, Brace & World, Inc., 1956.

GENTRY, LILLIAN. "A Study of the Vocabulary Load of Sixty-Six Preprimers," *Journal of Educational Research,* XLIII (March 1950), 525–32.

GATES, ARTHUR I. *The Improvement of Reading* (3d ed.). New York: The Macmillan Co., Publishers (a division of the Crowell-Collier Publishing Co.), 1947.

HARRIS, ALBERT J. *How To Increase Reading Ability* (4th ed.). New York: Longmans, Green & Co., Inc., 1961.

HILDRETH, GERTRUDE. *Teaching Reading.* New York: Holt, Rinehart & Winston, Inc., 1958.

HUSBANDS, KENNETH L. (ed.). *Teaching Elementary School Subjects.* New York: The Ronald Press Co., 1961.

KARLIN, ROBERT. "Machines and Reading: A Review of Research," *Clearing House,* XXXII (February 1958), 349–52.

McKEE, PAUL G. *The Teaching of Reading in the Elementary School.* Boston: Houghton Mifflin Co., 1948.

McKIM, MARGARET. *Guiding Growth in Reading.* New York: The Macmillan Co., 1955.

NATIONAL COMMITTEE ON READING. *A Report on the Teaching of Reading.* Part I. *The Twenty-fourth Yearbook.* Bloomington, Ill.: Public School Publishing Co., 1925.

NATIONAL SOCIETY FOR THE STUDY OF EDUCATION. *The Teaching of Reading in the Elementary School.* Part II. *Forty-eighth Yearbook.* Chicago: University of Chicago Press, 1949.

REEVE, OLIVE R. "The Vocabulary of Seven Primary Reading Series," *Elementary English,* XXXV (April 1958), 237–39.)

ROBINSON, HELEN M. *Materials of Reading.* Supplementary Educational Monographs, No. 86. Chicago: University of Chicago Press, 1958.

RUSSELL, DAVID H. *The Basic Program in the Modern School.* Contributions to Reading, No. 1. Boston: Ginn & Co., 1947.

YOAKAM, GERALD A. *Basal Reading Instruction.* New York: McGraw-Hill Book Co., Inc., 1955.

8

READING IN THE FIRST GRADE

During recent years a number of innovations have been introduced on an experimental basis at the first-grade level, to compete with the basal-reading-series approach. These new, highly individualized methods stress a one-to-one relationship between the teacher and the pupils. Depending upon the advocates and the locale, they are variously known as individual guidance or self-selective reading; the language-experience approach or the individual experience approach; and permissive grouping.

In quite a different direction, there has been a resurgence of interest in "rugged phonics," at the primary level particularly—a going back to drill, and denatured drill at that, on hundreds of words and "word families" (*ug, gug, nug, sug, zug,* etc.) before beginning any reading for thought.

In the course of this chapter these methods will receive attention. However, since the majority of first-grade teachers make use of the basic approach to teaching beginning reading, the greater part of the chapter will be devoted to such instruction. A tristate survey[1] (Ohio, Pennsylvania, and West Virginia) revealed typically that most teachers in the study preferred *systematic* provisions for word analysis and other reading skills, generally "in close conjunction with the material of the basic reader." The basic plan makes use of a graded series of first-grade readers, including the use of one or more reading-readiness books, several preprimers, a

[1] Barbara A. Purcell, "Methods of Teaching Reading: A Report on a Tristate Survey," *Elementary School Journal,* LVIII (May 1958), 449–53.

primer, and finally a book one. The chances are that many of the persons reading these words learned to read in the first grade by means of a basic primer and book one. The practice of using a basal series to provide for systematic growth in reading has evidently met a continuing need, for it has stood the test of time and, happily, does not fall into the category about which Eleanor M. Johnson[2] writes, "The history of American elementary education is strewn with the remains of potentially good ideas that had a brief popularity—and then disappeared, leaving scarcely a trace of influence on classroom practice." Today, in addition to the graded readers, a basic series provides a guidebook or manual, offering lesson plans for the teacher, and a workbook, presenting practice exercises for the children.

The first part of the first grade, however, is usually dedicated not to actual reading of print but to finding out if the children are ready for reading and, if they are not, to carrying on a program of activities designed to promote readiness. For some children, the process requires only a few weeks. For others, the period may extend into months. Since it would be misleading to start a discussion of the first-grade program with a discussion of actual reading instruction, when a gradual approach has been recommended, a review of the material on reading readiness in Chapters 5 and 6 is presented below. After a brief summation of the teacher's planning and the children's activities during the readiness period, this chapter will take up suggestions for actual basic instruction in reading at the first-grade level.

MOVING FROM READINESS TO READING

To avoid the error of asking children to read before they are equal to the task, the teacher employs a variety of mental and readiness tests, interviews, and conferences to appraise each child's degree of readiness in five areas. Intelligence tests discover whether the child has achieved the mental level required for dealing with symbols. Data concerning the child's general health, his vision, hearing, and speech round out the picture of his physical

[2] Curriculum Letter No. 35. File: Reading Grades 1–6, Middletown, Conn.: Department of School Services and Publications, Wesleyan University, 1958.

readiness. A number of tests of emotional reactions are available, if needed, though they are usually given not by the teacher but by the school psychologist. Actually, according to many studies, the teacher's own observation, supported by evidence gathered in parent conferences, helps to uncover most of the important facts about the child's emotional readiness. Such a conference also permits some insight into the child's social readiness and language background.

After appraising readiness in these five factors, the teacher makes use of a variety of activities to develop the language, visual, and mental skills directly related to reading, without introducing the act of reading itself. The teacher plans lessons to promote reading readiness in these skills, that include the use of both reading-readiness books and firsthand experiences such as field trips and other activities connected with the unit of work. Through both these types of experience, the children develop mental concepts and a meaningful vocabulary. Reading-readiness books also afford valuable practice in teaching left-to-right directional responses and visual observation of similarities and differences. They can also be used to encourage such mental skills as the ability to see relationships, to make associations, and to recognize a sequence of ideas. Emotional readiness, social readiness, and language readiness will develop as by-products of other activities if the teacher seizes every opportunity to build the child's self-confidence, arouse his interest, and help him to adjust to the group. Consultation with the parents is necessary during the readiness period so that they are informed of the reasons for delaying actual reading, in certain cases, until the child can adequately cope with this difficult skill.

Part of the program of reading readiness consists of the use of experience stories based on the children's group activities. The teacher prints these stories on large charts and the children "read" them back. Shortly after the chart work is initiated in the group, the teacher may screen out those who find it easy to read words, pronounce them, and recognize them the next time they see them after a few exposures—in short, those who can read most of the experience stories on the charts fluently. The teacher can give these children readiness work leading directly to the vocabulary of the preprimer. For example, she may ask the members of this top group to draw an airplane and a helicopter. She can then show the children how to label each drawing with appropriate phrases which they will soon find useful in reading the preprimer.

> Up, up, up.
> See it go up.
>
> Down, down, down.
> See it come down.

Or the teacher may urge the children in this accelerated group to draw pictures of themselves raking leaves in the yard, or doing something else to help at home, after which she can lead the children to label each drawing, perhaps after this fashion:

> See Bob.
> See Bob work.
> See Bob work, work, work.

INTRODUCING THE FIRST BOOK

It will not be long before the children in the top group are ready for their first book—the preprimer. The second group may need an additional few weeks of practice in more advanced reading-readiness books before starting the first preprimer, as well as additional work with experience stories. The slow group may continue with reading-readiness experiences at an easy level for several months, or even longer.

Class Arrangement. The teacher should arrange the beginning reading group quite close to her. Each pupil carries his chair from its accustomed place at the work table and places it in a semi-circle of chairs facing the teacher and the blackboard or big chart. This arrangement is usually known as the "reading circle" and is a very important part of the first-grade reading program (see illustrations in Chapter 3).

Before passing the preprimers to the members of this group, the teacher should provide quiet work for the other two groups who are still developing their readiness for reading. The middle group may be seated at the work tables, drawing pictures to illustrate its latest field trip or other group experiences. The slow group may be seated in the library corner, looking at the many picture storybooks available for their enjoyment on a low table or in nearby bookcases. The library corner, which is just as essential to the reading program as the reading circle, should be made as attractive as possible, with gaily painted table, chairs, bookshelves, and a variety of books to interest the children. Often flowers, plants, and gay figurines are placed on the table and bookcases to give an added note of attractiveness. Sometimes, as in this case, children are sent to the library corner; sometimes they are allowed to go there when they have completed their assignments.

With the class satisfactorily arranged, the teacher seats herself in a chair facing the accelerated group in the reading circle and hands each child a copy of the preprimer. She then encourages the children to glance through the pictures and ask questions about them.

Care of Books. The fun of becoming acquainted with new books should be supplemented by learning how to care for them. Slips of paper, each bearing a child's name, may be clipped to the books; then, assured of receiving the same one each day, the child will assume more responsibility for keeping it as clean as when he received it. The teacher should show the children how to open a book carefully, a few pages from front to back at a time, to avoid breaking the binding, and how to turn pages by lifting the upper right corner with the fingers of the right hand. She should caution the children against putting books on the floor or sitting on them while waiting for a lesson to start—both being abuses commonly accorded books in primary classrooms.

The Initial Lesson. Most children are delighted to begin reading from a book filled with printed words instead of pictures. If the children have had an interesting readiness program, they will be well prepared to start this reading. Since the initial lesson is of great importance in the child's mind, the teacher should handle this introduction with great skill.

STARTING THE FIRST STORY. The first story in a preprimer usually presents the most important boy and girl characters and contains a few short sentences about each. Let us say that the first picture shows Bob holding a large toy balloon shaped like an astronaut in a silver space suit. The caption reads: See Bob. The second picture shows his younger sister in a pretty dress. The caption reads: See Sue. The third picture shows the balloon starting to get away from Bob. The caption reads: See it go. The fourth picture shows Bob jumping every high and catching the balloon. Sue is standing by, laughing. The caption reads: Funny, funny Bob.

First the teacher leads an introductory discussion about the children and the action depicted in the pictures. The teacher says, "Look at the picture. Who can this boy be? What is he playing with? What is his name? The line under the picture tells us. It says, 'See Bob.'" (The teacher makes sure that all the children in the reading group frame the right part.) Next the teacher calls upon a child to reread the sentence orally. The teacher, of course, actually reads the lines in the first four-page story, and the children read back what they have just heard.

ENDING THE FIRST STORY. After the remaining three pages of the story have been "read" by a repetition of the technique described above, the teacher should make an interesting comment about the next day's story, concerning Bob and his pet dog. It is deflating to end the lesson with an unimaginative direction such as "Close your books and take your seats." Left with the anticipation of another story, the children return to their seats from the reading circle, feeling proud and happy that something very special has happened that day: They have read a real book!

Often overlooked by critics of easy beginning books, most of which contain much repetition, is the fact that reading simple little sentences gives the first-grade child, no matter how "sophisticated" (from having watched TV twenty hours a week), the same delight that an adult American enjoys when first he manages to read a simple little sentence in Spanish or French, for example. Needless to say, in reading a foreign language much repetition is welcomed for the security it permits. In a manner of speaking, print is like a new language to the child.

PLANNING THE READING PERIOD

Planning Seatwork. To ensure uninterrupted time with one reading group, a teacher must plan seatwork for the other two groups. She may prepare mimeographed assignment sheets and distribute these among the children who are not in the reading circle at the moment. Some suggestions for seatwork for the three ability groups (slow, average, fast) in the class follow:

Seatwork for the Reading-Readiness Group (Slow Group)

Sheet of objects.

The child circles the one that is different from the rest and colors all those that are alike the same color.

Sheet of animals or objects with missing parts.

Seatwork for the Preprimer Group (Middle Group)

The child draws the missing parts.

Paper folded or lined into four equal parts, top of each part labeled "one ball," "two balls," "three balls," "four balls."

The child draws a picture in each part to illustrate the caption. Their drawings will show the teacher whether they have read the terms correctly. (Creative drawing.)

Sheet with outline of a side view of a stairway with four steps, with caption "See Sue go up."

The child draws Sue going up.

The drawing will show the teacher whether the child has understood the caption.

Sheet with outline of a see saw, with caption "Bob is up. Sue is down."

The child draws Bob and Sue in their correct places. (Semi-creative drawing.)

Seatwork for the Primer Group (Top Group)

Sheets with sentences from stories in the primer, with blanks left in the sentences and several words below which can be used to fill in the blanks.

The child selects the word which best fits the blank space in the sentence and draws a line from the chosen word to the blank in the sentence. (Multiple choice.)

Sheet with printed or written directions such as "Draw the part of the story you liked best."

The child carries out the directions.

The foregoing suggestions for individually assigned seatwork are to supplement the exercises in the workbook accompanying the basic preprimer and primer. Whether made by the teacher or prepared commercially, seatwork assignments should afford the children practice in reading skills. These assignments are not mere stopgaps to keep the children quiet or busy. There is little educational value in such an assignment as passing around the outline of a pig or rabbit and requesting the children to fill in the color. This and similar techniques fall into the lamentable category of "busywork." The carefully planned assignment can only be one that helps children grow in reading skills.

Planning and Working with the Three Groups. To clarify the process of working with the three groups, a specific example of one method is presented here. In this case the slow group is reading the readiness booklet; the middle group, the preprimer; the top group, the primer or book one.

The teacher takes the slowest group to the reading circle for work in a reading-readiness booklet. After completing guided picture reading of one or two pages according to the lesson suggestions in the teacher's manual, the teacher explains the seatwork the children are to do and sends them back to their tables.

Then the teacher brings the middle group (average ability) to the reading circle. These children now are reading in the preprimer. She goes through the preparation step and the guided-reading step. (For a report of an actual preprimer lesson, see page 209.) The following day, or possibly that afternoon, this group may have rereading (part of the skills-and-drills step) or the follow-up step. The teacher explains their seatwork and dismisses the group to their tables.

The teacher now calls up the top group, which contains the best readers in the class. These children are reading in the primer or book one of the basic series used in that school district. She goes through the preparation and guided-reading steps with them. It may be that she had gone through these steps yesterday; in that case, she may be continuing with skills and drills and follow-up. She assigns seatwork to this group and tells the children they may go to the library corner to read when they have finished it. Though most children are not capable of much independent reading at this level, those in the top group are usually able to read in supplementary preprimers and primers.

Planning Additional Activities. Some first-grade teachers permit children a wide choice of activity after they have finished a reading assignment. They even permit children to hammer and saw in construction work, play with blocks, practice dramatizations, or engage in other activities which distract the other group trying to read with the teacher. But the best method is to let the children do seatwork, read library books, work on jigsaw puzzles with educational value, match words and numbers, or draw and paint quietly. An atmosphere of *reading quiet* should be established and maintained.

Another activity often used after the regular assignment is completed is the "flash-card drill." Children are paired to help each other recognize the words lettered or printed on the cards that the teacher flashes rapidly. Usually a skilled reader is paired with a poor reader. A repetition of this type may enable children to learn certain words, but it does so by sacrificing meaningful context. Constance McCullough, professor of education, San Francisco State College, has pointed out that sometimes children left to themselves with a set of flash cards learn to identify the correct words by the smudges or tears on the cards themselves.[3] It is better to choose from the variety of exercises found in the drills section of the manual than to rely on flash cards.

[3] "Flash Cards—The Opiate of the Reading Program," *Elementary English,* XXXII (October 1955), 379–81.

The Reading Program and the Daily Schedule. There are many ways of scheduling the school day in the first grade. The plan that follows is intended as a sample for beginning teachers. It shows how the three reading groups might be scheduled in the daily program in the first garde. This schedule differs from the daily program previously outlined for reading-readiness work.

9:00 to 9:10	Pledge to the flag, roll call, collection of money for morning milk and hot lunches.
9:10 to 9:25	Music, children singing rote songs.
9:25 to 9:30	Number work (also taught incidentally during the school day as children add papers, milk straws, and count for games).
9:30 to 10:00	Unit of work (such activities as drawing, painting, working in clay, building).
10:00 to 10:10	Evaluation of work done on the unit. Cleanup.
10:10 to 10:20	Recess.
10:20 to 11:20	Reading with three groups: one in primer, one in preprimer, and one in reading readiness..
11:20 to 11:40	Games, physical education.
11:40 to 12:00	Listening to stories by the teacher.
12:00 to 1:00	Lunch hour.
1:00 to 1:15	Listening to story reading.
1:15 to 1:35	Music and rhythms.
1:35 to 1:50	Drills-and-skills type of reading with three groups (includes doing seatwork and checking it).
1:50 to 2:00	Play time (outdoors if possible).
2:00 to 2:30	Story time, dramatization, poetry, record playing, art.

CONDUCTING A PREPRIMER LESSON

Appearing below is a basic reading *lesson plan*, written by a first-grade teacher. Following this is a *stenographic report* of the reading lesson in the preprimer which she taught from the plan. Both the lesson *plan* and the actual *lesson* taught from it show that this teacher is acquainted with recommended procedures and has kept her aims firmly in mind. This plan is shorter than the student teacher form on page 190. Not only is a preprimer story very short, but this teacher has had years of experience in teaching reading and does not need to write down all details.

A PREPRIMER LESSON PLAN

I. What (subject matter)

  A. Basic reader: *Fun with Pets and Toys* (preprimer)

  For Grade: One
  Title of story: Tips
  Pages of story: 5–8
  Pages of lesson plan in manual: 16–18

  B. Visual Aids: Picture clipped from magazine, showing a very clean-looking dog.

II. Why (aims)

  A. Contents of story and reading-skill aims

  To help the children:
  1. To visualize the characters: Bob, aged six, and his young dog named Tips.
  2. To visualize the time (the present) and place (a back yard).
  3. To identify with the emotions during oral reading, showing with the voice Bob's *eagerness* to get his pet clean, his *surprise* when the dog ran off and his *amusement* when the dog hid in the doghouse.
  4. To recognize the new words: "Tips," "come," and to review the words in yesterday's story: "Bob," "funny." (Pages 1–4.)

  B. Social aims

  1. To awaken a sense of responsibility in care of pets.

III. How (method)

  A. Preparation or motivation

  1. Show picture of the clean-looking dog and ask, "What do we do to help keep dogs clean?" Bring out the need for washing them. Ask what is used.
  2. Present the new words: "Tips," "come."
    a. Tell the children they will meet a new book friend—a black dog with white tips on his ears, nose, and tail, called *Tips*. Print word on the chalkboard. Have some child read the word after it is pronounced.
    b. Tell the children that our new friend Bob was the owner of Tips. Bob wanted to give Tips a bath one day. So he

called him. Insert the word "Come" in front of "Tips" to form "Come, Tips," and read phrase. Frame the whole phrase and have it read.

3. Checking retention of new words:
   a. Use riddles: I'm thinking of a word that tells the dog's name. (Have a child frame it and say it.)
   b. To have "come" identified, say it rhymes with "some" and means the opposite of "go," etc.

B. Guided reading (including guided picture study)

p. 5   Have the children look at the picture on this page and describe what they see. Ask what Bob is doing. Bring out what he has ready for the bath. Ask what Tips is doing. Then have the printed phrase "Come, Tips" read. Encourage a coaxing tone of voice when it is read aloud, after silent reading.

pp. 6–8 Continue similarly, asking purposeful guiding questions. Have all children in the group read silently to find the answer to question. Then call on one to read aloud.

C. Drills

1. Have the four-page story reread, this time without teacher guidance. Have each child who reads orally describe the action in the picture before reading aloud the printed words.

2. Write the new sight word "come" at the top of a column containing this word mixed in with "foils." Have a child underline and pronounce the word "come" every time he sees it:

come
corn
come
came
come
comb
come

3. Pass workbooks of seatwork and review the new words: "Tips," "come." Review two familiar words learned in the first lesson: "Sue," "funny." The word "and" was drilled on by use of rebus technique prior to preprimer work, i..e., pictures of familiar pairs—cake, pie; ham, eggs (with words "and" joining them).

D. Follow-up step

    1. Invite the children to discuss the point of the story, or the part they enjoyed reading the most. Ask them to describe attempts they have made to wash their pets. Stress kindness to animals.

    2. Sound out the class regarding any snapshots the members may have at home showing themselves photographed with their pets. If enough snapshots are available, a display may be set up, with captions to give opportunity for extra reading.

    3. Not only this particular reading group but the entire class will enjoy hearing read the amusing picture storybook by Gene Zion called *Harry, the Dirty Dog* (published by Harper & Row, New York).

IV. Evaluation

    A. Children's gains (to be filled in after lesson is taught.)

    B. Teacher's gains (to be filled in after lesson is taught.)

Now, having read the teacher's plan, it should prove of help to study next a stenographic report of the lesson as it was actually taught. It is worth noting that this experienced teacher kept rather closely to her original plan, with due allowance for important "leads" and contributions from her pupils. After studying the stenographic report of the lesson, why not try to fill in the *Evaluation* above? Consult the list of aims and then decide whether or not they were achieved.

STENOGRAPHIC REPORT OF A PREPRIMER LESSON

A. Preparation for Reading

    1. *Motivation or Approach to the Story*

        TEACHER (displaying a picture of a small dog, which she has clipped from a magazine): This dog is very clean looking. What do we do to help keep dogs clean? (Children discuss.) How do you give your dog a bath?

The teacher elicits the response that a pan of water, a cake of soap, and a scrubbing brush are needed.

        TEACHER: What does your dog do when you give him a bath?

The teacher encourages several children to contribute ideas drawn from their personal experience or observation.

2. *Presentation of New Words*

The teacher prints each new word on the board as she says it and calls on an individual child to read it back.

TEACHERS The boy in the story we will read today is named Bob. He has a dog. The dog is black all over except for white tips on his nose, ears, paws, and tail. So his name is (the teacher pauses and writes) *Tips*.

TEACHER: Bob wants to give Tips a bath. So Bob says, *Come, Tips*. (Teacher writes in print script.)

TEACHER: Then to make Tips hurry more, Bob says, *Come, come*. (Teacher writes.)

TEACHER: Then Tips does something funny. So Bob says, *Funny, funny Tips*.
Come, Tips, come. (Teacher writes.)

3. *Vocabulary Check*

The teacher calls on individual children to go to the blackboard to frame certain words or phrases with cupped hands. [Pointing is not recommended. It tends to focus attention on the word letter nearest the finger, instead of encouraging careful scrutiny of the entire word.]

TEACHER: Who can find the sentence on the board that tells:
What Bob says when he wants Tips to come?
What Bob says when Tips is slow in coming?
What Bob says when Tips is funny?
What Bob wants Tips to do when he is funny?
Find the name of Bob's dog.
Find the word *funny* as many times as you can.

B. Guiding the Reading: Picture Study

1. *Asking the Motivating Question*

TEACHER: We are going to read our story today to find out what funny thing happened when Bob wanted to give Tips a bath. (The preprimers are distributed.)
NOTE: The teacher makes certain that each child opens the book to the first picture. As the children discuss the pictures which carry the story, thus weaving a background for the few printed words, they make spontaneous comments. (The vocabulary possible at this level is so meager that the pictures must of necessity carry the thread of the plot. To help the children master the recognition of new words, only two or three are introduced each day. These new words receive a maximum of repetition.)

2. *Asking Guiding Questions, Page by Page.*

Come, Tips.

PICTURE STUDY

Teacher: Let's all look at this picture. Who is in the picture?
A child is called upon and answers.

Teacher: What is Bob doing?
A child expresses an opinion.

Teacher: What is Tips doing?
A child answers in detail, perhaps recalling the reason for the
    dog's name.

Teacher: What things do you see in the picture that show that
    Bob is going to give Tips a bath?
Several children list the articles, speaking one at a time, and an-
    swering in sentences.

GUIDED READING

Teacher: Bob wants Tips to come, so what does Bob say?
Child reads: *Come, Tips.*

Come, Tips.
Come, come.

Picture Study

> Teacher: Now we'll look at the picture on this page and see what is happening. What is Tips doing?
> A child describes the way the dog is jumping back.

> Teacher: How does Bob look?
> A child expresses an opinion, interpreting the picture.

> Teacher: What is Bob trying to do?
> A child answers that he is probably trying to coax the dog to come nearer to him.

Guided Reading

> Teacher: Bob is saying something to Tips. He is trying to get him to come. What does he say first?
> A child reads: *Come, Tips.*

> Teacher: Then Bob coaxes Tips to come. Read what Bob says next.
> A child reads: *Come, come.*

Funny Tips

PICTURE STUDY

> Teacher: I wonder if Tips will come! Let's look at this picture. What is happening?
> A child answers, probably enjoying the humor of the situation.

> Teacher: Tips looks funny running away, doesn't he? Why do you think Tips did that?
> A child explains that Tips doesn't like baths.

> Teacher: What is Bob doing?
> A child volunteers that Bob looks surprised.

> Teacher: How would you feel if you were Bob and your pet ran away when you wanted to give him a bath?

GUIDED READING

> Teacher: Now we'll read what Bob says when Tips is so funny. Who can read the line under the picture?
> A child reads: *Funny Tips.*

> Teacher (referring to the picture again): Yes, Tips certainly looks funny running away that fast.

Funny, funny Tips.
Come, Tips, come.

PICTURE STUDY

> Teacher: Let's look at the last picture in the story and see if Tips gets a bath.
>
> The children inspect the picture and chat together, enjoying the humor of the situation depicted.

> Teacher: What did Tips do?
>
> A child explains that Tips ran to hide so that he wouldn't have a bath.

> Teacher: How do you think Bob feels? Why is he laughing?
>
> A child volunteers an answer.

GUIDED READING

> Teacher: Tips is really funny, isn't he? Let's read and find out what Bob is saying to Tips. He is a funny, funny dog. So what is the first thing Bob says?
>
> A child reads: *Funny, funny Tips.*

> Teacher: Does Bob still want Tips to come? The last line tells us. What does it say? Read it.
>
> A child reads: *Come, Tips, come.*

3. *Conversing About the Story*

TEACHER: How do you suppose Tips is going to get a bath? Who helps you when you bathe your dog?

A child may respond that his father does.

TEACHER: Perhaps Bob's father will help him to give Tips a bath. Did you like this story? Which part did you think was the funniest? Has your dog ever played a trick on you? Does your dog have a doghouse? Do you put fresh water out for your dog every day? How else can we take care of our pets? Why is it necessary to keep them clean?

The children converse about these and other points they themselves raise, always being guided to speak one at a time, to keep to the point, and to listen politely as others talk. [The above steps in the lesson may consume fifteen or twenty minutes with an average group in the first grade.]

C. Skills and Drills

[This part of the lesson can be taught later in the day or perhaps the next day. It is used to promote fluency, enrich the vocabulary, and encourage retention of story facts in sequence. And, of course, this activity develops the imagination.]

1. *Procedures for Rereading*

Page 5

TEACHER (setting an example for dealing with the picture and verbal text): Bob had a cute little black and white dog named Tips. One warm summer day Bob thought to himself: This is a good day to give Tips a bath. So Bob got a basin of water, a cake of soap, and a scrubbing brush. He saw Tips playing on the green grass, so he called to him: *Come, Tips.* (Teacher sweeps hand under the line in the preprimer book and reads the line aloud.)

Page 6

A CHILD (imitating the teacher and weaving a narrative drawn from his imagination to go with the picture): Tips didn't like to take a bath, and when he saw the pan of water and the cake of soap he knew what they meant. So he jumped back just in time. Bob really wanted to give Tips a bath right away. So Bob called to him and said, *Come, Tips.* (Child indicates the line and reads it orally.) But Tips wouldn't come. Then Bob said: *Come, come.* (Child reads the line from the book.)

[The teacher continues similarly with the other two pages of the story. But such proficiency does not come without training—time and patience are needed to elicit fluent descriptions from the children (preferably in the past tense) of the action portrayed in the pictures. Actually, reading at this level deals with what might be termed "talking picture stories." Eventually the children develop the ability to exercise their imagination in describing the action in the picture, which is closely tied in with the few words of print below.]

2. Seatwork

[To give practice in recognizing the new words in this story and thus prevent memorization, a piece of seatwork (nine by twelve inches) may be given to each child in the group. A facsimile is presented below. The pupils underline the correct choice.]

D. Follow-up

[1. The children discuss the proper care of dogs or other pets. They elaborate stories about funny or clever tricks their dogs or other pets do. Then the teacher encourages the children to make illustrations in crayon or finger paint of their pets at play, or of the dog or cat next door or down the street.

2. Books such as those listed below can be displayed on the library table as a follow-up of the reading about Tips. The list consists of books about dogs which have pictures of interest to young children.

There Was Tamie. D. and M. Bryan, New York: Dodd, Mead & Co., Inc.

The Pup Himself. Morgan Dennis. New York: The Viking Press, Inc.

Angus and the Ducks. Marjorie Flack. New York: Doubleday & Co., Inc.

Harry, the Dirty Dog. Gene Zion. New York: Harper & Row.]

WORKING WITH FOREIGN-LANGUAGE-SPEAKING CHILDREN

When a language other than English is spoken in the home, children must learn to speak English in the first grade before they are ready to learn to read English. Theirs is a word-recognition as well as a readiness problem.

Whether the teacher has only a few children with foreign-language backgrounds or an entire class of such children, she should use the direct method of teaching. A procedure is outlined below for a lesson in a simple, everyday activity—getting ready for school—which illustrates the use of the direct method with a group of Spanish-speaking children. In applying this method the teacher must always speak slowly and clearly, repeating the phrase with a minimum of variation to assure the word the familiarity that fosters a feeling of security in the children. It is helpful if the teacher can use a Spanish phrase first; if she cannot, gestures and actions usually will convey the meaning to the children. Of course, after introducing the phrase, the teacher should discontinue her use of Spanish, or the children will not be motivated to learn English.

LESSON FOR FOREIGN-LANGUAGE CHILDREN

I. What (subject matter)

Visual aids: a pan of water, a bar of soap, a towel, paper towels, a washcloth, a comb, a hairbrush, a mirror. Pictures of children combing their hair, brushing their teeth, taking care of their clothes.

II. Why (aims)

1. To teach new words, such as water, soap, towel
2. To help the children use English idioms
3. To help the children pronounce words correctly
4. To replace the Spanish rising inflection with the American habit of dropping the voice at the end of a sentence
5. To teach American standards of grooming
6. To make the children feel at ease in the class

III. How (method)

TEACHER: Juanito, come here, please. (She motions to him and he comes to her.)
Look! (She indicates the pan of water.) This is water. Juanito, tell me *This is water.*

JUANITO: Dees ees oo–aw–ter.

TEACHER: Good! (The teacher does not correct his pronunciation at this point. This is not his last chance to pronounce the words correctly.)
Juanito, tell me *This is soap.* (The Spanish word for *soup* sounds much like the English word soap, and Juanito may appear surprised. It would help if the teacher knew the Spanish word for soap, *jabón* (pronounced hah-BONE).

JUANITO: Dees ees soap.

TEACHER: Good! (She motions him to his seat and uses the identical procedure with Lupe, Jorge, and Pedro.)

TEACHER: Look. This is a towel. (She shows it to Juanito.) Tell me *This is a towel.*

JUANITO: Dees ees a towel.

TEACHER: I wash my hands with soap and water. I dry my hands on a towel. (She suits the action to the words.)

JUANITO: (He imitates the actions of the teacher, using the same soap and water but a paper towel. He tries to fit the words to the action. The teacher cues him in pronouncing the sentences.)

TEACHER: *This is a toothbrush.* (She displays it.) Tell me *This is a toothbrush.*

(The lesson continues.)

After all the children in the group have had a turn acting out and pronouncing a given phrase, the teacher displays appropriate pictures which she has clipped from magazines and guides the

children in labeling them. She might display on the bulletin board
a picture of a boy washing his face. Over a period of a week the
following lines might be added under the picture—at the children's
halting dictation:

> The boy washes his face.
> The boy uses water.
> The boy uses soap.
> The boy uses a towel.
>
> He washes his neck.
> He washes his ears.
> He washes his hands.
> He brushes his teeth.
> He combs his hair.

The children will need a great deal of help in pronouncing English words correctly. Using a mirror, the teacher may help the
child compare his lip movements as he says certain words with
the way the teacher forms hers.

The direct method builds the meaning of English words and
sentences on a solid foundation consisting of acting out a phrase,
saying it, and dictating a little story for the teacher to record.
Later the children try to read back the stories they have helped to
compose.

At every stage in her teaching, the teacher must display a
friendly, warm-hearted attitude to put the children at ease. She
will be amply rewarded when she remembers that nothing makes
the child feel more lonely than being unable to understand what
people are saying. After sufficient vocabulary and concepts have
been learned, the children are ready for the first preprimer.

PLANNING THE YEAR'S PROGRAM

The Primer and Book One Period. Usually the top and middle
groups finish the preprimers and primer by the end of the first
grade. But they should not be forced to finish a certain number of
primary readers at the cost of skipping important lesson steps.
Quite frequently the top group will finish book one of the basic
series as well. At this level the stories are longer, the new words

are introduced faster, and the plot thickens a little as the number of concepts increases.

The Number of Books To Be Read. There are always some teachers who ask how many books children in the first grade should be expected to cover between September and June. In the past, first-grade teachers were supposed to guide children through as many primary books as possible. The emphasis in reading practice was upon quantity rather than quality. Today teaching practice is different, and represents a sensible improvement. Teachers are not so interested in how many books are read in the beginning levels; they are interested in how much the children have gained from their reading. It is pointless to hurry a child through three pre-primers, the primer, and book one of the basic series, plus six or seven supplementary preprimers and primers of other series, for he may miss the bulk of the meanings involved. Merely pronouncing words is not true reading. What is of prime value is the amount of personal enrichment gained by the child from his reading. For example, he can learn from a preprimer story that, when a big umbrella folded down over Sally, she was not a crybaby but took the mishap in stride, saw the joke on herself, and laughed. From this same four-page story, the children who read it meaningfully can be taught to note also how proud Sally's older brother and sister were when she did not cry. Even at the primary level the reading criterion should be: Does the child know more about himself and other people as a result of reading?

Duration of Time on a Story. In the past it was common practice to read a story a day and, in some cases, even two. Inevitably, the meaning of the content was neglected, since pronouncing words correctly, with little or no attention paid to the ideas, plot, and character, was the main concern. Today, the emphasis is rightly upon extracting all the values possible from a given story. Hence, to cover the four steps of a basic lesson with maximum profit to the children, at least three reading sessions are needed.

Word Recognition in the First Grade. Earlier in this chapter, mention was made of a resurgence of interest in "rugged phonics" to compete with an approach to beginning reading through the use of sight words plus easy types of phonetic and structural analysis. The latter method is usually associated with a basic series of readers. Sparks and Fay[4] conducted a study to evaluate the two methods of teaching reading. A pair of schools experimented with the *Phonetic Keys to Reading* versus a basic reading program in grades one and three. The *phonetic* series seemed to produce superior results in comprehension as tested through the end of grade two, but the initial lead in vocabulary for this group was not maintained. By the end of grade three and in grade four, no significant differences were found. The authors concluded that the standard basic method gave enough phonetic training to provide pupils with necessary word-attack skills. They cited the need for further research on methods which "tend to overstress a particular phase of mechanics of reading," i.e., the phonetic method, by itself. Certainly, the basic reading approach allows for better balance, since the drill on phonetic analysis is related to the use of familiar words learned by sight and is not isolated from content, but connected with the little stories in the basic readers.

The basic approach, then, makes use of a combination of word-recognition methods instead of relying upon any one method like the "alphabet-phonics." Parents who insist upon having their children begin reading with the alphabet because *they* did do not seem to realize that *they* learned to read the hard way. For every beginner who survives the unpsychological rigors of the alphabet-phonics approach, there may be thousands who never fully recover from the confusing ordeal, and spend the remainder of their lives with an intense dislike for reading.

Letters of the alphabet studied in isolation mean relatively little to beginning readers. They can see that "a" is in alphabet soup or on a toy block, but just saying it and the rest of the letters by rote is tedious and unchallenging. As a first-grade teacher pointed out, when a child is faced with the separate letters of the alphabet, the situation is roughly akin to being confronted with the ingredients of cake: flour, eggs, sugar, vanilla, etc. Separately, these do not hold much meaning for the child, but combine them into a cake

4 Paul E. Sparks and Leo C. Fay, "An Evaluation of Two Methods of Teaching Reading," *Elementary School Journal*, LVII (April 1957), 386–90.

and the child can "take hold." Similarly, "d," "g," and "o" are just abstract "somethings," but, joined together in the word "dog," they remind the child of a friendly animal he can pet, feed, and play with. In short, the word has meaningful associations for him, whereas isolated letters and sound fragments such as "ba," "be," "bo," and "bu" do not.

MODERN APPROACH GRADUAL. Research has shown that children learn more easily when they feel secure. In the modern basic program the approach to reading is therefore made gradually. Each skill is based on previous experience, to ensure that at each step of the way the child will be enabled to succeed and so to gain confidence. Since rhymes are easy for the child to identify—Mother Goose and other nursery rhymes have always been popular—the children are exposed to ear-training exercises as a first step in word analysis. After "Jill and "hill" have been identified through auditory perception of rhyme, and "down" with Jack's "crown," the children name the objects they see in pictures distinguished by rhymed endings, for example, "rose" and garden "hose." Listening to similar *endings* in this way sharpens the child's alertness to sounds. After working with rhymes, the children name pictured objects that *begin* with the same sound, for example, "*b*all," "*b*asket," "*b*oat."

Gaining sight vocabulary is next in line. During a varying interval, listening for rhyming and beginnings sounds, i.e., word analysis, is abandoned temporarily in order that the children may gain, by look-and-say, a stock of easy sight words through reading one or more preprimers. In this way the child would learn, for example, "hop," "help," "he." The teacher calls attention to the fact that they all *look* alike and *sound* alike at the beginning because they all start with the same letter. She then names the letter, *h* in this case, and the child has a start on associating letters with sounds.

Finally, the child is ready to combine all the above skills. Starting with a sight word such as "ball," he can recognize a list of new words by substituting different beginning consonants on the same rhymed ending. Thus the child is enabled to read the words "call," "fall," "tall," "small," "stall," and "wall." Easy structural analysis comes next with the addition, as the case may be, of "s," "ed," "ing" to familiar root words. Example: "calls," "called," "calling." This completes the typical first-grade basic reading program as far as word recognition is concerned. To summarize the year's work, the following verses may prove interesting:

Poem to an Alphabet Attached Parent[5]

My dear Parent, it's plain to see,
That about reading we don't agree.
You say your boy should start with the alphabet.
Why, Parent, in first grade, he's not ready yet.

Letters alone don't mean a thing.
To a small boy who has lots of zing.
He's not worried about "A" as a letter,
He has plenty of things he'd like to do better.

He should start with the easiest reading skill.
Rhyming is something that he can do well.
We build up his confidence first, you see,
And then we work on vocabulary.

He rhymes many words with the speed of lightning,
Says beginning sounds with a pace that's frightening.
Sight word vocabulary is next in line,
And he'll learn that in plenty of time.

Three preprimers are what he reads.
They will help care for some first grade needs.
He'll start reading books by "look-and-say."
To him, he's reading the adult way.

He doesn't need the alphabet yet.
He's learning all the skills that he should get.
If we go at this process gradually,
Johnny will read in no time—you'll see!

Enriching the First-Grade Program. To achieve the broad aims of reading instruction, other books in addition to the basic readers should be read in the first grade for information and enjoyment.

[5] By Judi Staffelbach, a student enrolled in the author's course in the teaching of reading at San Jose State College. This poem was written in fulfillment of an assignment to imagine a conversation between an alphabet-oriented parent and a first-grade teacher following a basal reading program.

SOCIAL-STUDIES READING AT THIS LEVEL. Stimulation for the children to carry on this type of reading can come from the use of a bulletin board, a news corner, a weather record, notices, greetings, safety rules, courtesy rules, signs for the "playtown grocery store" or "playtown bus," etc. Each holiday offers opportunities for teaching history informally. The teacher may read aloud selections about Hallowe'en, Thanksgiving, Christmas, St. Valentine's Day, May Day, Mother's Day, Memorial Day, and so on. The children themselves can enjoy looking at picture books featuring important holidays.

RECREATIONAL READING AT THIS LEVEL. To stimulate the child's desire to read, much can be done by placing on the table and shelves in the classroom library corner a display of colorful and amusing books such as *A Ring o' Roses* by Leslie Brooke (Warne), *Mike Mulligan and His Steam Shovel* by Virginia Burton (Houghton Mifflin), *The Tale of Peter Rabbit* and other charming stories by Beatrix Potter (Warne), *Make Way for Ducklings* by Robert McClosky (Viking), *Don't Count Your Chicks* by Ingri and Edgar d'Aulaire (Doubleday), *Madeline* by Ludwig Bemelmans (Simon & Schuster), *The Five Chinese Brothers* by Claire Huchet Bishop (Coward-McCann), *In the Forest* by Marie Ets (Viking), and *The ABC Bunny* by Wanda Gag (Coward-McCann).

A fine first-grade teacher once remarked, "Just as an enterprising storekeeper proudly displays his choicest merchandise in order to win customer attention, so I place within view a nice selection of books, labeling each group appropriately: EASY BOOKS, NEW BOOKS, FUNNY BOOKS, PICTURE BOOKS etc."

OTHER APPROACHES TO READING THAN THE BASIC

Though the plan of using a basic series in teaching first-grade reading is followed in the majority of our nation's schools, other plans to launch beginning reading are advanced from time to time. Of fairly recent development are those enumerated at the start of this chapter. Still in their experimental phase, these highly individualized plans will be described and informally evaluated below. At the close of this section, references to books and articles, featuring various points of view concerning self-selective reading, will be listed for the interested reader to consult.

Self-selective Reading, or Individual Guidance. In its present form this is a fairly new organization of the reading program. Rather than reading a basic reader in an ability group (fast-moving, average-moving, and slow-moving readers), the children read independently, each pupil selecting a different book, usually not a reader but a "trade" book. Instead of reading in groups, the pupils (twenty-five to thirty in the average first grade) take turns reading privately to the teacher. In some first grades, the teacher moves about, observing the children, helping with word recognition, listening to them read. In other primary classrooms, the teacher has the pupils come to her desk for individual reading. The time devoted to the individual conferences varies. It may be as little as three to five minutes daily or ten minutes a week, or more, "if the pupil needs greater help." The author has observed that, when several pupils need help simultaneously with word recognition, concept clarification, or meaning, the teacher, busy giving private lessons to the rest of her roomful, makes use of pupil-helpers, though the extent of aid a first-grade child can give to another is open to scrutiny. In a basic reader at the first-grade level, the vocabulary is controlled. Words are introduced gradually and given enough repetitions in different meaningful connections to make them familiar, but, in self-selective reading, with each child reading a different storybook, and needing to ask help to recognize many unfamiliar words, a real vocabulary problem exists, as even the most ardent advocates of this plan admit. Evidently, one teacher involved in an experiment with individual guidance experienced discontent, for she confessed somewhat paradoxically, "I find it necessary to *socialize* the *individual* guidance, and *group* the children for teaching certain skills like phonics which they all seem to need, in order to be able to read on their own."

The teacher who attempts to get around to individuals in the class might borrow from the counsel of Horace Mann, who pointed out that "If every child in the class learns to read in a different book, and if the teacher tries to get around the class to each one individually, the child will receive only a fraction of the teacher's time and instruction." Along this line, questions might be raised similar to the following: Does this procedure make good use of the teacher's time and instructional skill? Are children receiving enough teaching in basic reading skills under this plan, or are they practicing their mistakes? Are the children being denied the profitable experience of social sharing which comes during the follow-up step of a basic lesson when children exchange ideas about a selection enjoyed in common?

A recent field study of individual guidance, conducted by the author, seemed to suggest that (1) the children read more books, but they have a definite tendency to continue to read easy books rather than gradually moving to material of greater difficulty; (2) the children do not conscientiously attend to the required vocabulary work—more and more they become careless readers, omitting unfamiliar words instead of listing them for later identification when the teacher has time to get around to them; (3) as the teachers involved in this plan report, it is an absolute impossibility to discover the difficulties each of the children in an average class may be encountering, and to find time to give adequate instruction individually.

On the other hand, favorable accounts of the success of individualized procedures are given by Lazar,[6] Veatch,[7] Kirby,[8] and many others. The interested student may wish to read these for opposing points of view.

As the title of his article suggests,[9] the late Dr. William S. Gray adopted a moderate position. He advocated the use of basic group instruction to avoid haphazard development of reading skills but encouraged teachers to use individual guidance during the children's recreational-reading time. Witty[10] also suggests that indi-

[6] May Lazar, "Individualized Reading: A Dynamic Approach," *The Reading Teacher* (December 1957).

[7] Jeanette Veatch, "In Defense of Individualized Reading," *Elementary English* XXXVII (April 1960), 227–34.

[8] Margaret Kirby, "Tête-à-Tête Lessons Develop Independent Readers," *Elementary English* (May 1957) 302–10.

[9] William S. Gray, "Role of Group and Individualized Teaching in a Sound Reading Program," *The Reading Teacher* (December 1957).

[10] Paul A. Witty, "Individualized Reading: A Summary and Evaluation," *Elementary English*, XXXVI (October 1959) 401–12, 450.

vidualized reading be considered a "part of the total reading program," rather than used as a substitute for a well-organized basic series. Stauffer[11] points out that the recommendations for individualizing reading instruction go back to the 1880's and were mentioned in some of the yearbooks of the National Society for the Study of Education, in the 1920's.

As Dr. Gray suggested, the plan can profitably be used during recreational reading. While the children are reading library books, the teacher may move about from child to child, chatting informally, gaining insight concerning personal tastes, letting the children read aloud their favorite passage, furnishing lead-ons to other books, and otherwise giving worthwhile individual guidance, but not depending on this for basic instruction.

Permissive Grouping. Another form of experiment with instruction deviating from the basic approach is termed the *permissive grouping* plan. According to this plan, the class is divided into small groups of the children's own choosing. The teacher asks the children, "With whom would you like to read?" Each child then whispers to the teacher his first, second, and third choices, and as a result seven or eight groups are formed, ranging, one supposes, from two members for the unpopular children to half a dozen for the well liked. Then, to make the plan even more permissive, each child is allowed to select the book he would like to read. Once each week the teacher works individually with one child from each group and helps him to read one story. The next day this child becomes the leader of his group and reads his story orally to them. Thus, once each week the children receive individual guidance and the opportunity to be the leader-reader of the group. Advocates of the permissive grouping plan argue somewhat obliquely that, since the child is not reading orally each day, he has the "advantage of being able to participate extensively in an audience situation." But teachers in the field have raised a number of questions about this, such as: "Is being exposed to a book read by another child to the group as satisfactory in promoting growth in reading skill as reading it?" "Does participation in

[11] Russell G. Stauffer, "Individualizing Reading Instruction: A Backward Look," *Elementary English*, XXXVI (May 1959) 335–41.

'an extensive audience situation' promote growth in reading?" "Can the teacher do justice to seven or eight groups?" "Where can the teacher procure thirty-five different books for first-grade pupils who have had only a meager experience with reading so far?" "Will the teacher be able to do more than merely listen to each child read?" (This plan and the one described above make no mention of guiding the reading with purposeful questions.) "With each child reading in a different book, is it possible for the teacher to give needed repetition to fix new words?" The method suggests keeping a record for each individual child of the skills with which he needs help; it would seem that this would constitute a considerable burden in bookkeeping. Instead of receiving help about once a week, would the child not derive greater learning opportunities from the daily guidance by the teacher of his ability group?

The Language-Experience, or Individual-Experience, Approach. With this type of plan the children learn to read by reading what they have written individually—little stories of two or three lines about their personal experiences. The assumption is that "what they can say, they can write, and what they can write, they can read."[12] It is a little easier to "say" than to write, of course. The latter operation involves spelling and the forming of letters. For both spelling and writing, the child requires the individual attention of the teacher. Since the children at this early level need assistance in writing many, many words, the consequence is a long line of wiggling children, waiting for the teacher to write out the words they wish to include in their individual-experience stories. Usually these are lettered by the child on large, chart-sized sheets of unprinted newspaper. To write on these requires quite a bit of room. What with the crowding to find writing room on the floors and tables of the first-grade class, and the long lines of children waiting to have their words written for them, several problems seem apparent in the attempt to teach basic reading skills by this method. A final query arises regarding the "interest value" 'of reading one's own compositions. Certainly, the element of sus-

[12] R. Van Allen and Gladys C. Halvorsen, "The Language-Experience Approach to Reading Instruction," *Contributions in Reading* No. 27 (Boston: Ginn & Co., 1961).

pense is missing, whereas the four-page picture-and-print stories in the average preprimer have amusing and often surprising situations.

COMPARING METHODS. With regard to the above method, a teacher asked, "Why this approach instead of letting us use a basic reading program with all the helps in the teacher's manual and the children's workbook?" The answer is that the various individual methods described above have been worked out by well-meaning people in protest against the *abuse* of basic reading instructional practices, not against wise use of the program. Monotonous "round robin" reading, with the pupils taking turns and standing and reading aloud in response to uninspired directions from the teacher to "read the next line" are but dull paraphrases of what a purposeful guided-reading session with the basic reader *can* be in the hands of a teacher whose enthusiasm and careful planning (much of the latter can be derived from the basic guidebook) make the whole process come alive. But even in the hands of the most mediocre teacher, the basic program is a safer tool than other plans. For example, Safford[13] reports an evaluation of an individualized reading program in Los Angeles County, involving 72 classroom teachers serving 2,485 pupils from kindergarten through the sixth grade. The survey was made to locate all classes which had been taught during the past three years with individualized reading techniques, i.e., where this was *the* regular reading program. This was a survey of what *had* occurred.

Test scores were compared. The conclusions suggested that (1) for the majority of the individual pupils in the seven classes, the use of individualized reading techniques resulted in lower gains in reading achievement over a period of one calendar year, when contrasted with the results of other methods of reading instruction that are currently used in this district and throughout the nation (i.e., the basic program); (2) the use of self-selective reading methods achieved no significantly different results with superior students than with average students; (3) the use of individualized reading techniques resulted in no significant difference in growth between reading vocabulary and reading comprehension.

[13] Alton L. Safford, "Evaluation of an Individualized Reading Program," *The Reading Teacher* (April 1960), 266–70.

As Constance McCullough said in 1958, when she was one of the few expressing reservations concerning the enthusiastic claims made for individualized reading by its supporters, "Have we, as citizens of a country struggling for survival in a highly competitive world, the right to jeopardize the quality of education by the widespread use of an unproven method?"[14]

The basic program has the merit of giving systematic coverage of important reading skills to recommend it. Many of the story situations in the primary readers are entertaining. Organizing the children for basic reading instruction in three ability groups has moderation to sustain it. The plan neither goes to the extreme of forcing all children, whether top, average, or slow readers, to use a book of the same level, nor to that of expecting the impossible of the teacher by asking her to be a private tutor to each of thirty beginners reading in a different book.

The basic program is the most important part but not the *only* part of the first-grade reading program. It is possible at this level to make a start on content-field reading. The children gain their first concept of the community and its workers through easy books about the postman, policeman, milkman. Social-studies, nature-study, and health primers abound, replete with colorful illustrations. Ample time daily should also be given to recreational reading—at this level, looking at picture books, reading some, hearing stories read, acting them out, chatting about them. In connection with recreational reading, the principle of self-selection operates very effectively.

QUESTIONS AND ACTIVITIES

1. Why is it impossible to state the exact amount of time which should be devoted in first grade to reading readiness?
2. Describe differentiated assignments for three reading groups.
3. What are the standards for acceptable seatwork, as opposed to mere "busy work"?
4. What is the instructional sequence for teaching word recognition at the first-grade level?
5. What are some practical difficulties which occur in the attempt to

[14] Constance M. McCullough, "Opinions Differ on Individualized Reading," *National Education Association Journal,* XLVII, No. 3 (March 1958), 163.

individualize the teaching of fundamental skills in a class of twenty-five to thirty first graders?

6. How can individual guidance be adapted to the recreational program?

7. Stage a debate with two members of the class taking the affirmative and two defending the negative sides—Resolved: that protests against the basic reading program are aroused by uninspired, cut-and-dried instruction rather than by the basic program itself, including the lesson plans in the manual.

SELECTED REFERENCES

BOND, GUY L., and EVA BOND WAGNER. *Teaching the Child to Read.* New York: The Macmillan Co., Publishers (a division of the Crowell-Collier Publishing Co.), 1950.

GROFF, PATRICK J. "The Problem of Vocabulary Load In Individualized Reading," *The Reading Teacher* (January 1961), 188–90.

DAWSON, MILDRED A., and HENRY A. BAMMAN. *Fundamentals of Basic Reading Instruction.* New York: Longmans, Green & Co., 1959.

DOLCH, E. W. *Teaching Primary Reading* (3d ed.). Champaign, Ill.: Garrard Press, 1960.

DURKIN, DOLORES. *Phonics and the Teaching of Reading.* No. 22. New York: Bureau of Publications, Teachers College, Columbia University, 1962.

DURRELL, DONALD E. "Success in First Grade Reading," *Journal of Education,* CXL (February 1958), 1–48.

FAY, LEO C. *Improving the Teaching of Reading by Teacher Experimentation.* Bulletin of the Indiana University School of Education, 34, No. 5 (September 1958).

HOLCOMB, JAMES. "The Language Experience Approach," *Challenge and Experiment in Reading. International Reading Association Conference Proceedings.* New York: Scholastic Magazines, 1962, pp. 72–73.

LAZAR, MAY L. "Individualized Reading," *Education,* LXXVIII (January 1958), 281–88.

McKIM, MARGARET. *Guiding Growth in Reading in the Elementary School.* New York: The Macmillan Co., 1955.

SMITH, NILA BANTON. "What Research Says About Phonics Instruction," *Journal of Educational Research,* LI (September 1957), 1–9.

"Reading in the Elementary School." *Forty-eighth Yearbook,* Part II, National Society for the Study of Education. Chicago: University of Chicago Press, 1959.

TINKER, MILES A. *Teaching Elementary Reading.* New York: Appleton-Century-Crofts, Inc., 1952.

9

READING IN THE SECOND
AND THIRD GRADES

As the young child moves through the primary grades, learning to read is only one part of his development. Reading is so interwoven with the many other adjustments the child must make that it is essential that the teacher consider reading as a vital aspect of his over-all development. However, if the children at this level are reading the basic reader with ease and confidence, if they are enthusiastic about the reading necessary to help them carry on their class activities, if they can work cooperatively in the group, they are making satisfactory progress.

Although it is difficult to estimate the exact degree to which an adjustment in reading contributes to the child's self-confidence, teachers know that a child loses confidence if he fails in reading—he has an added insecurity to overcome in his daily embarrassment before his classmates. A child may be clumsy at jumping rope and thus feel inferior, but this is a seasonal play activity that the child can avoid. But if a child cannot read, he fails every day, and before the whole group. Should reading become a dreaded part of every school day it may have an adverse effect on the child's personality. For these reasons the teacher must pace the reading program to the child's ability.

READING SKILLS

In the second and third grades children should be able to read much longer thought units in achieving the purposes set for reading, that is, instead of requiring line-by-line prompting, as in their first contacts with books, they should now be able to read an entire page, occasionally even a whole story, in answer to a motivating question. They should also be able to read in relation to their problems. For example, if a group at this level is working on a farm unit, they should be able to learn what products are secured from the farm and to discover what buildings will be needed in the construction of a miniature farm in the classroom.

Since children in the second and third grades usually have wider meaning backgrounds than first-grade children, they should be able to make fuller comparisons between selections read, to draw more elaborate inferences, to apply more directly what they read. They should be encouraged to use library books to carry on more independent reading. They should be guided to develop individual interests in their reading.

The child at this level should be ready for more advanced word-recognition problems. The use of word-analysis skills can be taught in the daily skill-building period, integrated with the basic series of readers. Once the reading habit is well established, children can also be taught how to work out unfamiliar words instead of learning them merely as sight words. The majority of pupils at this level are capable of learning about vowels and syllables.

PLANNING FOR BASIC INSTRUCTION

How the teacher guides growth in reading skills is very important. Merely to say that interest in independent reading should be fostered or that work in phonetic and structural analysis can be accelerated does not answer the question as to how skills are taught. Perhaps the most economical way to give the student teacher a clear picture of the skill building involved in a basic reading lesson is to describe the steps taken in writing a basic lesson plan for the second or third grade.

Student Preparation for a Practice Plan. Because the lesson plans in the teacher's guidebook are designed primarily for teachers in the field, they appear in a slightly different form from those student teachers are required to prepare. To give conscious and deliberate purpose to instruction, the student teacher will need to list aims and procedures step by step, and add an evaluation at the close of her lesson plan. The terminology used in guidebooks may vary, but these four main steps of a reading lesson are usually presented: (1) preparation, (2) guided reading, (3) drills, (4) follow-up. No matter whether the first step is called "preparation" or "motivation" or "introduction," its purpose is to arouse *interest*, to present new words, and to check vocabulary. Similarly, the names of the other three parts may also vary, but the usefulness of each remains constant in most basic series. Hence, the guided-reading step, through the medium of stimulating questions, sets *purposes* for reading; the third, or drill, step gives *security* through repetition; and the fourth, or follow-up, step meets the child's need for *self-expression*. This part of the lesson also encourages him to apply what he reads.

Both student and experienced teachers should adapt the manual plan given, to the needs of their particular groups. However, since incidental emphasis is not a reliable teaching technique, it is desirable that the teacher follow most of the suggestions outlined in the teacher's manual.

In drawing up a practice plan the student teacher should

1. Read a story in the basic reader to become acquainted with the plot and characters.
2. Study the plan in the teacher's manual, observing how the story is motivated and making a note of the new words to be introduced.
3. Obtain suitable visual aids, either pictures or objects.
4. Consult the Form for a Basic Reading Lesson Plan for Student Teachers at the close of Chapter 7 in this textbook. Working from the story to the teacher's manual to the children's workbook, fill in as many blanks in the Form for a Basic Reading Lesson Plan for Student Teachers as lend themselves to such treatment. (Each story demands its own treatment, which is dictated by its content.)
5. Set up four categories of aims: story-content aims, dealing with character, scene, and action; reading-skill aims, comprising recognition, comprehension, reaction, and application of ideas in the story; social aims, treating of facts, manners, and attitudes;

and workbook aims, providing practical drill. Reread the story to extract all possible values for the children.

6. Study the suggestions given for guiding the reading of the story. Even though many of the manuals may suggest silent reading for the *whole* story, it is often wise to *guide* the reading silently, then orally, of at least the first two pages. This serves the dual purpose of arousing the pupil's interest in the plot and characters and allowing for necessary motivated oral-reading practice. (Make up appropriate guiding questions adapted from the many helpful questions usually given in the manual.)

7. Study the teacher's manual again to learn how to present the exercises in word analysis, critical thinking, etc.

8. Check from the library any books mentioned in the teacher's guidebook for use in the follow-up steps. Examine these books to become acquainted with their contents. Then place the books on the classroom library table in readiness for recommendation to the children at the close of the reading lesson.

An Example of an Actual Lesson Plan. A student teacher's lesson plan appears below for the story "The Twin Fawns." It divides into three lessons to be taught at different times. Compare the student's lesson plan with the Form for Student Teachers, and note how the prospective teacher adapted her plan. Reading her *plan* should provide a fairly clear picture of a third-grade basic reading *lesson* itself. She expanded the guidebook plan to meet her need as a student for including more details.

STUDENT TEACHER'S LESSON PLAN FOR THIRD-GRADE BASIC READER STORY

I. What (subject matter)

A. Name of reader: *Once upon a Storytime.*

Author of the series: Guy L. Bond and others.
Publisher: Lyons and Carnahan, 1962.
Title of the story: "The Twin Fawns."
Pages of the story: 161–172.
Pages of the teacher's guidebook: 87–91.
Name of reading series: Developmental Reading Series.

B. Visual aids: Pictures of doe and fawns, eagles, mountainous terrain, the Indian chief, etc.

II. Why

A. Story-content aims

1. To visualize the doe and her two white fawns; the children, Jim and Lucy, aged 8 and 9; their father; and the old Indian chief.
2. To visualize the scene in the mountains.
3. To visualize the action of the children seeing the four eagles and the baby deer through their field glasses, etc.
4. To lead the children to identify themselves with the emotions expressed by the characters in order to read meaningfully, showing with the voice whether or not the characters felt worried, anxious, relieved, etc.

B. Reading-skill aims

1. To guide the children to reason from cause to effect, i.e., the flying eagles were causing terror among the deer.

2. To lead the children to draw inferences about the kindness of Jim and Lucy, to judge by their eagerness to protect the baby animals.

3. To increase the child's stock of meanings regarding the rarity of white fawns, etc.

4. To notice picturesque choice of words, such as "eagles flying in wide circles," "thicket," etc.

5. To stimulate critical thinking by asking, "Could this story really happen? Would an Indian chief cook a dye from twigs at his lodge to turn the white fawns a dark color, to make it harder for the eagles to spot them?"

C. Social aims

1. To acquaint the children with the law that prevents people from keeping young wild animals unless there is no mother.

D. Workbook aims

1. To give practice in using phonetic clues. For example: The position of the "a" in "fawn" does not give it the short sound because of the consonant controller "w" following.
2. To promote knowledge of the names of other baby animals than fawns, i.e., piglet, calf, lamb, colt, chick, duckling.
3. To teach the syllabication rule about dividing a word when an "le" ending is preceded by a consonant, as in the new words: "eagle," "saddle."

III. How (method)

First day—first part of the story

A. Preparation for reading

1. To motivate interest, show pictures of baby deer and ask who can tell what they are. Explain that the story to be read today is about two little white fawns. Display a picture to show the thicket where they lived.

2. Write the title of the story on the board and say, "This is the title of our story today. Read the title silently and let us see who can get ready to read it aloud." Then have title read orally.

3. Frame the word "fawn" and ask, "Can you think of the names of any of the fawn's relatives?" As the children contribute words such as "doe," "buck," "stag," write them on the board. Ask what we have done to protect wildlife, to elicit the word "law." (Place it on the board.) Explain about the children in the story: names and ages. State there is also an Indian chief who appears. (Show picture.) Write the word "eagle" and have it read. (Show picture.)

B. Guiding the reading

1. To establish a purpose for reading say, "We have already learned that our story today is about twin fawns. They were unusual because they were white and so they showed up against the earth. The four eagles flying overhead could see them too easily. In the story, Jim and Lucy realized that the little fawns were in great danger. Let's read the story to see *if* Jim and Lucy are able to help them."

2. Motivating question repeated by one child.

3. Guiding the first three pages. (Silent, then oral, reading.)

Sequence for Guided Reading

Page 161: "Read to find out what the children are seeing through their field glasses." (Have all read silently to find the answer. Call on one to read orally. He shows the teacher the words he plans to emphasize, the "sock" words. Then he faces the class, and the teacher, and children in the group close their books, marking the place with a finger, and listen to see if he reads the right part orally. This is called the "only-one-book-open technique.")

Page 162: "Read to find the part that tells why the children could not go and take the fawns to their place." (Use same sequence as above for p. 161.)

Page 163: "What idea did Mr. Baker and the children have that might help the fawns?"

Pages 164 to 173: "Read the rest of the story to yourselves to find out if the Indian chief they went to was able to save the fawns by dyeing them a different color."

4. Have the children read the remainder of the story away from the reading circle, to find out if the chief's plan to save the fawns really worked.

Second day—second part of the story

1. Start with a recall motivation: "What did the chief cook with twigs, leaves, and roots over his lodge fire?" (Children find *again* this part which they *had read by themselves* at their seats.) Someone is called upon to stand and read the part that tells about cooking dye.

2. Ask, "What was unusual about the way the white deer were caught and dyed a protective dark color?" (Have the passages read aloud and discussed.)

C. Drills and skills—third day

1. Draw from the pupils descriptive terms to tell how the characters felt at different stages in the story, and write these on the board:

worried (about the fawns' danger from eagles)
anxious (to help the fawns)
eager (to ride to Warrior Mountain)
calm (how the Indian chief felt)
excited (when Lucy and Jim caught the doe and her fawns)
happy (when the mother deer accepted her fawns again)

2. Word analysis

a. Structural analysis (working with syllables, etc.) Present this word and have the children pronounce it: "ea/gle."

Write others on the board: "snuggle," "saddle," "giggle," "purple," "people." If no one can pronounce them, demonstrate how. Then place the syllabication vertical in each. Lead the children to see that words ending in "le" require the preceding consonant to form a syllable.

3. Transfer of vocabulary

   a. Arrange two columns on the board. On the left, under the heading *Everyday Way,* write the ordinary way of saying something; on the right, a better and more interesting way chosen from the story.

Everyday Way	*Book Way*
baby deer	fawns
he wanted	he intended
bushes	thicket
mother deer	doe

   b. Jumble these and have the children draw lines between the ones that match, finding the part in the story where used.

4. Explain the pages (50–51) in the *Fun and Do Workbook* which the children are to finish.

D. Follow-up

   1. Ask the children which part they thought was the most exciting. Let different children read aloud their choices.
   2. Ask the children to draw or paint their favorite scene. Review story happenings such as the episode when the Indian chief cooked dye to camouflage the white fawns and thus save them from the circling eagles, or the one in which the mother deer's acceptance of the fawns was in doubt.
   3. Show the stillfilm, "The Deer Family" (suggested in the teacher's guidebook).
   4. Read the poem "A Friend in the Garden" by Juliana Horatia Ewing. *Ring-A-Round.* Macmillan (suggested in the teacher's guidebook).
   5. Call attention to these books about animals on the library table (partial list quoted from a longer list in the teacher's guidebook):

      Billy and Blaze, C. W. Anderson. Macmillan.
      Angus and the Ducks, Marjorie Flack. Doubleday.

Dash and Dart, Mary and Conrad Buff. Viking.
Honk, the Moose, Phil Stong. Dodd.
Bambi, Felix Salten. Simon & Schuster.

IV. Evaluation

    A. Children's gains: after teaching a three-day lesson with the help of the lesson plan, answer these questions:

        1. Did the children grasp the facts and ideas presented?

        2. What gains did the children make in understanding the need for having a law to protect wildlife?

        3. What improvement in oral-reading skill was made by Betty Jean and Nita? (Usually they cannot be heard.) Did Tom again fail to bring out the "sock" words to lend meaningful interpretation to his oral reading?

        4. In what way did this story build up respect for American Indian lore?

        5. How many were able to apply the "le" ending syllabication to unfamiliar words, using the study of the new word "eagle"?

    B. Teacher's gains: in professional skills, etc.

        1. Is improvement being made in drawing more from the children and "lecturing" less, i.e., using "ten peeps to every cluck"?

        2. Is the timing of lesson steps improving?

LESSON REMINDER CARDS

Though the student teacher prepared a complete lesson plan for teaching the third-grade basic reader story, thus gaining security from a good background, she typed some of the main points on a series of "lesson reminder cards." These she kept close at hand while teaching the children. The first card contained notes on the preparation step. The second had a few notes for guided reading. (Two of the student teacher's cards are shown on page 241). The third card contained notes for conducting drill, and her fourth card had reminders in the form of questions to ask and books to show for the follow-up step.

Top reading group: The Twin Fawns
pp. 161-172. Manual pages: 87-91

New words: fawns, eagles, doe, law,
coyotes, Chief, starve, Warrior.

Preparation: Show pictures of fawns,
eagles, doe, Indian chief. Discuss.
Write new words on board. Check
back over them second time.

Motive: Read to find out if the
two children were able to save the
fawns from the eagles.

Guide the reading:
p. 161.: Read to find the part
that tells how many big
eagles were overhead.
p. 162 : Read to find out why the
two children could not
take the baby deer home.
What else might hurt the
twin fawns beside eagles?
p. 163 : How could the Chief
help save the fawns?

Have the children read the
rest of the story silently.

Lesson reminder cards.

ORGANIZATION FOR TEACHING

In both the second and third grades it is advisable to continue with a single basic reading series, rather than to use one publisher's series for the first grade, another for the second, and still another for the third. Under this plan the program in word analysis is apt to be more systematic. Skill in word recognition takes time, sequence, continuity, i.e., a graduated program. Children gain reading confidence more readily when the progression of difficulty is kept at a stable rate. For this reason, the teacher of reading must consider herself a teacher of many grades. In a second grade, she undoubtedly will have some children able to cope only with first-grade readers, some who are advanced enough to move rapidly through the second-grade readers and perhaps to begin the third, and some who are retarded in their reading. She will have to organize her groups to meet the needs of these varying levels.

If the class is divided into the customary three groups according to reading proficiency, the teacher should present new material to one group while the other two are doing exercises in the workbook, supplementary seatwork, or reading in social studies or library books. Here is a sample schedule:

	(20 minutes)	(20 minutes)	(20 minutes)
Group 1 (top readers)	Teacher presents new material	Pupils finish reading story alone	Pupils read social studies books
Group 2 (average readers)	Children finish story introduced the day before	Teacher asks questions to check comprehension of story	Pupils read library books
Group 3 (slow readers)	Teacher gives pupils easy seatwork	Children look at picture books or draw	Teacher presents new material

TEACHING THE RETARDED READER

Time must be found during the school day to give individual attention to the few children who need special assistance. (For a full discussion of remedial-reading work, see Chapter 14.)

The Remedial Session. It may be helpful to read how one third-grade teacher conducted a remedial session. A little girl was attempting to read a primer story entitled "Ride with Me." The teacher sat with her at the back of the classroom, out of the direct view of the other children, and used the following techniques to promote recognition of the words in the title and in the two sentences which the child read during the fifteen-minute private session:

1. When the child missed the word "ride," the teacher gave

   Context clue: It's what you do in a car.
   Rhyming clue: It rhymes with "slide."

2. When the child missed the word "with," the teacher gave

   Context clue: It's a connecting word.
   Opposites clue: It's the opposite of going by yourself.

   When the child could not get the word, in spite of these helpful clues, the teacher told her the word.

3. When the child missed the word "me," the teacher gave

   Definition clue: It's what you call yourself.
   Rhyming clue: It rhymes with "be," "we." (The teacher pronounced "be" and "we" and wrote these words on the board so that the child could see them.)

After this brief session with the child, the teacher spent the remaining time in trying to fix certain words. She wrote "hide" and pronounced it for the child. Then she erased the first letter and substituted "r" to form "ride" and had the child pronounce the word. Then she changed the word to read "wide" and, finally, to read "side." She used the drill to form a strong chain of associations among the rhyming elements in a series of words. (This process is variously termed "serial substitution" or "consonant substitution.")

To fix the connective "with," the teacher made use of "repetition with foils"—writing the word in a column several times, mixed with foils of similar profile or shape:

> with
> when
> with
> wild
> with
> wind
> with
> with
> width
> with

The child underlined and pronounced the word "with" every time she recognized it in the column, ignoring the other words. Because "with" is a difficult, abstract word, the teacher reinforced the practice with "kinesthetic tracing" and had the little girl trace and say the word until she could write it correctly without the model in front of her. (The theory is that the word pattern is imprinted in the muscles to such a degree that thereafter the word is written automatically (see Chapter 14).

After similar drill on other words the child missed, the teacher printed each word on a strip of paper and had the child file these in her own alphabetized word box.

Retarded readers at this level often reverse small words and persist in reading "was" for "saw," "dig" for "big," "felt" for "left," "tried" for "tired." Kinesthetic tracing is useful here, since the process sets up strong directional associations. As the children trace from left to right, a strong left-to-right orientation is being established. For some retarded children, remedial work consists primarily in directing the child's attention to the meaning of the passage. For example, if the child reads the sentence "The boy saw a dog" as "The boy was a dog," the teacher should carefully stress the fact that the way the child has read it simply does not make sense. For the child who confuses letters, the technique has been suggested of printing one letter on a card and the other on tracing paper, then superimposing the traced letter on the one printed on the card. The child is told to note that the two letters "b" and "d" (from the case cited above) go in different directions.

The Work with the Parents. Teachers are often heard to say, "If a child is already confused by his reading, an overanxious, nagging parent may be the last straw." As a first step the teacher must help the parent to realize that the child is not being poor in reading on purpose. Look for the underlying causes of poor performance in reading. Check vision, emotional balance, school attendance. If he has been absent from school too often, the child has inevitably missed sequential instruction and practice in reading.

Since remedial instruction is quite technical, parents should leave actual teaching to the child's teacher and restrict their efforts to supplementing her guidance. Parents are not acquainted with Gates's research, for example, which shows that "spelling should not be taught *during* reading because spelling interrupts the process of getting meaning from print. Stopping and studying the characteristics of words is inappropriate to continuous reading, but it is necessary to look at each letter in spelling."[1] Instead of talking about *how* a child is reading, the parent should talk about the story ideas, thus emphasizing *what* is being read. Parents should surround the child with easy books. Often these come organized in series, convenient for the parent to remember. Two examples, among many that might be cited if space permitted, are *The Beginner's Books* (Random House, Inc.) and the *I Can Read* books (Harper and Row). Second- and third-grade children who are having difficulty in reading enjoy these books. Indeed, though designed for beginners, they are popular with young children throughout the primary level. The first series above presents this list: *The Cat in the Hat, The Cat in the Hat Came Back, A Fly Went By, You Will Go to the Moon, Cowboy Andy, Stop That Ball, Bennett Cerf's Laugh Book,* and so on. The second series above offers this list: *The Little Bear, No Fighting, No Biting, Danny the Dinosaur, Sammy the Seal, Last One Home Is a Green Pig, Emmett's Pig, Seeds and More Seeds.*

[1] Arthur I. Gates, "Reading in Relation to Spelling," *Teachers Service Bulletin in Reading* VI (October 1944) (New York: Teachers College Contributions to Education, Columbia University).

Half the battle is won if the child's interest is attracted and if the reading is easy enough to permit him to succeed. Parents should never forget that the more the children read at home, the better readers they will be.

TEACHING SILENT AND ORAL READING

Since it is an easy transition from talking aloud to reading aloud, children in the first year should do a great deal of oral reading; but it is wise, even at this level, to have the children read a sentence through first silently. Silent reading in the beginning stages might be considered a "junior partner" of oral reading. Later the "junior partner" assumes full partnership status, and, in the second and third grades, the amount of silent reading increases. Because oral reading reflects the child's ability in silent reading, the teacher should not encourage children to do much independent silent reading until she knows they can read orally materials of appropriate difficulty with reasonable ease. If children hesitate or fail in oral reading, then silent reading will be equally faulty. And, whether reading silently or orally, children should have a purpose which the reading will satisfy; otherwise their interest is not properly motivated.

Silent independent reading or beginning library reading should utilize books with lower vocabulary difficulty than the materials used in class periods. Such books increase reading speed, and the child should be encouraged to read them. But such reading should be voluntary; if it is forced on the child, it may spoil his pleasure in reading for fun.

During and after the War of Independence, inspired by the fervor of Patrick Henry and other patriotic orators, schoolmasters demanded a great deal of expression in oral reading. Often, reading with expression was made the dominant emphasis in the reading process, replacing the functional motive of reading to perceive and then project meaning. The elocutionary aim set a pattern, and, during the decades that followed, teachers continued to admonish their pupils to read in a flamboyant and oratorical style.

But expression cannot be considered apart from thought. It cannot be gained from superficial drill. If a child comprehends what he is reading, if he recognizes the meaning or emotion of a passage, good expression follows naturally. Suppose a child were reading the section below. If he were deeply interested, his interpretation would probably be:

> Tips is not so *very* big.
> Is he as *big* as *your* dog?
> Oh, *much* bigger.
> Is he as *big* as *Tom's* dog?
> Oh, *much*, *much* bigger!

When a child does not read naturally, with meaningful expression and emphasis, the teacher may approach the problem by asking such questions as "Which word tells you about Tip's size? Read it so we can tell how big he is . . . Good! That time you showed us with your voice." "Which words tell us he is bigger than Tom's dog? Now make us hear it." In TV this is called bringing out "sock" words.

In this connection, it might be interesting to note that many well-known announcers, when preparing their scripts, underscore important words to help lend emphasis and interest to what they are reading. They also draw connecting lines to indicate the thought units which are to be delivered in one breath—on one rhythm, as it were. They term this process "casing" a sentence. Teachers can teach children to case sentences in a similar fashion, that is, to plan silently how they will read the sentences orally, deciding which words to emphasize in order to bring out the meaning.

It is especially important for teachers who guide the primary stages of reading to get the child accustomed to reading in meaningful units, because many of the child's permanent reading habits are being established during these early experiences. The teacher can increase the reading span by accustoming the child to look for meaning units. For example:

The children   were waiting   to see the circus

The teacher may ask the child to read each phrase orally as she indicates it, or she may write the phrases widely spaced for the child to read. Often it helps to ask a child to look away from the book and say the sentence. This is termed the "look-away" method.

TEACHING WORD ANALYSIS

The first problem in all reading is one of word recognition. At the first-grade level the problem is approached through the mastery of sight words. In the beginning stages of reading, children are exposed to certain useful words with such frequency that they learn the words by sight. At this stage much use is also made of picture and context clues. The children gradually develop the ability to use their stock of sight words for comparisons. They learn to substitute different beginning consonants—changing "ball" to "call" to "wall" to "fall," for example. Easy structural analysis is now within their grasp, and they are able to recognize the root "call," with an "s," "ed," or "ing" added.

With this background of first-grade instruction, the average second-grade pupil is ready to be introduced to phonetic analysis. The child must be given daily guidance in this aspect of word recognition. The third step of the lesson plans in the teacher's guidebook at this level should not be neglected. Word-analysis skill is the foundation on which is laid efficient, rapid silent reading of phrases and sentences.

Learning Vowel Rules: A Second-Grade Skill. Before guiding children in the formulation of the vowel rules, it is necessary to teach them to distinguish a vowel and a consonant. The teacher may ask the children how many printed tools are used in reading English. They will indicate that twenty-six letters of the alphabet are used. Then the teacher can emphasize that in working with these tools some are used more than others—that these are the ones most used: "a," "e," "i," "o," "u," and sometimes "y."

Beginning with sight words such as "pan," "cap," "hid," "pin," and "bit," the children will enjoy observing the change that occurs in the sound of the vowel in each when an "e" is added at the end to form "pane," "cape," "hide," "pine," and "bite." The teacher can explain that in this second list each vowel, which was short, now *says* its alphabet name.

Gradually, as the exercises in the teacher's guidebook for building vowel understandings are followed, the children will learn that the pronunciation of vowels varies in different words; that sometimes vowels are seen in a word, but not heard; that the position of a vowel has something to do with the way it is pronounced. To help the children formulate the rules with complete understanding, the teacher should keep presenting sight words and ask these extremely pertinent questions about them: "How many vowels do you *see* in this word?" "How many vowels do you *hear* in this word?" "What is the *position* of each vowel in the word?" "Does the position change its sound?" "Does the position of another letter near it change its sound?"

Finally, after working with a number of sight words which illustrate the principles of *variability, silentness,* and *position,* the teacher can help the children formulate the five vowel rules (see pages 312–314).

Learning Syllabication: A Third-Grade Skill. To determine the position of the vowel "u" in the word "pupil," for example, it is first necessary to find the syllables by structural analysis. Only then will it be evident that the first "u" is at the *end* of the first syllable and thus should be given the long sound of the vowel. If the teacher follows the instructional steps outlined in most third-grade teacher's manuals, she will find it quite easy to help the children with the syllabication rules (see pages 318–319).

Since there is a wide range of ability in the second and third grades, some of the pupils may still be collecting a vocabulary of sight words, while others may be able to recognize many sight words and their endings. Usually the average and top groups are able to perform serial substitution and can therefore move on to understanding and application of the vowel and syllabication rules. Thus, by easy stages, they achieve a means of attacking new words independently.

Word analysis is a useful but not exclusive means of word recognition. Children at all levels should be encouraged to make use of picture and context clues as well. A great deal of confusion exists regarding "phonics," as phonetic analysis is popularly called. Because previous systems of phonics were sometimes carried to extremes, the whole process of word analysis was condemned for a time. Today word analysis is regarded as *one* aid in word recognition. It is not used as an end in itself but serves as a tool for meaningful reading. Because phonetic and structural analysis are rather complicated, Chapter 11 is devoted to a thorough exploration of the topic.

A COMPARISON OF BASIC VS. INDIVIDUALIZED READING

An Experiment at the Second-Grade Level. Sartain[2] reports an experiment carried on in the public schools of Roseville, Minnesota, to determine "whether second-grade groups (660 pupils) would make greater progress in reading skills when taught for three months by the method of individualized self-selection or when taught for an equivalent period by a method of ability grouping using basic readers plus a variety of supplementary books." Lack of space prevents including a detailed report of the study here, but for the individualized program more than a hundred books were available. Skills and oral reading were taught during conferences between the teacher and individual children for approximately ten minutes twice a week. All the pupils kept detailed records of books read. For the basic program during the alternate three-month period three different ability groups, reading in suitable-level basic readers, met daily with the teacher, who used the teacher's manuals and basic workbooks for a thorough, sequential program of skills. All of the supplementary books mentioned in the follow-up step of the manual were grouped invitingly on shelves, and the children were encouraged to read them. Over two hours were scheduled for reading work, divided into morning and afternoon periods for both methods.

The teachers' observations of the strength of individualized self-selection were listed as follows:

(1) Individual conferences provide a valuable personal relationship with pupils. (2) Pupils are motivated to read more extensively. (3) There is a keen interest in sharing. (4) There is strong motivation for individual improvement. (5) Top readers are especially responsive.

Observations about the weaknesses of the individualized method were

[2] Harry W. Sartain, "The Roseville Experiment with Individualized Reading," *The Reading Teacher* (April 1960), 277–81.

(1) Slow pupils and others who cannot work well independently become restless and tend to waste time. (2) There is no opportunity to teach new vocabulary . . . needed *before* reading. (3) It is impossible to provide a systematic program of word analysis. (4) It is difficult to identify pupils' difficulties in short, infrequent conferences. (5) There seems to be some doubt about the permanence of skills taught so briefly. (6) The method is inefficient because of the time required to teach skills to individuals instead of teaching groups . . . (7) The conscientious teacher becomes frustrated at attempting to provide individual conferences for all of the pupils who need them each day.

Analysis of test data showed that the children made .25-year greater gain through basal reader instruction in ability groups than by the individualized method. It was felt that the "individual conference procedure" could well be transferred to the basic program in some form, rather than "forfeiting the advantages of a well-planned basic system" to obtain the benefits of individual conferences in a self-selective reading plan.

In addition to furnishing a very complete report on the Roseville experiment, only a small part of which was given here, Dr. Sartain has prepared a helpful bibliography of seventy-four books and articles concerning pros and cons of individualized reading programs. (This bibliography appears in *The Reading Teacher* magazine for April, 1960, on pages 262–265, and 270.) The interested student may wish to read some of the articles in order to obtain both points of view concerning this controversial method. The student would also do well to visit some classrooms, if possible, to observe both types of reading programs in operation, and to make up a list of strengths and weaknesses revealed by such visits.

SOCIAL STUDIES READING PROGRAM

During their first year in school, children are generally limited to a study of their immediate environment—the home, the school, and the neighborhood. In the second year, the circle widens to provide the children a broader understanding of the community in which they live. The third grade often studies a contrasting environment such as the way of life of the Eskimos or the Indians. Thus children moving through the first three grades learn how various types of communities meet the basic human needs of food, shelter, clothing, transportation, communication, work, play, self-expression, education, religion, and government.

Though the regular morning and afternoon periods are set aside for basic reading work, additional reading of social-studies content can be expected of the top and average groups. Suppose a third-grade class is studying the Pueblo Indians. It will read about their skill in building, weaving, beadwork, painting, and pottery making. This reading in reference materials has been assigned to enable the children to establish a replica of a Pueblo Indian trading post in one corner of the classroom. The children are organized into committees, each responsible for research in the different reference books provided by the teacher. Later the information collected by each committee will be shared with the rest of the children through oral and written reports. The children will show by their handwork—weaving, beadwork, basketry—how well they understand the descriptions and directions which they read. As the culmination of the study of Pueblo Indians, parents are invited to see a dramatization of the trading post in operation and to listen to passages the children have written summarizing the facts they have learned from their reference reading.

Supplementary Reading. While the basic series provides a foundation of systematic instruction, reading in subject-matter fields helps to broaden the children's informational background. Books are available in social studies, science, and health which many children in the second and third grades can read independently, following out interests aroused by the basic reader or by the social-studies unit of work. Space forbids the citation of more than a few of these books. Separate titles from a series can be chosen, of course.

The Unit Study Books. (To judge by the catalog, the titles must run into hundreds, including every possible topic from Alaska to zebras.) Columbus, Ohio: The American Education Press.

The American Adventure Series. (All about Davy Crockett, Daniel Boone, Kit Carson, Chief Black Hawk, etc.) New York: Harper & Row.

Childhood of Famous Americans Series. (Biographies of great Ameri-

cans: presidents, inventors, scientists, sports figures. Includes Lou
Gehrig, Luther Burbank, George Washington Carver, Clara Barton,
etc.) New York: The Bobbs-Merrill Co., Inc.
Cowboy Sam Series. (Eight books. All about Indians, cowboys, cattle
rustlers.) Chicago: Beckley-Cardy Co.
Junior Science Books. (Titles are explanatory of type of content in-
volved) *Junior Science Book of Beavers, Junior Science Book of
Electricity, Junior Science Book of Flying, Junior Science Book of
Stars, Junior Science Book of Trees*. Champaign, Ill.: Garrard Press.
The Reading Skill Texts. *Nicky* (grade two) *Uncle Funny Bunny*
(grade three). Columbus, Ohio: Charles E. Merrill Books, Inc.

RECREATIONAL READING PROGRAM

The classroom library is a useful supplement to the regular
school library. When the children have free time, they should be
encouraged to go to this reading corner and enjoy recreational
books of their choice. A special time for such reading may also be
set aside to ensure that the classroom library is used by all of the
pupils, and not just those capable of finishing their work early.

Library tables and bookshelves should be stocked with a wide
variety of materials, both fanciful and realistic. Stories about animals, whether realistic or make-believe, exercise a strong appeal
to children in these grades, as do those about cowboys and space-
men. Airplanes seem to fascinate children at all levels, including
this one. And, toward the latter part of the second and third
grades, many children begin to take an interest in books about
boys and girls their own age.

Most teachers follow the practice of staging recreational-reading
programs on Friday afternoons. Usually termed "book fun on
Friday," these session may be likened to the meetings of a little
literary club. Here stories may be acted out, poems read, puppet
shows staged, and dioramas exhibited to help advertise to classmates books individual children have enjoyed. Sometimes paper-
bag masks help in re-creating a character such as Mrs. Goose in
Mrs. Goose's Party and allow shy, self-conscious children to perform without actually facing the group until they have developed
the necessary readiness.

The children also enjoy making replicas of a radio or television
set and giving book reports to the "studio audience." A simple,

usable form of book report, as filled in by a third-grade child, follows:

> Title of book: *Sparkie and Puff Ball*
> Author: Paul Brown
> Main Characters: Puff Ball, Sparkie, Shep, Buffalo, Uncle Josh
> Plot: This story is about a horse, and his name is Puff Ball. He was a very tame horse. He had a partner who was a boy named Sparkie.
> Did you like the book? Yes x   No __
> Why? I liked the story because it seemed like an exciting movie on television.

Selected Favorites for the Classroom Library. Children's books are available in such rich abundance that the task of selecting a few books which have proved popular at the second- and third-grade levels almost becomes embarrassing. Visions come to mind of well-thumbed copies in different classrooms, and it is hard to know which to leave out. At any rate, the following seem to be *among* the long list of those that have given enjoyment.

The *Curious George* books (five so far), by H. A. Rey. Boston: Houghton Mifflin Co.

The *Little Eddie books,* by Carolyn Haywood. New York: William Morrow & Co., Inc.

The Beginner Books (very easy but liked by the entire primary level; Include *Bennett Cerf's Book of Laughs*). New York: Random House, Inc.

The Story of Ferdinand, by Munro Leaf. New York: The Viking Press, Inc.

Why Cowboys Sing in Texas, by Le Grand. South Nashville, Tenn.: Abingdon Press.

Flip, Flip and the Cows, by Wesley Dennis. New York: The Viking Press, Inc.

The Fast Sooner Hound, by Arna Bontemps and Jack Conroy. Boston: Houghton Mifflin Co.

Slappy Hooper, The Wonderful Sign Painter, by Arna Bontemps and Jack Conroy. Boston: Houghton Mifflin Co.

The Five Hundred Hats of Bartholomew Cubbins, by Dr. Seuss. New York: The Vanguard Press.

The Five Chinese Brothers, by Claire Huchet Bishop. New York: Coward-McCann, Inc.

Calico, The Wonder Horse, by Virginia Lee Burton. Boston: Houghton Mifflin Co.

Horton Hatches the Egg, by Dr. Seuss. New York: Random House, Inc.
Harry The Dirty Dog, by Gene Zion. New York: Harper & Row.
The Happy Lion, by Louise Fatio. New York: McGraw-Hill Book Co.,
Inc.

Available Sources. In connection with the recreational reading
program, teachers are fortunate to have available many antholo-
gies of children's literature, and other books which give guidance
in making selections for the schoolroom library and aid parents in
choosing books wisely for their children.

May Hill Arbuthnot. *Children and Books* (2d ed.). Chicago: Scott,
Foresman & Co., 1958.
Children's Catalogue. New York: The H. W. Wilson Co. Issued yearly.
Josette Frank. *Your Child's Reading Today.* New York: Holt, Rinehart
& Winston, Inc., 1951.
Lillian Hollowell. *A Book of Children's Literature.* New York: Double-
day & Co., 1954.
Stanley J. Kunitz and Howard Haycroft. *Junior Book of Authors.* New
York: The H. W. Wilson Co., 1951.
Nancy Larrick. *A Teacher's Guide to Children's Books.* Columbus,
Ohio. Charles E. Merrill Books, Inc., 1960.

QUESTIONS AND ACTIVITIES

1. What reading skills should the child be able to use at the second-
   and third-grade levels?
2. What are some of the contributions of the teacher's guidebook to
   lesson planning?
3. In what particulars does the student teacher's plan differ from the
   plan in the teacher's guidebook?
4. How is the reading work organized at this level?
5. Try to arrange to help a retarded reader in a nearby school by using
   some of the word-attack and word-fixing activities listed in this
   chapter.
6. How may parents be of help to retarded readers?
7. What is the modern position as to the amount of oral and silent
   reading to schedule at this level?
8. What practical techniques should the teacher use to promote meaningful oral reading, instead of admonishing children to "read with
   expression"?

9. What word-recognition skills are used at this level which go beyond the first grade?
10. What are the advantages of a session of "book fun on Friday"?

SELECTED REFERENCES

AARON, IRA A. "What Teachers and Prospective Teachers Know About Phonics Generalizations," *Journal of Education Research,* LIII (May 1960), 323–30.

ARBUTHNOT, MAY HILL. *Children and Books* (2d ed.). Chicago, Illinois: Scott, Foresman & Co., 1958.

ARTLEY, A. STERL. *Your Child Learns To Read.* Chicago: Scott, Foresman & Co., 1953.

BOND, GUY L., and MILES A. TINKER. *Reading Difficulties: Their Diagnosis and Correction.* New York: Appleton-Century-Crofts, Inc., 1957.

DOLCH, E. W. Teaching Primary Reading (3d ed.). Champaign, Ill.: Garrard Press, 1960.

DEBOER, JOHN J., and MARTHA DALLMANN. *The Teaching of Reading.* New York: Holt, Rinehart & Winston, Inc., 1960.

"Development in and Through Reading," National Society for the Study of Education. *The Sixtieth Yearbook,* Part I. Chicago: The University of Chicago Press, 1961.

HESTER, KATHLEEN B. *Teaching Every Child To Read.* New York: Harper & Row, 1955.

HEILMAN, ARTHUR W. *Principles and Practices of Teaching Reading.* Columbus, Ohio: Charles E. Merrill Books, Inc., 1961.

LARRICK, NANCY. *A Parent's Guide to Children's Reading.* New York: Pocket Books, Inc., 1958.

LARRICK, NANCY. *A Teacher's Guide to Children's Books.* Columbus, Ohio: Charles E. Merrill Books, Inc., 1960.

MCKEE, PAUL. *The Teaching of Reading in the Elementary School.* Boston: Houghton, Mifflin Co., 1948.

SHELDON, WILLIAM D. "Reading: Instruction," *Review of Educational Research,* XXV (April 1955), 92–106.

STONE, CLARENCE. *Progress in Primary Reading.* St. Louis: Webster Publishing Co., 1950.

WILLIAMS, GERTRUDE. "Provisions for Critical Reading in Basic Readers," *Elementary English,* XXXVI (May 1959), 323–30.

WHIPPLE, GERTRUDE. "Characteristics of a Sound Reading Program," *Reading in the Elementary School,* Forty-eighth Yearbook, Part II, National Society for the Study of Education. Chicago: University of Chicago Press, 1959. Pp. 33–53.

10

READING IN THE INTERMEDIATE AND UPPER GRADES

From time to time there appear on the reading horizon new and adventurous methods in reading instruction. Team teaching, educational or instructional television, and teaching machines are three of these. Since these methods are still in their experimental stages, elapsed-time studies must be made before judgment can be passed concerning their effectiveness in the total reading program.

SPECIALIZED METHODS IN READING INSTRUCTION

Team Teaching. The population explosion in the United States has produced far-reaching side effects. One of these has been a search for new patterns of instruction to cope with the problems of overcrowded schools (i.e., lack of classroom space) and, most important, a shortage of properly trained teachers. Team teaching is one method which its proponents hope will help to solve some of the problems. In a team program, instead of spending their entire day with the same thirty children, teachers are formed into teams varying in size from two to seven or eight teachers. For example, Mrs. A, Miss B, and Mrs. C might well be formed into a team responsible for the instruction of ninety or more fourth-grade children. Thus, the children have the benefit of Mrs. A's expertness in science and arithmetic, of Miss B's interest in reading and in written and oral English, and of Mrs. C's ability in music, physical education, and art. To see a social-studies movie or stillfilm or to hear a talk, all ninety children in the fourth grade will foregather in a large resource room with Mrs. A. in charge. This leaves the other two teachers in the team free to plan their own specific programs, or to work with smaller groups—remedial or special project. The teachers in the team plan the program cooperatively in a number of weekly meetings. Hence, team teaching is not like departmentalized teaching in which the teachers work separately and more or less in isolation.[1]

Instructional Television. Though this form of teaching is too costly to allow for the amount of repetition usually required in fixing *skills* such as reading, writing, spelling, and arithmetic, quite a few school systems throughout the country are enthusiastic about its use in teaching *content* areas such as social studies, science, art, and music appreciation. Experts in the latter fields bring carefully planned "visuals," demonstrations, explanations, and descriptions within the grasp of hundreds of pupils at one time. Connected with instructional television there is usually an "educational television center," equipped with its own "studio" for closed-circuit broadcasting. The "studio teacher" works from this studio. Her "telelesson" then goes out to various classrooms, fitted with enough television sets to accommodate the intermediate-grade children who will be viewing the lesson. The television teacher may thus take care of a total load for the day of from 400 to 600 pupils.

Combining Team Teaching and Instructional TV. As the author understands it, in the Anaheim, California, "redeployment plan"[2] basic skills such as reading, spelling, writing, and arithmetic are taught by a team of three teachers, each having a small group (average, twenty-five pupils) in a conventional self-contained class-

---

[1] This description is a digest from *Schools for Team Teaching*, published by Educational Facilities Laboratories, Inc., of New York (a non-profit organization of the Ford Foundation).

[2] Anaheim City School District, "The Redeployment Plan: A Report of Closed Circuit Instructional Television in the Anaheim City Elementary School District," Anaheim, Calif., 1960.

A basic reading lesson in the fifth grade, showing part of the top ability group doing the preparation step. The study of new words from the story to be read, coupled with a discussion of visual aids, helps to arouse interest. (*Bascom School, San Jose, Calif.*)

An upper-grade boy chose to make a model of Heyerdahl's "Kon-tiki" as his report for a social-studies unit on explorations. He also drew an accurate map depicting the voyage. (*Memorial Junior High School, South Huntington, N.Y.*)

room for half a day, while social studies, science, health, music, and art appreciation are taught by means of instructional television to large groups (ninety or more) in sizable resource rooms containing television receivers. A typical team may consist of five teachers, three of whom teach the basic skills while two "studio teachers" telecast lessons in the content areas to large groups. In order to make good use of teaching talent and room space, the small "skills groups" are alternated mornings and afternoons with the large "contents groups" receiving telelessons. A somewhat similar organization, with minor deviations, is utilized in educational television projects carried on in Hagerstown, Maryland, in Jefferson County, Kentucky, and in numerous other school systems. A composite of evaluations of such programs shows some strong and some weak points.

FAVORABLE REACTIONS. (1) Dividing up the work frees the elementary-school teacher from the obligation of trying to teach approximately nineteen subjects. (2) The plan makes possible smaller-sized skills groups. (3) While most teachers want to do their utmost, as members of a team they are spurred by the need for greater planning to develop extra teaching strengths. (4) The children pay better attention because of the compelling nature of the medium. (5) Enriched background accrues to the pupils from the elaborately prepared "visuals" and meticulously worked out lesson plans of the studio teachers. (6) Illustrations and objects can be used more effectively and efficiently, that is, seen by hundreds at once and enlarged in close-ups. (7) Teachers have time and incentive to collect resource materials for each lesson. (8) Community resources can be more successfully tapped; a speaker is willing to come once and address a large group. (9) The children are placed on their own responsibility by the "take it or leave it" challenge of instructional TV, whereas, in a situation with the teacher present "in person," the children are aware that they can ask for repetitions.

CRITICAL REACTIONS. (1) There is the danger of covering too much content because of the one-way nature of the communication, though in most situations the television viewing is followed by small-group discussions. (2) Pupils tend to become passive listeners, there is too little emphasis on doing. (3) Children in the intermediate grades are in a period of rapid physical and emotional change which makes them too restless to pay attention to lectures, even if accompanied by visual aids. (4) Sheer numbers tend to prevent the type of personal contact and guidance this age group should receive from a teacher responsible for their learning. (5) With so many teachers handling a group, a certain amount of detachment sets in. (6) Fewer "checks" result in false security on the part of pupils. As a result of the more or less passive viewing, they wind up thinking that they "know a lot" when they merely know a little *about* a lot of things. In other words they arrive at the "acquaintanceship" level instead of being called upon to achieve the "mastery" level. (7) The numerous planning sessions required of a team become onerous. (8) Many teachers are inevitably "inhibited" by the presence of other teachers while giving instruction. Interestingly enough, the points for and the points against a combination of team teaching and instructional TV seem to be almost equally balanced.

Teaching Machines. A number of school systems have been trying out another important and interesting trend, that of using "teaching machines" to improve instruction in reading and other subjects. Many different forms of teaching machines are being developed today. In size they may range from "a desk model about equal in size to a dictionary to a complicated electromechanical machine as large as a refrigerator." Some machines present teaching programs on sheets or strips of paper, while others use some form of sixteen- or thirty-five-millimeter film for the purpose. Some require the learner to write his response, while others require him to press a button or pull a lever to show his selection from several choices offered. Some machines are designed to record errors and the amount of time taken by a learner to answer a question. Depending on the "complexity of the machine and the instructional job it is supposed to do, the machines range in cost from about $15 to $4,000."

Regardless of differences in size, function, and cost, current research claims three advantages for this form of instruction: (1) Most machines make it impossible for the learner to peek ahead to find out the right answer. (2) The machines will give the learner a signal when he is on the wrong track in making use, for example, of such reading skills as recognition, comprehension, critical thinking, and application. (3) The machines will save the teacher's time by cutting down on the tedious necessity for correcting workbooks and skill texts.

It should be understood that, instead of reading the unit of information and questions on the pages of a workbook, the pupil sees both on a paper tape moving past a window on the front of the box-shaped container. The answers also appear on a paper tape but in a separate window on the front of the machine. With one of the best teaching machines which the author examined, a lever is pressed to move the tape and bring into view the right answer. The student then compares it with his own. Into view comes the next unit of information, then the questions about it, and so on.

The teaching machines seem to promote a high degree of attention—an element inseparable from learning. No doubt the novelty exerts strong appeal. Smith[3] makes the point, however, that in order to "use such programmed material to advantage the teacher will need to plan both preparatory and follow-up experiences to help students develop ways of processing, digesting and integrating the important facts and principles that have been programmed." Along this line a speaker at the May, 1962, conference of the International Reading Association, in San Francisco, complained that what teaching machines lack are "built-in praise dispensers and analyzers." Both of these educators stress the importance of the human element. Some requirements of teaching will probably never be met by mechanical means. However, team teaching, instructional television, and teaching machines represent worthy attempts to meet emerging educational problems. It seems likely that they will serve in a supplementary capacity to a well-balanced program of basic instruction and recreational and content-fields reading in the intermediate grades. History has shown us that it is usually more fruitful to use a combination of methods than to depend upon any one method.

[3] Philip G. Smith, "The Art of Asking Questions," *The Reading Teacher* (September 1961), 7.

THE READING PROGRAM

Regard for Interests and Needs. Children from the fourth through the eighth grades usually display a rich variety of reading interests. Having had more practice, they are no longer limited to reading at the experience level. Instead, they begin to develop the ability to read imaginatively about many people and places beyond their actual experience. Since new elements appear among the reading tasks, additional systematic teaching is required. In spite of this rapid progress, there is still so much room for improvement of reading abilities that social-studies texts cannot begin to substitute for basic instruction with standard basic readers, teacher's guidebooks, and children's workbooks. Teachers of the intermediate and upper grades are increasingly allotting regular daily periods to the type of continuous reading growth only basic materials can furnish. However, the well-balanced intermediate-grade program must include a great variety of reading in the content and recreational fields as well.

TEACHING PRACTICES

Intermediate-grade reading can be taught by widely opposed methods. However, the fundamental aims in reading instruction should underlie all basic lessons prepared for these levels. The teacher should

1. Continue to develop the skills of word and concept recognition
2. Develop the skills of comprehension, interpretation, and application of what is read
3. Guide the children to develop a wide variety of tastes and interests in reading
4. Help each child improve in vocabulary, fluency, speed of reading, etc.
5. Aid each pupil in developing habits suitable for (1) recreational reading and (2) informational study-type reading
6. Motivate practice in silent and oral reading

Two examples of differing teaching practices are cited below. These are by no means either *the* wrong way or *the* right way of teaching reading, but they do serve to illustrate a difference in aims and practices.

A Questionable Reading Practice. This lesson procedure was applied in an intermediate-grade classroom. Does it have a familiar ring? The teacher faced the class of thirty-six children who, in spite of varying abilities, were all reading, or attempting to read, the same reader.

> TEACHER: What story here have we been reading?
> CHILDREN (in a bored chorus): The one about the lighthouse.
> TEACHER: Who wants to tell us what had happened so far in the story? All right, Henry.

Henry stood and mumbled an elliptical account composed of an endless succession of *ands*. The children paid no attention to his recital, which ran as follows: "Well, there was some fellows and they worked on a boat and the boat was going to some lighthouse and was going to fix something wrong with the light and a storm came up and the pulley from the boat broke and one of the men was on it."

> TEACHER: All right. Now all open your books to page 129, and let's read the rest of the story. Betty, you may begin.

The children took turns, each reading a paragraph orally, at sight. The slow readers stumbled through their passages, being prompted frequently by the teacher. When she finally said, "That will do!" to each slow reader, he sat down looking abashed and miserable as a sigh of relief passed over the classroom.

> TEACHER (in a perfunctory tone, at the close of the reading): Did you like the story? Tomorrow we will read the next story. Answer the questions in the workbook on page 67. Class dismissed for recess.

What is wrong with such a reading lesson? The answer is *everything*. Lesson instruction requires express effort, and effort implies a plan; yet there is little evidence of planning here. A lesson is also learned by express effort. In such an unchallenging lesson as this, the greatest effort expended would be entailed in the children's attempts to remain awake.

It is no justification to state that many people who were taught reading by this "round robin" method are reading satisfactorily today. This may be true, but, exposed to more intelligent guidance, these same persons might have become more successful readers; or consider the fact that a great many of them apparently did not weather such reading lessons, if one is to judge by their frank distaste for books and reading.

What were the major flaws in this so-called lesson?

First of all, interest was not aroused before or during reading—truly unforgivable, since the story was a lively one about an automatic lighthouse whose powerful lamp, burning acetylene gas, had failed for some reason. A crew arrived during a stormy, foggy night to service the fuel tanks. Several times a crew member tried to approach the lighthouse by means of a line and pulley because rocks prevented bringing the boat closer. Eventually he lost his hold and dropped into the sea, whereupon a young crew member leaped from the tender to try to save the drowning man.

Secondly, no purposes were set for reading. The pupils were not reading to look for *ideas,* but merely reading *paragraphs.* And the material was beyond the recognition, comprehension, and interpretation powers of two-thirds of the children in the class. Thirty-six of them were kept in the same reader, when only the fast-moving ability group were able to cope with such phrases as "impenetrable fog," "heavily shrouded in blackness," "compressed fuel supply," etc.

In short, the teacher showed no familiarity with child needs and basic reading lesson steps. The children simply read without being led to interpret meanings in the light of their own backgrounds. And, most serious of all, such a lesson may instill feelings of inferiority and inadequacy in children who continually fail to gain the approval of their classmates and teacher.

A Desirable Lesson. Compare the preceding questionable practice with the following lesson, making use of the identical story in the same sixth-grade reader. This teacher, however, had divided her class into three ability groups and used the sixth-grade reader only with the top ability group. She carried on the lesson about the lighthouse—with considerable improvement in planning—

while the other two groups were engaged in silent-reading assignments. Here below is a stenographic report of her procedure, etc.

A. Preparation step

   1. Motivating interest

      TEACHER: Today we are going to read the next story in our basic reader. Here is the title. (The teacher writes *Adventure at the Lighthouse* on the board.) Everybody read it silently. Larry, will you read it aloud now. When you read the word "lighthouse," what does it make you children think of?

      CHILD: I think of how lonesome a lighthouse keeper is out there all alone. I saw a movie on television about one.

      TEACHER: That must have been a movie about long ago because today most lighthouses are *automatic*. (Teacher writes the word.) What do you suppose that means?

      CHILD: It means it works by itself.

      TEACHER: What would you like to find out about an automatic lighthouse? I'll write your questions on the board. (Three children ask questions as to how it would work without a keeper; how far away the light can be seen in heavy fog; who comes and fixes the light if it gets out of order.)

      TEACHER: You have asked some interesting questions. Let's see if you will find the answer to them when you read today's story. But first we must look at some of the new words.

   2. Presenting new words

      TEACHER: Today we have lighthouses with lamps that are *mechanically* operated. The lighthouse lamp can send a beam fifteen miles. It burns *acetylene* gas. The tanks of *compressed* fuel supply the light for two or three months. One night when it was stormy and foggy a *cable* to the shore station sent a signal that the gas supply had failed. The service boat and crew had to brave the storm to refuel the lighthouse lamp. Otherwise what might have happened to ships at sea on the rocky coast? (Discussion.)

3. Vocabulary check

The teacher had placed the above underlined words on the board as she wove them into her oral introduction. She now called on different pupils to go to the board and frame the words for which she gave meaning clues: "I'm thinking of a word on the board that means something under pressure." ("compressed"), etc.

B. Guided-reading step

1. Asking the major motivating question

TEACHER: One of the senior crew members of the service boat tried to get from the boat by a line and pulley to the dark lighthouse. Then something happened. What do you suppose it was? (Child guessed he lost his hold.)

TEACHER: Let's read the story to find out if he was able to fix the lighthouse lamp. Also, as you read, remember the questions you asked that are still on the board. Let's see how many things you can learn about the operation of an automatic lighthouse.

2. Guiding the reading for the first few pages silently then orally

Page 129: Read to find the part that tells what happened to make the lamp go out. (All read silently. One is called on to read part orally. Others close books and listen to see if the right part is read.)

Page 130: Read to find out why it was difficult for the service boat to reach the rocky point where the lighthouse stood. (See procedure above for silent followed by oral reading.)

Page 131: Read until you find out what happened to the senior crew member. (A child is called on. He reads *without* meaningful interpretation. The teacher asks him if the crew member was terrified or not. Child says he was scared to death. Teacher: "Well, show that terror with your voice.")

Page 132: Read to find out who jumped in when the senior crew member fell into the sea. The book uses

Pages
133–140:

three choice words to describe his actions. What are the words? ("courageous," "alert," "dependable").

Read the rest of the story to yourselves. Find out if both men were saved. Remember how foggy and dark it was, and how high the waves were rolling. When you finish reading the story, write the answers you have found to your questions about automatic lighthouses. Your questions are still on the chalkboard.

C. Drill

1. The next day the children read aloud the answers they had written in fulfillment of the assignment above.

2. They did the matching exercise in the workbook.

3. Three of the children had read with such nervous rapidity that their articulation suffered. The teacher worked with them, drilling patiently to help them to pronounce syllables and endings more clearly.

D. Follow-up

1. Conversation about the story: The teacher asked what was the difference between being alert and being dependable (qualities shown by the young crew-member hero). Synonyms "wide-awake" and "reliable" were discussed. The teacher displayed *Boys' Book of the Sea* by Charles Boff (E. P. Dutton & Co., Inc.) and *The Sea Around Us*, a version for young readers by Anne Terry White of Rachel Carson's book (Golden Press, Inc.). She invited the children to read both.

This lesson contained several essential elements absent from the first lesson described. In the second lesson, the children set their own purposes for reading the story by the questions they raised about automatic lighthouses as opposed to the old-fashioned kind. The children were grouped according to reading-ability levels. They were led to read accurately to locate information and critically to interpret, evaluate, and discuss what they had read. Since experience shows that clear oral reading carries over to improved speech, they were gaining extra values. Independent reading in supplementary books was fostered.

The Importance of Using Basic Readers. In the era of reliance on informal, incidental teaching, there was a strong tendency to abandon the use of basic readers in the middle grades and to depend on social-studies texts and reference books in this and other content areas for continued growth in reading habits, tastes, and skills. The program was not wholly successful, because the child at this level has seldom possessed the skill required to read reference books fluently. Today many schools use basic readers for the middle and upper grades. Educators now realize that they cannot assume that children emerge from the primary grades with a complete mastery of the mechanics of reading. They still need the systematic exercises provided by the basic workbook and the skills section in the teacher's guidebook. This type of sequential skill building is absent from materials dedicated exclusively to geographical and historical content, for example. In these, new terms and concepts are introduced at such a rapid rate that even gifted pupils are sometimes confused. If children are asked to deal with materials that are too difficult, they become discouraged and are apt to want to abandon reading altogether. Thus reading development is halted, and, instead of progressing, the children merely stand still and mark time or, worse, regress.

SELF-SELECTIVE READING. Even more questionable than relying on social-studies texts for growth in basic reading skills is the practice of allowing each pupil to read in a different book according to his interests. In this non-basic, or multibook, plan, there are no class sessions, no regular reading times, no periods at all when school readers are used to promote consecutive reading growth of a group as a whole. The children go to many books, reading with little supervision, often for only a brief time in each book. This informal practice does not prepare pupils to read specific selections, as does basic instruction. With each pupil reading a different book, there is literally not enough time for the teacher to give needed guidance. Is it possible to provide a class of thirty to forty pupils with adequate instruction in the informal program described above?

Contrast this lack of organization with the systematic approach of the group organization in which three ability groups will be using basic readers suitable for three different levels. With this plan the teacher is able to furnish each group the necessary instruction in the growth of skills.

Basic readers not only provide progress in skills and abilities but help to promote new interests and tastes by offering a systematic sampling of many types of reading content. Most basic readers at the intermediate levels introduce the children to both modern literature and excerpts from the classics. In the course of a basic series, children will read stories dealing with history, biography, science, travel, and sports. There is usually a bibliography at the end of each story or unit to spur the child to more good reading. For example, a child may acquire a lifelong interest in the superb writings of the great American humorist Mark Twain through an excerpt from *The Adventures of Tom Sawyer*, supplemented by a list of his books, in a sixth-grade reader.

All things considered, in handling reading at the intermediate and upper levels, it is highly desirable to continue the use of basic readers. It is the most reliable method of developing reading skills. The teacher will find many helpful suggestions in the teacher's guidebooks of the basic series for developing comprehension, vocabulary growth, and interpretation and application of meaning. The teacher can rely on a manual in teaching reading, much as a pilot relies on radio and signal beams. It contains directions to teachers for the sequential development of all the essential skills, not the least important of which is word analysis. Many children at these levels still do not know how to make out words on their own, and need help. If the intermediate teacher feels embarrassed at a lack of knowledge of phonetic and structural analysis, let her extract a little comfort from Aaron's[4] survey showing that "teachers at all levels need to acquaint themselves with phonics generalizations." One of the most effective ways to learn anything is to try to teach it. The basic manuals give step-by-step lesson plans for helping the children to develop skill in word analysis (see Chapter 11 in this text).

[4] Ira A. Aaron, "What Teachers and Prospective Teachers Know About Phonics Generalizations," *Journal of Educational Research*, LIII (May 1960), 323–30.

PROGRAM OF ORGANIZATION

On planning a program in intermediate- and upper-grade reading, the scope of the problem may seem staggering, but the work can be so organized that even the beginning teacher can enjoy the feeling of security which comes from an understanding of underlying purposes.

Materials. In such organization, materials are a prime consideration. The following are essential materials for all types of reading:

1. The basic sets of readers on three difficulty levels, with the accompanying children's workbooks. The teacher needs these for building skill in silent and oral reading.
2. Additional skill-building techniques the teacher works out—blackboard directions or mimeographed assignment sheets—for practice in comprehension skills such as recognizing the general significance of a selection, finding the central thought, recognizing words and abstracting their various meanings, reading for details, making inferences from what is read, and evaluating ideas acquired through reading.
3. Current-events papers (a subscription for each child if possible). The teacher uses these for the content fields (see chapter 12).
4. Library books with a range of difficulty in the fifth grade, for example, of from second-grade level to about eighth. The teacher uses these for silent recreational reading.
5. An abundant collection of books related to the social-studies unit currently occupying the attention of the children. Books on subjects such as food, clothing, shelter, work, play, transportation, communication, recreation, education, government, health, and religion.
6. A set of children's encyclopedias and other reference books at the intermediate and upper levels.
7. Dictionaries (at least one for every two children if it is not possible to have one for each child).
8. Children's magazines (at least three subscriptions for the class).

9. Books of poetry, choral-reading selections, recordings of poems and stories in the phonograph collection. These the teacher will need to help set high standards for oral reading in this type of material.

10. Paperbacks for children.

Plans for a Week's Work. Good organization involves planning. Each week's work should be set up to show how the aims for intermediate- and upper-grade reading are accomplished in the classroom situation. A suggested plan for a week's work follows:

Weekly Plan for Intermediate-Grade Reading

Monday

All groups first meet together to receive assignments. It is wise to have at least three difficulty levels. There may be several children in the class who require remedial help.

GROUP I	GROUP II	GROUP III
Silent recreational reading or independent reading related to the unit	Silent reading in basic reader, with word analysis in workbook	Teacher-guided silent and oral reading in basic reader

Tuesday

All groups meet together to receive assignments. Perhaps it is necessary to correct mistakes made in workbooks or to help some child find a reference for the unit.

GROUP I	GROUP II	GROUP III
Teacher-guided oral and silent reading in basic reader; word analysis or dictionary skills	Silent recreational reading or reading correlated with the unit	Silent study with workbook or dictionary or practice reader (Gates-Huber type), word analysis, etc.

Wednesday

All groups meet together for planning period, so the teacher can answer questions and make assignments.

GROUP I	GROUP II	GROUP III
Silent study in basic reader or workbook, or doing comprehension or rate exercises individually, followed by recreational reading	Same as Group I at their level of ability; teacher-guided oral and silent reading	Teacher-guided oral reading; work in structural and phonetic analysis

Thursday

GROUP I	GROUP II	GROUP III
Recreational reading to prepare for audience reading on Friday	Silent recreational reading, teacher-guided oral reading to prepare for Friday audience reading	Teacher-guided oral reading to prepare for Friday; study period, dictionary skills, etc.

Friday

All groups meet together. The program is varied to feature the following reading activities (Friday's session may resemble an informal literary club):

Current Events	Dramatizations
Audience Reading	Book Reports
Poetry Enjoyment	Play Radio Reading
Choral Reading	Teacher Presentation of Library Books

Plans for Grouping. The classes should be arranged into three general ability groups. Group I may be composed of independent readers. Although the teacher should guide their development in all skills, these accelerated pupils benefit especially from the opportunity to read independently. Group II may be made up of average readers who need much practice in silent work-study periods and in guided oral reading, yet are able to engage in some independent reading. Like Group I, they profit from direct guidance in study techniques, use of the dictionary, and reference skills. Group III may consist of slow readers who require a great deal of direct guidance and help in oral reading, in phonetic and structural analysis, in doing practice exercises in workbooks, in skimming, and in interpreting paragraphs. The average class usually has a number of children who do not fit into any of these three groups. Because of their retardation, they demand remedial guidance.

Each group should, of course, read in a basic reader at its level. It is absolutely counter to good modern practice to have all thirty or forty children in a room reading from the same reader. The teacher should be sure that she has selected the level at which each group can make the best progress. The individual interests of children should be fostered in the recreational-reading periods, when books of varying difficulty can be used. Extensive opportunity should also be provided for reading materials connected with any social-studies unit of work which may be in progress in the room.

TEACHING SKILLS

Before considering the relative emphasis to be given oral and silent reading in the middle and upper grades, the problem should be considered in its several aspects. Chronologically, oral reading comes first: Children make sounds and talk long before they learn to read. The transition from talking to oral reading is easy and natural; hence beginning readers should start with oral reading.

Studies carried on by Judd and Buswell[5] in the twenties seemed to indicate that oral reading tends to slow silent reading. The finding, through the use of eye-movement photography, that the eye of the average reader can recognize ideas four times as fast as they can be spoken was widely heralded, and a group of educators took alarm and resorted to the extreme of dropping oral reading almost completely from many intermediate- and upper-grade programs. Thus, once past the second grade, the children were denied such values of oral reading as sharing an interpretation, gaining skill in pronouncing new words, enunciating clearly, and so on. It is doubtful if the relatively small amount of time spent in reading aloud parts of the first two pages of a story in the basic reader will slow up the silent-reading rate, when the latter activ-

[5] Charles H. Judd and G. T. Buswell, *Silent Reading: A Study of Various Types,* Supplementary Educational Monograph, No. 23. (Chicago: University of Chicago, Department of Education, 1922).

ity takes up the larger proportion of reading time. Opposing the position of those who lean to major emphasis on silent reading is the linguistic view. Leonard Bloomfield, for example, believes that reading should be keyed to the oral language already mastered at a functional level when children enter school. He advocates using oral language through the medium of complicated phonetic instruction as the best way to learn to read. Linguists ask, "How can a child learn to read efficiently if he has failed to master the sounds of American English?" Dr. Morris Val Jones[6] writes, "I often combine oral reading and speech therapy. . . . Increased competency in one area will be reflected in the other."

The Role of Oral Reading. No matter what the emphasis, oral reading is used regularly in life, and children should be prepared in this skill. In fact, if the reading program is to contribute to effective reading and speech habits, oral reading must be given more attention than it has recently received. This, in turn, means oral-reading guidance of high quality, not the wasteful process of oral reading by lines and paragraphs around the class.

USES IN LIFE. The functional roles of oral reading in daily life include reading aloud notices, instructions, announcements, resolutions, reports, minutes of meetings; reading aloud to inform, amuse, or prove a point; reading aloud jokes or stories; reading radio or television commericals professionally; reading prepared speeches. These are the business and social uses of oral reading.

The practice of reading aloud will help the child later to

1. Provide entertainment in a social group
2. Verify a fact challenged by others in the group
3. Share an item to which all do not have access
4. Give directions for others to follow
5. Present announcements or questions, problems, or riddles for a group to answer or solve

[6] Dr. Jones is a professor of speech and hearing therapy, working with the California State Department of Education. The above statement was made in a communication to the author, replying to her question "Is there a carryover from clear oral reading to clear speech?"

STANDARDS FOR A GOOD ORAL READER. Authorities in the field are generally agreed upon the following characteristics of the good oral reader:

1. He prepares the reading in advance
2. He reads in idea units, not word by word
3. He reads with sufficient volume to be easily heard
4. He reads distinctly, never slurring ends of words
5. He uses his voice to transmit emotion, etc.
6. He reads at a suitable rate—neither too fast nor too slow
7. His reading shows that he wants to hold the interest of his audience (He exerts vitality.)
8. He brings out the "sock" words as television announcers do

VALUES OF ORAL READING IN SCHOOL. Various studies in the teaching of reading show that oral reading in school

1. Helps to show whether or not a child can recognize words and phrases quickly and accurately
2. Gives practice in correct pronunciation of words
3. Gives practice in using correct grammar
4. Stimulates interest in vocabulary enrichment (If a child reads a word aloud, he is more apt to use it in speech than if he has only read it silently.)
5. Permits sharing of literary enthusiasms
6. Sometimes helps to overcome speech defects
7. Aids in poetry appreciation
8. Develops poise in facing a group and holding its interest

INSTRUCTION AND PRACTICE IN ORAL READING. Before attempting to provide guidance in oral reading at the intermediate- and upper-grade levels, the teacher should determine how well her pupils—even the accelerated ones—can read orally. She should know, of course, that silent-reading scores do not necessarily indicate oral-reading achievement. A report of a supervisory visit to a school enrolling children from superior homes confirms this statement. The children in this particular school ranked high in standardized silent-reading tests, but they appeared to be unable to read orally with any degree of proficiency. They seemed to be uncomfortable and insecure, as though the activity were unfamiliar; they had difficulty pronouncing the words or reading with the emphasis, intonation, and articulation necessary to endow their oral reading with meaning.

The case of one boy was typical of the group's reaction to oral-reading demands. He knew the meaning of the word "cynosure" in the sentence "When Danny won a badge of merit he was the cynosure of all eyes." But his pronunciation was incorrect, and the word emerged as if spelled *signsir*. His ability to group words orally was considerably below standard, in spite of superior silent-reading scores in several tests.

It was found that his failure in oral reading was due to lack of practice. Beyond the second grade, the school had pinned its faith exclusively on silent reading. The children had been given no help in systematic word analysis, and, without planned oral-reading sessions to check their pronunciations, they had formed poor habits of word recognition. Thus a group of highly intelligent children had limited oral vocabularies. As Walter de la Mare the noted English writer once said, people refrain from using valuable words such as "gewgaw" and "awry" simply because they are uncertain of the correct way of pronouncing them. This class also had been denied experience in dramatic interpretation. One little girl in the group read a passage containing such forceful descriptive terms as "windstorm," "earthquake," "drought," "riot," and "flood" with no more feeling than if she had said, "Please pass the salt." Accustomed to reading only to herself in school, she ignored her listeners.

But practice without guidance can be, and often is, a waste of time. A good example of the need for guidance is the case of a sixth-grade boy who read three pages orally with apparently good interpretation. When he had concluded, the teacher said, "Now, tell us in your own words what you have just read to us." The boy looked sheepish. "I'm sorry, I can't," he confessed; "I wasn't listening." This, truly, is oral reading in a coma, divided from comprehension, and should serve as a warning against the misuse of oral reading which occurs when pupils take turns standing and reading out loud for better or for worse. In spite of all the criticism of this outmoded practice, it is still followed in many intermediate- and upper-grade classrooms. As one baffled child remarked, "The teacher told me to read that part right there. What does she want me to do that for?"

Definitely, children need a recognized purpose for reading aloud to others. A valid purpose is to share an interpretation. To do this, one child in the group may be asked to show with his voice how proud and happy the boy in the story was when he told his father he had won first prize for the colt he had raised. Another purpose might be to read to settle an argument. Suppose that half the group believes that Navaho Indians sit on the ground and weave from the bottom of the loom upward, while the other half of the group believes that the Navahos stand and weave from the top of the loom downward. Someone finds the place in the book and reads the answer. Still another purpose might be to satisfy a need, such as reading how in baseball to throw a fast curve. To call attention to plot and character, the teacher may direct the children to find the part that tells why Marty wanted a bird dog for a pet. Was it to help save his father's crops or to save Marty the trouble of chasing away hungry blackbirds himself?

After the children have read silently to find the passage which, they think, answers each question, the teacher calls on a child to read aloud the appropriate sentences. To approximate an audience situation, the other children and the teacher close their books (using a finger to mark the place) and listen attentively to determine whether the correct answer is read. With all books closed except his own, the reader must assume responsibility for reading clearly and meaningfully. Thus he gains practice in audience reading. This procedure is either called "practice audience reading" or the "only-one-book-open technique." Usually such guided reading continues for the first two or three pages of the story. By then the children's interest is aroused and several have enjoyed the values inherent in motivated oral reading.

Occasionally, in working with an individual pupil, the teacher may have a passage read aloud as a test of competence, since a child's oral reading gives some clues to his ability in silent reading. Oral reading *at sight* is recommended only for testing, the purposes being to find the difficulties which the child is meeting and to evaluate progress.[7] It is not so much a form of audience reading as a type of diagnostic study to lead to the improvement of general reading ability. This form of test may also reveal faulty habits of speech. If a child reads too rapidly, slurring words, the chances are that he will speak too rapidly, committing the same errors. Since the child uses talk a great deal in his daily life, it is important for him to speak clearly and well. The two oral activities, speaking and reading, are closely related. Use of a *tape recorder* enables the pupil to hear how he sounds to others. Often, after hearing a mumbled uneven reading, the pupil is more ready to launch a personal campaign of improvement. With the help of the teacher a plan may be evolved to help the student to correct deficiencies. A later tape recording will encourage the student by revealing areas of improvement.

The Role of Silent Reading. Competence in silent reading is indispensable. Silent reading is much more prevalent than oral reading, though people should be proficient in both. Silent reading, being much faster than oral reading, permits the covering of much more material. When reading silently, a competent reader makes only three fixations per line, whereas, when reading orally, he requires six, his fixations per line are shorter, and he takes in more letter spaces. The reading time of the passage is only twelve seconds as compared with twenty-six for oral.

INSTRUCTION AND PRACTICE IN SILENT READING. In developing silent-reading ability, as in improving other types of learning, children are helped by guidance, discussion, emphasis, practice, and appraisal. Firm, steady progress does not result from haphazard training. Only if careful and systematic attention is paid to growth in silent-reading habits, attitudes, and skills will the child be able to profit fully from his instruction. Even exceptionally able children read better with direct guidance than without it.

Teacher's manuals or guidebooks, without exception, stress the importance of teaching definite lessons that enable the child to interpret the meaning of a word, a sentence, or a paragraph. These

---

[7] Needless to say, this is a very informal test. See Chapter 15 for the names of standardized oral-reading tests to administer.

lessons should be just as tangible as lessons in adding, subtracting, multiplying, and dividing in arithmetic. Too often there is a tendency to rely on incidental emphasis. But this policy of laissez-faire is fatal to sequential growth.

At the intermediate-grade level, at least three kinds of reading experience should be provided daily to fulfill the ninety-minute requirement widely recommended in the schools for reading.

1. Basic reading—training in the skills connected with recognition, comprehension, reaction, and application through the use of silent and oral reading in the basic reader and accompanying workbook
2. Informational or study-type reading connected with reading in subject-matter areas (see Chapter 12)
3. Recreational reading following individual tastes and interests (see Chapter 13)

As was indicated in the example of a week's work in reading (see pages 271–272), children need active guidance in a balanced program of reading activities. Reading stories alone or confining reading to social-studies content is not enough to equip the child to cope with lifetime needs in reading. The intermediate and upper grades can help assure such long-range growth if children are given instruction in the wide variety of reading activities required in modern society. Two classic lists of typical situations requiring children and adults to read silently are presented here.[8]

Informational-Reading Activities.

1. *To read signs, notices, directions.* Getting needed information from railroad folders, maps, road guides, numbers on stores and houses, labels in grocery sections, etc.
2. *To understand assignments and written directions in both school and life activities.*
3. *To work out complicated problems or experiments.* Reading Scout manuals, materials on radio, cookbooks, problems in arithmetic or other textbooks, and science manuals. Adults also have

[8] *The Teaching of Reading: The Twenty-fourth Yearbook* of the National Society for the Study of Education, Part I (Chicago: University of Chicago Press, 1925), pp. 5–8.

to read income-tax blanks and materials relating to their vocations, homemaking, care of children, etc.

4. *To find or verify spelling, pronunciation, meaning, use of words.* Using the dictionary, encyclopedia, and other reference books.

5. *To gather materials for fuller understanding, for talking or writing on one's hobby, for assigned papers and discussions in school or club, and for experiments.* A common type of work in schools which have gone beyond the one-text stage, using all the facilities of the reference library, tables of contents, indexes, headings, charts, illustrations, graphs, and tables in books.

6. *To know what is going on.* Reading news items, comments on events, book and drama reviews; looking over publishers' lists; tracing quotations or allusions or tracing and verifying statements which help keep one up to date. In school this is represented by many assignments in civics, American problems, and current history, and by the reading of bulletins in rooms or halls and communications from other classes and schools. A common illustration among adults is reading or skimming trade, manufacturing, and professional journals and books or reports, to gain new information.

7. *To decide how to act in new situations.* Reading notices, warnings, youth-guidance articles, business offers, and advertisements. Pupils realize that they must meet new situations as they grow up. Such reading is done in school and needs to be done more often by assignments in which pupils learn to weigh the accuracy and reliability of statements and make choices or secure fuller information, and then decide what to continue and complete.

8. *To reach conclusions as to guiding principles, relative values, or cause and effect.* Reading conflicting opinions about school athletics, social behavior, politics, war, and the like; reading reports and editorials about strikes, elections, committee hearings, etc.

Recreational-Reading Activities.

1. *To relive common everyday experiences.* Enjoying stories of home and school, of one's own village or city.

2. *For fun or sheer enjoyment during leisure time.* Reading jokes, nonsense rhymes, humorous articles. More reading for this purpose is needed in the school.

3. *To enjoy sudden changes and sharp contrasts—positive excite-*

ment. Reading stories of adventure and accounts of travel and peril.

4. *To escape from real life.* Reading romances and accounts of almost impossible idealism.

5. *To enjoy ready-made emotional reactions.* Reading lurid, cheap romances and stories of insipid romantic love. Common as this reading is, it is questionable if it should be encouraged in school.

6. *To satisfy natural and valuable curiosity about human nature and motives.* Reading excellent character portrayals in fiction, play, and verse.

7. *To satisfy curiosity about animals, strange regions and distant times, and current happenings removed from one's own environment.* Reading encyclopedias, travel and nature books and magazines, histories, and miscellaneous portrayals of new experience. Here the shift to purposive (work type) reading occurs very often and satisfactorily.

8. *To enjoy sensory imagery.* Appreciating the word pictures, the feeling, the style, and the choice of words.

The chapter on Recreational Reading (Chapter 13) presents ways to realize goals for pleasure reading at the intermediate-grade level. Topics include book clubs, paperbacks and magazines for children, literature-appreciation programs, and lists of books suitable for grades four through eight.

Promoting Comprehension. Comprehension—the act of getting meaning—is basic to all reading activities. It is the teacher's challenging task to provide the children with experience which will help them comprehend their reading.

INCREASING VOCABULARY AND CONCEPTS. An adequate background of concepts is a basic factor in comprehension, for such a background is inevitably paralleled by growth in the meaning vocabulary. A group of seventh-grade children who have enjoyed the firsthand experience of a field trip to the mountains would comprehend more fully a passage in the science book containing references to "strata" and "talus." The teacher may be unable to increase the child's intellectual capacity, but, when it comes to increasing his stock of meanings and vocabulary, she can play a stellar role. Expanding the child's vocabulary may be accomplished in innumerable ways: by taking the children on excursions, by stimulating activities connected with the unit, by making frequent use of visual aids, by promoting interesting discussions and insisting upon clear explanations, by guiding the children to make intelligent use of the dictionary—to mention but a few.

DEVELOPING SPECIFIC SKILLS. Experimental studies have shown that many skills are involved in comprehension and that the development of each is aided by specific instruction from the teacher. As a rule, children do not spontaneously practice all these complicated skills. They profit immensely from guided practice in organizing, outlining, summarizing, and recognizing main ideas and supporting details, culling material for a sequential list, etc. Worthwhile exercises should be planned by the teacher to help children find the climax in a story, novel, or play; to recognize relationships between ideas; to recognize the sequence of events— the list is almost inexhaustible.

PROMOTING CRITICAL READING. Most authorities point out that comprehension is not limited to assimilation.[9] They universally deplore passive reading and recommend critical and reflective reading, reading characterized by the reader's desire to gain the fullest possible meaning from a passage. The teacher should be constantly alert to help the child to interpret the facts, to demand clear ideas from everything that he reads. Children formulate only vague ideas when they meet such unfamiliar words as "façade," "alluvial fan," or "Puritan." One educator has amusingly described the plight of an immigrant boy who was reading with apparent understanding about the Pilgrims and Thanksgiving turkeys. However, when he was called on to give an oral report of his silent reading, it became clear he had confused the words "Pilgrim" and "turkey"—both terms being new and strange to him. Confronted with unintelligible terms, children cannot think, they cannot reason, and naturally they cannot assimilate. Many books

[9] E. Elona Sochor, A. Sterl Artley, William Eller, Robert Dykstra, and Gertrude Williams, *Critical Reading: An Introduction* (Champaign, Ill.: National Council of Teachers of English, 1959).

in the content fields are so difficult that children form the habit of mouthing a superficially memorized passage here and there or copying it down for the unit. It has been found, for example, that some geographies and histories intended for the use of middle- and upper-grade children contain over 2,000 topics. To learn the concepts and vocabulary involved would require that the children master at least ten a day during the year's work.

PURPOSEFUL QUESTIONING. Many teachers do not understand how important the quality of their questions is to the child's comprehension. A great many experiments have shown that intelligent questioning improves the quality of comprehension in both immediate and delayed recall to a greater extent than do careful reading and rereading without purposeful questions. For example, two pioneers in educational psychology, Judd and Buswell, of the University of Chicago, pointed out as early as 1922 that questions "help the child to make a more organized attack on print."[10]

Unplanned, obscure, vague, or perfunctory questions do little to motivate the type of interest in reading which ensures active understanding. Indeed, it might well be said that the quality of comprehension will not be much better than the quality of questions set to guide the reading. Compare the trite question "How many tickets were sold by the boys?" with the stimulating query "When did you get the first hint that the circus would be a success?" The latter question calls for judgment and requires the pupils to reason about the probable success of the boys' pet circus in terms of the number of tickets sold. To restate this point, which of the following purposes set by the teacher would be more effective in directing attention to meaning: "Read to find out what happened at the end of the story" or "Read to find out if the young cowboy was able to keep all 2,000 cattle from stampeding?" Questions or directives that contain an exciting human-interest value make a broad appeal to intermediate- and upper-grade children. The teacher eager to improve the children's skill in comprehension will pay close attention to the kind of questions she prepares

[10] Charles H. Judd and G. T. Buswell, *Silent Reading: A Study of Various Types,* Supplementary Educational Monograph No. 23 (Chicago: University of Chicago, Department of Education, 1922), p. 11.

to guide the reading. She should strive to plan her questions so that the child will be required to think more critically, to prove statements, to assemble facts, and to give more extended answers than "yes" or "no." Ideally, questions should help the child to link his own experience with the content of his reading. It is desirable to ask a question with deliberation and to phrase it to bring out essentials rather than meager details. "What about Cuba?" is typical of the obscure question. There should be variety in questioning. The teacher has a wealth of question types at her disposal: memory, evaluation, comparison, recall, reasoning, summary, discussion, analysis, decision, outline, illustration, refutation. All questions should be worth answering; otherwise children will lack interest in seeking the answer. For instance, who cares how many shelves were in Mother Hubbard's cupboard? The main point of interest is that the cupboard was bare, with her dog facing virtual starvation.

COMPREHENSION EXERCISES. In addition to the reaserch and reference reading in the social-studies unit, reading in the basic reader and workbook, and reading for pleasure, children gain valuable practice in comprehension through other activities. Comprehension exercises are one such activity and can be assigned to one group while the teacher guides the reading activities of another group. A few examples of such comprehension exercises are listed here:

1. *To increase ability to read and follow directions,* have the children study a how-to book in a hobby area, subsequently encouraging them to make appropriate party decorations, room displays, etc.
2. *To improve their ability to classify and organize ideas,* have the children read silently a story in the basic reader; then write a direction on the board telling them to list the actions of the main characters in three columns:

The Hopi child	*The Hopi father*	*The Hopi mother*
1. ate piki bread	1. ate piki bread	1. washed the wool
2. gathered reeds	2. gathered reeds	2. dyed the wool
3. played	3. soaked reeds	3. wove baskets
4. slept	4. killed rabbits	4. made clay jars
	5. wove blankets	5. cooked piki bread

3. *To promote growth in reading to select materials for specific purposes,* have the children prepare suitable holiday programs or programs for various community or school drives. The children read silently to gather material from various sources to prepare their speeches, advertising placards, etc.

4. *To improve comprehension of details,* write a series of questions on the board and have the children find sentences that relate to each in the story.

5. *To teach comprehension of facts in sequence,* write directions for a new game and let the children determine who is to serve as captain, what rules must be observed, where on the playground the game is to take place, and, step-by-step, how it is to be played.

6. *To teach children to arrange material logically,* give them a jumbled set of directions for doing various types of magic tricks, puzzles, etc. Comprehension is measured by how the children rearrange them.

7. *To improve their ability to organize,* have the children read silently a paragraph in a geography (Choose one that has a boldface topic heading, but do not call the children's attention to it); after the reading, ask the children to close their books and write in their own words what the topic of the paragraph was; then have them check by looking back at the topic heading in boldface type.

8. *To promote the ability to organize what is read and to teach children to classify ideas,* have them list phrases in the story having to do with time, place, action words, picture words.

9. *To promote the ability to classify,* write a list such as the following and have the children cross out the words which do not belong: "hand," "foot," "head," "hat," "finger," "toe"; or "Red Cross," "YMCA," "Boy Scouts," "field trips," "Camp Fire Girls."

PURPOSIVE REREADING. When a specific purpose is set for rereading a selection, comprehension is deepened. It is common for adults to reread to verify a point, to re-encounter particularly satisfying sensory imagery, or to meet some other personal interest or need. Asking the children to read the story again to determine whether they know all the words is a futile assignment, as has been emphasized repeatedly. Children require a better reason for rereading than mere word repetition. Below are valid purposes which have been developed for use in school situations where rereading of a selection seems desirable.

1. To prepare a dramatization, puppet show, or simulated television broadcast to a "studio audience" (It is necessary to reread to note the number of scenes in the story, the number of characters needed, and the types of simple properties desirable in creating the illusion of reality.)
2. To select beautifully worded passages to share with others
3. To memorize the apt phraseology and particularly the nub of a joke or anecdote in order to tell it to someone
4. To select points relevant to the topic heading or to select a new topic heading in a passage read
5. To judge the suitability of a title of a story or poem
6. Te reread a passage in order to settle a point in controversy
7. To reread to verify a point only partially grasped
8. To reread to get a set of directions straight

Children should be taught that people value the companionship of those who express themselves well. The teacher should frequently stress the value of transferring some of the new words and phrases from their reading to their permanent vocabulary. Children can be taught to expect to read a passage more than once where verbal retention is desirable.

Improving the Rate of Silent Reading. When the teacher considers the enormous amount of interesting material available, the temptation is strong to work primarily for speed. But it is well to remember that comprehension must never be sacrificed to speed. What is the advantage of reading rapidly if nothing is retained?

The child who is progressing normally in reading usually achieves increased speed along with an improvement in comprehension. At the intermediate level, the average silent reading rate for materials of average difficulty ranges from 140 words per minute in the fourth grade to 210 in the sixth grade. Yet, many children are still reading below their potential speed levels, that is, they are reading all types of materials more slowly than the purpose and content warrant.

IMPORTANCE OF ATTITUDE. The first step in guidance to increase the rate of silent reading is to motivate the children to reading rapidly. The teacher should point out the advantages of being able to cover a great deal of interesting material; demonstrate that the pupil who is equipped to read materials at 200 words per minute has a decided advantage over the pupil who is able to read only 100 words per minute; and emphasize that the pupil who reads more slowly must either spend many more hours reading or do less of it.

Perception Span. Many authorities agree that increasing eye perception span improves reading speed. Some define perception as the *visual* process and recognition as the *mental* process of associating the word with its meaning. According to this definition, the perception span is the number of words that can be seen at a single fixation on a printed line. The number of words which can be recognized, that is, the meaning understood, is the recognition span. Other authorities use the terms interchangeably. For the teacher the important thing to remember is that the children should be taught to read phrase by phrase rather than word by word, not only to improve rate but to increase comprehension. The two should never be considered separately.

Because of faulty early training, perhaps from a premature introduction to the alphabet, some children form the habit of looking at every letter in a word. The teacher should demonstrate that it is possible to read quite efficiently the word "basketball," for example, when some of the letters are omitted, as follows: "b sk tb ll."

The teacher should help children understand that the skillful reader reads three or four words at once. She can demonstrate this by having the child compare his rate when reading word by word with his rate when reading phrases. To introduce the habit of reading in phrases, the teacher may use machines such as the tachistoscope (Keystone View Co., Meadville, Pa.), which flashes phrases from a projector onto a screen, or the SRA (Science Research Associates of Chicago) accelerator, which has a device that travels down the page at adjustable rates. Research was cited in Chapter 7 of this textbook which showed the motivational value of such machines. They demonstrate to the child the value of reading in phrases and convince him that it is possible to push himself to read faster. Teachers should, however, realize the limitations in the mechanical training of the eye movements. Since the individual reads with the "mind's eye," rate should not be considered apart from comprehension. As someone has aptly said, "Rate is not improved by stretching the eye span but by hastening the mind."

READING MATERIALS. A sound and effective means of improving speed is to give the child a great deal of easy material to read. If this material is stimulating and absorbing, interest is clearly heightened. The value of interest in sparking fluent reading is well known to readers of mystery stories, to cite an obvious example. Almost inevitably, the larger the vocabulary, the more fluent the reading, since fewer words offer obstacles to quick comprehension. Similarly, efficient habits of word recognition improve reading rate. The child who must puzzle over every word, hunting wildly for meaning clues in such simple connecting words as "then," "the," "is," "are," "was," "to," "it," and "up" is not likely to read at a satisfactory speed. Therefore, attention to guidance in word analysis and other aids to word recognition helps improve speed.

Some investigators recommend setting a time limit for reading a given selection to improve rate. Others advocate reading with a sort of blotter-like movement of the eyes along just the upper half of the letters in words. Others suggest reading just a little below the line of print. This last group also claims that rate can be increased by omitting recognition of small connecting words. Some authorities even recommend reading down the center of the page, in spite of doubts raised as to whether this gain in speed results in a similar gain in comprehension. Again, it should be emphasized, rate and comprehension must go together. Although some persons may profit from the use of these high-speed techniques, there are many others who do not. But to read a great deal seems to be the method most likely to increase reading rate in most cases.

STUDY HABITS AND CONDITIONS

A great many academic hairs have been split over the question of the difference between reading and study. One school of thought seems to believe that when the reading act is purposive, it is study, when non-purposive, reading. In other words, this group does not consider study and reading as synonymous or interchangeable concepts. Other authorities maintain that all reading is done for meaning and hence is purposive. Since reading habits are used in study, the middle ground—the position adopted here—considers study as an intensive type of silent reading.

Gerald A. Yoakam, in his classic work on the subject,[11] has analyzed the kinds of reading involved in study as follows: (1) In *observational* reading the student notes the ideas of the author and accepts them as they stand. The reader, more or less as a spectator, simply observes the thoughts of the author. (2) In *assimilative* reading the reader wishes to understand the thoughts of the author and make them his own. Intense purposive mastery is his desire. He does not assume a critical attitude, however, but sits at the feet of the author to learn. (3) In *analytical* reading the reader judges the worth of the ideas and tends to challenge the authors statements one by one. Yoakam does not classify recreational reading as study. He may have eliminated it because of his impressive findings concerning the differences in retention for narrative and factual materials. He demonstrated that 70 per cent of the content of narrative material is retained after a single reading, as compared with 25 per cent of factual content. Obviously, factual materials require *study*.

Retention and memory are of fundamental importance in study, since the aim of study is usually to remember, for use in thinking and speaking, an essential proportion of what the author wrote. Yoakam pointed out that it is possible to comprehend what one reads and to forget it immediately, or to retain it so imperfectly that it is of no use either immediately or later. He also reminded us of a problem with which teachers are all too familiar: the child's ability to remember words without understanding the ideas.

The Relation of Retention to Study Habits. In study situations reading must be discriminative. For retention children must be taught to label ideas: Who is involved in this particular history

[11] *Reading and Study* (New York: The Macmillan Co., Publishers [a division of the Crowell-Collier Publishing Co.], 1929), p. 118.

chapter? When did these events take place? Where? How? Why? Good memory is aided by interest, clear original impression, frequent recall with good attention, distributed practice, and a determination to remember.

THE NEED FOR TEACHER MOTIVATION AND DIRECTION. Retention is greatly aided by preparation and motivation. Most experienced teachers will agree that it is necessary to give the children oral preparation before launching a study assignment—to give them facts and ideas for complete understanding of the selection. In assigning lessons teachers should make the object of the lesson clear and try to relate the materials to the interests and needs of the children. No teacher should delude herself by believing that she is motivating good study when she merely admonishes the children to read the selection through carefully. Research on this problem has clearly revealed that a single undirected reading of factual material yields the following depressing results: The reader obtains a comparatively small number of ideas approximately correct; the reader obtains a number of definitely wrong ideas; or the reader shows no evidence that the printed matter has made any impression whatever. This last has been termed the "nobody home" response, and it is not as rare as it should be. Fortunate, indeed, is the reader who has not had the experience of reading three or four pages and suddenly realizing that he has not remembered anything but has merely been passing his eyes over lines of print.

Even a second undirected reading frequently secures no better results. If the purpose of reading is retention, children need to be motivated to expend effort; and, since effort is dependent on interest, it is the teacher's task to set purposes or, better still, to lead her pupils to set purposes of their own. The self-posed question has undoubted value.

It is the teacher's responsibility to help children make the best use of a single reading by directing their own study. The pressure of modern life is so intense that it often leaves time only for a single reading; hence it is important for the child to learn how to make the most of it. Yoakam showed that retention after a single reading is improved if the reader forms the following study habits:

1. *The habit of questioning.* What is the main idea here? Is it true? What question does this paragraph answer?
2. *The habit of visualizing.* Trying to picture actions, conditions, and people to make memory associations more vivid.
3. *The habit of supplementing thought.* Adding to the author's material from one's own experiences.
4. *The habit of recording ideas.* Underlining, outlining, and summarizing.
5. *The habit of evaluating.* Judging the worth of the material. Did it serve the reader's purpose? Which reference was the most worthwhile?[12]

Many children, as well as adults, understand only partially how to study. One reason an embarrassing majority of Americans dislike to be questioned about details of history is that too often their study habits, like Topsy, "just growed," without much cultivation or guidance, and they have retained few facts. For example, several teachers who observed the study activities of children in elementary grades found that children gave the following wide variety of answers to explain what they did when they studied:

I pick out main ideas.
I look hard at words.
I think to myself.
I look up words in the dictionary.
I recite and say things over and over.
I sit up tall and close my lips.
I review a lot.
I write down everything.

Showing laudable retention, a group of junior-college women explained how they studied a textbook assignment by the use of the "SQ3R" technique. This method is widely used in high schools, colleges, and universities. The symbols stand for: survey, questioning, reading, reciting, and rereading. Increasingly, students are being helped to see the importance of topic heads as guides to reading, the use of self-recitations, outlining, taking organized notes, writing summaries, and linking new materials with past experiences. However, some students at these upper levels still tend to pin their faith on merely reading a lesson through several times.

[12] *Ibid.,* pp. 234–38.

From these and similar examples, it is apparent that children must be helped with their study problems by giving them practice in actual study techniques at the intermediate level.

THE NEED FOR TEACHER GUIDANCE. Guidance in interpretation helps the child retain materials by directing his attention to relationships and ideas that might otherwise escape him. Unless rich meaning associations are aroused, the reader's comprehension and memory of a passage are meager and incomplete. For example, if some of the children have been to the zoo, they should be encouraged to contribute what they know to a story about zoo animals. This helps build vivid personal associations. Encouraging children to discuss previous experiences will help to develop understanding in new situations.

To achieve depth of understanding and permanence of retention, guide the children to make real meaning associations by stressing human-interest values in the story content. Recalling an important date, such as that of the founding of the Jamestown settlement (1607), is easier if the children are impressed by the dramatic story of the problems facing the people of England at that time which led them to seek homes in the New World. Giving children a background of human-interest meanings helps them to remember facts.

Children's study habits are improved if they are encouraged to challenge the author, to carry on a running fire of agreement or disagreement with the statements they read. Retention in study is improved if children are encourage to apply what they read. It is estimated that at least half of the information acquired is forgotten unless put to immediate use.

ADAPTATION OF RATE OF READING. Children at the intermediate level are not too immature to be told that it is necessary to adapt their style of reading to given content and purpose. Too often instruction in this fundamental of study is neglected until high school or college, only to have poor habits become set through years of practice. Children should be helped to understand that they should expect to read some things more slowly and attentively than others, for example, reading to follow directions, as contrasted with skimming less emphatic material.

A teacher should point out that it is desirable to read rapidly in comparing one reference with another, in looking for answers to a series of definite problems, and in reading current magazines, newspapers, comics, mysteries, and most fiction. On the other hand, children should be encouraged to adopt a slower rate for reading directions, factual materials, or fine literature. To comprehend fine literature, the child must be able to follow the author's thought, notice the beauty of his style, and react emotionally to his ideas. Appreciational reading and study have two principal aspects: the intellectual and the emotional. Some appreciations concern content style; others, thought. Such reading requires ample time to think about the ideas presented, to compare them with one's own word choice or preferred arrangement, to admire them.

The reading rate of both good and poor readers will vary with different materials and purposes. Thus a very good reader may read Carl Sandburg's poetry at a slow pace in order to enjoy his evocative choice of words. Research has shown that the good reader has several distinct reading rates: a rapid rate for familiar easy prose materials, a careful, slower rate for noting main ideas and supporting details (study rate), a very rapid rate for skimming, and a slower one for appreciation.

To test the pupil's ability to adapt reading rate to content and purpose, the teacher may have him describe what rate of reading he would use for each of the following: memorizing a joke, looking up a bus schedule, taking medicine according to instructions on the label, reading *Caddie Woodlawn,* and forming an idea of the content of a new history book.

Reading Atmosphere and Environment. Even children at the primary level learn the rudiments of establishing a favorable atmosphere for reading. Early in the first grade the primary teacher sets a standard of "reading quiet" to be observed by the two groups engaged in working at their seats while she is giving direct guidance in reading to the third group. Quiet activities, which will not tempt the children to talk about what they are doing or to make distracting noises, are assigned to foster the habit of keeping quiet while others are reading. Of course, quiet should not be made a fetish, as was the case in former years. Courteous consideration of the rights of others to enjoy reading quiet is developed by group decision and maintained by group action.

Teachers who feel that construction activities are a satisfactory concomitant to reading would do well to realize that even classical music distracts from reading efficiency. One study showed to what extent popular music distracted a group of subjects during the paragraph section of the Nelson-Denny reading test.[13] Another experiment, reported at a teachers' convention, indicated that the loss of efficiency in study was 80 per cent for popular and rock-and-roll music as compared with 60 per cent for classical music—the greatest loss occurring during vocal passages.

Children can be taught to cultivate a quiet study atmosphere at home and in school, and they can profit from noting the importance of concentration in retention. To help the child to limit the field of attention, the teacher may tell him to imagine that he has put a "mental frame" around himself and his book.

READING TOOLS. Children in the intermediate and upper grades are ready to learn to expedite their study. With such instruction provided at this level, they will tend to form better study habits. It is improvident to postpone guidance in study techniques until children reach high school or college.

Children should be taught to set up good study conditions by surrounding themselves with the tools of study. The teacher should encourage them to have a definite table or desk to which they regularly go to study. Books, pencils, pens, ink, papers, erasers, and dictionary should be close at hand. Their chairs should support the back but not occasion lounging. The study area should be well ventilated though not drafty. The teacher should train the children in the care of their eyes—to read with sufficient light coming over the left shoulder—and demonstrate how tilting a book causes less eyestrain than placing it flat on the desk or table. She may prescribe Voltaire's habit of prolonging reading time by refreshing the eyes occasionally with a dash of cold water.

[13] M. T. Henderson, A. Tinnes, and J. Barlow, "A Study of the Effect of Music Distraction on Reading Efficiency," *Journal of Applied Psychology,* XXIX (August 1945), 313–17.

The Library. Although the use of the classroom, school, and neighborhood libraries is related to the development of study habits—through reference reading and the search for pertinent data—the role of libraries will be considered later. It may be said here, however, that each class should be conducted to the school or local library. The teacher should enlist the aid of the librarian in helping children learn how to apply locational skills, such as the use of library indexes, book indexes, encyclopedias, call numbers, and the *Reader's Guide*, in connection with both research and recreational reading.

The Use of Books. Teachers should offer children practice both in locating reference materials independently and in using a dictionary accurately.

Reference Books. Children need experience in learning how to evaluate a book before taking notes. Introduced early enough, it might minimize the tendency to copy indiscriminately vast quantities of notes. Instruction should be designed to give children practice in

1. Stating the general contents of the book after looking through the table of contents
2. Finding pages dealing with a particular topic from the index
3. Compiling a bibliography on a subject
4. Noting titles and center and sideheads to determine the nature of the content and organization
5. Reading silently directions given in basic readers; explaining orally the meaning of these directions
6. Familiarizing oneself with captions of illustrations
7. Suggesting the wording of an outline or set of notes on a particular topic as the teacher records such dictation on the blackboard

Dictionaries. Many children in the intermediate and upper grades reject the dictionary as a learning tool because they have not been taught how to utilize it effectively. Research has shown that, when a casual method of dictionary instruction is compared with a planned method, it is found that systematic instruction is far superior.

Authors in the field of reading are generally agreed that establishing a favorable attitude is essential to growth in dictionary skills. The child who demands meaning from all that he reads will be more inclined to turn to the dictionary for clarification than the child who has not been guided to demand understanding from print. Once the attitude of wanting certainty of meaning is established, the way is paved for guidance in the use of the dictionary. A great deal is heard about establishing a "spelling conscience"; in the same way, it may be said that there is such a thing as a "dictionary conscience."

Basic dictionary skills to be taught should include locational, pronunciation, and meanings skills. Any word that causes the reader to consult the dictionary is known as an "entry" word. To locate such words, the children need to be able to use alphabetical order and must be able to use the guide words according to the sequential position of their letters. These are basic locational skills. The child who comes across the unfamiliar word "baffle" in his reading and hunts for it on a page with the guide word "battle" at the top is not using the requisite skill. Command of structural analysis is often necessary in using locational skills—a further justification of training in systematic word analysis. If the entry word is "filing," the child must be able to recognize that this is an inflected form of a root word. He must be able to remove the "ing" ending mentally, understand that the final "e" was dropped when the ending was added, restore it, and then consult the word "file" in the dictionary.

Children need definite instruction in interpreting dictionary pronunciations. For example, it has been found that, if the child recognizes the long, short, and unstressed vowel sounds, he can accurately solve the pronunciation of at least 75 per cent of the words he will seek in a juvenile dictionary.

A third important skill is that of selecting the correct meaning from among the dictionary definitions. Definite instruction in this skill is important; otherwise children often seize upon the first definition listed. Much guidance is needed in helping children to comprehend defined meanings and to adapt these meanings accurately to a given context. And, of course, the dictionary also helps the children to verify spelling and syllabic divisions encountered in his reading.

Space does not permit the inclusion of sample procedures in teaching dictionary skills. But in the better junior dictionaries the teacher will find ample notes to the teacher that are helpful in planning lessons in dictionary skills. The dictionary's value in word recognition, itself a basic need in reading, is of vital importance, and competent usage here should be planned systematically at every level. Children should become "double book" readers, that is, have the dictionary at hand when reading a book.

QUESTIONS AND ACTIVITIES

1. To appraise understanding of the motivating value of questions which include a personal, human-interest emphasis, compare the following pairs of questions and decide, in each case, which has more merit. Defend your choice.

   A. What kind of little girl was Lisbeth?
   B. How did Lisbeth show she was shy?

   A. How many foods did the noble ladies eat?
   B. How could they have balanced their diet instead of concentrating on boar's meat, meat pasties, clotted cream, and sweetmeats?

   A. Is this a nonsense story?
   B. Which sentence first tells you this is not a serious story?

   A. What does a raccoon look like?
   B. How can you recognize a raccoon when you see one on your next camping trip?

2. Evaluate the two contrasting types of reading lessons described at the beginning of this chapter.
3. What are the values of oral reading for the intermediate and upper levels? For daily adult living?
4. List acceptable standards for good oral reading. What is the objection to excessive audience contact, i.e., looking up often from the book?
5. What skills are involved in comprehension?
6. How can good study habits be developed?
7. Outline a week's work at the intermediate and upper levels to include basic reading, social studies, and recreational reading.

SELECTED REFERENCES

AARON, IRA A. "What Teachers and Prospective Teachers Know About Phonics Generalizations," *Journal of Educational Research*, LIII (May 1960), 323–30.

BOTEL, MORTON. "We Need a Total Approach to Reading," *The Reading Teacher* (April 1960), 254–57.

CHALL, JEANNE. "The Encyclopedia as an Educational Tool," *Teachers' College Record* (February 1961).

CENTER, STELLA. *The Art of Book Reading*. New York: Charles Scribner's Sons, 1953.

COHN, WERNER. "On the Language of Lower-Class Children," *School Review* (Winter 1959).

"Development in and Through Reading. *The Sixtieth Yearbook of the National Society for the Study of Education*, Part I. Chicago: University of Chicago Press, 1961.

GRAY, WILLIAM S., and A. STERL ARTLEY. *100 Good Ways To Strengthen Reading Skills*. Chicago: Scott, Foresman & Co., 1956.

HARRIS, ALBERT J. *How To Increase Reading Ability* (4th ed.). New York: Longmans, Green & Co., Inc., 1961.

HANNA, GENEVA R., and MARIANNA K. McALLISTER. *Books, Young People and Reading Guidance*. New York: Harper & Row, 1960.

PRESTON, RALPH C., and MORTON BOTEL. *How To Study*. Chicago: Science Research Associates, Inc., 1957.

RAGAN, WILLIAM B. *Modern Elementary Curriculum* (rev. ed.). New York: Holt, Rinehart & Winston, Inc., 1960.

ROBINSON, F. P. *Effective Study* (rev. ed.). New York: Harper & Row, 1961.

SPITZER, H. F. "Studies in Retention," *Journal of Educational Psychology* XXX, 1939.

STORDAHL, K. E., and C. M. CHRISTENSON. "The Effect of Study Techniques on Comprehension and Retention," *Journal of Educational Research* XLVI (1956), 561–70.

ZIRBES, LAURA. *Spurs to Creative Teaching*. New York: G. P. Putnam's Sons, Inc., 1959.

SMITH, LOIS, and JANE BECHER. "Self-selection with Intermediate Children," *The Reading Teacher* (November 1960), 83–86.

11

PHONICS AND OTHER AIDS
TO WORD RECOGNITION

Today, when it comes to beginning reading, modern educators believe in using both "sight words" learned by the look-say method and phonics.[1] The work in phonics, however, is introduced gradually. Since detecting rhymes is relatively simple for little children ("Jill," "hill"; "down," "crown"), ear training is begun in the first grade. The children listen for rhyming sounds as they name familiar objects they see in pictures. For example, the children name items pictured in a row—a car, a star, a cat—and listen for those that have the same *ending* sound, i.e., rhyme. Next the children follow a similar procedure in learning to recognize *beginning* sounds as they name items in pictures. So far no demands are made upon the children to deal either with beginning or ending sounds in *print*. To reiterate, only spoken words and pictures are used at this stage.

As the children are guided through easy preprimers, in which pictures carry the plot and printed words below represent the conversations, a modest stock of sight words is collected through repetition and meaning. The children are taught to recognize the words as "wholes" by looking at them and saying them a number of times. As soon as the children can recognize such words as "mother," "me," "make," and "my" when they see them, they

[1] James B. Conant *et al., Learning To Read: A Report of a Conference of Reading Experts* (Princeton, N.J.: Educational Testing Service, 1962).

are ready for some analysis. As regards these four words, attention should be drawn to the similarity of the first part of each. The teacher asks, "Do these words *sound* alike at the beginning?" (Time out for checking, followed by confirmation.) "Do these words *look* alike at the beginning?" (The teacher indicates the "m" in each and receives confirmation from the children.) "They all begin with the letter 'm,'" summarizes the teacher. Now it is possible for the children to recognize the usefulness of "m." It starts four words they know by sight and will help them to start other words they meet that have a similar beginning.

To modern educators, this gradual approach through sight words to associating sounds with letter symbols seems infinitely less confusing than presenting beforehand a string of letters or a combination of letters (phonograms) to be memorized in narrow arbitrary drill, isolated from function. To advise the children, as some phonics "systems" do, "Whenever you see *ug* say 'ug'" can have repercussions. Suppose the children have laboriously learned this "word family" some members of which chance to form words and some, nonsense syllables: *bug, cug, dug, gug, hug, nug, sug, pug*, etc. Now what happens when the children later come across the word "pugilist"? How would the above isolated drill help them to pronounce the "u" in the first syllable? Soffietti[2] points out that "The English *letter* is not a primary clue to vocalization as it is in Italian." Witness what happens to "a" in "father," "hat," "ate," "any," "tall," "village," "sofa." The same query as to the value of attempting to use phonograms may be raised. A functional program of word analysis of the type presented by the majority of teacher's manuals, integrated with reading for *meaning* in the basic readers, is recommended by many leading educators working in the field of reading.[3]

Beginners who can use a few of the techniques of phonetic analysis enjoy an initial advantage in the number of words they can read by using as a "key" a sight word they know. A specific example at the first-grade level will be offered in the paragraph below to indicate the value of *phonetic and structural analysis.*

---

[2] James P. Soffietti, "Why Children Fail To Read: A Linguistic Analysis," *Harvard Educational Review*, XXV (Spring 1955), 63–94.

[3] James B. Conant *et al., op. cit.*, p. 10.

These are the twin stars in the crown of the comprehensive, over-all process of word analysis. Because of its former association with questionable "systems," the terms *phonics* is not quite as acceptable as the more accurate term *phonetic analysis*, but usage has firmly established *phonics* in the public mind to denote the sounds represented by letters and combinations of letters called *phonograms*. In this chapter, the terms *phonics* and *phonetic analysis* will be used interchangeably. The comprehensive term *word analysis* may refer either to phonics, phonetic analysis, or structural analysis. In the last, instead of focusing attention upon *sounds* of letters and letter combinations, attention is given to prefixes, suffixes, syllables, and endings added to a root word. Upon first introduction all this technical terminology is apt to prove overwhelming, but, as examples of exercises are given in the chapter, using sight words, phonics, and structural analysis, it is hoped that any confusion regarding the meaning of these terms will be dispelled.

To proceed, then, to our first example. If the child knows the word "ball" by sight, having met it in several of the preprimer stories, as Sue and Bob throw the ball to their dog, Tips, who brings it back once, then changes the game and carries it off and loses it, experience in word analysis is gained through phonetic analysis (new beginning consonants on same rhymed ending) and structural analysis (endings added to the root word) as follows:

Phonetic Analysis:	Structural Analysis:
ball (sight word)	ball (sight word)
fall (new beginning sound)	falls, falling (new ending)
tall (new beginning sound)	taller, tallest (new ending)
call (new beginning sound)	calls, called, calling
wall (new beginning sound)	walls, walled
stall (new beginning sound)	stalls, stalled, stalling
small (new beginning sound)	smaller, smallest
hall (new beginning sound)	halls

This, typically, in almost all of the widely used basic reading series on the market, represents an early stage of word analysis. Sometimes, to figure out the words that are rhymed with his sight word, the child may need a context, or meaning, clue to help him, for example, "It rhymes with 'ball' and means the opposite

of a short person" ("tall"). However, if the teacher follows the
sequential pattern in the average teacher's manual and children's
workbook for a basic reading series, the child is soon able to recognize fifteen of the most used beginning consonants and can
quite easily figure out new words that rhyme with his sight words,
as above. Consonants such as "q," "x," "z," etc., are not introduced
very early, since their use is comparatively infrequent in beginning words.

A SEQUENTIAL PROGRAM IN WORD RECOGNITION

The need for augmenting the use of sight words and context
clues with definite guidance in word analysis is now a recognized
part of the basic reading program. Today, even former advocates
of the "no-analysis-at-all" policy accept the fact that children need
systematic guidance in word attack, if they are to be self-reliant,
efficient readers.

The philosophy of modern reading does not condone an isolated
program of word-analysis techniques at either the primary or
the intermediate level. To isolate word recognition and to make
use of irrelevant phonics work is to repeat the mistakes of the
past. As far as possible, the teacher should follow a program that
is consistent with that recommended in the teacher's guidebook or
manual of the basic reading series. She should not have the children merely memorize a list of rules in phonetic and structural
analysis; rather, the children should make generalizations inductively, as the explanations in this chapter will show.

As a guide to methods of word attack at the first three proficiency levels, the three charts on pages 310, 316–317, and 320–321
may prove helpful. The teacher can consult them to find placement of levels. Two other proficiency levels—the fourth, dealing
with the use of the dictionary, and the fifth, dealing with the reading of figurative language—do not require charts for clarification
but will also be discussed. Though the first level of proficiency in
word analysis should be achieved in the first grade, the second
level in the second grade, this ideal is by no means attained by
all pupils. A child may need two years of training to understand

consonant substitution, for example. Thus, he will be learning a first-level skill in the second grade.

Instruction in various word-analysis skills is no longer solely the responsibility of the primary teacher. Word analysis is a skill that must be developed gradually, a skill which requires nurture at each level. Thus, in some cases, sixth-grade teachers may need to teach first- or second-grade word-analysis skills. Even though the teacher must know what the achievement goals are for each level, she must lead each child toward these goals at his own pace. The sequence for the five proficiency levels, however, must be kept intact. Since each skill develops from a skill previously learned, it is impossible, for example, to teach children the use of the dictionary and diacritical marking (a fourth-level skill) until they know how to recognize syllables (a third-level skill), which, in turn, is based upon recognition of vowels (a second-level skill).

First Grade. At this first level, seven steps are used to introduce the children gradually to the complicated process of recognizing symbols. Each step is built on knowledge the children have already acquired about words. At first the children listen to rhyming sounds and read pictures; then they listen for the beginning sounds of the words for things in pictures. In this way the children are gradually led to identify letters with sounds. (Being able to associate sounds with letter symbols is an important phonetic skill.) Now the stock of approximately 100 sight words, built up through reading preprimers, can be used by the children to make comparisons, and the children are ready to recognize new words by using consonant substitution and structural analysis.

The seven steps in word analysis in the first grade are presented on the following pages.

Step 1. Recognizing Rhyming Sounds.

    a. Through experiences in *ear training*
    b. Through experiences in *picture reading*

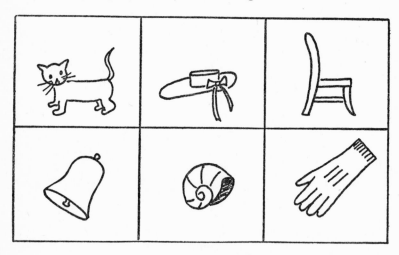

The first step in teaching the child to read is to help him to distinguish rhyme. This is auditory preparation. Since all children have experienced auditory communication, it is only natural that the first step in reading readiness begins with this aspect. Teaching the child to hear rhyming elements is also done by means of "reading" pictures containing familiar objects. For example, the child is guided to find the picture in the first row above showing something that rhymes with "cat." He is directed to say these two words, "cat" and "hat" and to listen to decide whether or not they rhyme. In each row of the illustration, a third pictured object is inserted as a foil. If the child is able to recognize that the words "cat" and "hat" sound alike but that "chair" sounds different, he is ready for the next stage (see Step 2 below).

Before a child can associate printed words with familiar spoken sounds he must be able to *hear* similarities and differences. If he is not ready to respond to pictures and the spoken word, he will not be ready to recognize abstract symbols in print. Beginning formally with letters of the alphabet does not help the child in hearing sounds, since the letter does not always take its alphabet name.

STEP 2. RECOGNIZING BEGINNING SOUNDS.

a. Through experiences in *ear training*
b. Through experiences in *picture reading*

The second step in teaching children to recognize words is to give them practice in listening for words that begin with the same sound. In the first row above, the names of the objects in the first two pictures begin with the same sound, *b*. The foil, "fish," in the third picture begins with a different sound. After the children have been asked to look at the pictures in each row and name the objects that begin with the same sound, they may be exposed to similar experiences. Colorful advertisements may be clipped from magazines and mounted. Five or six pictured objects may be used instead of two. More foils may be inserted to furnish additional practice in detecting likenesses and differences in the beginning sounds of words. Experiments have shown that auditory sensitivity to rhyming sounds is more easily developed than is recognition of beginning sounds. However, the latter is a strategic skill, as it constitutes a bridge from the perception of the first sound to the name of the first letter in a word.

STEP 3. RECOGNIZING WORDS AT SIGHT.

a. Through *looking* at each word many times in experience stories and preprimers

    b. Through *saying* each word while looking at it in experience stories and preprimers

During the reading-readiness period, children enjoy many experiences in common. Some of these are recorded in brief five- or six-line stories by the teacher and read back from blackboard and chart by the children. The children become familiar with such words as "we," "had," "fun," "play," "saw," "pet," which are used frequently in various experience stories. The "look-and-say" method does not require children to deal with letters or sounds at this initial reading stage; they simply know the word as a unit, having seen it and pronounced it many times. No feeling of strangeness or insecurity is attached to these sight words because they are drawn from the children's own experiences.

The look-and-say method dominates the early stages of reading in the preprimers. Word analysis is incidentally utilized. Colorful pictures show the action, and they are accompanied by the natural speech patterns used by children. The words "Oh!" "look," "something" and other everyday words appear with sufficient frequency to be learned as sight words if the teacher uses the type of guidance required for fixing them. Directing attention to words as units and to word-form clues helps the child to build a useful sight-word vocabulary.

In presenting the new word "run," the teacher may say, "When Bob wanted Tips to run, he said, '*Run, Tips.*'" As the teacher pronounces the word "run," she prints it on the blackboard or chart. After a number of exposures to the word "run" in a variety of meaningful settings, the children know it as a sight word.

While children are developing a vocabulary of sight words in the early stages of first-grade reading, they must be helped to make visual discriminations. Guidance is given in helping them notice more than the general appearance of the word, that is, they learn to look for word-form clues. For example, they should notice the difference in the height of such words as "me" and "little," the striking up-and-down character of "tall," and "ball," the length of the word "something," the shortness of "in," the part of "big" that goes below the line.

To help the children discover likenesses and differences in word forms, the teacher directs attention to their shape, contour, and

size. For example, the child may be asked to look for the uneven-
ness of the word "laughed." Attention to word-form clues helps
the child distinguish the words in his rapidly expanding sight-
word vocabulary. If the child confuses the word "mother" for
"makes," as often happens, the teacher may point out that there
are two tall parts in the word "mother" and only one in "makes."
Although this method is of value during the initial period of reading, it loses its effectiveness as soon as too many words of similar
shape are met by the child. When that occurs he must progress to
word analysis.

STEP 4. ASSOCIATING LETTERS AND SOUNDS.

The child knows the words "he," "help," "hello" as sight words,
having encountered them very often during the reading in three
preprimers. The fourth step consists of teaching him to associate
sounds with visual letter symbols—an important phonetic skill. To
perform this complicated step, the teacher asks the child to look
at these sight words and pronounce them. She then asks, "Do
these words all *sound* alike at the beginning? Do they all *look*

alike at the beginning? Yes, they all start with the same letter. We call that letter "h." That is its alphabet name. But when we sound the letter "h" in a word such as "hello" or "hop," it sounds different. It does not say its alphabet name. Now let us look at the pictures (on page 307) and name the things in the pictures that have names that begin with the same sound as the words on the top line. Yes, "house," "horn," and "hen" sound the same at the beginning. So they must start with what letter? Yes, "h." Similarly, sight words and pictures are used to teach the recognition of "b," "c," "d," and others.

Step 5. Substituting Consonants in Words.

| Sight words: | must | jump | ball |
| New words: | dust | bump | call |

During this fifth step children have fun with words. They learn to sound out new words from the words they already know by sight. In the word "must," which they know at sight from having seen it many times in their experience and preprimer stories, they can substitute beginning consonant "d" and read the brand new word "dust." They can proceed from the recognition of their old friend "jump" to the new word "bump" by mentally substituting the consonant "b" at the beginning. If this last operation proves too difficult, the teacher may have "jump" recognized and then let the children watch her erase the consonant "j" and substitute the consonant "b." Consonant substitution thus provides children with a useful control over the endless variety of new words encountered in print. In this process the children use a sight word, never a meaningless fragment, as the point of departure. They actually read new words.

Step 6. Substituting Medial Vowel and Ending Consonants.

In this sixth step, through the use of the substitution principle, the children may proceed from the recognition of a sight word such as "cap" to the reading of "cup" or "cop" by substituting different medial vowels. Similarly, children may use the sight word "Ted" as a basis for recognizing the new word "ten," with serial substitution of a different ending consonant.

STEP 7. EXPANDING WORD ATTACK.

a. Through structural analysis
b. Through combining substitution and structural analysis.

If a child knows the sight word "bring," consonant substitution enables him to read "wing," "ring," "string," "king," "fling," "ding-a-ling." Thus, by the use of consonant substitution in a series (i.e., serial substitution), his ability to recognize words in print has been enlarged. In the *seventh* step, then, the teacher adds structural analysis to the substitution skill. Now the child is enabled to read the root words above with several different endings: "wings"; "rings," "ringing"; "strings," "stringing"; "kings"; "flings," "flinging'; etc. Many additional words have been expanded from the sight word "bring" by the application of consonant substitution and structural analysis.

However, there is an important difference between teaching the child to find the root "bring" in the new word "bringing" and teaching him to look indiscriminately for small words in larger words. Finding root words is legitimate structural analysis; finding small words such as "ash" in "wash" or "as" in "wash" or "was" in "wash" is faulty practice. Not only are these little words not roots (meaning units) of the word "wash," but they are not pronunciation units. Finding these smaller words in "wash" will not help in pronouncing the word—it will have quite the opposite effect. Another danger in teaching children to recognize a new word in this way should be noted. If children are taught to look for "an" in "man," for example, they tend to pronounce it "muh-an," thus making a two-syllable word of a monosyllable. This, too, runs counter to accepted practice in structural analysis.

Second Grade. As the children advance to the second proficiency level, they achieve increased independence in word attack. They are now ready to learn the five vowel rules. This is a major step forward in developing the ability to read new words independently. Progress in phonetic analysis should be accompanied, of course, by growth in structural analysis. Therefore, at this level the children are introduced to more complicated variant endings than "s," "ed," and "ing," which were learned at the beginning level.

FIRST-GRADE PROGRAM IN PHONETIC AND STRUCTURAL ANALYSIS

PREPRIMER LEVEL	PRIMER LEVEL	BOOK-ONE LEVEL
Phonetic Analysis:	Phonetic Analysis:	Phonetic Analysis:
Ear training for rhymes or ending sounds (*day, way*)	Visual-auditory perception of rhyme (*to, do*)	Recognizing final consonants: (*get, let*, etc.)
Ear training for beginning consonants (*Sue, see*)	Visual perception of beginning consonants (*baby, ball, big*)	Substituting final consonants (*ran* to *rat*; *can* to *cat*)
Structural Analysis:	Visual-auditory perception of beginning consonants—hearing sound and naming letter in sight words (*he, big, see, pet, run, mother, do, come, time, now, we, go, fun, jump*)	Combining consonant substitution with use of meaning clues and study of word form
Recognizing the root word plus endings "s," "ed," "ing" (*work, works, worked, working*)	Understanding substitution of beginning consonants (*ball* to *call* to *fall* to *tall*)	Recognizing new word "night" from resemblance to sight word "right" and checking meaning clue
	Structural Analysis:	Structural Analysis:
	Recognizing the root words plus endings (*see, sees; tip, tips*)	Recognizing root word plus endings (*help, helps, helping*)
		Identifying parts of compounds (*some/thing, birth/day*)

The long-range lesson plan below suggests how the teacher may introduce the five vowel principles to the children. Toward the close of the plan, procedures are given for introducing the skills in structural analysis which should be taught at this second level. For more detailed information concerning the program of phonetic and structural analysis at the second proficiency level, see the second-grade chart on pages 316–317.

LONG-RANGE PLAN FOR SECOND GRADE

SUBJECT MATTER

> Five vowel rules
> Variant endings

AIMS

> To teach the five vowel rules inductively, beginning with words the children know by sight
> To stress the importance of the *position* of the vowel
> To teach the principle of *silentness* applied to vowels
> To teach the principle of *variety* in vowel sounds
> To teach recognition of variant endings such as "ies," "es," "est," "ly"

Learning To Identify Vowels

> Expose the children to a cardboard strip entitled Vowels, containing a row of vowels set apart by commas, including y in parentheses because it is sometimes a vowel, as follows: *a, e, i, o, u, (y)*.
> Ask the children what they see on the cardboard strip. If one child says, "letters," acknowledge that they are indeed letters but add that they have another name. Say, "They are called *vowels.*"
> Write on the blackboard a row of sight words containing the letter "a": "at," "ate," "car," "ball." Have these words pronounced by different children in the group.
> Help the children to identify the vowel in each word. Lead the children to look from the word "at" to the letters on the vowel chart. Ask, "Do you see a vowel in the word 'at'? What is it?" Proceeding similarly, lead the children through a recognition of the vowels in the other three words above. Prepare them to notice variations in the sounds of vowels by pointing out that "a" has a shorter sound in "at" than in "ate." Next, call attention to the different sounds of "a" in "car" and "ball."
> Teach the vowel "e" in the same manner, beginning with sight words featuring "e": "met," "me," "her."

Teach the vowel "i" through reference to such easy sight words as "it," "ice," "bird."

Teach the vowel "o" by reference to easy sight words such as "hot," "go," "or." Again, the variation in sound is pointed out: the short "o" in "hot," the longer "o" in "go," the different sound of "o" in "or."

Teach the vowel "u" through use of the sight words "up," "use," "hurt," in the same way.

TEACHING THE SHORT-VOWEL RULE

Learning How the Initial and Middle Positions Affect Vowels

Write in a column the words "am," "an," "back," "can." Call on different pupils to pronounce each and place a little "v" close under the vowel to identify it. (If necessary use the vowel card as a reminder: *a, e, i, o, u, (y)*.

Then, taking one word at a time, call on different pupils to answer the questions in the following recognition routine (Child's answers are indicated in parentheses):

Teacher: The word is "am." How many vowels do you see? (One.) What is its position in the word—at the beginning, middle, or end? (Beginning.) Does it say its alphabet name? (No.) How would it sound if the vowel said its alphabet name? (a-a-am.) What does the vowel say? (Short sound of the vowel as in "cat.") How do you mark the short "a"? (With a breve, or sort of little rocker that means the short-vowel mark.)

To identify the sound of the vowel in "back," the same recognition routine is used but for answer: "The vowel is in the middle." After working with the four words above in this fashion, the children are ready to draw up

1. THE SHORT-VOWEL RULE

When there is only one vowel in a word and that vowel comes at the beginning or middle of the word, it usually takes its short sound.

Present some new words such as "bang," "glad," to test the children's ability to apply the rule. Lead them to notice that there is only one vowel, that it is in the middle, and ask what sound it should be given. Have the children say the short sound of "a," which they will remember from the key word "cat." (They "tune in" the vowel rule and say the word. As soon as they say each word they recall a spoken counterpart. The rule is functioning to help them to make out words on their own.)

TEACHING THE LONG-VOWEL RULE

Learning How the End Position Affects the Vowel

Write on the board a column of words the children know by sight, such as "me," "my," "no," "she." Have the children pronounce them. Then call on a child to place a little "v" under the vowel in each to identify it.

Taking one word at a time, call on different children to answer the following questions in the "recognition routine" (correct answers are indicated in parentheses):

Teacher: The word is "me." How many vowels do you see? (One.) What is its position: beginning, middle, or end? (End.) Does it say its alphabet name? (Yes.) What kind of a vowel is it? (Long.) How do we mark the long vowel? (With a macron, or straight line over the letter. It shows the long-vowel mark.)

After the same recognition routine has been asked, using the other three words above, the children are ready to draw up

2. THE LONG-VOWEL RULE

When there is only one vowel in a word and that vowel comes at the end of the word, it usually takes its long sound.

TEACHING THE TWO-VOWELS-TOGETHER RULE

Learning About Silent Vowels

Building on the understandings which the children have gained during the previous drills that (a) there are certain letters called vowels and that (b) their *position* in the word makes a difference in the way they are sounded, proceed to the teaching of the next principle governing the pronunciation of words—the principle of silentness.

Present these words: "read," "pie," "seem," "day." Have them pronounced. Call on different children to follow the "recognition routine" which will lead toward the generalization (rule) inductively: "How many vowels do you see in 'read'"? ("Two.") "How many do you hear?" ("The first one.") "Does it say its alphabet name?" ("Yes.") "What happens to the second vowel?" ("Silent.") "How do we mark the vowel we hear, since it says its alphabet name?" ("Macron.") "What do we do with the silent vowel?" ("Cross it out.") Proceed similarly with the other words above. Then lead the children to form

3. THE TWO VOWELS-TOGETHER RULE

When there are two vowels together in a word, the first vowel usually takes its long sound and the second vowel is silent.

Present new words to check the ability to deal with new words containing two vowels together. (If the third step in the basic lesson plan outlined in the teacher's manual for a given basic series is followed, ample practice will be given in figuring out new words in this category.)

TEACHING THE FINAL-"E" RULE

Continue to develop understanding of the principle of silentness by presenting the following sight words and having them pronounced by the children: "ate," "bake," "game," "late," "made," "rake," "ride," "time." In each case have the children tell how many vowels they see and how many they hear. Then ask for the position of each vowel. Lead the children to see that it is the vowel "e" on the end which is always silent. Tell the children that it is referred to frequently as final "e," and help them to form

4. THE FINAL-"E" RULE

When there are two vowels in a word and one of them is final "e," the first vowel usually takes its long sound and final "e" is silent.

Test the children's grasp of this rule by having them read "cap" and "tap." Then show how the pronunciation is changed when an "e" is added to each to form "cape" and "tape."

TEACHING THE CONSONANT-CONTROLLER-VOWEL RULE

Learning How Consonants Control Vowel Sounds

Review the vowel rules about position and silentness, then develop awareness that the strong consonant "r" changes, or controls, the sound of vowels which come immediately in front of it. Present this list of sight words and have them recognized: "bird," "first," "third," "or," "start," "far," "fur." Tell the children to consider the word "bird," for example. Then ask, "How many vowels do you see?" ("Only one.") "What is its position?" ("In the middle.") "What sound do we usually give to vowels in the middle of a word?" ("The short sound.") "Try this word with the short sound." ("bid.") "But you said that the word was "bird." What happened to the vowel? What strong consonant comes after it?" ("r.") Yes, "r" changes vowels that come right in front of it and gives them a new sound. Let's pronounce some of the other words in the list and see what "r" does to the vowel in each." Then lead the children to formulate

5. The Consonant-Controller-Vowel Rule

When there is only one vowel in a word and it is followed by "r," the sound of the vowel is neither long nor short but changed, or controlled, by the consonant "r."

Later, use other sight words such as "crawl," "call," "saw," "straw," and "cell," to show that "a" is affected by two other consonant controllers—"w" and "l." For contrast, have the children compare what the "l" does to "a" in "call," and the way the "e" in "cell" is unaffected by the "l." Then add to the consonant-controller-vowel rule, "The vowel 'a' is affected also by 'l' and 'w.'"

Learning How Endings Change Words

Review the recognition of simple variant endings such as "s," "ed," and "ing." Then carry on the following second-level types of structural analysis:

Write the root word "stop" and have it pronounced. Write "stopping" and have it pronounced. Call attention to the fact that the consonant is doubled before the ending.

Write "try." Then write "tries" and have it used in a sentence. Call attention to the changed ending ("y" changes to "i" and "es" is added).

Write the word "pile" and have it recognized. Erase the "e" and add "ing" to form "piling." Have the word pronounced. Call attention to the dropped "e" (harder than simply adding "ing").

Write the words "box," "fox," "fix." Have the words read. Add "es" in each case to form "boxes," "foxes," and "fixes." Have the words pronounced and call attention to the ending.

Write the word "tall" and have it pronounced. Add "est" to form "tallest." Have it pronounced and the ending noted.

Write the words "friend," "string," "farm." Add endings to form "friendly," "stringy," "farmer." Ask the children to read these and name the root word and the ending in each case.

The above simplified handling of vowels is designed for the elementary-school level, where most children are unable to cope with the refinements of diacritical marks. Thus it is not desirable to baffle children with such terms as *diaeresis* or *circumflex*. Instead of using the terms *macron* and *breve,* most teachers refer to them as the "long-vowel mark" and the "short-vowel mark." A simple way to handle the consonant controller is to draw an arrow *from* the top of the "r" in "car," for example, *to* the top of the "a."

THE CONTENT OF A PROGRAM IN PHONETIC

Developing Phonetic Skills

Visual-auditory perception of special two-letter consonants (*wh, ch, sh,* and *th,* as in *why, chick, she, think, that*).

Visual-auditory perception of consonant blenders (*st* in *stop, store, stay;* the *l* blended in *play, slow, black, cluck, flew;* and the *r* blended in *friend, gray, trick, train*).

Auditory perception of vowels (short *a* in *fat, bat;* long *a* in *cake, lake*).

Visual-auditory perception of vowels (long *i* in *pie, mine, time;* short *i* in *dig, sit, did; i* modified in sound by *r* in *sir, dirt, stir, third; ay* in *way, gray, day; ai* in *train, tail, paint*—only first vowel heard; *a* followed by *r, w, l* with neither short nor long sound in *car, caw, fall*).

Blending known consonant and vowel sounds (*trip, sly*).

Developing Phonetic Understandings

Consonants in words may be silent (second *l* in *pull;* second *n* in *dinner;* second *b* in *rabbit,* etc.).

Silent vowels are phonetic clues (*paint, train, wait, tail*).

Vowels stand for more than one sound (*y* sounds like short *i* in *Sally, poky, very, party;* like long *i* in *try, buy, why, fly*).

Using Phonetic Analysis in Attacking New Words

Consonant substitution (*corn, thorn*). Vowel substitution (*his, has*).

Using Structural Analysis in Attacking New Words

Recognizing verbs formed by doubling final consonant before adding ending (*pull* to *pulled*—no doubling; *stop* to *stopping*—doubling consonant).

Changing "y" to "i" before adding ending (*try–tried; hurry–hurries,* etc.).

Recognizing derivatives formed by adding "y" (*wind* to *windy*).

Third Grade. The main task at the third proficiency level is to learn to use syllabication skills in pronouncing and making out the new words met in reading. The long-range plan below describes how the teacher may introduce the children to the three syllabication rules over a period of several weeks. For added details concerning this important skill in structural analysis, see the Third-Grade Chart, pages 320–321. It will be noted that ability to perform syllabication rests on ability to recognize vowels and consonants. For example, it is obvious that the child must first scrutinize the word "pupil" for the visual clue consisting of a single consonant surrounded by vowels before he is able to syllabicate the word "pupil" correctly.

AND STRUCTURAL ANALYSIS—SECOND GRADE

Developing Phonetic Skills

Auditory perception of special vowel combinations including diphthongs (*oo* in *food, book; ow* in *know, cow; ou* in *outside, through; oi* in *soil, boil; oy* in *boy, joy,* etc.).

Developing Phonetic Understandings

Variability: Some consonants have variable sounds (hard *c* in *cut, candy;* soft *c* in *cinder;* hard *g* in *gate, get;* soft *g* in *germ*).

Different letters may represent the same sound (*c* in *cut; k* in *kitten*).

Principles for Determining Vowel Sounds

Position: If there is only one vowel in a word, it usually has its short sound unless it comes at the end of the word (*bit, Tips*).

Silent vowels: If there are two vowels together in a word, usually the first takes its long sound and the second is silent (*each,* only *e* is heard; *peep,* only first *e* is heard; comparing *got* and *goat; ran* and *rain,* etc.).

If there are two vowels in a word, one of which is final "e," usually the first vowel takes its long sound and the final "e" is silent (*bite, rose, cane, rope, wife, whole, taste*).

Consonant controllers: If the only vowel in a word is followed by "r," the sound of the vowel is usually controlled by "r" (*far, fir*).

If the only vowel in a word is "a" followed by "l" or "w," the "a" usually takes neither the long nor short sound.

Using Phonetic Analysis in Attacking New Words

Making use of consonant substitution, medial vowel substitution; applying understanding of vowel position, consonant controllers, silent vowels, etc.

LONG-RANGE PLAN FOR THIRD GRADE

Subject Matter: Three syllabication rules

Aims: To teach these syllabication rules inductively

Begin with an activity to promote auditory perception of syllables. At first use the term *parts of words,* then gradually introduce the correct term, *syllables.* Say the word "train" and clap hands to show that the word has only one part. Then say the word "button" and have the children clap hands twice to designate the syllables.

Pronounce several words such as "please," "hurry," "happy," and "automobile," and ask the children to pronounce them after you and clap for the parts, or syllables, each contains.

TEACHING THE TWO-CONSONANT RULE

Dividing Between Two Consonants Surrounded by Vowels

To promote understanding of how to determine syllabic units in the words "enter," "admit," "button," ask the children to pronounce them and clap for the number of parts, or syllables, each contains.

Having elicited the answer from the children that each word contains two syllables, write the words on the board and ask the children where a line should be drawn to show the syllables. (The children may give various answers.) Ask, "How do you know where to draw a line?" (The children probably have no idea.) Then tell them that they can learn how to divide words and be sure that they are right each time. Offer to show them how.

Write the word "button" on the board and point out that there are two consonants in the middle. (Use small *c*'s to designate consonant under the letters.) Then indicate the vowels "u" and "o" surrounding the consonants, and divide between the consonants to form syllables. Proceed similarly with such words as "puppet," "problem," "welcome," showing the children that each contains two consonants in the middle surrounded by vowels. Finally help the children to draw up

1. THE TWO-CONSONANT RULE

When there are two consonants surrounded by vowels in a word, split between the two consonants to form syllables.

Present the children with a list of new words such as "ladder," "Tippy," "shoulder," "circus," "winter," and guide them to recognize each by applying the two-consonant rule.

TEACHING THE SINGLE-CONSONANT RULE

Dividing in Front of a Single Consonant

Have the children clap for the parts, or syllables, they hear in "clover," "tiger," "lady."

Then write these words on the board and ask the children where they should be divided. (Again, various answers may indicate the children are not certain.)

Suggest that the children look for the number of consonants in the middle of each word that are surrounded by vowels, and lead them to see that in each case there is a single consonant with a vowel on each side. Draw the vertical syllabication line in front of the single consonant to form: "clo/ver," "ti/ger," "la/dy."

Show how structural analysis (syllabication) has put the "o" in "clover" at the end of the syllable. Lead the children to compare the long sound at the end of a syllable with the long sound of the vowel at the end of a word, and to see the similarity.

Then say, "You see, it is important to divide words into syllables to find out what the position of the vowel will be, so you will know how to pronounce it."

Lead the children to formulate

2. The Single-Consonant Rule

When there is a single consonant surrounded by vowels, the word is usually divided in front of the single consonant to form syllables.

TEACHING THE "LE" ENDING RULE

Dividing before the "le" Ending Plus the Preceding Consonant

Say the words "table" and "middle" and ask the children to pronounce them after you and clap for the number of syllables they hear.

Write the words on the board as follows: "ta/ble," "mid/dle." Call attention to the fact that they both end in "le" and have a consonant in front of the "le" ending.

Ask the children to dictate more "le" ending words to write on the board, and elicit "people," "giggle," "purple," "kettle," "rattle," "gobble," "maple." Have the children take turns finding the "le" ending and the preceding consonant, and drawing the vertical syllabication line. Guide them to note that the accent is never on the "le" ending.

Write the word "whole" on the board and ask how to divide it. If a child says, "In front of the 'le,'" draw the vertical line as "who/le," and say, "Now it has two syllables. Pronounce it the way it is divided." (The child should then realize that it has a *vowel* instead of a consonant preceding the "le" ending, and should *not* be divided.)

As the understanding of syllables grows, guide the children to apply the vowel principles learned at the second level to the pronunciation of vowels in syllables.

After giving sufficient practice in syllabicating words which utilize the "le" ending, help the children draw up

3. The "le" Ending Rule

When a word ends in "le" preceded by a consonant, the word is split in front of the consonant preceding "le."

THE CONTENT OF A PROGRAM IN PHONETIC

Developing Phonetic Skills

Auditory perception of vowels (*a* unstressed as in *ago, again*).

Auditory perception of syllables (single-syllable words).

Visual-auditory perception of syllables (approach by comparing *bunch* with *es* ending in *bunches,* after work with single-syllable words).

Developing Phonetic Understandings

Silent: Consonants in words may be silent (*w* in *wren, wrong, wrap*).

Variability: Some consonants have variable sounds (*ch* in *Christmas* sounds like *k;* has another sound in *chocolate*).

Different letters may represent the same sound (*pound, crowd*).

Relation of vowel sounds and syllables: A word or part of a word in which there is one vowel sound is called a syllable. There are as many syllables as there are vowel sounds in a word. (Location of vowels in *lady, tonight, planning,* etc., to show number of syllables correspond.)

Principles for Determining Vowel Sounds

Position: If there is only one vowel in a word or syllable, that letter usually has the short sound unless it comes at the end of the word or syllable (*rent, cup, lot, gift; Tip/py, lad/der, sec/ond, ti/ger, la/dy*).

Silent vowels: If there are two vowels together in a word or syllable, usually the first has its long sound (*bea/ver, eat/en, teach/er*).

If there are two vowels in a word or syllable, one of which is final "e," usually the first vowel takes its long sound and the final "e" is silent (*rode, close, bye, ate, amuse*).

Consonant controllers: If the only vowel in a word or syllable is followed by "r," the sound of the vowel is usually controlled by "r" (*circus, winter, shoulder*).

If the only vowel in a word or syllable is "a" followed by "l" or "w," the "a" usually has neither the long nor the short sound (*almost, crawl*).

Using Structural Analysis in Attacking New Words

Recognizing words formed by adding prefixes and suffixes (*ly* and *y* as in *safely, airy; en* as in *golden, eaten; un* in *untied, unkind; ful* in *wonderful, helpful; er* of agent, *farmer, teacher, driver; ish* in *foolish, boyish; dis* in *dislike; re* in *reread*).

Recognizing words formed by doubling the final consonant, changing "y" to "i," or dropping final "e" before the ending (*trim, trimmed; fairy, fairies; file, filing*).

Recognizing compound words (*moonlight, pancakes, cardboard, storekeeper*).

Identifying root words in variants and derivatives (*fish* in *fisherman, fish* in *fishing; load* in *loaded; bob* in *bobbing; welcome* in *unwelcome; appear* in *disappear*).

Combining Structural and Phonetic Analysis

Identifying and attacking root words in variants and derivatives.

Identifying and attacking parts of compounds.

Identifying and attacking one syllable in a two-syllable word.

AND STRUCTURAL ANALYSIS—THIRD GRADE

Developing Phonetic Skills

Auditory perception of syllables and accent.

Developing Phonetic Understandings

Relation of vowel sounds and syllables: A word or a part of a word in which there is one vowel sound is called a syllable.

Awareness of syllabic division aids in determining vowel sounds in a word of more than one syllable (*de/cide, de/tec/tive*).

Principles for Determining Vowel Sounds

Position: If there is only one vowel in a word or syllable, that letter usually takes its short sound unless it comes at the end of the word or syllable (*win/ner, fas/ten; no/tion, la/zy*).

Silent vowels: If there are two vowels together in a word or syllable, usually the first takes its long sound and the second is silent (*easy*).

If there are two vowels in a word or syllable, one of which is final "e," usually the first vowel takes its long sound and the final "e" is silent (*blaze, disrobe, amuse*).

Consonant controllers: If the only vowel in a word or syllable is followed by "r," the sound of the vowel is usually controlled by "r."

If the only vowel in a word or syllable is "a" followed by "l" or "w," the "a" usually takes neither the long nor the short sound (*law, fall*).

Accent: In words of two or more syllables, one syllable is stressed or accented more than the other or others. Accent affects vowel sounds (compare *y* in *try* and *tiny*). Accent tends to shorten all vowels except "u."

Using Phonetic Analysis in Attacking New Words

Blending syllables into word wholes. Noting and using visual clues that aid in determining accented syllables in words: In most two-syllable words which end in a consonant followed by "y," the first syllable is accented and the second is unaccented.

If "de," "re," "be," "ex," "in," or "a" is first syllable, it is usually unaccented. Final "le" is usually not accented.

Using Structural Analysis in Attacking New Words

Recognizing words formed by adding prefixes or suffixes (*im, un, dis, ful*).

Understanding and Using the Principles of Syllabication

If the first vowel in a word is followed by two consonants, the first syllable usually ends with the first of the two consonants (*but/ton, prob/lem*).

If the first vowel letter in a word is followed by a single consonant, that consonant usually begins the second syllable (*be/gin, pu/pil, lo/cate*).

If the last syllable of a word ends in "le," the consonant preceding the "le" begins the last syllable (*cir/cle, pur/ple*).

Combining Structural and Phonetic Analysis

Identifying and attacking root words in variants and derivatives.

Identifying and attacking parts of compounds.

Identifying and attacking one syllable in a two-syllable word.

Fourth Grade. Because the English language is only partially phonetic, the children will soon discover that the application of vowel and syllabication rules does not always help them in recognizing and pronouncing unfamiliar words. The exceptions to the rule call for the next step, that is, turning to the dictionary for help in pronunciation. The children will also meet many words which follow the vowel and syllabication rules but which are unfamiliar in *meaning*. Here, again, recourse must be had to the dictionary. The teacher's major task, then, at the fourth-grade level is that of giving instruction in dictionary skills. These skills, with recommended teaching procedures, are listed below. The teacher should schedule as many lessons to introduce these dictionary skills as her particular group of children seems to require.

Learning Locational Skills for the Dictionary

To guide the children in the use of locational skills, explain that the word that sends people to the dictionary is technically known as the "entry" word. Write the term *entry word* on the blackboard, and explain that people look up words because they are uncertain of meaning, uncertain of pronunciation, or uncertain of both.

Place the unfamiliar word "baffle" on the blackboard and ask a child to look it up. Suppose he wastes time looking for it on a page with the guide word "battle" at the top; then show him how necessary it is to learn the alphabet consecutively, in order to know whether to look ahead or to look back from the page opened.

Show that it is important to have a command of structural analysis (endings, prefixes, suffixes, syllabication) in order to know what the root form of an entry word may be. Explain that, since the dictionary does not list "filing" but only "file," it is necessary to know the final "e" is dropped when "ing" is added. Tell the children to take off the "ing" ending mentally, understand that final "e" was dropped when the new ending was added, restore it, and get the word "file" listed in the dictionary.

Learning Pronunciation Skills for the Dictionary

Give the children definite guidance in interpreting dictionary pronunciations. Show that, if they can recognize the long, short, and unstressed vowel sounds alone, they can accurately determine the pronunciation of at least 75 per cent of the words they have to look up in a juvenile dictionary.[4]

[4] Particularly recommended are the *Thorndike-Barnhart Beginning Dictionary* (grades 4–5) and the *Thorndike-Barnhart Junior Dictionary* (grades 5–8), (Chicago: Scott, Foresman & Co., 1959).

Teach the children the difference between primary and secondary accents. Have them test a word orally by repeating it until the accent is satisfactorily placed.

Learning To Select Pertinent Meanings

Give the children definite instructions in this skill. They often confuse meanings by seizing upon the first definition listed instead of selecting one appropriate to a given context.

Give thorough guidance in helping children to comprehend defined meanings and to adapt these to the given context.

Fifth Grade. The two main word-recognition skills to be taught children at this closing level of the sequential program are (1) understanding figurative language and (2) recognizing multiple meanings of words.

Understanding Figurative Language

Since it is not possible to enumerate examples of figurative language —their number is legion—as one enumerates the five vowel rules, lesson steps cannot be outlined here for teaching this skill. But the teacher should seize every opportunity to help the children in their daily reading to go beyond the literal meaning of a word used figuratively. Figurative phrases such as "The grocer was *running out of flour*" or "He *hit the ceiling*" seem to adults easy to understand. But these phrases demand more than mere recognition of words: It is necessary to go beyond the literal meaning of "running" and "hit" to more complicated mental images. Imaginative visualization is required. The best practice seems to be first to clarify the literal meaning of words used in a figure of speech and then to lead the children to establish some understanding of the figurative meaning. Lesson plans in the teacher's guidebook for the basic series make provision for growth in these skills as figurative words and phrases arise in context.

Recognizing Multiple Meanings of Words

Many children reach the fifth proficiency level in the middle grades. At this time teachers can begin to help children to detect "loaded" or "weighted" words which arouse emotional reactions and impede clear thinking. It is quite easy for them to understand why such derogatory nicknames as "Jap" and "Wop" are more than mere words. Children can be helped to realize that such a word as "democracy" means many things to many people when they are given the opportunity to tell what democracy means to each of them. Multiple meanings of words, or semantics, require a mental skill which develops even more gradually than the understanding of figurative language. Lesson plans in the basic manuals provide for growth in this skill as words and phrases arise in context. To gain background concerning the implications of semantics for straight thinking, the teacher should read Stuart Chase's *The Proper Study of Mankind* (New York: Harper & Row, 1948).

QUESTIONS AND ACTIVITIES

1. Now that you have studied the chapter, underline the term in the following list of choices which means the same as phonics: sight words, structural analysis, phonetic analysis.
2. In the following, which is the most inclusive, comprehensive process? structural analysis, word analysis, phonetic analysis?
3. Fill in the blanks below:

   a. The first step in word analysis involves listening for r———— sounds and naming items in pictures.
   b. The second step involves naming items in pictures but this time listening for b———— sounds.
   c. In between *b* above and *d* below, children learn some sight w———— by the look-say method as they read easy reading books called p————.
   d. This step develops from the three above. The newly learned s———— words are recognized. Suppose they consist of "do," "did," "dog." The teacher asks, "Do they l———— alike at the beginning? Do they s———— alike the beginning? They all start with the l———— *d*."
   e. When the child substitutes a new beginning on a familiar rhymed ending the process is called c———— substitution. Sometimes if a whole series of words is used, as in going from "rest" to "pest" to "west" to "crest," the process has another name, i.e., serial s————.

4. What confuses some students is the order of learning the first two ear-training steps in early stages of word analysis. Because rhymes are easy for children to detect, the analysis *begins* with them, but rhymes, of course, occur at the *end* of a word. On the other hand, *beginning* consonants are harder to deal with and come *last*. It would therefore be more convenient for the prospective teacher to remember if the second step b———— sounds came first and the first step dealing with e———— sounds came last! True or False?
5. What would be the danger of depending on sight words alone for word recognition?

6. At what grade level and for what particular job do the children need to learn the whole alphabet *consecutively?* At what stage do the children learn fifteen of the most used beginning consonants by name? Which consonants are not stressed at this point? Why not? At what level do the children learn the six vowels?

7. Underline the roots in "calling," "uncalled-for," "unforgettable." Name the simple ending; name two prefixes used here; name two suffixes used. What is this process: phonetic analysis or structural analysis?

8. Here are some made-up words: "parx," "cax," "mo," "greach," "zene."

    a. Which word is pronounced according to the consonant-controller-vowel rule?
    b. Which words make use of the long-vowel rule?
    c. What two words follow the principle of silentness (i.e., have some silent vowels)?
    d. Which word follows the short-vowel rule?
    e. Which two words follow the principle of position with the place of the vowel in the word affecting the way it is pronounced?

9. Here are some made-up words of two syllables: "slobax," "swurple," "witdem." Look toward the middle of the first word. Have you found a visual clue? Where do you usually split to form syllables when there is a single consonant surrounded by vowels? How do you split the second word to form syllables? Is the "le" a sufficient visual clue to indicate syllabication, or what else must be considered? Mark vowels in each of the syllables for pronunciation. Why do you have to know the position of the vowels through syllabication before you can give their correct pronunciation in the third word?

10. Pronounce the word "awful." Divide it into syllables by using the single-consonant rule. Now, what is the first syllable? Why is "a" neither long nor short but pronounced in a different way? What is controlling this vowel? How many vowels are controlled by "l," "w"?

11. All but one of the reading experts who aided in preparing the Conant report condemned a formal phonics approach and recommended following the sequential program in the teacher's manual for the basic reading series in use. Do you agree with them? Examine some books exclusively devoted to phonics, and compare them with a teacher's manual for any one of the primary readers

of a basic series. (See the third lesson plan step—drills, related practice, etc.) Muster your final arguments.

SELECTED REFERENCES

CONANT, JAMES B., *et al. Learning To Read: A Report of a Conference of Reading Experts.* Princeton, N.J.: Educational Testing Service, June, 1962.

DURKIN, DOLORES. *Phonics and the Teaching of Reading,* No. 22. New York: Bureau of Publications, Teachers College, Columbia University, 1962.

GATES, ARTHUR I. "Results of Teaching a *System* of Phonics," *The Reading Teacher* (March 1961), 248–52.

GATES, ARTHUR I. "A Review of *Tomorrow's Illiterates* by Charles C. Walcutt, and *What Ivan Knows that John Doesn't* by Arthur S. Trace, Jr." New York: Bureau of Publications, Teachers College, Columbia University, 1962.

GATES, ARTHUR I. *Reading Attainment in Elementary Schools: 1957– 1937.* New York: Teachers College, Bureau of Publications, Columbia University, 1961.

GRAY, WILLIAM S. *On Their Own in Reading* (2d ed.). Chicago: Scott, Foresman & Co., 1960.

HARRIS, ALBERT J. *How To Increase Reading Ability* (4th ed.). New York: Longmans, Green & Co., Inc., 1961.

HILDRETH, GERTRUDE. *Teaching Reading.* New York: Holt, Rinehart & Winston, Inc., 1958.

RUSSELL, DAVID H., and ETTA E. KARP. *Reading Aids Through the Grades.* New York: Bureau of Publications, Teachers College, Columbia University, 1955.

Reading for Today's Children, Thirty-fourth Yearbook of the Department of Elementary School Principals, Washington, D.C.: National Education Association of the United States, XXXV (September 1955).

WALPOLE, HUGH. *Semantics: The Nature of Words and Their Meanings.* New York: W. W. Norton & Co., Inc., 1941.

SAPIR, EDWARD. *Language: An Introduction to the Study of Speech.* New York: Harcourt, Brace & World, Inc., 1949.

SOFFIETTI, JAMES P. "Why Children Fail To Read: A Linguistic Analysis," *Harvard Educational Review,* XXV (Spring 1955), 63–94.

PART IV

ADDITIONAL ASPECTS
OF THE READING PROGRAM

12

READING IN THE CONTENT FIELDS

In the education profession, the term *content-fields reading* usually refers to the reading of books devoted to special fields such as geography, history, and home economics. The layman seldom uses the term or, indeed, ever thinks of its implications. Nevertheless, when he reads an item in the newspaper, a recipe in a cookbook, or the information on a traffic citation, he is reading content pertaining to the fields of current history, home economics, and civics. During the course of an ordinary day, the average adult may be called upon to read restaurant menus, insurance policies, professional magazines—to mention a few more examples of specialized content—and, if he is a skilled reader, he will gear his reading to suit varying purposes and materials, in somewhat the same way that he drives a car at different rates, depending upon the nature of the errand and the type of traffic encountered.

Some kinds of materials require only the briefest skimming; others warrant lengthy study. In reading an editorial tirade in a partisan newspaper, the individual has every right to interpret it freely; obviously, this does not apply to reading a telephone number. Think how handicapped an adult would be if he used the same set of habits and attitudes in reading income-tax instructions and in reading a partisan newspaper. In the first instance, verbatim retention is essential; in the second, he can interpret as freely as he pleases. If anyone doubts this point, he has only to visualize the federal government's disapproval of such personal interpretation of an income-tax blank.

As in life, many kinds of content reading are demanded in school. Only that reading program is valid which gives children direct, planned guidance in using the many types of reading demanded by our complicated civilization. Without definite training, how can children learn to utilize all the different reading skills they will be expected to apply to content reading in life?

CONTENT-READING PROBLEMS

In schoolwork, few areas place as many demands on reading as the content fields of social studies, science, arithmetic, and so on. When, in the fourth grade, reading in the content fields is taken up in earnest, children should be so guided that they will enter upon a period of discovery and broadening horizons. Many teachers, however, fail to comprehend the enlarged task which the children face at this level—which is sometimes aptly referred to as the "great divide"—and a seeming lack of interest on the part of a child in social studies or other content fields may not be recognized for what it is: sheer inability to meet new and complex reading demands.

Reading in the basic reader constitutes an easier task for children than reading in the content fields. Various important factors are controlled in the basic reader which cannot be similarly controlled in books dealing with subject-matter content. For example: vocabulary in the content fields is usually more difficult; new terms are introduced faster and with fewer repetitions; more facts are presented to the reader; greater retention is expected; and references to previous facts occur with more frequency in historical, geographical, and other such materials.

At one time it was considered sufficient for the teacher to concern herself solely with the subject matter of the geography, history, civics, or natural-science textbook. But, more and more, the needs and abilities of children as individuals are being recognized and considered. This trend has focused increasing attention on the method to be used in reading various types of content. In other words, pupils require instruction of one type for reading social-studies content; of another, for dealing with arithmetic problems; of still another, for coping with materials that bristle with scientific terms. Different reading techniques are demanded by each content field, and these techniques must be taught in the period set aside for the subject. No matter how excellent the instruction in basic reading, children need additional definite guidance in handling curricular reading, and some children will need more guidance than others. A detailed discussion of some of the major content-reading problems is presented below.

The Challenge of Specialized Vocabularies. A certain technical vocabulary characterizes each of the subject-matter fields. Children must be prepared for reading such materials. Unless they have a background of clear concepts, children cannot read with sufficient comprehension. It is the teacher's job to define technical terms in language that the child can understand. When the dictionary is used, as it should be almost constantly, it is the teacher's task to help the child to interpret the various definitions presented and to select the one applicable to a given passage. Denied such guidance, children obtain vague and fuzzy ideas or, worse still, completely erroneous concepts. In geography, for example, words are found with connotations peculiar to the subject, such as "alluvial *fan*," "*relief* map," "river *mouth*."

This need for clarification of terminology extends to all content areas. In arithmetic, the child encounters *subtract, dividend,* and other equally technical terms. In civics, he is asked to deal with the *minutes* of the last meeting, with members addressing the *chair,* and the *carrying* of a motion. Faced with these distinctive vocabularies, the child must not be left to his own resources.

Rapid Introduction of Concepts. Content books often overwhelm the child by presenting too many concepts with too few explanations. One geography book, for example, actually contains 200 new terms in one section. These are introduced with machine-gun rapidity and are given little or no development or clarification. One paragraph in another current geography uses such terms as *cenote, limestone formation, Mayan civilization, maize,* and *milpa* in dealing with a study of Yucatan. Obviously, the teacher must prepare the child to understand such reading through discussion and visual aids. To treat geographical content as if it were general reading matter is a major error. One investigator was astonished to find children in the fifth grade pronouncing words such as "peninsula," "piedmont," and "delta" without being able to identify them on the nearby landscape. What complicates the problem is that there are no accurate synonyms to use with slower readers. Would anyone, for example, be satisfied to call *tropical jungles* "hot woods"?

Special Study Skills Required. The nature of each subject in the content fields makes it obligatory to read them in various ways. When doing supplementary reading in civics, history, and geography, for instance, children need to learn the art of skimming, of ignoring words or topics encountered along the way in favor of concentrating on the search for the needed information in the reference book, dictionary, or encyclopedia. Experience shows that children also need to be taught how to take notes from different books in preparing social-studies reports. Moreover, they need definite instructions in collecting and synthesizing materials from a variety of sources. Unless such training is forthcoming, children tend to copy reams of notes verbatim.

Geographical achievement requires geographical thinking. To read about Mexico and conclude the lesson by asking questions such as "How big is a burro?" or "How many baskets do you see in this picture?" is a waste of valuable teaching and learning time. Make geographical *use* of these facts. For example, the teacher might ask, "How has the small size of the burro contributed to the problem of transporting heavy goods in mountain areas?" "What income is received from the fine baskets made at Toluca?" "How does this income raise the standard of living of the people in that region of Mexico?"

Extra Demands on the Teacher. With the content subjects especially, the teacher must supplement the textbook from her own background and experience. She will need to clarify concepts for the child, to help him interpret what he reads in terms of his experience, and to suggest further reading and study. When dealing with natural science or the social sciences, it is necessary to supplement the spoken and written word with excursions, pictures, objects, museum trips, and construction activities. Low accomplishment in social-studies reading frequently is not so much evidence of poor instruction in basic reading as it is an indication of insufficient background in the specific subject-matter areas involved—though, of course, social studies and reading reinforce each other here. In short, children are not usually poor in reading and good in social studies. However, they may be good in reading and poor in social studies if they need additional help with study skills and background, and do not get it. The social-studies teacher must not sidestep her responsibility here if the students cannot read effectively. Helping them with reading difficulties will result in progress in social studies.

It is also part of the teacher's task to enlarge her own background by mastering a wide range of accurate factual information. As someone interested particularly in natural science has complained, the ignorance of teachers regarding plants, animals, and flowers is proverbial. This type of accusation could also be made against many other teachers who have collected superficial facts connected with a given unit of work, for example, those in the social studies who have not informed themselves about various political, social, and economic events in the news which would add depth to the school unit.

To help the teacher to understand the complexities associated with guiding reading in the content fields, it may prove useful to consider each field in turn, listing the reading skills and habits required and the special problems encountered. Actual lesson plans will be presented in several of the content areas: a lesson involving geography reading in a single text book, geography reading through the use of reference books, a history-reading lesson, two lessons in reading current-events papers, and a science-reading lesson. Space precludes lesson plans in other content fields, but it is hoped that the examples offered may be sufficient to show how many problems are involved in giving effective instruction. In general, this type of reading requires patience with technical terms, a willingness to reread, a certain discipline in confronting a great deal of factual data, and a readiness to make practical appliction of the content.

READING GEOGRAPHY CONTENT

Although most schools now integrate geography, history, and civics, teaching them as social studies, or handle them in relation to a major unit, the teacher must still prepare children to read materials in these areas adequately. Regardless of the curriculum plan in use, experimentation has shown that the children need to be taught directly, rather than incidentally, to understand concepts which are primarily geographical in nature. In reading geography content children need to be taught to

1. Sense space relationships. *A thousand miles* is a distance difficult for children to understand even though they can easily read the words. To give children an accurate notion of this distance, it is necessary to compare it with the distance to the farthest places to which they have been. To teach directions, children must be taught the location and significance of *north,* and not conceive of it, for example, as the "top of the map."

2. Understand how geography influences people and events. In this instance it may be helpful to remind children how lazy they feel on a very hot day. Thus they will be enabled to understand the attitude of tropical natives and their comparative lack of progress, in the Congo region, for example.

3. Prepare detailed, well-organized reports for class discussion from materials read in different books.

4. Get the facts straight. No fact is worth learning unless its importance is understood and it is accurately assimilated.

5. Sense cause-and-effect relationships. For example, the heavy rainfall and high temperature in the Amazon region cause impenetrable jungles, which in turn make transportation and communication difficult, which in turn impedes progress.

6. Recognize generalities such as the fact that increased altitude indicates a cooler climate.

7. Find the main ideas in an involved paragraph containing cross-references and extraneous details.

8. Recognize supporting details.

9. Understand terminology. One investigator has shown, for instances, that present-day geographies average a special geographical vocabulary of 60 terms in the third grade, 100 in the fourth, 150 in the fifth, and 250 in the sixth.

10. Classify geographical concepts according to basic human needs: food, shelter, clothing, occupations, recreation, communication, transportation, aesthetic expression, government, education, and religion.
11. Compare statements and draw accurate conclusions.
12. Read graphs, maps. For example, the teacher may direct attention to the map as follows: "Look at the scale on the map. What distance represents 100 miles? Now estimate the distance between Buenos Aires and Rio de Janeiro. Compare it with some distance you've actually traveled."

Many teachers are still using ruinously sterile methods in the teaching of geography. That extra touch, that added attention to careful and creative preparation for adequate reading, that planning that would make the geography lesson a real contribution to the children's development, is often lacking.

Deeper meanings and implications of the subject should greatly concern the teacher. Attitudes and interests and habits of thought about the world are involved when children attempt to deal with geographical material. All too often, a child reading about a custom in Brazil ends by provincially congratulating himself because *he* is not as strange and different as some Brazilians are.

During the conduct of a unit organized for the study of a particular country, several types of reading lessons may be used. Sometimes there are appreciation lessons, as when children read a strikingly beautiful description of the harbor at Rio de Janeiro. At other times, work-type lessons may help the children to acquire increased skill in the use of the index and table of contents or in fusing ideas gained from a variety of sources. Almost certainly, the state text in geography will be used for part of the work. One sixth-grade geography lesson plan for dealing with a section in a textbook about the Amazon region of Brazil is presented below. This lesson plan differs from a basic developmental plan, for, as the teacher guides the reading, she elicits points from the children to use in making an outline of the material on the board. Later this outline is used to help the children write summarizing paragraphs of the content. Another difference is that a check test is given at the close of the reading to determine the degree of retention of factual data.

LESSON PLAN FOR TEACHING GEOGRAPHY READING

I. What (subject matter) The Amazon Jungle

Human Geography by J. Russell Smith
Visual aids: Maps, flat pictures

II. Why (aims)

A. Fact aims

To help the children

1. Understand how the Amazon Jungle has influenced the economic development of Brazil
2. Recognize the advantages and disadvantages of the Amazon Jungle to Brazil
3. Learn new words and concepts such as "navigable," "tributaries," "tropical," "boa constrictor," "vampire bats," "alligator"

B. Skill aims

To teach the children how to

1. Make an outline
2. Reason from effect back to cause
3. Pay attention to topic headings in organizing thinking
4. Respect accurate retention of significant facts which should be common knowledge
5. Understand the meaning of geographical terms and to transfer them to their permanent stock
6. Summarize material after it is read

C. Social aims

To guide the children to

1. Appreciate the advantages to man of a favorable geographical environment by showing that the United States has been more fortunate in its climate, topography, and natural resources than Brazil
2. Develop an interest in actual travel
3. Develop an interest in traveling vicariously through reading books and magazines

III. How (method)

  A. Motivating the reading

    1. Arouse interest in the geography content to be ready by

      a. Writing on the blackboard population figures for the United States (over 180 million) and Brazil (80 million), revealing that the United States has approximately 100 million more people

      b. Superimposing a map of the United States over a map of Brazil (both drawn to scale), showing that the latter exceeds the United States in area by the size of the state of Texas

    2. Raise the problem question:

    Why is it that, though Brazil is larger than the United States in land area, it has so few people in comparison?

      a. Cannot people live there comfortably?

      b. Is there much uninhabitable land going to waste?

    3. Make the assignment:

      a. Turn to the section on Brazil in the geography book.

      b. Find the part labeled "The Amazon Region: An Equatorial Rain Forest." To study this may help to answer the problem question.

  B. Guiding the reading and making an outline simultaneously

    1. Ask the pupils to look at the first topic heading again (see 3b above). Discuss the meaning of "equatorial rain forest," and show pictures to clarify it.

    2. Begin to incorporate in an outline on the board the facts discovered during the reading (any outline form is acceptable, but for this particular selection the content divided into two main sections, "Advantages of the Amazon Jungle to Brazil" and Disadvantages of the Amazon Jungle to Brazil"):

      I. Advantages of the Amazon Jungle to Brazil

        A. Products

          (a) Small amounts of rubber
          (b) Small amounts of mahogany
          (c) Brazil nuts in abundance
          (d) Cacao production

B. Amazon River navigable for almost 3,000 miles

II. Disadvantages of the Amazon Jungle to Brazil

    A. Position near the equator causes

        1. Tropical heat
        2. Floods
        3. Dense foliage

           a. Hard to farm
           b. Hard to build roads

        4. Many pests

           a. Insects: mosquitoes, army ants, etc.
           b. Mammals: jaguars, vampire bats, etc.
           c. Reptiles: boa constrictors, crocodiles

        5. Presence of savage tribes who alone seem able to withstand heat, etc.

C. Writing a composite paragraph

    1. Call on various children to suggest sentences to summarize the material of the outline on the blackboard.

        a. *First Version* (Children's unedited suggestions)

        Are you thinking of going to the Amazon to live? Well, stop to think what it is like. There are a lot of things that are hard to take down there. The climate is hot and rainy. There are a lot of floods. There aren't any roads, only trees and other things growing. There are mosquitoes, tsetse flies, army ants, alligators, vampire bats, tapirs, boa constrictors, and savage Indian tribes. But the Amazon region has three good things. You can raise rubber. You can raise cacao. You can raise Brazil nuts.

        b. *Second version* (after children have been helped to improve syntax by combining sentences, balancing phrases, reorganizing facts, and selecting words with more precision)

        Before moving to the Amazon region of Brazil, jungle enthusiasts should investigate living conditions. Since this third of Brazil is located near the equator, there are almost insurmountable disadvantages. Though the immigrant can enter the region quite easily by boat, because of the navigability of the Amazon for almost 3,000 miles, once the river is left for land, the dense forest makes traveling very nearly impossible. The heavy rainfall causes such a dense growth of vegetation that it is difficult to clear the land for farming. In addition to savage tribes, there are other dangers from the numerous insect, reptile, and mammal pests. To offset these disadvantages, a small profit is gained from the production of rubber, cacao, and Brazil nuts. All in all, the region is not appealing to civilized men. No wonder this vast area is largely wasted! These disadvantages help to account for the smaller population of a giant country like Brazil, as compared with the large population of the United States.

D. Following up the reading
   1. Give a factual test to check retention.
   2. Invite the children to read supplementary books about the Amazon region and other parts of Brazil.

IV. Evaluating the Lesson

List the children's gains. Compare these gains with the original aims. Which were achieved? Which require more teaching?

A guided-reading session in a geography textbook resembles supervised study. During the guidance session the teacher might ask questions such as "What two main things do you expect to find in this paragraph after reading the topic heading in boldface type?" "Do all the facts seem to you to belong to this heading?" "What is the next topic heading?" "What will you expect to find here?" "Now that you have read the paragraph, does it seem to you that this is a good topic heading?" "What heading would you suggest instead?"

As the pupil analyzes the paragraph, naming its separate parts and looking for relationships, he is learning to think clearly about data and is building the habit of selecting facts to organize into an outline. After several such supervised periods, the more accelerated pupils can proceed independently, reading to make reports for the social-studies unit of work on pertinent problems which arise.

The last-named type of reading involves research, the process of locating content related to a given topic and rejecting irrelevant material. In the early stages—in fourth, fifth, and possibly in a slow-moving sixth grade—the teacher herself looks up reference materials, directing children to them by means of typed or printed direction cards (which give the title of the book and page references) as well as by guiding questions, or directions, to lend purpose to the reading.

An example of a research reading lesson related to a fifth- or sixth-grade unit on Brazil is given below. Some topic, such as coffee production, attracts the attention of the committee studying occupations in different parts of Brazil, and the teacher prepares a reference-reading lesson to meet the needs of this committee.

A REFERENCE-READING LESSON USED WITH A UNIT ON BRAZIL

1. The teacher locates books which contain references to the topic "Coffee Production in Brazil." She notes paragraphs and sections which deal with such subtopics as the coffee plant, soil, climate, planting, harvesting, drying, hulling, grading, storing, shipping, roasting, and marketing.

2. The teacher types the title of the reference book, the pages, and a few questions on three-by-five-inch cards. For instance, if the committee investigating occupations in Brazil is composed of four children, there would be four direction cards containing material such as

First reference: *The Fertile Land of Brazil* by Sydney Greenbie (New York: Harper & Row), p. 8.
What do coffee berries resemble? How are they picked? Where does coffee grow best?

Second reference: *Coffee: The Story of a Good Neighbor Product* (New York: Pan American Coffee Bureau), p. 8.
How is coffee stored? Shipped?

Third reference: *Brazil; Land of Surprises,* by Ralph Haefner (Chicago: Lyons & Carnahan), p. 100.
Read what this reference says about coffee coming to Brazil from French Guiana. Which member of the governor's family allegedly smuggled the coffee plant to the Brazilian army officer?

Fourth reference: *Our Good Neighbors in Latin America* by Wallace West (New York: Barnes & Noble, Inc.), p. 52.
Read what this reference says about coffee coming to Brazil from Dutch Guiana. Which member of the governor's family allegedly smuggled the coffee plant to the Brazilian

major? Since this reference disagrees with the third reference, to discover the true facts, look up the main topic "Brazil" the subtopic "Coffee," and the second subtopic "History of Coffee Growing in Brazil" in the encyclopedia.

3. The teacher hands the direction cards containing the above material to the committee.
4. Each child takes his direction card and finds his reference among the many books on the reading table.
5. A period of study follows while the children follow the directions appearing on the cards and prepare to read aloud. The teacher helps with difficult words.
6. Each member of the committee reads to the other members of the group.
7. With books closed, the children test each other informally, chatting and discussing points such as the conflicting data on the exportation of coffee from one of the Guianas to Brazil. A point is made concerning the need for looking in many places for data.
8. The children *individually* write up the topic and the best write-up goes into the Class Record Book for the unit of work. As an alternative, the entire committee may dictate a *composite* summary for the teacher to write on the blackboard, after which it is copied, and the best one included in the Class Record Book. A typical composite paragraph, which shows the effects of necessary help given by the teacher in transferring some of the new words, follows:

Brazil's Biggest Crop

Although three-fourths of the world's coffee comes from Brazil, the coffee plant was not native to Brazil but brought from one of the Guianas. The trees grow nine feet high and require a subtropical climate and well-drained uplands. Since coffee berries must be picked by hand, many workers are needed on a coffee *finca*. After the coffee is harvested, it is dried, hulled, graded, and stored in São Paulo. From there it goes to Santos on the coast. This is the port from which coffee is sent to the United States and other countries.

READING HISTORY CONTENT

The purposes of reading history content vary according to the viewpoint of the teacher or the textbook in use. One teacher may feel that the chief goal of history study is to acquire knowledge of the progress and culture of man; another may insist that the primary purpose is to help to interpret life today; a third may feel that the ultimate goal is to help each child build a philosophy of life that will develop the high ideals of democratic citizenship. Whatever the viewpoint of the teacher, her objectives will usually become the goals of her pupils, and these goals will become the purposes which motivate reading. The progressive teacher will strive for a combination of such purposes in teaching her children to read history meaningfully. In reading history, children need to be taught to

1. Read history as a true story with implications important to the individual living today
2. Sense cause and effect relationships, to trace results back to causes and to predict results from events
3. Become acquainted with sources of materials in this field
4. Read historical materials voluntarily
5. Compare parallel materials in different books
6. Know the difference between original source materials and secondary sources
7. Compare the past and present
8. Distinguish between relevant and irrelevant materials
9. Develop an interest in fascimiles of historical documents
10. Understand "internal evidence" and its fascinating role in exposing historical hoaxes (This should appeal to the detective instinct in each individual.)
11. Note the time of the occurrence of events
12. Pay attention to chronological sequence
13. Apply old knowledge to new situations
14 Select and organize materials for outlining
15 Understand the significance of factual data
16 Group items to be learned in a meaningful association instead of memorizing them singly (For example, children should be encouraged to form the habit of thinking in terms of key persons, key events, key periods, key topics.)
17. Form the habit of associating personalities with events instead of attempting to remember isolated facts
18. Understand the special vocabulary of this field

Reading to gain information to solve a problem involves a reading ability so necessary that it calls for more complete discussion than a mere listing of facts. The society in which American children are growing today is charged with problems which need to be solved by citizens free of prejudice or bias, citizens who can think objectively and critically. In the schoolroom this democratic function can be stressed and practiced during social studies. Below is an example of an eighth-grade lesson plan in the content field of history, with problem solving as its main goal.

LESSON PLAN FOR TEACHING HISTORY READING

I. What (subject matter)

Section in the eighth-grade history book concerning the Constitution of the United States. Facsimile of the Constitution.

Section in the history book dealing with the Articles of Confederation. Fascimile of this document.

Section in the history book concerning the United Nations Charter. Fascimile of the Charter.

Maps of the thirteen original colonies, map of the southern states, map of the United States, world map.

II. Why (aims)

To teach the children to

A. Sense cause and effect relationships, to trace results back to causes and to predict results from events
B. Compare parallel materials, for example, the great documents being studied
C. Compare the past and present
D. Apply history to new situations
E. Organize or *group* items to be learned into a meaningful association

III. How (method)

A. Display the fascimiles of the three documents named above and lead the children to discuss them. Use maps freely during this discussion. Explain new words incidentally. Raise two problem questions: (1) "Why was it that the Articles of Confederation failed, while the Constitution has stood the test of almost two centuries?" (2) "Will the fate of the United Nations Charter be that of the Constitution or the Articles of Confederation?"

B. Refer the children to pertinent sections in their history books, and make available several other reliable sources, marking the pages dealing with the first two documents being compared.

C. Lead the children to analyze the information they have read during a study period and to explain how they relate it to the first problem question above.

D. Help the children to reach some conclusion about the first question, both individually and as a group.

E. Lead the children from the conclusion above to the application step. Ask them, "How can we apply what we have learned about the past to situations today? Is there any relationship between this struggle for a better type of national government and the efforts of the United Nations to become a successful world organization?" (To answer these further, meaningful reading about the two documents and the United Nations Charter is necessary.)

IV. Evaluating the Lesson

A. What went right in the lesson? What evidence proves this?

B. How could the learning situation have been improved?

Suppose that, after teaching the above history lesson, the teacher wrote in her evaluation that the children had been interested in the facsimiles of the three documents but had been puzzled by a great many terms met in their reading. Her next move might be to clarify these terms by every means possible.

When considering the problems of reading textbooks in history, the late Henry Johnson of Columbia University, the dean of history teachers in the United States, pointed out how difficult the involved style of some history books is to the young student unless guidance is given in interpretation. He quoted a passage concerning the founding of Massachusetts in 1629 which read

Unlike the poor and humble Pilgrims were the founders of Massachusetts. They were men of wealth and social position, as, for instance, John Winthrop and Sir Richard Saltonstall. They left comfortable homes in England to found a Pilgrim State in America. . . .

Johnson's comment on this in his text is interesting:

The words are simple. Children even in the sixth grade can read them and give them back in the class recitation. The routine teacher, content to rest the matter there, will get the impression that the book is adequate. However, do children see or feel anything except words? Do they *see* any Pilgrims? Do they *see* what was happening to America?

What are comfortable homes? Wealth? And social position? . . . Obviously, one thing to children in the crowded tenements of New York, and another thing to the children in the mansions on Fifth Avenue, and still another to the children on a farm. . . . What do the words actually tell them about the circumstances of the Puritans? What is gained by naming John Winthrop and Sir Richard Saltonstall in passing? What does it mean to a sixth-grade child?[1]

The teacher of history who is eager to stimulate the habit of extensive reading for information, understanding, and experience will take steps to make the subject matter as lucid and interesting as possible. The following suggestions may offer some practical ideas in conducting the work in history. Although activities are an essential part of the modern program, ample time must be provided for guided reading in the group and for interpretative discussion.

EXAMPLES OF HISTORY ACTIVITIES

1. Children, particularly in the intermediate and upper grades, enjoy rewriting history as though designed for a modern newspaper, with headlines such as "COLUMBUS DISCOVERS AMERICA!" This follows the ingenious example set in a book called *News of the Nation: A Newspaper History of the United States.*[2] For example, a sixth grade, studying the history of California and the establishment of a series of missions by the Franciscan priest Father Junipero Serra, wrote the event as a modern newspaper might:

Final Edition

San Diego   July 2, 1769

Weather: No Smog Today

FATHER SERRA IS HERE!

Following a record-breaking 400-mile walk from Mexico, Padre Junipero Serra has arrived in San Diego and will build a chain of super-missions.

---

[1] *The Teaching of History* (rev. ed.; New York: The Macmillan Co., 1940), pp. 243–44.
[2] Sylvan Hoffman and C. Hartley Grattan (2d ed.; New York: Garden City Books).

2. It is often valuable to introduce biographies as a background to purely textbook material. In studying the achievements of Columbus, Jefferson, Franklin, and others, it is possible to humanize the heroes and yet remain faithful to fact. As someone has sternly pointed out, "Characters greatly distorted for moral or patriotic ends can serve no definite historical purpose." On the other hand, the practice of "debunking" (mentioning slightly questionable facts that have no real significance in or bearing on a great leader's true contribution) is not to be recommended either. Children may profitably seek answers to such questions as What kind of home did Franklin come from? What educational advantages did he enjoy? What was his occupation? Who were his friends? What were his hobbies?

3. It is desirable to arrange trips to museums to view the interesting display of historical objects. These trips furnish additional background for understanding the past and appreciating the present.

4. Historical fiction and historical movies may increase interest in famous figures and events described in history books.

5. Children should be encouraged to bring family keepsakes of historical value for temporary exhibit in the school museum.

6. The display of photostats of original documents helps to build respect for the progress our country has made toward enlightenment. This, coupled with the desire to promote a closer bond of unity among our people, was the motivating purpose for the long pilgrimage of the "freedom train." The display of original documents also develops respect for written records as compared with verbal reports.

7. Checking out pictures and books with historical implications from the visual-aids center and the library will do much to enliven the reading in the history text. The children should be stimulated to get ideas, not just blurred images, from the pictures. The teacher must lead them to observe, compare, classify, and generalize what they see in pictures.

8. Children may stage historical pageants and plays to make the past more vivid and to help clarify their understanding of men, both as causes and as pawns of great movements.

9. Children should be encouraged to evolve time charts, tracing the history of the development of transportation, of the westward

movement, of aviation. (One group of children approached the problem by making time charts of outstanding events in their own lives. Thus one boy's chart listed, "Born, 1950. Family moved from Iowa to California, 1956. My rooster won Fourth prize in the county fair in 1962.")

10. Children may enjoy painting murals to illustrate famous historical happenings or historical sequence.

11. Children should be encouraged to learn *some* facts about history. While few teachers would want to return children to the barren custom of learning long lists of battle dates, they would like the children to understand the causes of some of the major wars, in the hope that, if the motivating factors which brought on wars in the past are widely understood, future conflicts may be avoided. It is impossible to think in a vacuum; a factual background is needed. Only by mastering certain factual data connected with the development of the United States, for example, can children learn to appreciate forces and ideals which have shaped its growth.

12. Children should be given much experience in research reading. The history textbook may be used as a point of departure for the reading of many reference books. It is certainly a valuable experience for the children to be taught not to regard unreflectingly everything they see in print as true. If one reference book on the history of coffee production in Brazil states that the plant was brought there from French Guiana, while another maintains just as firmly that the plant was brought to Brazil from Dutch Guiana, the true facts should be sought in some reputable reference like the *Encyclopaedia Britannica*.

READING CURRENT-EVENTS CONTENT

In reading newspapers, news magazines, or current-events periodicals designed for school use (*My Weekly Reader, The Junior Review, Current Events,* and the like), children should be taught how to discern the essentials in such content. They should know how to

1. Gain and remember news materials that may prove useful in discussion

2. Classify news items (local, national, international, human interest) to promote clearer thinking
3. Learn to label facts according to the "nose-for-news" formula
4. Develop the power to associate facts being learned with facts already known
5. Link reading with action (If a notice about renewing a traffic license is announced in the newspaper, the sensible reader owning a car will react.)
6. Analyze pictures and match captions with them
7. Read material with opposing opinions, that is, seek out the different sides of a question
8. Form the habit of being on guard against an attitude that is too favorable or too hostile (Children may be encouraged to ask, Who wrote this article? What is his record? Where did he get his information? What is the date line? Where did he write it? How does it fit in with what else I have read?)
9. Get facts straight in reading and be able to pass them on with their original meaning, rather than distorting them
10 Avoid what has fittingly been termed the "grasshopper conclusion," that is, jumping to a conclusion based on one example
11. Gain more accurate understandings from reading by being on the alert for

    a. Misleading headlines (Example: A friendly newspaper may report, "400 Attend Democratic Meeting." An unfriendly paper may treat the meeting in an unfavorable light with the headline: "Only 400 Attend Democratic Meeting.")

    b. Glittering generalities (Example: "All the world loves a lover." As a matter of fact this is not true. Part of the world may envy them; part may condemn them for their self-centeredness; part may criticize them for lack of taste if they are too demonstrative in public.)

    c. Bandwagon appeals (Example: Torso Tom, champion of TV wrestlers, eats Puffled What for breakfast, so why don't you?)

    d. Questionable logic (Example: The moon is light, feathers are light; therefore the moon sheds feathers.)

    e. Questionable sampling (Example: More than five times as many women use this detergent.)

    f. Prejudice (Example: Calling minority groups uncomplimentary nicknames.)

The experts agree that nearly all Americans are newspaper readers, though only 75 per cent purchase newspapers. (The rest read them as "counter" papers, or read them over people's shoulders in streetcars and buses or on the newsstands.) Yet in spite of the avid attention to the daily news, it does not necessarily follow that the American people have a high "newspaper-reading quotient." In fact, figures show that 90 per cent read the comics; 60 per cent, the sports page; 56 per cent glance at the front page; and only 5 per cent read the editorials.

Since there is a general dislike in a democracy for having someone else do the individual's thinking, teachers must teach children to be discerning when they read the newspapers, to obtain precise, instead of vague and sketchy, information. The sad fact, however, is that large numbers of American children will leave school without being able to read the newspaper well enough to get meanings straight and to retain accurately what they read. Yet, as critics have pointed out, educators cannot say that the schools have discharged their responsibility if millions of American citizens confine their reading to the comics and sports pages, the cheap tabloid press, and exposé magazines. Much of the poor quality of newspaper reading can be traced to perfunctory current-events lessons in the classroom. If any lesson warrants thoughtful preparation, it is this one. It trains children in the skill of reading two of democracy's most important media of communication—the newspaper and the news magazine. Since the recognition of propaganda and an analysis of the methods of propaganda will develop an understanding of how facts may be slanted to obtain a desired effect, this phase of reading the news should not be neglected.

In setting up standards of effective reading in current events, the teacher may profit from studying successful procedures. Three examples of efficient lessons promoting skill in dealing with current-events content follow:

PLAN FOR A CLASS NEWSPAPER

After the teacher of a sixth grade had led a discussion of news and news reporting according to the famous "nose-for-news" formula, her pupils decided to launch a class newspaper. They made a poster to inspire "reporters" and displayed it in the corner of the classroom which was designated as the "news room." An editor-in-chief was elected. (He had access to a portable type-writer.) Many rich learning opportunities were enjoyed by these children as they published quarterly, hectographed issues of the *Sixth Grade News.* Included in their paper were reports of class scholarship and sports events, reviews of favorite books, a column of jokes and riddles, human-interest items, etc.

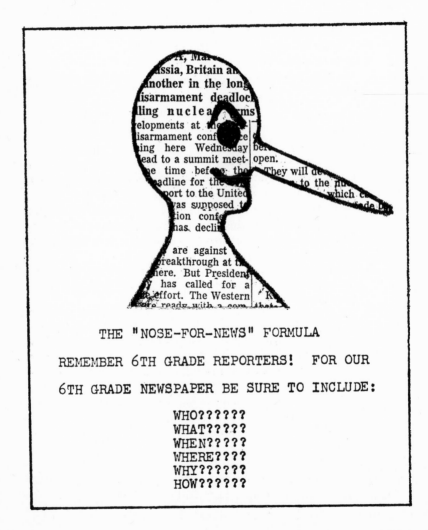

THE "NOSE-FOR-NEWS" FORMULA

REMEMBER 6TH GRADE REPORTERS! FOR OUR

6TH GRADE NEWSPAPER BE SURE TO INCLUDE:

WHO??????
WHAT?????
WHEN?????
WHERE????
WHY??????
HOW??????

LESSON PLAN FOR TEACHING CURRENT-EVENTS READING

I. What (subject matter)

Copies of *My Weekly Reader,* one for each child in the sixth grade. Maps to locate places mentioned.

II. Why (aims)

To teach the children to

A. Classify the news
B. Scan headlines and opening paragraphs
C. Use the "nose-for-news" formula in retaining facts read in the news

III. How (method)

A. After distributing a copy of *My Weekly Reader* to each of the children, refer to the list below and guide the children to scan the headlines of various articles to try to decide under which classification each belongs: national, international, or local news; science and invention; human interest; sports.
B. Write the nose-for-news formula on the blackboard. Explain that a good reporter must include in his news story of an event: *who* was involved, *what* took place, *when* it took place, *where* it occurred, *how* and *why* it happened.
C. Lead the children to realize that, if such facts are included in the article by the reporter, the same facts should be obtained from the article by the reader.
D. To give the children practice in the skill, ask them to turn to an article entitled "By-Products of Cotton." Have the children scan it and classify it under the topics *science* and *invention.* Have them match labels from the nose-for-news formula to the facts mentioned in the item, and, after this, look away from the paper and try to recall who invented the process of using seed oil for making phonograph records, lipsticks, cold cream, men's felt hats, and so on. If they forget a fact, have them reread the article to locate it.

The practice described in this current-events reading plan of consciously labeling factual data according to the *who, what, why, how, when,* and *where* facts in the content would improve both comprehension and retention, thus training future newspaper readers in two strategic skills.

The following example of a way one teacher handled the reading of a weekly newspaper in a seventh-grade lesson illustrates still another teaching approach.

A SEVENTH-GRADE LESSON

1. The teacher distributed copies of *The Junior Review* to a low-seventh-grade social-studies class consisting of thirty-two children.

2. She had members of the class skim the paper to determine the classification of each news item.

3. The teacher and pupils together surveyed one item entitled "The American Southwest." They noted and discussed new words. They referred to a map to locate the region accurately. The children then read silently to get the facts, using the nose-for-news formula. After the silent reading, they took turns quizzing each other on the factual data contained in the article.

4. The teacher suggested that the children select their favorites in the joke section and get ready to tell them. The teacher emphasized that it is essential to master the wording of the main point verbatim. She reminded the children that it is important to reread and carry on self-recitation to master the joke for retelling the next day.

5. Various children volunteered to report on representative articles, and a study period followed.

6. The next day, the teacher set up a play microphone and the children gave a simulated television news broadcast as follows:

Classification	Title of Article	Pupil
Science	*New Insect Powder Works*	Mary H.
Persons in the News	*The Baseball King*	Tom B.
Humor	*Jokes and Puns*	Bob, Ann
Hemispheric News	*Mexico's Mechanization*	Vivian L.
Food	*Sugar from Underground*	John H.

7. After each child had given his report, he quizzed his listeners, asking them *whom* his article had been about, *where* the event had taken place, and so on.

According to the seventh-grade teacher, the response to this news reading was impressive, particularly because the class was made up of children who had been reading mechanically only a short time before. Indeed, the teacher reported that the children were at first "insulted" when she expected them to get the meaning of what they read. Accustomed to take turns in oral reading round the room, they appeared to be saying to themselves, "We're reading this out loud. What else do you want?"

READING ARITHMETIC CONTENT

Reading in arithmetic is so difficult and specialized that the child must be given special guidance in this field. Studies on how to make arithmetic reading more meaningful have demonstrated the value of direct and systematic presentation of key words. One authority suggests that the problem be stated orally without numbers being mentioned to help communicate meaning; that graphic drawings be used; that vocabulary exercises precede the arithmetic reading, to sharpen and broaden the understanding of words in arithmetic problems.[3] Others have recommended that the new words be looked up in the dictionary, that they be used in sentences, matched in pictures, etc. The use of concrete experience to give meaning and add interest to arithmetical concepts also is advocated. This might include having the children divide possessions equally, plan what to buy with a given amount of money, plan refreshments for a party, time classmates to see who runs fastest, go on errands to the store. These experiences will help them to read meaning into problems. In order for the child to fully comprehend arithmetic content and to understand every word he reads, the teacher should train him to read the problem rapidly first to gain an over-all picture of what it contains. Then she should teach him to reread it carefully and ask himself these questions:

> What facts am I given?
> What am I asked to find out?
> What facts do I need to solve the problem?

[3] Leo J. Brueckner and F. E. Grossnickle, *Making Arithmetic Meaningful* (New York: Holt, Rinehart & Winston, Inc., 1953).

What is the first step to take to solve it?
What is the next step? The next?
What is the probable answer?

Finally, the teacher should train the child to reread the problem to determine whether or not it has been completely solved.

In reading arithmetic content, pupils need to be taught to

1. Recognize such arithmetical symbols as plus and minus
2. Know the meanings of such arithmetical terms as fraction, invert, subtrahend
3. Alter their reading speed (Arithmetic problems have to be read at a slower rate and usually require more than one reading.)
4. Learn to read both quantitative terms and qualitive terms with meaning

In guiding the children through a series of problems in arithmetic, the teacher should keep in mind the aims of reading, the type of guidance needed for full comprehension, and the principles used in all reading work. Preparation for concepts is needed. Abstractions in arithmetic must be made concrete, difficult as this sometimes is. Demonstrations, activities involving number and measurement, pictorial aids, and actual objects will help here. Proper motivation for reading quantitative material is equally important.

READING SCIENCE CONTENT

In reading science content, children should be taught to look for facts supported by scientific data. A great many terms must first be clarified—usually five or six before the guided reading— and the rest taught in context as they are reached in the guided reading. Since facts are presented rapidly, motivation and discussion are needed to hold interest. As in any content reading, an outline of the facts should appear on the blackboard to be used with the guided reading. Children need to watch for topic headings and relate relevant facts to each from the paragraphs involved. Many visual aids will be needed (use more actual objects and diagrams than pictured representations) if clarity of scientific concepts is to be achieved. Many experiments must be demonstrated by the teacher. If a child can successfully perform an experiment after reading a passage dealing with it, this is proof of his ability to understand printed directions.

In reading science content, pupils need to be taught to

1. Develop the scientific attitude of demanding proof
2. Rid themselves of erroneous impressions
3. Learn to distinguish between popular and scientific terms
4. Develop patience in studying technical materials
5. Separate fact from fiction in reading
6. Get background for appreciating the achievements in the field of science by reading about the lives of scientists
7. Form the habit of looking up scientific terms in the dictionary
8. Form the habit of rereading directions for laboratory work

LESSON PLAN FOR TEACHING SCIENCE READING

I. What (subject matter) "Our Ocean of Air"

Contemporary Science Series—Grade Six by Neil J. Odettes *et al.*

Visual aids: Diagram showing kinds of air: troposphere, stratosphere, ionosphere, exosphere.

Picture of Mount Everest to illustrate the highest point *on* earth. Map of Tibet and the Himalayas.

Globe of the world.

Photographs from *Life* magazine for March 2, 1962, and March 9, 1962, showing John Glenn, the first American astronaut to orbit the earth.

II. Why (aims)

A. Fact aims

To help the children to understand

1. The relation between altitude and air pressure. i.e., the farther away an object is from earth, the less the pull of gravity (To illustrate the weightlessness of objects in the ionosphere, describe how the astronaut "parked" his camera on air.)
2. How the lack of oxygen affects the human body

B. Reading-skill aims

To teach the children how to

1. Recognize new words and concepts: *stratosphere, gravity,*

weightless, oxygen, boiling point (212° for water at sea level; how lowering pressure lowers the boiling point and vice versa)

2. Make an outline and compose a summarizing paragraph from it about the section covered in the science text

C. Social aims:

To lead the children to

1. Appreciate the victory achieved by science in making it possible for a man to ascend to outer space, where there is no oxygen, i.e., no pure air to breathe
2. Value the self-discipline and courage of the astronaut

III. How (method)

A. Motivating the reading

1. Show picture of John Glenn, in astronaut suit, taken on February 20, 1962, the day he orbited three times around the earth in 4 hours and 56 minutes, going 17,500 miles an hour, and flying 160 miles up into outer space. Emphasize the peril he faced when he slowed down the space capsule to ram back into the atmosphere, where there is pressure instead of the weightlessness of the ionosphere. Describe how the friction of the air heated the shield on his space capsule to nearly 3,000 degrees.
2. Raising the problem: "Read to find out why it is such a remarkable feat for a man to survive a trip to outer space."
3. Making the assignment: "Turn to the table of contents and find the section 'Our Ocean of Air' "

B. Guiding the reading and making an outline

(Though, in actual teaching, these two activities occur simultaneously, with material being added to the outline at the board as soon as it has been read in the science book and discussed, it is more convenient to place all the guiding questions together and follow with the unbroken outline.)

P. 37: "Read the topic heading in dark type. When it says 'below the stratosphere' what is meant? At what altitude does the lack of oxygen begin to affect the body?" (All read silently. Then one pupil reads the answering part orally. Discussion follows. The outline is begun.)

P. 38: "Read to find out at what altitude a person needs 50 per cent oxygen. A person dies at a certain level without oxygen. What altitude is that? Find out if death occurs at an altitude below that of Mount Everest. Let's find the map of Asia. Now locate Tibet. Now the Himalaya Mountains. How high does it say Mount Everest is? Is this below the altitude when a flier must have pure oxygen? (Discussion. Facts added to outline.)

P. 39: "Read to find at what altitude the stratosphere begins. What must planes carry now? What would happen to a man at 40,000 feet without a pressure cabin?" (All read silently to find the facts. One reads answer aloud. Discussion. Outline augmented.)

P. 40: "Now I am going to ask you to read until you find a sentence that tells about something almost unbelievable. (Class reads silently to find it. One pupil reads aloud. Discussion. Outline augmented.)

End of the first day's guided reading and work on the outline, which appears as follows:

Outline of Science Content Read

I. Relation between altitude, oxygen, and life

  A. How altitude affects the body below the stratosphere

    1. At 10,000 feet, lack of oxygen affects a person; he may become faint and dizzy.

    2. At 20,000 feet, a person needs oxygen 50 per cent.

    3. At 25,000 feet (below the height of Mt. Everest, at 29,002 feet the highest point *on* earth), man dies without oxygen.

    4. At 35,000 feet, a flier must have pure oxygen.

  B. How altitude affects the body in the stratosphere and ionosphere.

    1. At 40,000 feet, the stratosphere begins.

    2. At 45,000 feet, all spaceships must have pressure equipment.

    3. At 65,000 feet, the boiling point is so low that blood boils.

C. Drill or review: To review the facts in the outline, have the children dictate a summary for the teacher to write on the blackboard. Either the teacher or some of the pupils may make suggestions for improving grammar, choice of words, or organization, *as* the summarizing paragraph is being composed by the class.

D. Follow-up

    1. Display the book *Space Satellite* by Lee Beeland and Robert Wells (Englewood Cliffs, N.J.: Prentice-Hall, Inc., 1958). Invite the children to read it.

    2. Give a factual test to check retention of facts. (A few examples are given below.)

       a. Fill in blanks:

          The stratosphere begins at ⎯⎯⎯⎯⎯
          The troposphere, where we live,
          is ⎯⎯⎯⎯⎯ the stratosphere.

       b. True or False (Circle one.):

          T F Air pressure decreases with altitude.
          T F Temperature goes down with altitude. etc.

IV. Evaluation

    A. Children's gains

       1. In facts:
       2. In habits:
       3. In skills:
       4. In attitudes:

QUESTIONS AND ACTIVITIES

1. What are some of the special problems connected with giving instruction in reading in subject-matter fields?

2. Why is reading in textbooks in the content fields more difficult than reading in basic readers?

3. Whether the content be geography, history, civics, current events, or natural science, what is the purpose of guiding the reading and placing an outline on the board simultaneously?

4. What is the purpose of the composite paragraph? Discuss the value of this form of integrating written work with reading, if any.

5. What are some of the differences between a lesson plan designed for use with a single textbook and a plan making use of several references?

6. Of the three lessons in current events, which one seemed superior to you? Why?

7. What must teachers in the content fields teach besides subject matter? Re-examine some of the broader aims in the fields of geography, history, and science before composing an answer.

SELECTED REFERENCES

Five Steps to Reading Success in Science, Social Studies and Mathematics. Metropolitan School Study Council, Affiliate of the Institute of Administration Research. New York: Teachers College, Columbia University, 1960.

GRAY, WILLIAM S. *Improving Reading in All Curriculum Areas.* Supplementary Educational Monographs, No. 76. Chicago, University of Chicago Press, 1952.

HANNA, PAUL R. "Generalizations and Universal Values: Their Implications for the Social Studies Program." *Social Studies in the Elementary School.* The Fifth-sixth Yearbook, Part II, National Society for the Study of Education. Chicago: University of Chicago Press, 1957.

HOSELITZ, BERT. *Reader's Guide to the Social Sciences.* New York: The Free Press of Glencoe, 1952.

JAROLIMEK, JOHN. *Social Studies in Elementary Education.* New York: The Macmillan Co., Publishers (a division of the Crowell-Collier Publishing Co.), 1959.

MERRITT, EDITH. *Working with Children in Social Studies.* San Francisco: Warsworth Publishing Co., Inc., 1961.

MICHAELIS, JOHN. *Social Studies for Children in a Democracy* (2d ed.), Englewood Cliffs, N.J.: Prentice-Hall, Inc., 1956.

MICHAELIS, JOHN. *The Social Studies in the Elementary Schools.* Thirty-second Yearbook, National Council for the Social Studies. Washington D.C., 1962.

PETERSON, THEODORE. "The Social Functions of the Press," Chapter 3 in *Mass Media and Education.* Fifty-third Yearbook, National Society for the Study of Education. Chicago: University of Chicago Press, 1954.

PIEKARZ, JOSEPHINE. "Getting Meaning from Reading," *Elementary English,* LVI (March 1956), 303–9.

PRESTON, RALPH C. *Teaching Social Studies in the Elementary Schools* (rev. ed.), New York: Holt, Rinehart & Winston, Inc., 1958.

SCHWAB, JOSEPH C. *Teaching Science* (rev. ed.). Cambridge, Mass.: Harvard University Press, 1962.

SOCHOR, E. ELONA, *et al. Critical Reading: An Introduction.* Champaign, Ill.: National Council of Teachers of English, 1959.

TIEGS, ERNEST W., and FAY ADAMS. *Teaching Social Studies: A Guide to Better Citizenship.* Boston: Ginn & Co., 1959.

WESLEY, EDGAR B., and MARY ADAMS. *Teaching Social Studies in Elementary Schools* (rev. ed.). Boston: D. C. Heath & Co., 1952.

WHIPPLE, GERTRUDE. "Controversial Issues Relating to Reading in Curricular Areas," *The Reading Teacher,* VIII (April 1955), 298–300.

13

RECREATIONAL READING

Although this chapter bears the title "recreational" reading, it could equally as well be called "pleasure," "leisure," or "voluntary" reading. All these terms are used interchangeably by teachers and librarians. The tearm *recreational* was chosen by the author because of the root word it contains, namely, "re-create." It suggests the kind of reading which brings new life to the reader, perhaps from two directions. Such reading might offer counsel to help a person *face* life, by instilling a higher level of aspirations. Equally, it might help the individual to *escape* from life's daily cares, thus allowing him rest and refreshment so satisfying as to re-create energy and vitality for returning to the daily round.

Many teachers indorse the entertainment values of recreational reading but quarrel at the mere thought of considering pleasure reading as an instrument of personal development. They insist upon a condition of pure enjoyment without any ulterior motive —akin to the thinking behind the familiar slogan "art for art's sake." However, it is possible to use reading as recreation—to read in a carefree, wholehearted mood of enjoyment—and yet wind up with some very valuable by-products. By a similar token some people eat for enjoyment but at the same time manage to obtain nourishment. Who has not sat down to enjoy a book by Mark Twain only to emerge after two hours of entertainment with a more humorous point of view toward life? Perhaps the difference is that of original intention. It would be paradoxical to begin a session of pleasure reading with the grim intent of improving one's sense of humor.

STATUS OF READING AS RECREATION

Do many people who have passed through American schools choose reading as a form of pleasure? Naturally, the effectiveness of any recreational-reading program is judged by the number and kinds of readers it helps to produce. Can it be claimed that the recreational-reading program in American schools has been successful? As librarians point out, "Many children can read but do not." In a recent study of the voluntary reading of young people, reported by Hanna and McAllister,[1] it was found that reading ranked fourth in recreational preferences, with radio, television, and movies ranked ahead of it in that order. There are a great many adults who would prefer to have reading ranked first. As David Russell[2] has written, "The acid test of any reading program is whether or not the children in it or graduated from it read for themselves. There is little value in developing competent reading ability unless it is voluntarily put to use."

GUIDING GROWTH IN RECREATIONAL READING

The mere existence of a lack of appreciation of the value of reading as recreation is, of course, no justification for its continuance. Teachers may properly be disturbed by the prevailing tendency to prefer other, less rewarding forms of recreation to reading, but their responsibility to children does not allow them to accept defeat. Granted that some factors such as the lack of reading in the home, the hurried pace of living that causes nervous tension, and the competition by mass media for leisure time are beyond the teacher's control, she can at least minimize them by dealing sympathetically with individual children. Then, too, she can remember that standards held too low may be raised; failure to emphasize recreational reading enough in the schools may be remedied; delaying the formation of interests and tastes until the

[1] Geneva R. Hanna and Marian K. McAllister, *Books, Young People and Reading* (New York: Harper & Row, 1960).
[2] David Russell, *Children Learn To Read* (2d ed.; Boston: Ginn & Co., 1961), p. 362.

secondary-school literature class may be corrected by providing the necessary guidance much earlier.

Setting Goals. What should be the goals of the teacher who is eager to improve the recreational-reading habits, attitudes, and interests of her pupils in her term's work? At the very minimum, she would probably aim to

1. Convince children by every means at her command that reading is a wonderfully rewarding form of recreation
2. Encourage children to engage in some recreational reading every day
3. Stimulate children to obtain a library card
4. Urge children to use it to check out a wide variety of recreational-reading matter
5. Guide children by every means possible to realize the values of recreational reading in helping the individual to relax and escape from daily cares, face personal problems with renewed perspective, relive past experiences, and extend and enrich experience vicariously

In other words, the teacher would guide the children to an understanding of the twofold service performed by recreational reading, namely, to promote enjoyment and to stimulate personal development.

Determining Children's Interests. Before attempting to introduce new reading interests to children, the teacher should take soundings and try to discover the number and depth of interests the children already have on hand. This can be done through informal observation of the children in the classroom and on the school grounds—through informal interviews, through questionnaires, and through noting the child's choice of hobbies, his preferences in motion pictures, comics, and television programs, and his library borrowings.

To obtain a broader background of understanding, the teacher should examine various methods which have been successfully used to elicit evidence of children's appreciation or enjoyment of reading. The teacher should also acquaint herself with studies already made of children's reading interests. Space permits the citation of only a few examples in each area.

Time provided for independent reading is a vital part of recreational-reading growth at all levels. Children enjoy belonging to book clubs. Naturally, a bookworm makes a suitable mascot. (*Bascom School, San Jose, Calif.*)

Through the use of a scroll theater, this boy dramatizes some exciting action in his favorite book, *The Wild Little Honker*. He shows how it is possible to visit the outdoor world of fields and streams with the help of reading. (*El Rancho Unified School District, Pico Rivera, Calif.*)

An Intermediate-Grade Questionnaire. Questions compiled by a group of teachers in a summer-session class were put to 260 sixth-grade children in the fall of the year, and the results were summarized and sent to the author. As one teacher phrased it at the close of her summary, "When children put in a plug for a book indirectly through answering a question, the response must be considered sincere, rather than made to please any adult." The teacher was referring to the questionnaire addressed to children which appears below.

Can you remember the name of any book that made you:

1. Feel patriotic? _____
2. Want to help other people? _____
3. Think that people in other times and places felt the way people do now? _____
4. Laugh out loud? _____
5. Cry? _____
6. Want to see other places? _____
7. Live in other times? _____
8. Read more books by the same author? _____
9. Love your family and home more? _____
10. Want to know how the author happened to write the book? _____

A great many books were mentioned by the sixth-grade children who answered the questions, but those that received most frequent mention in each category included: for question 1, *Johnny Tremain;* for question 2, *Sue Barton, Senior Nurse;* for 3, 4, and 8, *Tom Sawyer;* for 5 and 9, *Little Women;* for 7, *Drums Along the Mohawk;* for 6, *Treasure Island.* Question 10 was not answered, showing that connecting the author's motivation with his writing was beyond the ken of the children in the group involved. It is a tribute to Mark Twain that his boy Tom Sawyer seems real to children of today though his book was written in 1876 about a boy who went through all the colorful adventures described in the 1840's.

Incomplete Sentences. Sometimes the use of the completion technique can furnish clues to children's interests—if they trust the teacher enough to give frank and open answers. Incomplete sentences are mimeographed, space is left for answers, and the children are asked to fill out the blanks.

1. I like reading better than _____
2. I like a book that makes me feel _____
3. I would rather read than _____
4. The difference between comic books and real books is _____

5. The kind of book I like the teacher to read to us every day after lunch is _____

A RESEARCH STUDY OF CHILDREN'S RATINGS OF READING MATE-RIALS. Coleman and Jungeblut.[3] report a study to determine children's reading interests and to discover which selections should be retained in a collection on the basis of interest. A group of 750 children, aged eight to twelve, in grades four, five, and six in several moderate-sized cities on the east coast, were the subjects of this study. The procedure was to use some selections in books dealing with nature study and social studies. The selections (rated on the Lorge Readability Index with scores of 3.1 to 7.0) were rated by children whose reading ability was at, above, and below the difficulty level of the material.

The children rated the material by marking phrases ranging along a six-point scale from "like very very much" to "dislike very very much." There was also opportunity for the child to check when he was unable to read a selection. For the one selection on which the results of the study were reported in detail, more than 80 per cent of 202 fifth-grade children rated a selection on lichens favorably. Most of those who disliked it came from one industrial community in a city. Evidently they did not have much background about lichens and thought it safer to "dislike" something they did not know than to "like" it. There were also differences in strength of appeal by grade levels. One generally liked selection described an exciting incident involving the Pony Express. This finding confirms previous studies—children enjoy suspense and excitement, a minimum of descriptive and expository matter, and heroes with whom the reader can identify personally. They also like dialog and humor.

[3] J. H. Coleman and Ann Jungeblut, "Children's Likes and Dislikes About What They Read," *Journal of Educational Research* (February 1961).

DIFFERENCES IN BOYS' AND GIRLS' READING INTERESTS. A study by Wolfson[4] examined the reading interests of approximately 2,000 boys and girls in grades three through six in Norwalk, Connecticut. A Reading Interest Inventory consisting of 120 questions was administered orally. Among answers to the questions on the inventory, boys' choices, as a group, were significantly different from girls' choices, except in the category of social studies. The twelve categories covered were adventure, animals, fine and applied arts, fantasy, family life and children, famous people, machines and applied science, personal problems, physical science, plants, social studies, and sports. The boys gave a high number of "yes" responses for adventure, animals, famous people, machines and applied science (*much* higher here), physical science, and sports. The girls gave more "yes" responses to show interest in fantasy, family life and children, personal problems, and plants.

The value of this study lies in the fact that it underscores once again the wide range and variety of children's interests—a finding which has implications for the selection of materials to capitalize on the children's existing interests. It also suggests that new interests be encouraged.

A great responsibility rests upon the teacher to encourage among youngsters the habit of reading and to guide their reading tastes and interests. These are not fixed for all time but are subject to change. When children are given some yardstick for judging the worth of a book, their choices in books are found to be superior to those revealed in Rankin's study[5] of the library books most frequently checked out. Popular themes in the study were revealed to be tomboyish escapades, aviation, adventure at sea, "loyal dog," and careers for girls. A large part of the guidance program consists of making the best selection of books easily available to children.

Selecting Recreational-Reading Materials. Every year, a flood of approximately 2,000 children's books of good, bad, or indifferent

[4] Bernice J. Wolfson, "What Do Children Say Their Reading Interests Are?" *The Reading Teacher* (November 1960), 81–82.

[5] Mary Rankin, *Children's Interests in Library Books of Fiction,* Teachers College Contributions to Education, No. 906 (New York: Teachers College, Columbia University, 1944).

quality are published in the United States to add to the multitude of children's books already in stores and libraries. How does the teacher "separate the wheat from the chaff?" Below are listed some sources to guide the teacher in the important job of selecting "the right book for the right child."

Anthology of Children's Literature (3d ed.) by Edna Johnson, Evelyn R. Sickels, and Frances Clarke Sayers. Boston: Houghton Mifflin Co.

"Bequest of Wings": A Family's Pleasure in Books by Annis Duff. New York: The Viking Press, Inc.

Best Books for Children—3,000 of the best children's books in print up to and including the year 1960. Very helpful to teachers as the titles are arranged by grade and by subject, etc. New York: R. R. Bowker Co.

Books, Children & Men by Paul Hazard, translated by Marguerite Mitchell from the French. Boston: Horn Book, Inc.

Bibliography of Books for Children (1960 ed.), suggesting quality books for children from four through twelve years of age. Bulletin No. 37, Association for Childhood Education International, Washington, D.C.

Children's Books Too Good To Miss (1959 ed.) by May Hill Arbuthnot *et al.* Cleveland: Press of Western Reserve University.

Children and Books by May Hill Arbuthnot (2d ed.) Chicago: Scott, Foresman & Co.

Helping Children Discover Books by Doris Gates. Chicago: Science Research Associates, Inc.

A Parent's Guide to Children's Reading by Nancy Larrick. New York: Doubleday & Co., Inc. Also out in a Pocketbook edition.

A Teacher's Guide to Children's Reading by Nancy Larrick. Columbus, Ohio: Charles E. Merrill Books, Inc.

The Proof of the Pudding: What Children Read by Phyllis Fenner. New York: John Day Co., Inc.

Reader's Choice Book List (1960–61) annotated list includes more than 500 of the best paperbacks for elementary, junior, and senior high school use. New York: Reader's Choice.

Your Children Want To Read: A Guide for Teachers and Parents by Ruth Tooze. Englewood Cliffs, N.J.: Prentice-Hall, Inc.

Your Child's Reading Today by Josette Frank. New York: Doubleday & Co., Inc.

As Phyllis Fenner writes,[6] "Actually the best list is one for each individual child." However, when eighteen librarians from all

[6] Phyllis Fenner, *The Proof of the Pudding: What Children Read* (New York: John Day Co., Inc., 1957).

parts of the country were asked to make a list of fifty books for the child's *home* library, they managed to produce a very fine list useful as well in guiding the teacher to make a wise selection of books for the *schoolroom* library. They also compiled a list of alternates. These are presented in Chapter 17 of Fenner's book, under the title "The Habit of Owning Books." Thus she makes available a list of "100 Tested Books Old and New Which Children Should Not Miss." It would be difficult to find a better aid for making a quick selection for the classroom library. Most school departments circulate the bibliographies presented in the section above.

AWARD-WINNING BOOKS. Two dependable lists of preselected books available to teachers in choosing books for the classroom or school library are those of the award-winning Newbery Medal books and Caldecott Medal books. The first award is given annually for the book published in the United States which is voted "the most distinguished literature" for children. When the list of Newbery Medal books is posted in the classroom book corner, a note should explain that John Newbery, for whom the prize was named, was an English publisher of children's books who lived from 1713 to 1767. The Caldecott Medal is given for the best picture book of the year. R. Caldecott lived from 1846 to 1886, also in England. Instead of publishing books as Newbery did, he was an artist and illustrator who believed that pictures for children "should be merry and gay." Below are lists of the books for children which have received the honor of these awards.

Newbery Medal Books

1922—Van Loon, Hendrik. *The Story of Mankind.* Liveright.
1923—Lofting, Hugh. *The Voyages of Dr. Dolittle.* Stokes.
1924—Hawes, Charles Boardman. *The Dark Frigate.* Little.
1925—Finger, Charles J. *Tales from Silver Lands.* Doubleday.
1926—Chrisman, Arthur. *Shen of the Sea.* Dutton.
1927—James, Will. *Smoky.* Scribner.
1928—Mukerji, Dhan Gopal. *Gay-Neck.* Dutton.
1929—Kelly, Eric P. *The Trumpeter of Krakow.* Macmillan
1930—Field, Rachel. *Hitty, Her First Hundred Years.* Macmillan.
1931—Coatsworth, Elizabeth. *The Cat Who Went to Heaven.* Macmillan.

1932—Armer, Laura Adams. *Waterless Mountain*. Longmans.
1933—Lewis, Elizabeth Foreman. *Young Fu of the Upper Yangtze*. Holt.
1934—Meigs, Cornelia, *Invincible Louisa*. Little.
1935—Shannon, Monica. *Dobry*. Viking.
1936—Brink, Carol Ryrie. *Caddie Woodlawn*. Macmillan.
1937—Sawyer, Ruth. *Roller Skates*. Viking.
1938—Seredy, Kate, *The White Stag*. Viking.
1939—Enright, Elizabeth. *Thimble Summer*. Holt.
1940—Daugherty, James. *Daniel Boone*. Viking.
1941—Sperry, Armstrong. *Call it Courage*. Macmillan.
1942—Edmonds, Walter. *The Matchlock Gun*. Dodd.
1943—Gray, Elizabeth Janet. *Adam of the Road*. Viking.
1944—Forbes, Esther. *Johnny Tremain*. Houghton.
1945—Lawson, Robert. *Rabbit Hill*. Viking.
1946—Lenski, Lois. *Strawberry Girl*. Lippincott.
1947—Bailey, Carolyn Sherwin. *Miss Hickory*. Viking.
1948—DuBois, William Pène. *The Twenty-one Balloons*. Viking.
1949—Henry, Marguerite. *King of the Wind*. Rand McNally.
1950—De Angeli, Marguerite. *The Door in the Wall*. Doubleday.
1951—Yates, Elizabeth. *Amos Fortune, Free Man*. Aladdin.
1952—Estes, Eleanor. *Ginger Pye*. Harcourt.
1953—Clark, Ann Nolan. *Secret of the Andes*. Viking.
1954—Krumgold, Joseph. . . . *and now Miguel*. Crowell.
1955—DeJong, Meindert. *The Wheel on the School*. Harper.
1956—Latham, Jean Lee. *Carry On, Mr. Bowditch*. Houghton.
1957—Sorensen, Virginia. *Miracles on Maple Hill*. Harcourt.
1958—Keith, Harold. *Rifles for Watie*. Crowell.
1959—Speare, Elizabeth G. *Witch of Blackbird Pond*. Houghton.
1960—Krumgold, Joseph. *Onion John*. Crowell.
1961—O'Dell, Scott. *Island of Blue Dolphins*. Houghton.
1962—Speare, Elizabeth George. *The Bronze Bow*. Houghton.

Caldecott Medal Books

1938—Lathrop, Dorothy. *Animals of the Bible*. Stokes.
1939—Handforth, Thomas. *Mei Li*. Doubleday.
1940—Aulaire, Ingri and Edgar d'. *Abraham Lincoln*. Doubleday.
1941—Lawson, Robert. *They Were Strong and Good*. Viking.
1942—McCloskey, Robert. *Make Way for Ducklings*. Viking.
1943—Burton, Virginia Lee. *The Little House*. Houghton.
1944—Slobodkin, Louis, ill. Thurber, James. *Many Moons*. Harcourt.
1945—Jones, Elizabeth Orton, ill. Field, Rachel. *Prayer for a Child*. Macmillan.
1946—Petersham, Maud and Miska. *The Rooster Crows*. Macmillan.

1947—Weisgard, Leonard, ill. MacDonald, Golden. *The Little Island.*
Doubleday.
1948—Duvoisin, Roger, ill. Tresselt, Alvin. *White Snow, Bright Snow.*
Lothrop.
1949—Hader, Berta and Elmer. *The Big Snow.* Macmillan.
1950—Politi, Leo. *Song of the Swallows.* Scribner.
1951—Milhous, Katherine. *The Egg Tree.* Scribner.
1952—Mordvinoff, Nicolas, ill. [Nicolas, pseud.]. Lipkind, William
[Will, pseud.]. *Finders Keepers.* Harcourt.
1953—Ward, Lynd. *The Biggest Bear.* Houghton.
1954—Bemelmans, Ludwig. *Madeline's Rescue.* Viking.
1955—Brown, Marcia, ill. Perrault, Charles. *Cinderella.* Scribner.
1956—Rojankovsky, Feodor, ill. Langstaff, John. *Frog Went A-courtin'.*
Harcourt.
1957—Simont, Marc. *A Tree Is Nice.* Harper.
1958—McClosky, Robert. *Time of Wonder.* Viking.
1959—Cooney, Barbara. *Chanticleer and the Fox.* Crowell.
1960—Ets, Marie Hall. *Nine Days to Christmas.* Viking.
1961—Sidjakov, Nicholas. *Baboushaka and the Tree Kings.* Parnassus
Press.
1962—Brown, Marcia. *Once a Mouse.* Scribner.

Stimulating Interest. To turn the children's attention to recreational reading, it is important to establish favorable conditions. As a means of doing this, the teacher might

1. Provide an attractive library corner, well stocked with books to meet many interests at the three different ability levels
2. Arrange for colorful displays of book jackets to advertise new books
3. Schedule a daily session of recreational reading
4. Schedule a regular weekly period in the school library
5. Schedule a trip once each term to the branch library in the neighborhood, to encourage the pupils to apply for library cards and to listen to talks by the librarian about recreational-reading resources
6. Set up book exhibits
7. Display pictures of children reading their favorite books
8. Display book reviews written by the children
9. Encourage the children to bring their books to share with others
10. Observe book-week celebrations
11. Organize a class book club to furnish an outlet for the children's recreational-reading activities

12. Read orally to the children, making each of these oral-reading sessions a lesson in literature appreciation by encouraging the children to discuss the significance of the selection being read

13. Talk about the lives of authors, and compare books by the same or different authors

14. Encourage the children to own books, to buy them with their own earnings

15. Make it possible for the children to read freely, without interruption or the threat of a test (Granted that the teacher's guidance in the development of appreciation is important, a nice balance of comment and of keeping quiet must be observed. If a child is to develop a taste for good reading, he must not be nagged by the unending comment and query of a teacher like James Thurber's "Miss Groby," who was "forever climbing up the margins of books, crawling between the lines, hunting figures of speech through the clangorous halls of Shakespeare and the green forests of Scott.")

THE CLASSROOM BOOK CLUB. A potent aid in guiding growth in recreational reading is the carefully prepared lesson in literature appreciation. Programed as book-club meetings, such sessions are usually scheduled for Friday afternoons. A program may be prepared jointly by the teacher and the children. The teacher herself may publicize a new book to the children. However, the greater part of the program is devoted to a series of book recommendations by appreciative children through various activities, either individually or in groups. These book advertisements take the form of puppet shows, simulated television interviews with famous book characters, book reviews, dramatizations, and the like. Suggestions for a rich variety of activities for the children to use in sharing their enthusiasm for certain books will follow the presentation of the lesson, planned for a meeting of a sixth-grade book club.

RECREATIONAL-READING LESSON PLAN FOR A BOOK-CLUB MEETING

I. What (subject matter)

1. *The Wind in the Willows* by Kenneth Grahame
2. *Mr. Popper's Penguins* by Richard and Florence Atwater

3. *Children and Books* by May Hill Arbuthnot
4. Pictures of Mole, Ratty, Toad displayed from *The Wind in the Willows*
5. Black paper cutouts of penguin face mask and wings attached to a pillowcase; pictures of the Antarctic

II. Why (aims)

1. To advertise *The Wind in the Willows*
2. To advertise *Mr. Popper's Penguins* and other books
3. To help children to become acquainted with modern classics
4. To guide children to share their reading enthusiasms
5. To give children practice in talking effectively about books, authors, and ideas
6. To stimulate children to learn facts about authors
7. To promote the transfer of new words from reading
8. To reduce indiscriminate use of television, by showing how much entertainment and pleasure comes from books
9. To stimulate the use of library cards

III. How (methods)

A. The teacher's part (first five minutes of the book-club meeting)

1. Write the title *The Wind in the Willows* on the board. Tell the children it was written in the form of letters to his young son by an Englishman named Kenneth Grahame. (This and other interesting facts about the author can be found in May Hill Arbuthnot's *Children and Books*.)
2. Hold the book up to display pictures of Mole, Ratty, and Toad.
3. Read the part of the story which describes "The Piper at the Gates of Dawn." After creating suspense by telling about the lost baby otter and the long, worrisome search for him, start reading aloud to the children. Stop reading when an exciting point has been reached.
4. Make use of the "unfinished incident" technique, and say, "if you want to know whether or not the lost baby otter was found, read *The Wind in the Willows*. I'll put it on the library table."
5. Announce that now the children who have worked out an advertisement for *Mr. Popper's Penguins* will take over the program. (One boy in the class has read it and has drafted

several of his classmates to help him show the other children how interesting the book is.)

B. The children's part (next twenty minutes or more)

1. Billy goes to a "play" television set bearing the letters "BOOK" and announces, "Today TV-B-O-O-K brings you a program to advertise a very funny book." (A cardboard frame with controls painted on serves as a TV.)

2. Billy says, "Here are some pictures of the ice-bound Antarctic region, or South Pole, where penguins live. We have a guest in the studio who has a penguin from the South Pole. His name is Mr. Popper. Would you care to introduce your pet penguin to the studio audience, Mr. Popper?"

3. Another boy comes forward leading a third child who is wearing the penguin outfit (pillowcase over the shoulders, black paper wings attached, and a penguin mask over his face, tied back of the ears).

4. The second boy reads from his script, describing how he had to flood the basement with water and let it freeze to make his penguin feel at home.

5. The first boy then tells the names of the two authors of the book and reads a short funny scene. He stops in the middle of the most exciting part and, like the teacher, invites the children to read the rest for themselves.

6. Either individually or in small groups, other children advertise books they have enjoyed, by one activity or another. For example, two imaginative boys stage an interview between Robinson Crusoe and a master of ceremonies on a simulated television show. Later Gulliver and the Swiss Family Robinson are interviewed to decide whether or not they, too, deserve membership in the "explorers' club."

7. Dramatization of the whitewashing scene from *Tom Sawyer* and the mad tea party scene from *Alice in Wonderland* follow.

8. Other children display dioramas, use a flannel board to help tell a story graphically, and present a puppet show.

There is really no limit to the number and kinds of recreational-reading activities which may be used successfully to advertise books during sessions of book fun on Friday. The children are urged to write the titles and authors on the board, no matter what activity is used, and great emphasis is placed on transferring new words from reading to oral book reports, discussion, and plays.

IV. Evaluation

The children stop to take inventory. They evaluate the advertisements they have witnessed, ask questions, describe what they liked best, and comment on the scenes chosen and the properties prepared; in short, they become amateur drama critics, deciding which are the strong and weak features of a program. On this particular day, they decide that the dramatization could have been better. With the help of the teacher, the children evolve to their satisfaction the following:

Suggestions for a Dramatization

1. Decide on a good story to act out.
2. Review the story happenings.

   a. Count the characters needed.
   b. Decide on the number of scenes.

3. Choose characters

   a. By tryouts
   b. By volunteers
   c. By seeing who can tell the most about what a character said and did, and choosing him for the part

4. Select stage properties and simple costumes.

   a. Decide what to use to represent a scene.
   b. Decide what to use for costumes.

5. Rehearse and then present the dramatization.

   a. Have the narrator announce scenes into which the story is divided.
   b. Have the children act their parts.

6. Evaluate the dramatization by asking

   a. Could the players be heard easily?
   b. Did they remain in character and not act silly?
   c. Did they face the audience?
   d. Did they use some new words from the story?
   e. Did they make the audience want to read the story or book they dramatized?

OTHER READING ACTIVITIES. For children, the most potent factor in promoting interest in reading a given book is the recommendation of a friend. How the first friend happened to read the book is not important, but the teacher very often will probably supply the *original* motivation. In the previous lesson, for example, there is little doubt that the teacher's enthusiastic indorsement of *The Wind in the Willows* will inspire several children to undertake a delightful new reading experience. Since the children's word-of-mouth advertisements also exert such a strong influence, it is important to encourage them to share their enthusiasm for various books with their classmates. Activities in which the children may engage to express appreciation of recreational reading include

1. *Presenting informal dramatizations.* In this way a number of children who have enjoyed a selection can disseminate its value to the rest of the class. Recently a sixth grade dramatized a story entitled "For the Emperor of China." What mattered that the "emperor" was wearing tennis shoes, blue jeans, and a very red American sweater: He had a gold paper crown on his head, and, as the children said, he was "an emperor from the neck up anyway." Ordinary grocery-store paper bags make good masks. With holes cut for eyes, nose, and mouth and interestingly painted, they add much to a dramatization.

2. *Reproducing books.* Children may present puppet shows or reproduce the action of stories with dioramas, or three-dimensional scenes, or by means of "movies" made up of long strips of wrapping-paper "film" on which consecutive action is pictured. The "film" is wound on pins that rotate, permitting interesting scenes from books to appear in an open space, or "screen," as the child commentator tells the story or makes necessary explanations.

3. *Mounting clippings* of book reviews written by the children about good books found in the classroom or school library. In their book "blurbs" the children tell what they liked about the book, which was their favorite character; what problem faced him, how he solved it, whether or not the ending was satisfactory, what was learned from reading the book. In these reviews, the children are encouraged to form good bibliographical habits, listing the author's full name, the complete title, the publishing company, place of publication, and date. Writing these should not be obligatory, but strictly on a voluntary basis. The object should be to *share* information.

As a variation, photograph children reading their favorite books. These snapshots are then mounted on the bulletin board with a brief book review written by a child using a vocabulary of appropriate terms that express appreciation more exactly than "It's a keen book," or the reverse, "It was lousy."

4. *Collecting picture dictionaries* of useful new words gleaned from outside reading. For example, a child finds the word "fathom" in Mark Twain's *Life on the Mississippi*. From the regular dictionary he learns that it means six feet of water. He then brings in a picture clipped from a magazine showing a body of water, with "six feet" indicated in his own script. Incidentally, this technique often reveals misconceptions harbored by pupils concerning word meanings. To illustrate the meaning of "fathom," one boy cut out six shoes pictured in an advertisement and set them up in a row. The class was quick to point out that "fathom" involved six feet of *water*, not six human feet.

5. *Using literary models.* After children have attempted to express themselves, they are prepared to appreciate how thoughts similar to their own have been aptly expressed by authors. One group of upper-grade boys who scornfully dismissed poetry as "sissy stuff" were led by their teacher to rewrite Noyes's "The Highwayman" in prose. After comparing their meager products with the power of the original, the boys were more inclined to appreciate poetry. If used skillfully, the literary model influences subsequent expression.

6. *Drawing imaginary bookcases.* The children may draw a three-shelf book case on large-sized paper, coloring it with crayon, showing which books they would *like* to own in a personal library. The title is lettered on the spine of each book drawn in. One group labeled these drawings "MY DREAM BOOKCASE."

7. *Serving as classroom librarian.* Each child in the room should be given a turn at holding this responsible office.

8. *Writing on a selected topic.* From "My Reading Autobiography" or "My Reading Time Line" much can be learned concerning the child's home, past reading, current preferences, and style of expression.

9. *Inviting authors* of children's books to class to talk about their writing.

10. *Going to the children's library* in the neighborhood or inviting the librarian to school to talk about books.

11. *Making bookmarks, bookplates, and artistic dust jackets* to stimulate an interest in taking good care of books.

12. *Staging an exhibit* of the books owned by the children in the class, for book week or other celebrations.

13. *Making a list* of the popular books currently published and selecting one which the class feels should be awarded the Newbery Medal Award.

14. *Discussing books* under the teacher's guidance, but not mulling over the story too much. Overanalysis is fatal to enjoyment. However, children can be encouraged to discuss the author's probable aim in writing the book, to report experiences similar to those read about, to hunt for clues in the story that help to build up an idea of the character, to select the funniest part, to remember pithy sayings, etc.

15. *Staging a "book auction,"* with one pupil holding up a favorite book, extolling its good qualities, taking "bids" and "selling it to the highest bidder," that is, turning it over to him to read.

Book Clubs, Magazines, and Paperbacks for Children. Aiding the teacher in her efforts to stimulate children's interest in voluntary reading are nationally organized book clubs for children, and magazines and paperbacks published especially for them. Each will be briefly discussed below.

Book Clubs. In 1960 approximately 12,000,000 children belonged to book clubs and received books on a regular basis, monthly or otherwise. Some of these clubs such as the Arrow Book Club and the Teen Age Book Club distribute paperback books through the schools. (These will be described in more detail). The other children's book clubs mail hardcover books directly to the child's home. Parents are interested in gaining book-club information, and it behooves the teacher to give as much guidance as possible. Information about the cost of memberships may be obtained from the clubs themselves (See the list below).

Arrow Book Club, New York. Five times during the school year each child may choose from a list of eighteen books. Age level: nine–

eleven. The books are paperback editions of favorite children's books, both fiction and non-fiction. The paper and type seem of a higher quality than in adult paper books. This club is joined through schools.

Junior Literary Guild, Garden City, New York. Join by writing to Doubleday & Co., Inc., Institutional Department.

Parent's Magazine's Book Club for Beginning Readers, Bergenfield, N.J.

Teen Age Book Club, New York. Eight times during a school year the members may choose from a list of eighteen books. Age level: twelve–sixteen. The books are paperbacks of juvenile and adult books popular with teen-agers.

Weekly Reader Children's Book Club, Education Center, Columbus, Ohio. Five books a year mailed, plus a "dividend book." Age levels: early readers, five–eight; star readers, eight–twelve.

Young Readers of America (Division of Book-of-the-Month Club), New York.

Children's Magazines.

American Girl. Girl Scouts, Inc., New York.
Boy's Life. Boy Scouts of America, Inc., New York.
Child Life. O. H. Rodman, Boston.
Children's Digest. New York.
Jack and Jill. Curtis Publishing Co., Philadelphia.
Nature Magazine. American Nature Association, Washington, D.C.
Popular Science. New York.
Space Magazines: "Aerospace Periodicals for Teachers and Pupils" by Willis C. Brown lists forty-one titles about space science as well as helicopters and planes. Publication Inquiry Unit, Office of Education, Washington, D.C.

Paperbacks for Children. Increasingly, paperbacks are available now for use at intermediate- and upper-grade levels. Mention has already been made above of the Arrow Book Club and the Teen Age Book Club paperbound books. Teachers will find many books suitable for intermediate-grade levels on the regular paperback racks in supermarkets and drugstores, under such section titles as "Sports," "Birds," "Boats," etc. Classics for these age levels are also to be found in cheap covers. This is a growing phase of book publishing for children, and paperback editions of modern classics may be in the offing. However, there is the very apparent drawback: the lack of durability of such editions.

SPECIAL PHASES OF RECREATIONAL READING

How can the teacher interest a child in a recreational-reading program which will counter the pervasive influence of comic books and television and which will develop surrogate tastes by acquainting him with the classics? Working out a reasonable solution to this complex problem is an important part of the teacher's guidance program in recreational reading. Few questions are asked more frequently by parents and teachers eager to improve children's reading tastes than those concerning the respective roles of the comics, television, and the classics. A reading textbook must, therefore, attempt to present partial solutions, if not complete answers.

The Problem of Comics. Over 25 billion of these books are sold each year, and, although many children's books sell fewer than 5,000 copies, more than 15 million comics are sold every month. Because comics are loaned and traded, it is estimated that children actually read 90 million of them monthly. At last report, the Comics Magazine Association was composed of twenty-three large publishing firms, four engraving companies, five printing houses, and seven of the largest distributing agencies. In short, comics are big business.

Why have comics achieved the enormous popularity indicated by these figures? It is not their humor which draws millions to them, including one-fifth of the adult population of the United States. These books are seldom funny. First of all, people like them because they are so easy to read; the pictures carry the story, thus eliminating the need to cope with a quantity of words. Second, the content is characterized by action, adventure, danger, and speed—ever popular features. Third, through the comics people can achieve escape to a world of fantasy. Indeed, this last point seems to be an extremely important factor in the success of comic books. To many children the comics contain absolutely no reality—a fact which may or may not refute the claim of Dr. Frederic Wertham[7] that American adults will never fully under-

[7] Frederic Wertham, *Seduction of the Innocent* (New York: Holt, Rinehart & Winston, Inc., 1954), p. 118.

stand juvenile delinquency until they realize the effect of comics on the minds of children. Some psychologists maintain that comics do not directly promote juvenile delinquency, but only accelerate propensities toward crime which are already present. Research by Blakely[8] indicated that the children who read numerous comics also read a great deal of other, better materials and were not discernibly different emotionally or scholastically. On the other hand, a study by Slover,[9] consisting of a questionnaire of eighteen items requiring ability to read and check responses, was used with the fourth-grade population of the schools of Mattoon, Illinois. There were 346 respondents. To the question "Do you read comic books?" 90 per cent of the children checked "Yes." Boys preferred comic books to storybooks in a ratio of two to one, a ratio reversed among the girls. *Poor readers preferred comics to storybooks in almost the same proportions.*

OBJECTIONS TO THE COMICS. Though most critics of the comics do not view them with the alarm expressed by Wertham, they usually condemn the slang, the incorrect grammar, the tasteless quality of the themes, and the miserable print and garish color. Sensitive and perceptive people have lamented the harm done by the stereotypes concerning race, nationality, morality, and ethics in comics, which seem to popularize such assumptions as the following: People are either all good or all bad; Oriental people are sinister villains; white people are superior; it is natural to seek revenge; foreign customs are inferior to American customs; education and serious books are dull business.

IMPROVEMENT OF THE COMICS. Thanks to the efforts of organized groups of parents, teachers, and other responsible citizens, the Comics Magazine Association was eventually forced to adopt a new code, barring depravity, obscenity, and violence of the ice-pick-in-the-eye, etc., type. Many of the "horror" and "weird" comics have disappeared from the newsstands.

[8] W. Paul Blakely, "A Study of Seventh Grade Children's Reading of Comic Books as Related to Certain Other Variables" (Doctoral dissertation, State University of Iowa, 1957).

[9] Vera Slover, "Comic Books Versus Story Books," *Elementary English* (May 1959).

As far as the teacher is concerned, the problem of the comics is a forceful reminder that children must be taught not only *how* to read but also to *discriminate* as they read. One fifth-grade teacher urged her pupils to appraise the comics themselves and, as a first step, to transfer their reading from unwholesome comics about murder, hatred, and revenge to the informational or funny-animal type. She also recommended "classic" comics to the children. It has been found that some of the better comics have a vocabulary equivalent to the sixth-grade level and therefore possibly promote a certain degree of fluency.

THE TEACHER'S GUIDANCE. Teachers can do much to help children evaluate differences in quality between comics and more rewarding types of reading. Teachers can persuade parents to set aside more time for good reading. Often the child's day is filled with television, piano and dancing lessons, and other activities which consume so much time that his reading becomes confined to the brevity of comic books. Teachers can also challenge children to evaluate the ridiculous antics of characters in comic books according to common-sense standards. And teachers can use the type of comic books which are adaptations of classics or history as an entering wedge to reading better books. Teachers can also try to keep comic books from dominating the reading interest of children. Usually comic books are a passing phase which is eventually outgrown; however, if the phase threatens to become a permanent habit, the teacher can insure a less one-sided development by seeing to it that the child has access to many good and interesting books at his ability level. The teacher's main concern should not be the fact the child is fascinated with comic books now; rather, it should be that his interest in them must not be allowed to set his reading taste for life. What must be done is to extend the child's interest gradually from an adventure comic book, featuring pirates, to *Treasure Island,* for example.

Competition from Television. Television is a commercial medium designed for a mass audience. It aims to entertain rather than to educate. Performing this main function more or less successfully, it is clearly a boon to elderly people and shut-ins. Since television helps to keep children quiet and entertained, many harassed mothers also consider it a boon to children. But television is not an unmixed blessing. Aside from curtailing time for wholesome out-of-doors play, television curtails time for reading. Children view such a quantity of programs that there is little time or energy left to devote to practice in reading.

The schools are responsible for teaching many skills in addition to reading. Even though ninety minutes are allocated to daily reading activities in the majority of American schools, only twenty or thirty minutes, on the average, are devoted to learning under the direct instruction of the teacher. To learn to read well, the children must supplement the period of direct instruction they receive with much individual practice. Former generations gained supplementary practice after school by doing a considerable amount of reading in the home. Two or three hours an evening were once devoted as a matter of course to reading. Now, according to research, that time is spent in watching television. Reading is a difficult skill to learn, requiring years of practice and much concentration, but a child needs no skill to turn on a television set. And, once it is turned on, the continual challenge offered by reading is missing, for televiewing is comparatively effortless.

TAKING STOCK. Some points are cited in favor of television, nevertheless: It keeps the family home (though they do not talk to each other but are engrossed in looking at the screen); the distinct speech of announcers *may* promote improved articulation (though an example is, of course, not nearly so effective as practice); the observation of the manner in which performers handle themselves helps people to attain more poise, improved posture, gracious deportment, and better grooming.

While the networks themselves call the attention of critics to the fact that television shows suitable for children *are* being produced to comply with parental and pedagogical demands, there are, unfortunately, many programs intended for adults which children also watch. Even when a childhood classic such as *Huckleberry Finn* is presented, its main effect on the discriminating reader is often to convince him that children would do better to *read* Mark Twain's original masterpiece. Moreover, in the presentation of children's classics, there is a deplorable tendency to inject contemporary references and even colloquial expressions, in the hope of catering to popular taste.

In spite of occasional excursions into the classics, many television programs for children are noisy and marred by a great deal of shouting, shooting, and general surging about. Admittedly, there are some educational programs that feature science, music, news, history, hobbies, or a variety of crafts, but it is also true that each field is hurried over and allotted superficial treatment. The cost of television productions is so exorbitant that sponsors cannot afford to pay for the time required to develop any concept thoroughly. At best, television does not develop ideas—it can only introduce them. Skimming over the surface, merely dipping into the topic, does not result in real learning. It is significant that reading and study go together.

A recent book by Schramm, Lyle, and Parker[10] shows the results of a number of surveys. "The average North American child," Schramm reports, "from age 3 to age 16, spends one-sixth of his waking hours on television, as much time as he spends in school, and more time than he devotes to anything else except sleep and play." An interesting feature of the Schramm report is a detailed analysis of a typical week (five weekdays) of television fare seen in a major city during the period from 4:00 to 9:00 P.M. Results of the study showed that in this time slot—the so-called children's hour—more than half the 100 hours monitored was given to programs in which extreme violence (murders, assaults, etc.) played an important part. The book represents three years' research on 6,000 children and is also based on information from 2,300 parents, teachers, and school officials.

Even if television is not guilty of creating fears, it is at least partially to blame for precipitating anxieties which lie near the surface. Visual realism on television probably has a greater impact upon the emotions than does realism stimulated in a person's imagination by reading. Therefore some psychologists consider television an adverse influence on sensitive, easily disturbed children.

[10] Wilbur Schramm, Jack Lyle, and Edwin B. Parker, *Television in the Lives of Our Children* (Stanford, Calif.: Stanford University Press, 1961).

Another group of critics deplores the flagrant manner in which television commercials—viewed by all age levels—encourage the use of sleeping pills, headache remedies as daily "pepper-uppers," cigarettes, beer, hair oils, cosmetics boasting "secret ingredients," and all the rest. Even people who work in the medium sometimes express disgust at examples of bad taste on television. Goodman Ace, writer of several major shows, facetiously described how his family has learned to enjoy television: "We do it with a six-foot screen . . . ," he declared; "we place it directly in front of the TV set." Of course, television writers work fast and labor under pressures; consequently, their output is often marked by defects. This becomes apparent when one compares their creative efforts with the writing of a classic which may have taken the author a lifetime to produce.

In addition to very meager returns for children in the way of ideas for the amount of time invested, there is some indication of eyestrain experienced after several hours of viewing the bright television screen, with its flickering images. Staring at a light— even at a thirty-watt bulb—for a few minutes will cause a strong after-image to appear when the eyes are subsequently closed.

MEETING THE PROBLEM. Cultural taste grows slowly through exposure to fine music, literature, art, ethics—the enduring, rewarding expressions of a great cultural heritage. But when this heritage is neglected, children lack standards for comparison and continue to be satisfied with "trash." Letters of protest written by parents and teachers to the heads of networks are one answer to the current crop of mediocre programs for children. This type of informal supervision has helped in the past to eliminate some undesirable programs.

Establishing the habit of good reading is an even more effective approach to the television problem. To accomplish this worthy goal, parents should set a personal example for their children by buying good books and reading a great deal themselves; by gently but firmly budgeting the children's televiewing time and demanding that, in all fairness, it be balanced with reading time. Leading the children to appraise the rewards of good reading, that is, to assess the comparative value of one book hour and one television hour is often extremely effective.

Assuming that television is here to stay—and that seems to be a rather safe assumption—we must live with it yet not allow ourselves or our children to lose contact with the heritage of books, and the rich experiences that only books can promote. Some teachers have found it helpful to lead the children to recognize the *advantages* of book reading over televiewing. During discussion, lists are composed by the children, such as the one which follows, elicited from a seventh-grade group:

1. Reading is handy.
2. You do not need expensive repairs.
3. The picture tube does not blow out.
4. No equipment is needed except a book, and maybe reading glasses.
5. You can read without interference from long-winded commercials.
6. You can pace and control the speed.
7. You can stop and think.
8. You can go back.
9. If you do not get it the first time you can re-read.
10. You can "make your own pictures" in your mind.
11. You get more ideas from reading.
12. The person who reads can talk about more ideas. He will also be more able to draw out others. With all the background reading gives, he will know how to ask interesting questions.

Another effective technique to use in reducing the indiscriminate watching of television is for parents and teachers to go over the weekly television guides or logs in the newspapers with the children. If the adults put in a good word for a worthwhile show, some influence may be felt, provided it is done in a permissive rather than preaching manner. Enlisting the children's cooperation and common sense in televiewing has been tried by both parents and teachers with varying degrees of success. "For every TV hour, a book hour" is the motto in some homes, and the fairness of it appeals to many children.

Acquainting Children with Classics. In *The Spectator,* Joseph Addison (1672–1719) the English poet and essayist defined a classic as follows: "A classic is the legacy that a great genius leaves to mankind, which is delivered down from generation to generation, as a present to the posterity of those who are yet unborn."

The teacher who has extracted some of her greatest happiness from reading, and who looks upon the classics as sources of pleasure and wisdom, is ever hopeful that she can, in one way or another, persuade children to experience some of the same advantages through a fondness for reading. As someone has aptly put it, victory over individual ignorance is the first major step toward victory over mass ignorance.

The classics represent a vast storehouse of the wisdom of the ages, and children should not be deprived of them. Critic Jack Gould once said, "Television's appetite for material is so huge that not even the supply of mediocrity is large enough to go around." The opposite is true of classics. So the books that have survived often bear the stamp of greatness. The classics provide profound insight into character, richly imaginative descriptions, and practical, helpful philosophy.

In this connection, Josette Frank asks with deep concern, "Will the literary allusions which come so readily to our lips have meaning for the children of today? Will they know what is implied when they hear someone labeled a Man Friday, or a Cassandra? Will they recognize a Mrs. Malaprop or know what to expect from Pandora's box?"

Of course, some children—talented readers with discriminating parents and teachers—*are* reading the classics. Librarians report that accelerated children continue to read the unabridged versions of *Oliver Twist, Moby Dick, Treasure Island, The Adventures of Tom Sawyer, The Last of the Mohicans,* and other classics, once so familiar and so cherished by older generations. However, thanks to the impatient tempo of the twentieth century, even the gifted children confess to skipping descriptive passages and concentrating on action and conversation.

IMPLICATIONS FOR PERSONAL DEVELOPMENT. Reading the classics is not enough; children must be guided to think about the implications for them personally of such reading. One teacher, working with an upper grade composed of very bright children, aroused a gratifying response to the classics by staging a "treasure hunt." She set her children to "prospecting" for books of permanent value, books that had been read by their grandparents when they were children.

The children began to "dig" for information. They consulted a number of sources for lists of interesting classics, with the object of choosing one from the list to "mine" for "pay dirt" (personally enriching ideas). Their sources included recommendations of friends who had read a certain classic and liked it; recommendations of parents and grandparents; book reviews of classics; knowledge of other books by the same author.

The children "staked their claims" by visiting the library and checking out the books finally decided upon. As the children read the books, each looked for a "rich strike" or "pay dirt" such as a rewarding idea or a picturesque phrase. These were then transferred to the "bank," a notebook containing the quotations and their sources, along with the child's personal reaction of agreement, disagreement, or supplementary thinking.

One boy who began in the fifth grade to keep one such "pay dirt" notebook continued it as a college freshman. The following, from his notebook, is one of the quotations which appealed to him most from *The Ramayana:*

> Rama wanted to know what his purpose was here below. . . . He wanted to know if he ought to be a great man, or a saint. . . . What was man doing here? . . . Should he rejoice or despair? Was the way of renunciation the right way? Should he seize this chance to give up the world?[11]

Below this quotation in his notebook he had jotted down his reaction to the passage. He related the ideas met in his reading to his own problems. This represents critical thinking of a high order, of course.

The notebook practice should be started when voluntary reading of good books begins. All through the grades, teachers should guide children to ask personal questions of books: Is there anything in this helpful to my development? To live by? If children are helped to observe the values for everyday living in their reading, they cannot but help develop better tastes and standards, for, thus challenged, they will realize that cheap and tawdry books yield but little that is rewarding.

[11] Aubrey Mennen, *The Ramayana* (New York: Charles Scribner's Sons, 1954), p. 68.

ADAPTING THE CLASSICS. Teachers often ask these questions regarding classics: Should we try to make all modern children read the classics, when so many have a difficult time with them? To present them to as many children as possible, should we assign abridged versions or comic-book "classics" to those who lack the ability to cope with the original work? For the upper half of the school population, familiarity with our great literary heritage should be axiomatic. The child cannot tell whether he will like or dislike such reading unless he has been exposed to it by a skillful and cultured teacher. Under such a teacher children can make great strides in appreciation of fine literature. The beauty of language in the classics, their vigorous style, will tend to affect the children's style and vocabulary. To quote a boy of twelve:

Well, I guess we ought to have a go at all those books that have lasted so long, like *Rip Van Winkle, The Three Musketeers,* and *The Deerslayer.* I'm kind of glad my teacher encouraged me to read Benjamin Franklin's *Poor Richard's Almanac.* It was interesting to read how Franklin didn't believe in spending money you don't have. I wonder what he would think of longtime payments for cars and refrigerators?

Certainly this boy, at his own level, was applying the same kind of critical thinking as the college freshman cited above. Perhaps modern students would be able to express their meanings more effectively if they were exposed to a wider selection of the great works of literature. The ever present phrases "I mean . . ." and "You know what I mean . . ." testify to the lack of precision in the thinking and speaking of many American students. Undoubtedly, the classics (in addition to enlarging vision and clarifying thought) supplement and extend vocabulary and contribute to the mastery of logical sentence structure. To appreciate wordlessly is not to appreciate fully.

There are diverse opinions concerning the desirability of abridgments and adaptations of classics. Many regard it as a desecration to tamper with them, even in the interests of furthering wider readership. They think that the child will be content with the glimpse he has had of the work and will never read the original.

Many teachers and parents hold the opposite view and maintain that such reading is better than none at all. They favor a brief acquaintance with *The Count of Monte Cristo,* for example, even if it is in a garishly illustrated comic classic, with the vocabulary greatly reduced, wise observations about life omitted, and only sketchy characterization.

Perhaps it is better to be guided by the individual child's preferences and abilities when deciding whether to provide him with the original or the abridgment. Stories have been retold in various ways since the beginning of time, and perhaps such a rattling good adventure tale as *Robinson Crusoe,* made available in an easy edition, can withstand such treatment to compete with television.

QUESTIONS AND ACTIVITIES

1. How does reading rank in the list of recreational preferences expressed by young people?
2. What are some of the goals of the teacher anxious to improve the recreational-reading habits of her pupils?
3. What can be learned from research studies of children's interests that is of value in selecting recreational-reading materials?
4. How would you go about finding a suitable collection of books for your classrom library?
5. Compare two of the bibliographies listed which help parents and children select suitable children's books. Evaluate them and decide which is of greater value to the teacher.
6. Check out several of the recent award-winning books and get acquainted with them.
7. How can the teacher stimulate interest in recreational reading? Of the fifteen activities listed which would you like to try?
8. Describe a typical classroom book-club meeting. Why is the teacher allowed a place on the program?
9. Notice the lesson plan for a dramatization, which follows the lesson plan in this chapter. During student teaching, ask your resident teacher to let you try out the dramatization.
10. What is your opinion of the value of children's book clubs?
11. What are some of the problems connected with the choice of recreational materials which teachers can partially solve?
12. How can the teacher promote "selective televiewing"? Of the facts in Schramm's study, which surprised you the most?
13. Which group of children should be challenged to read the classics? What is your opinion of "revised classics"?

14. How many minutes did you spend yesterday viewing television? What did you learn concerning a philosophy of life? List any valuable ideas gained to sustain you, should you wake up depressed at 4:00 A.M. Compare the yield here with that of some recent serious reading like *The Ramayana*.

15. Why is it important to know each child as an individual in order to guide his growth in interests and tastes in reading?

SELECTED REFERENCES

ARBUTHNOT, MAY HILL. *Children and Books* (2d ed.). Chicago: Scott, Foresman & Co., 1957.

CERF, BENNETT. *Reading for Pleasure*. Harper & Row, 1958.

DEBOER, JOHN, and MARTHA DALLMAN. *The Teaching of Reading*. New York: Holt, Rinehart & Winston, Inc., 1960.

FADIMAN, CLIFTON. *The Lifetime Reading Plan*. Cleveland, Ohio: The World Publishing Co., 1958.

FRANK, JOSETTE. *Your Child's Reading Today*. New York: Doubleday & Co., Inc., 1954.

HOLLOWELL, LILLIAN. *A Book of Children's Literature*. New York: Holt, Rinehart & Winston, Inc., 1950.

HOLMES, DORIS F. "Standards Are Goals," *American Library Association Bulletin* (February 1960), 119–23.

JACOBS, LELAND B. "Historical Fiction for Children," *The Reading Teacher* (January 1961), 191–94.

LARRICK, NANCY. *A Teacher's Guide to Children's Books*. Columbus, Ohio: Charles E. Merrill Books, Inc., 1960.

NORVELL, GEORGE W. *What Boys and Girls Like To Read*. Morristown, N.J.: Silver Burdett Co., 1958.

SCHRAMM, WILBUR, *et al. Television in the Lives of Our Children*. Stanford, Calif.: Stanford University Press, 1961.

SHERBOURNE, J. F. *Toward Better Reading*. Boston: D. C. Heath & Co., 1959.

SIMPSON, ELIZABETH. "Why Shouldn't Young People Jam the Public Library?" *Junior Libraries*, VII (September 1960), 4–6.

WELLS, CHARLES A., and TIMOTHY J. LYNCH. "The Amount of Free Reading Engaged in by Intermediate Grade Pupils Who Have Viewed Television for One Year or More," *Journal of Educational Research* (February 1954), 473–77.

WITTY, PAUL. "Children, Television and Reading," *The Reading Teacher* (October 1957), 11–16.

WITTY, PAUL, and ROBERT A. SIZEMORE. "Reading the Comics: A Summary of Studies and an Evaluation"—I, II, and III. *Elementary English*, XXXI (December 1954), 501–6; XXXII (January, February, 1955), 43–49, 109–14.

14

REMEDIAL READING
IN THE CLASSROOM

A child suffering from reading disabilities is educationally ill. No
sensible person would say to a physically sick child, "I think it is
time for you to get busy and get well. Just look how well your
younger sister is, and she isn't as old as you are." Yet a paraphrase
of this foolish statement is heard about reading failure in many
homes and classrooms throughout the United States. No child is a
remedial-reading case because he wants to be—even though he
may sometimes protect his ego by acting as if he did not care.

If it were possible to teach each day so that every child progressed at a rate consistent with his abilities, the necessity for
remedial reading would be greatly curtailed and teachers would
not be faced with the difficult task of trying to carry on individual
tutoring in reading amidst the hubbub of a crowded classroom.
The unpleasant fact is that, today, a fifth or more of beginning
school children will develop reading problems before they reach
high school, unless the teaching and learning of reading are greatly
improved.

Reading difficulties stem from many causes, but, no matter what
the cause, any child having difficulty with reading needs special
help. Perhaps the child is socially immature or lacks experience.
He may not have mastered sufficient words to express his own
ideas or understand the ideas of others. Perhaps he comes from
an underprivileged family, and poverty has affected his health,

leaving him undernourished or undersized. Perhaps his mind too is undernourished because his parents read very little or speak English imperfectly. He may lack security because his father keeps moving from job to job, thus interrupting his schoolwork. It may be that his parents neglect him or favor a brighter child in the family. Or he may lack emotional maturity and, therefore, be unable to concentrate on a difficult abstract skill such as reading, because he is anxious, unhappy, hostile, or depressed.

Before he can be taught to read, the child must be able to see and hear adequately. Again, these factors are often decisive in the child's progress. Perhaps his eyes are not functioning normally. Perhaps he cannot hear sounds distinctly. Perhaps he has been absent from school a great deal with whooping cough, measles, and colds. Or his reading difficulty may be due to inadequate teaching. He may have been taught by harassed, overworked teachers in large classes where the stipulation to individualize instruction was an empty phrase.

TEACHING PROCEDURES

Preview. "What can you do when you just have fifteen minutes to sit down with a child and try to help him with his reading?" This desperate query was put by a conscientious sixth-grade teacher who had thirty-nine children in her class, three ability groups, and four children achieving so poorly that they did not fit into even the lowest reading group. With the cooperation of a number of classroom teachers and principals, the author and several student teachers embarked on a modest project to determine the most efficient remedial procedure we could find to use in a fifteen-minute period. After trying a number of more ambitious plans, the following simple but realistic three-step procedure yielded the best results: Step 1—Ask a question to guide the silent reading of a passage of interest to the pupil. Step 2—If he cannot read a certain word, provide an oral clue to its pronunciation or meaning. This is not meant to give permanent aid to the learner. It is merely a stopgap measure to use until the word can be *fixed* through repetition. He is not supposed to remember which clues to use in recalling each word. Giving a clue saves him the humiliation of being *told* each word outright. When the word is fixed through drill, he will not need clues to recognition.) After giving the oral clue, have the child "tune in" the whole sentence orally to preserve meaning, as part of the second step. Step 3—To meet the child's need for repetition in some form to fix the word, use a method appropriate to the word. If the word has rhymes, get repetition through calling attention to the similar rhymed ending; if the word has no rhymes and is short enough, repeat the word itself in a column mixed in with foils; etc. (The words he misses as he tries to read thus become the basis of drill. No irrelevant, isolated lists of unfamiliar words or fragments of words are used.)

Discovering Those in the Group Who Need Help. Before discussing the application of the above three-step technique to the case of a retarded twelve-year-old boy by a classroom teacher, it may prove fruitful to survey briefly the problem of screening: Which of forty children need special help in reading?

1. The teacher gives an intelligence test such as the Lorge-Thorndike Group Test.[1] Next she uses a reading-survey test such as the Gates Reading Survey (see Chapter 15) to determine which children belong in the fast-moving, average-moving, and slow-moving reading-ability groups. By this means, the teacher learns which of the children in her class fall so far below standard that they do not fit into any group, and require special help.

2. Having discovered through the use of standardized tests the three or four children who fall far below standard, the teacher's next task is to find time to attend to these children individually. While the regular ability groups are busy doing reading workbook assignments or social-studies or recreational reading, the teacher takes the screened-out readers aside, one by one, and briefly interviews them.

3. After the interview has revealed the child's special line of interest—helicopters, dogs, or whatnot—the teacher locates reading matter featuring his center of interest and written in a simple easy vocabulary. Then the individual remedial work begins on

---

[1] The Lorge-Thorndike I.Q. Tests (Boston: Houghton Mifflin Co., 1957). Level 2, non-verbal, for grades 2–3, 35 minutes; level 4 for grades 4–6, verbal battery 44–49 minutes, non-verbal, 27 minutes.

the basis of fifteen-minute sessions daily, using the three-step technique outlined above or some other plan.

The Remedial Work with Ron. It is hoped that the study of an actual case will serve to make clear the use of at least one type of remedial-reading technique in a regular classroom situation where the teacher has many children and very little time for individual instruction.

Ron, a boy of twelve, entered an overcrowded sixth-grade classroom one Monday morning in October, too late to take the formal standardized tests administered to the other pupils. The teacher interviewed Ron and learned that he lived with his family in a trailer, which was convenient, since his father kept moving westward, leaving one job after another as a garage repairman. Ron, therefore, had a history of interrupted education. Altogether he had thus far been enrolled in eleven schools. At one time the family lived near a large ranch in Texas. This experience resulted in his ambition to be a cowboy someday and prompted his only apparent hobby, watching cowboy films on television.

INFORMAL TESTING. While awaiting the standardized tests for which she had to send, the teacher determined Ron's approximate reading level by giving him two informal tests—the 100-words test and the Dolch Basic Sight Vocabulary Test (Garrard Press, Champaign, Ill.). Trying Ron out at reading a paragraph of 100 words in the sixth-grade reader, she learned that he made more than 5 mistakes per 100 words. The same poor showing occurred when Ron read aloud, at sight, paragraphs of 100 words in the fifth-, fourth-, and third-grade readers. Not until Ron read from a second-grade basic reader could he read 100 words and make fewer than 5 mistakes in word recognition. He knew only a third of the 220 easy, everyday words in the Dolch test. Not all of the 220 were tested at a single session.

THE START OF REMEDIAL WORK. The teacher realized that she must secure more data to determine Ron's specific reading abilities. But, in the two brief sessions she had held, she had discovered that he seemed alert enough but lacked experience, that is, practice, in reading. He had missed the training which makes sight words a permanent possession of a child and enables him to distinguish them easily. From the manner in which he blocked on certain words during the 100-words test, the teacher suspected that he knew very little about consonant substitution or word analysis. Indeed, she gathered that all he could do was to name consonants and vowels by rote; he did not understand them in a functional setting.

Since she could spare only ten or fifteen minutes for each private session with Ron—because of the needs of others in her group —the teacher wished to make every minute count in giving the child something he sorely needed: practice in reading.

THE EXPERIENCE METHOD. The teacher had not yet found a book with a second-grade vocabulary that dealt with cowboys, but, knowing about his interest, she invited Ron to tell her about his ambition to be a cowboy, and also to tell something about the ranch he had seen. She suggested that he dictate his "story" to her while she took it down. (They sat at the back of the schoolroom, working at a table.) Below is the "story" Ron dictated, aided by prompting in the form of questions sympathetically put by the teacher.

> I want to be a cowboy.
> I want to work on a ranch.
> Horses are fun to ride.
> I like the song "Home on the Range."
> It tells about where the deer and
> the antelope play.

The teacher typed the story, and, the next day, Ron tried to "read it back." Though he had dictated this story based on his own experience, he failed to recognize several words. For one thing, he misread the last phrase as "where the deer and the cantaloupe play." To correct this error, the teacher asked what a cantaloupe is and pointed out that it would not make sense to think of fruit playing. (Ron had formed the habit of regarding reading as the pronunciation of words, which alone was such a staggering task that he had seldom been able to concentrate upon the meaning of a passage.)

To make remedial procedures clear, a lesson plan is offered below, equally applicable whether the child's own experience stories or unfamiliar content is involved. It should be noted that it is brief and, as far as the method is concerned, consists of three parts. It would not be realistic to expect an elaborate plan for one child in a roomful of forty children. Therefore this is kept simple by design.

LESSON PLAN FOR REMEDIAL READING

I. What (subject matter)

    A. Ron's own experience story about cowboys, since they are his main interest

    B. Other easy materials located by the teacher, featuring cowboys

II. Why (aims)

    A. To improve Ron's reading skills

    B. To improve his attitude toward reading

III. How (method)

Guidance

    A. Guiding the reading: Ask Ron to read to find certain definite parts of the passage. Have him read silently; then, after indicating words he does not know and giving clues as to their pronunciation, have him read orally.

Attack clues

    B. Giving attack clues: When Ron does not know a word, furnish a clue instead of humiliating him by telling him every word outright. (Some common words such as "was," "this," etc., are difficult to "cue" and should be furnished.)

Fixing methods

    C. Fixing the words: Every word that troubles Ron during the guided reading will be used for drill. The essence of fixing is to secure mastery through some form of repetition: repeating the word itself or the rhymed ending, tracing over and over the word, etc. It depends on the word. If it has many rhymes as in the case of "call" ("ball," "fall," "stall," "wall," "small," "tall"), repetition is secured in the rhymed ending. But if the word is "this," which has no exact rhymes, the word itself has to be repeated for the child and he finds it in a column mixed with "foils": *"this," "the," "this,"* "then," *"this,"* "then," *"this."* (It would be very convenient to concentrate on teaching a pupil words that could be learned by the application of one or two fixing techniques, but that would mean the words would have to be preselected instead of occurring in a piece of reading matter that interests him.) Whatever word in the reading matter turns out to be a problem, must be fixed by appropriate means. Since all this sounds more complicated than it actually proves to be in practice, it is best to show a graphic chart of (1) the words Ron missed while reading his own experience story, (2) the attack clues given by the teacher, and (3) the specific fixing methods used.

INTERIM INSTRUCTION. For several days, Ron's own experience story and the words which he missed in the Dolch Basic Word Test of 220 words provided Ron's reading matter. The words he had trouble with during the guided reading were used for drills. Each word he missed was written for him on cards, in both print and cursive writing, and filed in an alphabetized "WORD BOX FILE" which the teacher had helped him make. His name was affixed to this box. When the teacher called for one of his words such as "want" or "antelope," he would look under "w" and "a," respectively, to find the word. After this he would name the beginning letter and tell whether it was a consonant or a vowel. The words he did not recognize during this review were drilled on again and "fixed," i.e., *mastered* by appropriate methods. *One* fixing method was used *per* word *not* all of them on all the words.

1. Sight word with foils
2. Consonant substitution (The policy is to use rhymes for a word if rhymes exist.)
3. Visual scrutiny (look-say method)
4. Kinesthetic tracing (see page 401)
5. Clapping for and pronouncing syllables, followed by pronouncing word without any break
6. Looking for root words plus endings
7. Applying vowel-recognition routines (see page 397).

Words Missed	*Attack Clues Given*	*Fixing Methods Used*
"want"	Since "want" has no rhyme and is difficult to define, the teacher told Ron the word. (Helping Ron to pronounce the word is the goal here. This oral clue is *not* meant to *fix* the word.)	"Sight word with foils" to secure repetition: *want* what *want* were wash *want* went *want*
"horses"	Picture clue. After Ron had dictated his experience story, the teacher hunted up pictures of horses and cowboys for him.	Repetition secured by "look-say": The child was directed to inspect the word "horse" (the root word) from left to right half a dozen times to get a mental picture of it. Then the ending "s" was added to form "horses."
"ride"	Definition clue: The teacher asked, "What is it you do with a horse that you said was fun?"	Repetition secured with rhymed endings: *ride* *wide* *side* *tide* After the teacher led the boy to pronounce each word, she asked him to underline the part that was the same, i.e., the rhymed ending.
"ranch"	Experience clue from the teacher: "The place you liked in Texas."	Use of short-vowel recognition routine composed of a series of questions for the child to answer, all leading toward a vowel rule inductively: "How many vowels do you see in 'ranch'?" ("One.") "What is its position—beginning, middle, or end?" ("Middle.") "Does it say its alphabet name?" ("No.") "How would it sound if it did?" ("R-a-anch.") "What does it say?" ("Ranch.") "How will you mark the vowel?" ("Short-vowel mark.")
"antelope"	Context and common-sense clue. (He had called it "cantaloupe.")	The teacher wrote it on the board as "an/te/lope." Then she said it, clapping at the same time to indicate syllables, and had Ron imitate.

VOWEL RECOGNITION ROUTINES

1. Short-vowel recognition (See "ranch" on chart.)

2. Long-vowel recognition routine for *no*—a word missed by Ron in a test

   "How many vowels do you see?" ("One.") "What is its position in the word—beginning, middle, or end?" ("End.") "Does it say its alphabet name?" ("Yes.") "What mark do we place over it?" ("Long-vowel mark, the macron.") (If Ron can pronounce "maverick," and he can, he is capable of pronouncing "macron" —even if the "a" is long—provided he knows its meaning.)

3. Two-vowels-together recognition routine for "team"

   "How many vowels do you see?" ("Two.") "How many vowels do you hear?" ("First one.") "Does it say its alphabet name?" ("Yes the 'e' does.") "What do you place over it?" ("Long-vowel mark.") "What happens to the second vowel?" ("Silent. Cross it out.")

4. Final-"e" recognition routine for "ride"

   "How many vowels do you see?" ("Two.") "How many do you hear?" ("First one: 'i' ") "Does it say its alphabet name?" ("Yes.") "What do we place over it?" ("Long-vowel mark—the macron.") "Where is the other vowel?" ("End of word.") "Do we hear that final 'e'?" ("No, it is silent.") (Change "cap" to "cape," "rid" to "ride," to show Ron how final "e" makes the preceding vowel say its alphabet name.)

5. Consonant-controller recognition routine for "car"

   Go through the routine. Point out that, even though the vowel "a" is in the middle of "car," it does *not* have a short-vowel sound as in "cat." The vowel is changed, or controlled, by the consonant "r" following and has a new sound.

READING FROM A BOOK. By now, at the end of a week, the teacher had located a book featuring Ron's interest. The book was entitled *From Town Boy to Cowboy*. The teacher told Ron that in this storybook he would read about a boy like himself, living in a town but wanting to be a cowboy and live on a ranch. The teacher suggested that Ron read the story to see how the boy got his wish (motivating question). To prepare for the story further, she mentioned that, though Ron lived in a trailer, the boy in the story lived in an apartment house in a big city like New York. She then handed him the book *"From Town Boy to Cowboy."*

The teacher asked Ron to read the title silently and indicate any word he didn't know. Ron did not know the word "town" in the title. The teacher gave him a definition clue, "It is another word you use instead of saying 'city.'" Ron furnished "town" without hesitation, but, if he had not, the teacher would have furnished the word. The title having been read silently then orally, the teacher now prepared to guide the reading by meaning units: "Read to find out where Tom lived." "Read to find out what he saw from the window," etc.

Tom Bond lived on the top floor of an apartment house in a big, big town. When he looked out the window he saw many roof tops. Way below he saw the busy streets. Cars and trucks went by. There were no horses. There were no cows. Tom wanted to be a cowboy and live on a ranch. He wanted to ride horses and round up "dogies." Tom did not want to be a town boy.

The teacher continued to guide the reading by short passages, on this day and on the day following. She had Ron read silently to find the answers, inviting him to ask for the pronunciation of any words he did not know. She gave appropriate attack clues or, in the absence of them, told him the words. Then she had him "tune in" the whole sentence in which the troublesome word or words occurred by reading it aloud. To stress meaning, she led Ron to discuss some of the ideas in the passage by relating them to his experience.

OTHER REMEDIAL WORK. Since Ron "chopped wood," i.e., read one word at a time, the teacher told him to look ahead, try to scoop up a phrase with his eyes, look away from the book, and *say* it to obtain a more natural interpretation. The teacher kept reminding Ron to "read the way people talk"—a far more effective method than admonishing the child to "read with expression." She also helped Ron to figure out which were the "sock" words so that he could read as clearly as TV-commercial announcers.

CHART SHOWING REMEDIAL METHODS USED IN DEALING
WITH THE WORDS RON MISSED IN BOOK READING

Words Missed	Meaning Clues Given	Fixing Methods Used
"lived"	The teacher under-lined the root, "live."	Since the word does not have many rhymes, and since it does not follow the "final-'e' " rule, the teacher used "look-say" method for repetition. She had him look hard at the beginning, middle, and end several times, saying the word each time. Then added the "d" and had the word read.
"top"	Ron read it as "to." The teacher told him it meant the opposite of bottom.	Since the word has rhymes she wrote them in a column: "top," "stop," "pop," "bop," "flop," "crop," "drop." She called attention to the similar ending.
"apartment"	Definition clue: "It is a place with many floors where people live in large cities."	The teacher clapped for the three syllables as she pronounced each. She had Ron imitate her. Then she marked the word on the board: "a/part/ment" and had Ron pronounce each syllable and then say the whole word quickly.
"window"	Object clue: Pointing to a window in the classroom, the teacher asked, "What is that called?"	The teacher clapped for the two syllables as she pronounced the word. She wrote it on the board: "win/dow." Then she showed that the vowel in the first syllable follows the short-vowel rule. (By the time a child has said this much of a word and tentatively said the "o," the pronunciation has triggered his memory of a word he knows: "window." Even if most English words are only partly phonetic, knowing the first part often "triggers" the rest, especially if the context in which the word occurs is observed.)

When Ron read the sentence below all in one tone, without any emphasis, the teacher indicated certain words to stress and showed him how the sentence should be "thought-grouped" for oral reading.

Tom Bond lived   on the *top* floor
of an *apartment* house   in a *big*, big town.

After Ron finished his first cowboy book, his teacher secured another, entitled *The Ranch Round-up*. Since it was written at a slightly higher difficulty level, Ron found it more interesting but also more challenging. With this the teacher continued to use the three-step sequence: guiding the reading, giving attack clues, helping the child fix words. She also provided other valuable types of reading experience. She helped him file words alphabetically in his word box, talked over ideas in the passages, and guided him to relate them to his personal experience. At the slightest sign of improvement in any aspect of his reading— whether attitude, habits, or skills—she praised him warmly, "celebrating each success."

KINESTHETIC TRACING. Since the other fixing methods employed by Ron's teacher have been described above, attention should also be drawn to the use of kinesthetic tracing, before describing the third-level skill which deals with syllabication principles. Though Dr. Grace Fernald, originator of the method, used kinesthetic tracing to fix polysyllables, many teachers think that beyond two syllables it loses some effectiveness.

In using kinesthetic tracing with Ron, his teacher wrote the word "wagon" (missed in his second cowboy book) on the board in cursive writing. Then she asked him if he would like to know that word "for sure" so he would not have to ask for it again. He nodded, and she told him that it might help him to recognize the word next time he saw it if he traced it several times. She showed Ron how to hold his index and middle finger together (for firmer contact) and use them to trace the word "wagon" on the board. Ron's teacher encouraged him to sound out the word as he traced it and to try to make the two processes "come out even." Ron traced and sounded the word about six times. Then, indicating that he thought he knew it, he erased the word and wrote "wagon" without the model. The word seemed almost to write itself, as if the tracing had impressed itself in a pattern upon his muscles.

However, his teacher reported that he seemed to retain words of several syllables better through the use of clapping for the syllables, pronouncing them, and indicating the syllables already marked off for him by the teacher in the words written on the board. In fact, the teacher felt that Ron had achieved readiness for learning the three syllabication principles inductively. She was anxious for him to go beyond the "baby level" of clapping for the syllables of the words written for him on the board and pronouncing them after her.

TEACHING THE THREE SYLLABICATION RULES. Below are the plans Ron's teacher used in order to teach him how to syllabicate.

1. The two-consonant syllabication rule: Present the word "window," and have Ron look toward the middle of the word for two consonants together. Have him mark under each with a small "c" to designate consonant. Then have him inspect the word to see if there is a vowel on each side of the two consonants. Have Ron mark the two vowels with "v" placed close up under each. Pronounce the word, clapping for the two syllables. Then place the syllabication vertical: "win/dow." Show Ron that it comes between the two consonants, surrounded by the two vowels. Present other words such as "welcome," "contest," "suggest," and follow the above routine to help him to form the habit of looking toward the middle of a word for two consonants surrounded by vowels. Tell him that almost all of the time the rule to split between two consonants works. Continue by showing him that in the word "important" there are two sets of consonants surrounded by two sets of vowels. Show how the word divides: "im/por/tant." Have him mark the consonants and vowels under each with c's or v's.

2. The single-consonant syllabication rule: Follow the above routine except to have the child inspect the middle of the word for the presence of a *single* consonant surrounded by vowels. Present the word "pupil." Have him label the letter "p" in the middle with a "c" underneath. Then label the "u" and "i" with a "v" underneath. Show him how the word divides: "pu/pil."

3. The "le"-ending syllabication rule: Present such words as "saddle," "stable." Teach him to look for the "le" ending with a consonant in front of it. Clap and show how both of these words divide: "sad/dle," "sta/ble." Then, to see if he can apply the "le"-ending rule, present the word "bridle" and have him show how it divides: "bri/dle."

Generalizations. The teacher's remedial plan for Ron represents one example of the kind of remedial lesson which may be prepared for use in a classroom. (Remedial instruction of the type which can be given in a clinic where there is more time available, as well as the expert help of trained specialists using the newest equipment and materials, lies beyond the scope of this discussion.) But, no matter what plan is used in the remedial guidance given to individual children in the classroom, the following considerations should be kept in mind as instruction is carried forward:

1. The child should be given the opportunity to read considerable material based on his own experiences and recorded by the teacher at his dictation, not only to start him off but also to lend variety to the remedial work later.

2. A sight vocabulary should be developed. Independence in reading rests on this ability.

3. The pupil should be given a secure method of word attack. After the child understands that reading is engaged in solely to get *meaning* from the printed page, he is ready to use his stock of sight words for purposes of comparison in learning to recognize new words through serial substitution, structural analysis, and phonetic analysis.

4. Easy reading a grade below the child's basic reading level should be provided to develop interest and fluency. This should not be forced on the child. When he is successful in basic reading, he usually takes a voluntary interest in independent reading.

5. The child's basic reading ability should be built up by every means possible. Starting at the level at which he is now successful, he should be led gradually toward increased power and fluency in reading—the goal, of course, being to bring him up to standard.

Teachers are dealing with precious commodities when they work with children. Although the progress of remediation just outlined may appear exceedingly complex, so little of this total program is required in any one case that it is much less formidable than it appears. And most remedial-reading teachers will agree that, although such guidance constitutes a real challenge, the satisfaction experienced is equally great as results become apparent. However, the teacher should recognize that she can do only so much in giving remedial aid and not demand the impossible of herself. The important thing is to understand what *can* be done, and then to attack the problem efficiently. As a matter of policy, the teacher should

1. Regard remedial reading not as a magic hocus pocus of special methods but as a more intense and personal application of the techniques used with all children
2. Try to improve the child's attitude toward reading, since retarded readers are generally either apathetic or hostile
3. Conduct each remedial session so that the child will be well aware of the purpose of each drill or other reading activity
4. Avoid too much routine in conducting remedial sessions; instead, provide a variety of activities, and emphasize human values by occasionally arranging little surprises
5. Bear in mind that retarded readers are especially prone to show ups and downs from day to day in their reading, and offer them needed encouragement
6. Be optimistic and patient
7. Help the child to experience *some* success at each corrective session (Since the child has met defeat repeatedly, it is especially important that he develop confidence in his ability to learn to read.)

COLLECTING INFORMATION ABOUT THE CHILD

The teacher should assemble as much information about each remedial child from as many sources as possible, in order to understand his needs and to provide the type of reading aid he needs. Forms of various types are available for use in selecting remedial-reading material that will complement the child's interests.

Interest Inventory. One such form, an interest inventory, is effective in determining the child's main interests. The one outlined here indicates the teacher's procedure in her interview with the child.

1. Teacher: "Here are some things you might do after school. I will put double 'xx' by the thing you tell me you would like to do best. I will put an 'x' by all other things you tell me you might like to do."

Play ball
Build an airplane
Go to Scout meetings
Go to the movies
Watch television
Listen to the radio
Practice your music lesson
Listen to records
Make collections
Play with your dog
Have a paper route
Ride a bicycle
Go swimming
Read comic books
Read other books
What else do you do? ————————————

2. Teacher: "Here are some trips you might like to take. I will put double 'xx' by the trip you tell me you would like most. I will put an 'x' by the ones you tell me you might also like to take."

Go to a farm
Go to the city
Take a trip on a boat
Take a trip on an airplane
Take a trip with your family in the car
Go to the mountains
Go to the ocean
Visit children in other lands such as France, Norway, and Mexico
Visit an Indian Reservation
Visit a ranch
Visit some historical place like Mount Vernon
Visit an old fort
Visit a place where all kinds of plants are growing
Go to a park and see all kinds of animals
What other trip might you like?————————————

3. Teacher: "Here are some things you might do on Saturday or Sunday. I will put double 'xx' by the thing you tell me you would like to do best. I will put an 'x' by the other things you tell me you might like to do."

Read a book by yourself
Have someone read a book to you

Have someone tell you stories
Go to the library
Read a comic book or funny paper
Look at pictures but not read
Play outdoors
Watch television

4. Teacher: "When you go to school, you have many things to do. I will put double 'xx' by the thing you tell me you like to do best. I will put an 'x' by anything else you tell me you also like to do."

Have reading class
Do arithmetic problems
Learn spelling
Draw and paint pictures
Write stories and letters
Give reports
Tell the rest of the class about things
Do experiments
Play games
Take physical education
Learn music and singing
Practice folk dancing
Attend book club
Attend library club
Make things
What else do you like in school? _____

After the teacher has checked the child's interests, she proceeds to ask him these questions and fills in the blanks:

Have you a nickname? _____ What is it? _____
If you had just one wish what would it be? _____
Whom do you like to play with in your family? _____
Do you have a pet? _____ What is it? _____
If you could have another pet, what would it be? _____

Reading Tests. Group tests are of value in giving an estimate of the reading levels in the class. Those who fall far below the norm are screened out for remedial help. Both standardized reading-survey tests and other, more informal types of individual tests may be used. Some examples follow.

Gates Reading Survey Test (Bureau of Publications, Teachers College, Columbia University, New York). Arthur I. Gates designed this group test in two forms for grades three to ten. The test requires fifty minutes to give and includes measures of speed, accuracy, level of comprehension, and vocabulary.

Basic Sight Vocabulary Cards Test (Garrard Press, Champaign, Ill.). This individual test, prepared by Edward Dolch, consists of a set of 220 cards which test the ability to recognize automatically some of the most frequently used words in the language.

Gray's Oral Reading Paragraphs (see Chapter 15).

Personal Inventory. The type of form reproduced below is very useful to the teacher in making a survey of specific factors which affect reading. The factors to be surveyed appear on the left, and the corresponding sources of information for each are on the right.

Factors	*Sources of Information*
1. Home Conditions. Evidence of insecurity (financial or emotional), family friction, discord, illness.	Home visits and parent conferences.
2. Emotional and social adjustment to school, to the teacher, to the children. Shyness, showing off, bullying, nervous tension.	Observation of child in classroom, on playground, home visits and parent conferences.
3. School Experiences. Chronological and mental age at time of entering school. School history: difficulties, attitudes, work habits, retentions, teachers' methods.	Reports from previous teachers. Study of cumulative record. Conference with child. Conference with parent.
4. Physical Condition. Vision and Hearing.	Health report. Results of examinations.
5. Mental Maturity.	Results of the individual intelligence test given by special examiner.
6. Reading Ability.	Results of Gates Reading Survey. Results of 100-words test. Results of Dolch Basic Sight Vocabulary Test, etc.
7. Interests.	Results of interest inventory.

After the teacher has collected, by the use of this form, all the information relating to the child's reading success, she is in a strategic position to help the remedial child to make a better adjustment to the work in reading. Ofter the information about each of the factors listed is written up in the form of a summary or profile and filed in the child's cumulative record. Even though it may require some time to round out the total picture of the child, remedial work can be begun as soon as the teacher has obtained some information concerning the child's interests and his reading level.

REMEDIAL-READING MATERIALS

Source Materials. One of the most helpful source books of titles of books for pupils whose interest is at a more mature level than their reading ability is *Good Reading for Poor Readers* by George B. Spache, now out in a revised edition (Champaign, Ill.: Garrard Press, 1959). The author has literally never seen a teacher's copy of Spache's book which has not appeared well thumbed and even worn out from constant use.

A much needed but heretofore rather rare list of books, compiled by Donald N. Bentz, appears in his article "Sports Books, Grade Seven Up" (*Junior Libraries* 6, November, 1959. Pages 11–13). The list of fiction and non-fiction is arranged under these headings: Boxing; Golf; Hockey; Judo, Wrestling, Body Building; Sports Cars and Racing; Swimming–Skin Diving; Tennis; Track and Field. (Some of the books can be enjoyed by fifth and sixth graders as well as by seventh and eighth graders, if slightly paraphrased by the remedial-reading teacher.)

Gateways to Readable Books, Ruth Strang *et al.* (The H. W. Wilson Co., New York). A short bibliography for retarded readers in the upper grades. The annotations are written simply enough to be read by the pupils themselves as they browse for a book they might like to read.

Curriculum Correlation of Cadmus Books with Basic Readers (E. M. Hale & Co., Eau Claire, Wis.). This provides teachers with available books to correlate with the basic series being used.

A Survey of Corrective and Remedial Reading Materials, compiled by Dora J. Reese (Bookstore, Eastern Montana College of Education, Billings, Mont.). Very complete and helpful.

RECREATIONAL BOOKS.

A. *Beginner Books*

  1. *The Cat in the Hat*. Random House. First grade.
  2. *The Cat in the Hat Comes Back*. Random House. Second.
  3. *The Big Ball of String*. Random House. Second.
  4. *Sam and the Firefly*. Random House. First, second.
  5. *A Fly Went By*. Random House. First, second.

B. *I Can Read Books*

  1. *Little Bear*. Harper. First.
  2. *Danny and the Dinosaur*. Harper. First.
  3. *Nobody Listens to Andrew*. Harper. First.

C. *Rockets, Satellites, and Space Travel*, etc. (Very Modern)

  1. *The True Book of Space*. Childrens Press. First.
  2. *The Earth Satellite*. Knopf. First.
  3. *You Will Go to the Moon*. Random House. Second.
  4. *Rockets into Space*. Random House. First, second.
  5. *Miss Sue, the Nurse*. Melmont Pubs. Second.
  6. *The Biggest Salmon*. Melmont Pubs. Third.
  7. *Navaho Land—Today and Yesterday*. Melmont Pubs. Third.
  8. *Atoms for Junior*. Melmont Pubs. Third to sixth.
  9. *Off into Space*. Whittlesey House. Fourth.
  10. *Man-made Moons*. Day. Fifth.
  11. *Freddy and the Space Ship*. Knopf. Sixth.

D. *The Walt Disney Books*

  1. *Here They Are*. Heath. Primer.
  2. *Donald Duck and His Nephews*. Heath. First.
  3. *Pinocchio*. Heath. Second.
  4. *Little Pig's Picnic and Other Stories*. Heath. Third.
  5. *Dumbo of the Circus*. Heath. Third.
  6. *Bambi*. Heath. Fifth.
  7. *Mickey Sees the U.S.A.* Heath. Fifth.
  8. *Donald Duck Sees South America*. Heath. Fifth.

E. *Easy Reading Books*

  1. *Surprise*. Macmillan. Primer.
  2. *In Came Pinky*. Macmillan. Primer.
  3. *Animal Parade*. Macmillan. First.
  4. *Animals Are Fun*. Macmillan. First.
  5. *Elsie Elephant*. Macmillan. First.
  6. *Animals Work Too*. Macmillan. Second.

    7. *The Pueblo Indian Stories.* Macmillan. Second.
    8. *Year Round Fun.* Macmillan. Second.

F. *Books About the West*

    1. *Cowboy Tommy.* Doubleday. Third.
    2. *Jerry and the Pony Express.* Doubleday. Third.
    3. *Cowboy Tommy's Round-up.* Houghton. Fourth.

G. *The Junior Every Reader Series*

    1. *The Robin Hood Stories.* Webster. Third.
    2. *Old Testament Stories.* Webster. Third.

H. *Young Readers Bookshelf*

    1. *Young Reader Animal Stories.* Grosset. Fourth.
    2. *Young Reader Baseball Stories.* Grosset. Fourth.
    3. *Young Reader Cowboy Stories.* Grossett. Fourth.
    4. *Young Reader Dog Stories.* Grossett. Fourth.
    5. *Young Reader Football Stories.* Grossett. Fourth.
    6. *Young Reader Pioneer Stories.* Grossett. Fourth.

I. *Books To Stretch on (Chuckle Stories)*

    1. *Repair It, Fix It, Make It Right.* Harper. Easy primary.
    2. *Danger, Danger All Around.* Harper. Easy primary.
    3. *Two Birthday Presents for Father.* Harper. Easy primary.

J. *Miscellaneous Recreational Reading*

    1. *Susannah, the Pioneer Cow.* Macmillan. Second.
    2. *Runaway Sardine.* Knopf. Second.
    3. *Shep the Farm Dog.* Heath. Second.
    4. *Caboose.* Lothrop. Third.
    5. *Andy, the Musical Ant.* Aladdin. Third.
    6. *Licorice.* Aladdin. Third.
    7. *Mr. Doodle.* Harcourt. Third.
    8. *Great Whales.* Morrow. Third.

SELECTED SERIES OF BOOKS (INFORMATIONAL AND PLEASURE READING).

A. *Aladdin Books.* Random House. First to sixth (science).

B. *All About Books.* Random House. Fifth and sixth (science).

C. *American Adventure Series.* Harper. Third through junior high (social studies).

D. *Around the World Series.* Macmillan. Fourth through eighth (geography).

E. *Aviation Series.* Macmillan. First through sixth.

F. *Basic Science Education Series.* Harper. First through ninth.

G. *The Basic Vocabulary Series.* Garrard. First through third.

H. *Childhood of Famous American Series.* Bobbs. Third through fifth.

I. *The Every Reader Library and Junior Every Readers.* Webster. Fourth through sixth (simplified classics).

J. *Cowboy Sam Books.* Beckley-Cardy. Primer through third (boys particularly like these eight books).

K. *Landmark Books.* Random House. Sixth through eighth (almost one hundred titles, including one on the FBI).

L. *Pleasure Reading Series.* Garrard. Third through sixth (fables, folk tales, etc.).

M. *How To Series.* Knopf. Fourth through seventh (making and doing).

N. *Inter-American Readers.* Macmillan. Third through sixth (title explanatory—many customs of Latin America, etc.).

O. *Living Literature Series.* Macmillan. Third through eighth.

P. *My Hobby Is Series.* Hart. Second through eighth.

Q. *Reading for Independence Series.* Scott Foresman. First through third (funny stories, including "tall tales").

R. *Real Books.* Garden City Bks. Fourth through sixth (topics include space travel, stars, pirates, camping, etc.).

S. *Wonder-Wonder Series.* Steck. First through sixth (pets and nature).

T. *Woodland Frolics Series.* Steck. First through sixth.

U. *Signature Books.* Grosset. Intermediate and junior high (many books about world-famous figures—inventors, scientists, authors, explorers, presidents).

V. *World Landmark Books.* Random House. Fourth and up (excellent).

W. *The Reading Laboratory.* Science Res. First through high (short complete stories).

PHONICS MATERIALS.

A. *Reading for Independence Series.* Scott Foresman. First through Third (humorous stories and tall tales, accompanied by integrated word-analysis program).

B. *Eye and Ear Fun* by Clarence Stone. Webster. First through sixth.

C. Filmstrips.

    1. *Let's Start with Key Words* (Soc. for Visual Education).
    2. *Word Analysis* (Scott Foresman).

        a. *Rhyme Time*
        b. *Beginning Sounds*
        c. *Letters and Sounds*
        d. *Fun with Words* (consonant substitution)

PRACTICE MATERIALS.

A. *Reader's Digest Reading Skill Builder Series* (Reader's).

B. *Reading Skill Texts* (Merrill).

    1. *Bibs.* First grade.
    2. *Nicky.* Second grade.
    3. *Uncle Funny Bunny.* Third grade.
    4. *Uncle Ben.* Fourth grade.
    5. *Tom Trott.* Fifth grade.
    6. *Pat, the Pilot.* Sixth grade.

C. *Diagnostic Reading Books* (Am. Educ. Press).

    1. *Nip, the Bear.* First grade.
    2. *Red Deer, the Indian Boy.* Second grade.
    3. *Scottie and His Friends.* Third grade.
    4. *Adventure Trails.* Fourth grade.
    5. *Exploring Today.* Fifth grade.

QUESTIONS AND ACTIVITIES

1. Explain in detail how you might proceed at the beginning of a new school year to discover the children in your room who need remedial-reading help.
2. What are the most important things a teacher should know about a child beginning remedial-reading instruction?
3. Describe the procedures that an intermediate-grade teacher might use in diagnosing the difficulties of a child who needs help.
4. Prepare a program that an intermediate-grade teacher might use in helping a retarded reader increase his reading proficiency.
5. List the values of the experience-story technique for remedial-reading children of any grade level. What quality is present in experience material that is not found in any other?
6. What is the purpose of each of the three main steps in the remedial technique used with Ron in this chapter?

7. How does the vowel-recognition routine help to teach rules inductively?

8. What would be the best fixing method to use with "garden"? Why?

   kinesthetic tracing?   rhyming?   sight word with foils?

9. What would be the best fixing method to use in fixing "team"? Why?

   sight word with foils?   rhyming?   kinesthetic tracing?

10. What would be the best fixing method to use with the word "this"? Why?

   rhyming?   syllabication?   sight word with foils?

SELECTED REFERENCES

BOND, GUY L., and MILES A. TINKER. *Reading Difficulties: Their Diagnosis and Correction.* New York: Appleton-Century-Crofts, Inc., 1957.

DOLCH, EDWARD W. "Success in Remedial Reading," *Elementary English,* XXX (March 1953), 133–37.

FEINBERG, H., and C. L. REED. "Reading Level of a Group of Socially Maladjusted Boys," *Journal of Educational Psychology,* XII (1940), 31–38.

HEILMAN, ARTHUR W. *Principles and Practices of Teaching Reading.* Columbus, Ohio: Charles E. Merrill Books, Inc., 1961.

HILDRETH, GERTRUDE. *Teaching Reading.* New York: Holt, Rinehart & Winston, Inc., 1958.

JERSILD, A. T. *Child Psychology* (5th ed.). Englewood Cliffs, N.J.: Prentice-Hall, Inc., 1960.

KEPHART, NEWELL CARLYLE. *The Slow Learner in the Classroom.* Columbus, Ohio: Charles E. Merrill Books, Inc., 1960.

RUSSELL, DAVID H. *Children Learn To Read* (2d ed.). Boston: Ginn & Co., 1961.

SPACHE, GEORGE D. *Good Reading for Poor Readers.* Champaign, Ill.: Garrard Press, 1959.

VAN ALTA, FREIDA E. *How To Help Your Children in Reading, Writing and Arithmetic.* New York: Random House, Inc., 1959.

VERNON, M. D. *Backwardness in Reading: A Study of Its Natures and Origins.* London: Cambridge University Press, 1958.

WITTY, PAUL. *Reading in Modern Education.* Boston: D. C. Heath & Co., 1949.

WOOLF, MAURICE D., and JEANNE A. WOOLF. *Remedial Reading: Teaching and Treatment.* New York: McGraw-Hill Book Co., Inc., 1957.

15

EVALUATING PUPIL PROGRESS
IN READING

During the past decade, though standardized tests have maintained pre-eminence, there has been a growing interest in teacher-made tests. It is natural that, after setting up objectives and choosing methods to achieve them, the teacher should want to evaluate changes in her pupils' *reading* behavior, for example. However, testing is not the only instrument of appraisal. Evaluation is descriptive as well as quantitative, and, since human behavior is too complex to be accurately assessed by a test score, other measures must also be used. Additional appraisals of pupil progress in reading can be collected by means of rating scales, inventories, check lists, questionnaires, anecdotal records, etc. This chapter will deal, therefore, not only with teacher-made and standardized tests but also with other measures of evaluation.

TESTING IN AN EVALUATION PROGRAM

Teacher-made Tests. There are three large classes of tests which can be prepared by teachers for evaluating various phases of growth in reading: first, the *essay;* second, the *recall;* third, the *recognition.* Each will be considered in turn.

THE ESSAY TEST. This form has been somewhat discredited because of the lack of objectivity and the limited sampling which it permits. However, nothing is more relevant and helpful than an essay test in determining ability in such mental skills as recognizing relationships, expressing ideas in a logical and interesting manner, etc.

Variety in essay-type questions that will involve certain mental processes, ranging from simple memory to complicated reasoning, can be achieved by using such introductory terms as list, outline, describe, contrast, compare, discuss, explain, and summarize.

RECALL TEST. There are two forms of recall which the teacher can utilize in preparing a test—the simple recall and the completion exercise.

An example of *simple recall* is the following:

Who wrote Tom Sawyer? _____

An example of *completion* is

Mark Twain was born in the year _____ in the state of _____.

(The teacher should avoid mutilating a completion test with so many blanks to denote omissions that there is not enough of the statement left for the student to go by.)

RECOGNITION TEST. This form of test involves the use of true-false responses, multiple choice, matching, and situation and problem solving. All the above forms except situation and problem solving are quite well known at the present time. An example of the latter will serve to clarify this type.

In the story, Huckleberry Finn helped the runaway Jim to escape.

Did he break a law of the state?
Did he break a law of humanity?
If you had been in his place, which law would you have kept?

Standardized Tests. Since the appearance of the Army Alpha tests at the beginning of World War I, standardized tests have dominated the field of educational appraisal. Authorities in this field have held their standards high, maintaining that reading ability, as well as other abilities, is measurable only in the result and cannot be accurately appraised by merely watching the process and noting how pupils study, how they enjoy reading, and so on—although these factors are important in the *learning process.* Nor are subjective evaluations accepted as forms of valid appraisal by workers in this field. According to these authorities, the only way to appraise reading ability and progress is periodically to measure the child's ability in terms of each reading objective and to note gains. (Of course, more informal methods of appraisal used in day-to-day checking are not utterly frowned upon by this group but are not considered valid.)

RELATION BETWEEN STANDARDS AND TESTS. Among the general rules to observe in educational appraisal, including the measurement of reading progress, the following are usually laid down as a minimum by authorities in the field of standardized tests:

1. There must be clear-cut objectives which can be described, upon which there is virtual agreement, and which can be proved to vary (increase, decrease, rise, or fall) in relation to some other factor (such as teaching).
2. There must be units of measure to tell *how much, how many, how long* (for example, how many books the child reads and how many words he recognizes can be counted).
3. There must be standards to tell whether the "much," the "many," and the "long" are satisfactory, reasonable, and attainable.
4. There should be analysis and diagnosis to tell *why,* so that the teacher can do something about the findings.

To meet this set of criteria, standardized forms of measurement are required. There are two valid types of standardized tests available for appraising educational growth: the standardized *survey* test and the standardized *diagnostic* test. An example of the reading-survey test is the *Gates Reading Survey* (1958 revision. New York: Bureau of Publications, Teachers College, Columbia University). For grades three to ten, and requiring approximately fifty minutes to give, this survey includes measures of the level of comprehension, word knowledge, and speed of reading. The function of the survey test is to show grade placements, a measure very important for administrative appraisal and activities. An example of the second type, the diagnostic test, is the Progressive Reading Test by E. W. Tiegs and W. W. Clark

(Hollywood, Calif.: California Test Bureau). This test comes in forms suitable for administering to primary-, intermediate-, and upper-grade levels. A group test, it requires fifty minutes to give and appraises such basic reading abilities as vocabulary in the fields of literature and natural and social sciences, comprehension, interpretation of meanings, and ability to follow directions. All this information can be obtained from the diagnostic analysis. Hence, the test supplies valuable data for pupil guidance.

The survey test gives the grade placement. (But, again, if the teacher does not know *why* a child ranks at the 5.6 level in reading, she will not know what to do to help him.) The teacher should be able to distinguish between these two types of tests and should place stress on diagnostic tests as the basis of pupil guidance.

EVALUATING SPECIFIC READING SKILLS. According to informed thinking in the field, the teacher should appraise reading progress in these important skills: word-recognition ability, comprehension and interpretation, study skills, oral reading, and vocabulary achievement. Standardized diagnostic tests in reading should be given to determine the pupils' abilities in these areas because such tests yield a maximum of information in a short space of time, measure the attribute being tested, are easily scored, and help the teacher to compare a child's score in one phase of reading with his status in other phases. Some diagnostic tests also furnish grade-place data.

The diagnostic test should be given early in the term of instruction to find out the initial status of the pupils in the many objectives of reading they measure. Then, after a period of teaching, another form of the test should be administered to appraise increments of growth. The purpose of securing evidence is twofold—to note the degree of attainment and to identify points where improvement is weak. Yet some school systems are guilty of giving periodic tests in a routine manner, without attempting to interpret the data obtained or to implement future instruction. The cooperation of the entire teaching staff, from first grade through eighth, must be enlisted if a testing program is to accomplish its purpose. The diagnostic test is very important from the teacher's standpoint, since it aids in identifying specific types of difficulties—hence, probable reasons for lack of progress.

Below are listed some well-known reading tests:

1. *Gates Primary Reading Tests* (1958 edition. New York: Bureau of Publications, Teachers College, Columbia University): For grade one and first half of grade two. Three tests, each requiring fifteen minutes to administer. Type PWR—a test of word recognition; Type PSR—a test of sentence reading; Type PPR—a test of paragraph comprehension.

2. *Gates Advanced Primary Reading Tests:* For second half of grade two and first half of three. Type AWR—word recognition; Type APR—paragraph reading (for rest of data see above).

3. *Gates Basic Reading Tests:* For grade three, second half of year, to grade eight. Type GS—reading to appreciate general significance; Type ND—noting details; Type UD—understanding directions; Type LC—level of comprehension; Type RV—reading vocabulary (for rest of data see number 1 above).

4. *Iowa Tests of Basic Skills* (1955–56 edition. Boston: Houghton Mifflin Co.): For grades three to nine, this achievement battery yields eleven separate scores in these important skills: vocabulary, reading comprehension, language, work-study skills, and arithmetic skills. The reading-comprehension test requires approximately one hour for administration at each grade level and offers a number of stories of graduated length and difficulty. Multiple choice test comprehension—best answer out of four available. (The only way to obtain the reading-comprehension test is to get the entire Basic Skills Battery.)

5. *Iowa Every-Pupil Tests of Basic Skills* (By Ernest Horn, Maude McBroom, and others. Boston: Houghton Mifflin Co.): For grades three to five, Elementary Battery; for grades five to nine, Advanced Battery. Test A—Silent Reading Comprehension; Test B—Work-Study Skills.

6. *Iowa Tests of Educational Development* (Chicago: Science Research Associates, 1958): Test 5—Ability To Interpret Reading Materials in the Social Studies; Test 6—Ability To Interpret Reading Materials in the Natural Sciences; Test 9—Use of Sources of Information.

7. *Metropolitan Achievement Tests, Elementary, Intermediate and Advanced Reading Test* (1959–60 edition. New York: Harcourt, Brace & World, Inc.): For grades three to four Elementary, Forms A and B. For grades five to six, Intermediate, Forms Am and Bm. For grades seven to nine, Advanced, Forms Am and Bm.

8. *STEP or Sequential Tests of Educational Progress: Reading* (1956–57 edition. Princeton, N.J.: Cooperative Test Division, Educational Testing Service): For the elementary grades, four to six, Level 4. Forms A and B yield one over-all score. For upper grades, seven to nine, Level 3.

9. *Gilmore Oral Reading Test* (1952 edition. New York: Harcourt, Brace & World, Inc): For grades one to eight this test consists of ten paragraphs, arranged in order of difficulty, which form a continuous story. Each paragraph, representing a grade level, is followed by five comprehension questions. There are two forms of the test. The test yields separate scores on rate of reading, comprehension, and accuracy (pronunciation of vocabulary). The test is given individually, and the individual record blank which comes with the spiral-bound booklet permits a detailed record of reading errors.

10. *Gray's Oral Reading Paragraph Test* (Bloomington, Ill.: Public School Publishing Co.): This instrument, used individually for grades one to eight, measures speed and competence in oral reading. There is a time limit of two minutes for each paragraph. The children read a series of paragraphs orally, while the teacher makes note of mispronunciations, omissions, substitutions, reversals, and blocks. The test affords a rapid means of screening out those in need of remediation. It also helps in sorting out the three ability groups in reading.

OTHER MEASURES FOR APPRAISING READING GROWTH

Check Lists. It is exceedingly difficult to make precise measurements of tastes and interests. However, the teacher may state what pupils on different levels should do, enjoy, and appreciate. A teacher may fill out a check list similar to the one below after she has made certain subjective observations of her pupils. Of course the assertions she makes do not represent clear-cut gains but merely indicate tendencies.

1. Ascertain the amount of reading the child does in and out of school.
2. Check on the voluntary use of a library card and library privileges.
3. Determine the amount of time spent in reading both in and out of school.
4. Ascertain the number of books read, their type, their range of topics, their quality, and the breadth of reading interests they reflect.

5. Observe topics of conversation and comments made indicating information gained through reading.
6. Watch for growth of desirable character traits that may result from reading.
7. Observe references to books read, comparisons voluntarily drawn between a character in one book and a character in another.
8. Ascertain the amount of vicarious experiences gained through reading.
9. Discover the number of books owned by each pupil.
10. Observe whether reading is preferred to other activities.

The Individual Interview. Of similar aid in discovering the child's reading likes, dislikes, interests, and reactions to books is the individual interview, conducted more or less informally by the teacher. Through such a conference, one teacher found that a girl in her seventh-grade class viewed all poetry with suspicion. She invariably associated poetry with a former teacher who had required her pupils to master a "memory gem" of poetry every Friday morning. On the basis of the interview, the new teacher subsequently helped the child to sense the joyous melody and movement to be found in rhymes and ballads by inviting her to join a speaking choir group. Later, the teacher encouraged the child to appreciate more subtle types of poetry. The girl, who had begun by hating poetry, ended by writing rather lovely verse.

There are three different approaches to the appraisal of growth in reading tastes. To determine whether or not children's tastes and interests are developing satisfactorily, experiments have been made to discover possible criteria which will prove useful in the selection of children's literature. (1) Several investigators have tried to cull from the works of famous authors lists of book titles and authors which they themselves claimed had been of great value to them. However, such use of adult opinion has been criticized because there is little agreement among adults concerning a common body of literature to be required, and because the plan does not recognize the child's present interests. (2) The judgments of children in selecting their own reading have formed the basis of a number of other investigations. Several early studies concluded that children's free reading selections were a valid criterion. But a later study of the reading choices of several hundred students seemed to indicate just as forcibly the futility of unguided free reading in developing refinement of taste and the expansion of interests. Many authorities now argue that it is the teacher's responsibility not only to ascertain in interviews the present level of interests and tastes of the children but also to foster potential interests. How can a child possibly know whether or not he is interested in a travel book or classic unless he is motivated to read it? The child who does not appreciate excellent literature at first may gradually acquire a taste for it. (3) Children's needs are a valid criterion for selecting children's books. These needs, or basic hungers, include the need for security and the ambivalent need for change, new experiences, and adventure; the need for achievement and recognition; the need to love and be loved. By this criterion, if a girl of ten or eleven chose *Little Women,* her teacher would approve her choice, since the book helps the young reader to satisfy the basic need for enjoying, if only vicariously, the warmth and security of the March family.

The teacher may want to use all three criteria above in judging the growth of her pupils' tastes and interests in reading and literature. Individual guidance conferences should follow any individual evaluation of reading appreciations and interests. For example, if the teacher discovers that a pupil is reading comics to escape from reality, she should attempt tactfully to discover what his anxieties are and to help him to understand that, while comics may provide an easy temporary escape from life's problems, they offer no insight for dealing with them. She might also attempt to improve the child's taste (from a taste for the spectacular and unrealistic *Superman,* for example) by offering him books which are not only full of action but believable and well written.

Informal Records Kept by Pupils. Authorities in the field urge that pupils be asked to keep an informal record containing brief notations about their reading, both to interest them in the amount they do and to enable teachers to help in improving the children's reading tastes. The data called for in the form used by the Progressive Education Association Eight-Year Study are as follows: title of the book, author's name, whether the book was required or voluntary reading, amount of the book read, type of book, where obtained, reaction to the book. If the teacher wishes, she may expand the last point to call for answers to such questions as Did you like the story? Why or why not? Were there any parts you particularly liked? Disliked? Why? Were there any characters you particularly liked? Disliked? Why? Would you want to recommend this book to a friend? What would you say in urging him to read it?

Anecdotal Records. To give perspective concerning significant samplings of pupil behavior, anecdotal records can profitably be kept by the teacher. The following are indicative:

> John groans as if in pain whenever Tom arises to read, even though Tom always prepares his reading.
>
> Jane reads for three minutes in the library corner, then begins to daydream.
>
> The only time Eloise does not stammer is during oral reading. She reads well aloud and it seems to lend her confidence.
>
> Jim has never volunteered to give a book report or join in giving a skit for the Friday Book Club program.
>
> Emmett brings books from home.
>
> Ernestine has not used her library card for two months.

Reading Autobiographies and Interest Inventories. Both of these techniques are effective in helping the teacher to appraise her pupils' attitudes and interests. These measures will not be discussed here, since the first was taken up in the chapter on recreational reading and the second was described in detail in the chapter devoted to remedial reading.

THE RELATION BETWEEN OBJECTIVES, INSTRUCTION, AND EVALUATION

Evaluation should be a more or less continuous process. After determining the initial status of her pupils' progress in reading, by means of standardized diagnostic tests, thus discovering needs as well as attainments, the teacher sets up objectives and selects the materials and methods of instruction suitable to the realization of desirable goals. After any period of instruction such as a daily reading lesson, some form of appraisal is made to determine the amount of progress toward realization of goals.

Evaluation of a Lesson Plan. Inasmuch as the relationship between objectives, instruction, and evaluation can best be examined in a practical situation, it may be helpful to consider how the teacher should prepare and evaluate a daily lesson plan in basic reading. Since well-defined aims are essential to an effective teaching-learning situation, the teacher should start the reading lesson with her immediate objectives clearly in mind. A written plan, designed for use on several days, is almost indispensable for the beginning and experienced teacher alike. Suggestions offered in the teacher's manual or guidebook for the basic series should be consulted and appropriate procedures then adapted to meet the needs of the pupils. Frequently, several days are needed for complete coverage of all essential steps.

In establishing her aims, the teacher should ask herself, "What, exactly, am I going to try to accomplish during the time I give my children guidance in reading?" After she has listed her reading skill aims, as well as the socially significant aims, related to the content to be read, the teacher should outline the method she will use in realizing those aims. The teacher's opinion of pupil performance inevitably forms during the lesson, but it is not until the entire lesson has been taught that the teacher can sum up the attained and unattained objectives. Space should be provided at the end of the lesson plan for the evaluation. In this section, the teacher answers such questions as Did I accomplish what I set out to do? What evidence do I have that my pupils learned new facts, gained practice in needed habits and skills, and emerged from this reading experience with enriched social understandings?

The plan for a fifth-grade lesson presented here illustrates the relation between aims, instruction, and evaluation. The form, which is a good deal shorter than the Form for a Basic Reading Lesson Plan for Student Teachers (see Chapter 7), is one widely used by teachers of sufficient experience, as an alternative to the longer plan. Naturally, not all the steps should be covered on the same day. While studying the plan, the student should note the close relationship between gains in growth made by the children and the original aims listed in the lesson plan by the teacher.

A FIFTH-GRADE LESSON PLAN

(Average Reading Group)

I. What (subject matter)

Book: *Days to Remember*
Story: "Handsome Heart"

II. Why (aims)

A. Story-content aims

1. To visualize character
2. To visualize setting (time and place)
3. To visualize the action

B. Reading-skill aims

1. To learn to use the dictionary
2. To grow in oral-reading skill (projection)
3. To recognize an apt choice of words

C. Socially significant aims

1. To be able to list ways in which dogs help people
2. To be able to list ways in which people care for animals

III. How (method)

A. Preparation for reading

1. Recall the story read yesterday about Rusty and discuss why he was a winner.
2. Develop meaning and recognition of new words by having the children use the dictionary to find the pronunciation and meaning of underlined words in sentences on the blackboard:

   a. The *gallant* man risked his life.
   b. The man had *launched* the boat.
   c. The Coast Guard was *summoned*.
   d. The crowd *roared* its approval.

3. Motivating question
   "Today we have a story about Todd, a young boy, and Major, his dog. The story tells us about some of their ex-

periences. As we read the story let's try to find out why the author gave it the title 'Handsome Heart.' "

B. Guided reading

The children read silently to find the answer to each question. Then some child is called upon to read the part orally:

1. "Why didn't Aunt Mattie think she'd like a dog?"
2. "Why wasn't it practical for Todd to have a dog?"
3. "What did the sea captain teach Major?"
4. "Why did Aunt Mattie dread storms?"
5. "Why was the crowd on the beach?"
6. "Why was it useless for a lifeboat to go out?"
7. "What was the plan of the Coast Guard?"
8. "Why did the crowd stand breathless?"
9. "How do we know Aunt Mattie had changed?"
10. "Why is 'Handsome Heart' a good title for this story?'

C. Skills and drills

1. Ask the children to glance through the story quickly to find the part or parts that (1) help them to picture the place where the story happened and (2) help them picture Todd, his dog, and Aunt Mattie. These parts will be read aloud.
2. Direct the children to find the most exciting part of the story. Then ask different pupils to read aloud the words that help build up a picture of tense excitement: "gallant," "breathless," "roared," etc. To call attention to the appropriateness of these words, ask the children to substitute "proud," "out of breath," and "yelled" in sentences containing the above words and compare the less striking effect produced.

D. Follow-up activities related to the story

1. Language development
   Ask the children to compare Major and Rusty, a dog in another story they have read.
2. Art correlation
   Invite the children to illustrate their favorite scene or character in the story, labeling it with a sentence caption from the book.
3. Natural-science and social-science correlations

   a. Ask the children to list habits and traits of dogs that make them useful to man.

        b. Ask the pupils to enumerate their responsibilities to animals, particularly their own pets.

IV. Evaluation (achievements)

    1. The children, with the exception of three in the group, were able to find in the dictionary, during the time allotted, the four new words they were asked to look up. Those who were called upon were able to pronounce the words and explain their meaning in sentences on the blackboard.

    2. Those called upon read aloud *all* the sentences which described the place where the story transpired, and were able to compare its typical features with coast towns with which they were familiar. In the drawings made, coast towns were represented with reasonable accuracy, showing an understanding of the locale. Those called upon read aloud *all* the phrases which pictured the main characters. The oral reading, in response to questions about story happenings, showed that those who were called upon to read recognized the sequence of action in the narrative.

    3. Nine of the children who read aloud held the attention of the others, to all appearances, but, while Billy J. was reading orally in his halting, monotonous way, signs of inattention and boredom were shown by many children.

    4. Ability to recognize an appropriate choice of words was shown when more members of the group expressed a preference for the words "gallant," "launched," "summoned," and "roared" than for the less discriminating substitutes "brave," "got the boat out," "called," and "yelled."

The Supervisor's Evaluation. A different type of appraisal, of great interest particularly to beginning teachers, is the evaluative check list often used by supervisors in observing a reading lesson. As the poet Robert Burns pointed out, the power to see ourselves as others see us is denied to human beings. Self-appraisal is often ineffective because of subjective factors or a lack of perspective. For a clear view it is very helpful, therefore, to have the benefit of a supervisor's evaluation of a session of reading instruction. Examination of the appraisal form presented below reveals that other aspects than the teacher's ability to give instruction are evaluated. Some might argue that her enthusiasm or the degree of her emotional security or her grooming has little direct bearing on her ability to teach reading. But, at any rate, it is interesting to learn the various items a supervisor checks in evaluating a reading lesson. The student teacher should try to appraise her own performance according to this example of a supervisor's check list.

CHECK LIST FOR EVALUATING A READING LESSON

(To Be Used by Supervisor)

Name of teacher:
Grade:
Reading group:
Books:

A. Type of lesson? (Check in the space below.)

   1. Basic developmental (   )
   2. Content-fields reading (   )

      a. Textbook type (   )
      b. Reference type (   )

   3. Recreational reading (   )
   4. Remedial reading (   )

B. Type of planning? (Check Yes or No.)

   1. Was there a definite plan in writing? (Yes) (No)
   2. Were three classes of reading aims listed? (Yes) (No)
   3. Were the four main steps of method listed? (Yes) (No)
   4. Had the teacher's guidebook been used? (Yes) (No)
   5. Was there evidence of written evaluation of previous lessons? (Yes) (No)

C. Lesson step observed? (Check in the space provided.)

   1. Preparation? (   ) Guided Reading? (   ) Skills and Drills? (   ) Follow-up? (   )

D. Teaching techniques (Check Yes or No.)

   1. Was enjoyment stressed? (Yes) (No)
   2. Were visual aids used to motivate the reading? (Yes) (No)
   3. Was discussion used to motivate the reading? (Yes) (No)
   4. Were guiding questions asked to cause children to visualize character, scene, and action? (Yes) (No)
   5. Did the teacher call attention to picturesque choice of words, and attempt to transfer them to the children's permanent stock? (Yes) (No)

6. Did thoughtful discussion relate story ideas to life? (Yes) (No)
7. Was the seatwork carefully explained? (Yes) (No)
8. Was the seatwork accurately checked? (Yes) (No)
9. Was the drill at the blackboard based on needs? (Yes) (No)
10. Did the teacher consult the teacher's guidebook to help to ensure regular, systematic practice? (Yes) (No)
11. Was the drill full of interesting variety? (Yes) (No)
12. Was the drill kept short and zestful? (Yes) (No)
13. Does the teacher understand phonetic and structural analysis? (Yes) (No)
14. Was the follow-up step interesting and worthwhile? (Yes) (No)

E. Other aspects of instruction (Check Yes or No.)
1. Does the teacher command facts? (Yes) (No)
2. Does the teacher use acceptable English? (Yes) (No)
3. Does the teacher show originality? (Yes) (No)
4. Does the teacher secure pupil participation? (Yes) (No)
5. Does the teacher have the respect of the pupils? (Yes) (No)
6. Does the teacher understand classroom management? (Yes) (No)

F. Personality and appearance of the teacher (Check Yes or No.)
1. Was the teacher friendly? (Yes) (No)
2. Was the teacher enthusiastic while teaching? (Yes) (No)
3. Was the teacher tactful? (Yes) (No)
4. Was the teacher alert and intelligent? (Yes) (No)
5. Does the teacher seem to be emotionally secure, that is, does her basic attitude seem to be one of self-respect as opposed to self-pity? (Yes) (No)
6. Was the teacher well groomed? (Yes) (No)

Evaluation of Reading Growth. The teacher who can list concretely some daily attainments of the pupils, whether through self-appraisal or with the help of the supervisor, can be said to have *taught* a lesson. The teacher may be revealing more about her own ability than that of her children if she says, "I taught a lesson today, but nobody learned anything." Nor is anything accomplished by the teacher who writes in her lesson plan the empty phrase "everything went smoothly," without a shred of evidence to document her claim. Such failure to set forth clear objectives and to evaluate the attainment of those objectives in terms of tangible evidence of pupil learning reflects inadequate teaching habits. Competent teaching implies changes for the better in the learner, changes that are not brought about haphazardly but require definite planning. The efficient lesson plan lists specific reasonable objectives and, just as specifically, attempts to evaluate the achievement of those objectives. In the case presented above, the teacher used her own powers of observation in evaluating pupil performance, trying to be as definite and realistic about it as possible. She might also have used written tests to check comprehension, interpretation, and control of new word meanings, but these are most effective, as a rule, after a series of lessons or after a group of related objectives has been attacked.

Most teachers are conscientious and deeply interested in the results of their instruction. Knowledge of what has been accomplished and of what remains to be done is essential in setting up plans for future teaching; hence, the competent teacher constantly checks the progress made by her pupils. Eager to determine what changes, if any, have occurred in the thinking and acting of her pupils, she uses every means at her command to appraise the effectiveness of her instruction. Systematic appraisals not only enable the teacher to gauge reading growth for her own information but aid the school supervisor, the school administrator, and the general public to learn important facts regarding the progress of American children toward mastery of the "first R."

Guidance and evaluation must proceed together, just as evaluation and objectives must be considered in relation to each other. The guidance attitude of seeking to know the child in order to meet his needs should go hand in hand with the evaluation attitude of wishing to discover what values the child gains from specific types of educational activities. Information about the efficacy of methods and materials is indispensable to an adequate evaluation attitude. And only by appraisal is it possible to obtain an index of method and material effectiveness.

QUESTIONS AND ACTIVITIES

1. Discuss the relationship between reading objectives and evaluation.
2. What advantage has a teacher-made test over a standardized test?
3. What are some of the advantages to be secured from an essay test?
4. Compare a recall test with a recognition test. Which is more difficult?

5. What is the main function of a standardized survey test and a standardized diagnostic test?

6. What are some of the rules outlined by authorities in the field of appraisal? Do you agree or disagree with them? Defend your position.

7. Discuss the relationship between the teacher's professional conscience and the habit of evaluating her work.

8. Why is it essential to measure results to judge effectiveness of teaching?

9. Which of the other measures of evaluation besides testing appealed to you as the most interesting to use?

10. Suppose this item appears in a teacher-made test, mark the best choice: If a child cannot attack initial sounds of words or substitute initial sound or find the root word when endings are added, he is deficient in:

     sight words   vocabulary   general reading   word analysis

11. How could you reword the statement in number 10 to make it more positive?

SELECTED REFERENCES

Austin, Mary C., Clifford L. Bush, and Mildred H. Huebner. *Reading Evaluation: Appraisal Techniques for School and Classroom.* New York: The Ronald Press Co., 1961.

Bond, Guy L., and Eva B. Wagner. *Teaching the Child To Read* (3d ed.). New York: The Macmillan Co., Publishers (a division of the Crowell-Collier Publishing Co.), 1960.

Freeman, Frank N. *Theory and Practice of Psychological Testing.* New York: Holt, Rinehart & Winston, Inc., 1955.

Furst, E. G. *Constructing Evaluation Instruments.* New York: Longmans, Green & Co., Inc., 1958.

Greene, Harry A., Albert N. Jorgensen, and J. Raymond Gerberich. *Measurement and Evaluation in the Elementary School* (rev. ed.). New York: Longmans, Green & Co., Inc., 1953.

Herrick, Vergil E. "Criteria for Appraising Procedures Used to Promote Reading Development," *Elementary School Journal*, XLVI (December 1945, January 1946), 191–99; 258–65.

Robinson, Helen M. (ed.). *Evaluation of Reading.* Supplementary Educational Monographs, No. 88. Chicago: University of Chicago Press, 1958.

Shane, Harold G., and E. T. McSwain. *Evaluation and the Elementary Curriculum.* New York: Holt, Rinehart & Winston, Inc., 1951.

STRANG, RUTH, CONSTANCE M. McCULLOUGH, and ARTHUR E. TRAX-LER. *The Improvement of Reading* (3d ed.). New York: McGraw-Hill Book Co., Inc., 1961.

THOMAS, R. MURRAY. *Judging Pupil Progress.* New York: Longmans, Green & Co., Inc., 1960.

WRIGHTSTONE, J. W., J. JUSTMAN, and I. ROBBINS. *Evaluation in Modern Education.* New York: American Book Co., 1956.

APPENDIX—A BOOK LIST

Operating on the theory that accessibility of book lists is an important factor in stimulating readership, the author offers a list below which seems to appeal to college students. These books are available in the majority of public, university, and college libraries. Most of them are famous enough to be secured in both hardcover and paperback editions.

FAMOUS NOVELS AROUND THE WORLD

American Novels.

Looking Backward by Edward Bellamy
The Good Earth by Pearl Buck
Death Comes to the Archbishop by Willa Cather
Windswept by Mary Ellen Chase
Guard of Honor by James Gould Cozzens
The Red Badge of Courage by Stephen Crane
U.S.A. (trilogy, 1930, 1932, 1936) by John Dos Passos
An American Tragedy by Theodore Dreiser
The Sound and the Fury by William Faulkner
The Great Gatsby by F. Scott Fitzgerald
The Scarlet Letter by Nathaniel Hawthorne
A Farewell to Arms by Ernest Hemingway
Ramona by Helen Hunt Jackson
The Portrait of a Lady by Henry James
Babbitt by Sinclair Lewis
Moby Dick by Herman Melville
The Catcher in the Rye by J. D. Salinger
Going Away by Clancy Sigal
The Grapes of Wrath by John Steinbeck
Uncle Tom's Cabin by Harriet Beecher Stowe
Huckleberry Finn by Mark Twain (Samuel L. Clemens)

Ben Hur by Lew Wallace
All the King's Men by Robert Penn Warren
Ethan Frome by Edith Wharton
Look Homeward Angel by Thomas Wolfe

English Novels.

Pride and Prejudice by Jane Austin
The Little Minister by James M. Barrie
Jane Eyre by Charlotte Bronte
Lord Jim by Joseph Conrad
Great Expectations by Charles Dickens
The Adventures of Sherlock Holmes by Arthur Conan Doyle
The Mill on the Floss by George Eliot
A Passage to India by E. M. Forster
The Forsyte Saga by John Galsworthy
The Vicar of Wakefield by Oliver Goldsmith
The Heart of the Matter by Graham Greene
The Return of the Native by Thomas Hardy
Green Mansions by W. H. Hudson
Brave New World by Aldous Huxley
Bliss (a novelette with other stories) by Katherine Mansfield
Of Human Bondage by Somerset Maugham
Animal Farm (also *1984*) by George Orwell
The Cloister and the Hearth by Charles Reade
The Story of an African Farm by Olive Schreiner
Frankenstein by Mary Shelley
Dr. Jekyll and Mr. Hyde by Robert Louis Stevenson
Gulliver's Travels by Jonathan Swift
Barchester Towers by Anthony Trollope
The Picture of Dorian Gray by Oscar Wilde

French Novels.

Père Goriot by Honoré de Balzac
The Stranger by Albert Camus
Sappho by Alphonse Daudet
The Count of Monte Cristo by Alexandre Dumas
Madame Bovary by Gustave Flaubert
Mlle. De Maupin by Théophile Gautier
The Counterfeiters by André Gide
Les Miserables by Victor Hugo
Gil Blas by Alain René Lesage
A Life by Guy de Maupassant
Remembrance of Things Past by Marcel Proust

Jean Christophe by Romaine Rolland
Paul and Virginia by Jacques Henri Bernardin de Saint-Pierre
The Red and the Black by Stendhal (Henri Beyle)
The Wandering Jew by Eugene Sue
Candide by Voltaire
Germinal by Emile Zola

Novels of Spain, Sweden, Russia, Germany, Czechoslovakia.

Don Quixote by Miguel de Cervantes Saavedra
Crime and Punishment by Fëdor Dostoevski
Wilhelm Meister by Johann Wolfgang von Goethe
Mother by Maxim Gorky
The Castle (also *The Trial*) by Franz Kafka
Story of Gosta Berling by Selma Lagerlöf
The Magic Mountain by Thomas Mann
All Quiet on the Western Front by Erich Maria Remarque
Quo Vadis by Henry Sienkiewicz
Anna Karenina by Leo Tolstoy
Father and Sons by Ivan Turgenev

INDEX